355.02 TARROW
Tarrow, Sidney G,
War, states, and contention :a
 comparative historical study /

WAI
AND CONTENTION

WAR, STATES, AND CONTENTION

A Comparative Historical Study

Sidney Tarrow

CORNELL UNIVERSITY PRESS   **ITHACA AND LONDON**

First published 2015 by Cornell University Press

First printing, Cornell Paperbacks, 2015
Printed in the United States of America

Library of Congress Cataloging-in-Publication Data

Tarrow, Sidney G., author.
  War, states, and contention : a comparative historical study / Sidney Tarrow.
    pages cm
  Includes bibliographical references and index.
  ISBN 978-0-8014-5317-5 (cloth : alk. paper)
  ISBN 978-0-8014-7962-5 (pbk. : alk. paper)
  1. Politics and war. 2. War on Terrorism, 2001–2009—Political aspects. I. Title.
  JZ6385.T36   2015
  355.02—dc23   2014042952

Cornell University Press strives to use environmentally responsible suppliers and materials to the fullest extent possible in the publishing of its books. Such materials include vegetable-based, low-VOC inks and acid-free papers that are recycled, totally chlorine-free, or partly composed of nonwood fibers. For further information, visit our website at www.cornellpress.cornell.edu.

Cloth printing   10 9 8 7 6 5 4 3 2 1
Paperback printing   10 9 8 7 6 5 4 3 2 1

For Chuck—Still a teacher!

Contents

Figures and Maps

Tables

Preface

This book has personal, intellectual, and political origins.

Two decades ago, when Charles Tilly published his major work on war and state building, *Coercion, Capital, and European States* (1992a), I had the bad grace to complain that he had left out the subject he practically invented during his long and distinguished career—contentious politics. How did Tilly respond when charged with this sin of omission? "I have written many books on contention," he cracked, his tongue deeply embedded in his cheek. "It's time I wrote about something else." In deciding to write this book, I wanted to try to complete the work Tilly had left undone: connecting contention to war and state-building. If I could do this, I thought, it would be a fitting homage to the great social scientist to whom the book is dedicated.

The book has intellectual origins, too, dating from my collaboration with Tilly and one of sociology's eminent scholars of contentious politics, Doug McAdam. Our book *Dynamics of Contention* (2001) was an attempt to address many different forms of contention: too many for some of our sociological colleagues. We did not want to produce yet another book on "social movements," the subject on which we had cut our intellectual teeth. We thought much could be gained and little lost by embedding movements in a broader framework of strikes, protest waves, nationalism, democratization, and revolution—and connecting them to states. This was what we called *contentious politics*.

But where to draw the line around our subject? McAdam and I saw war in a separate category from contention. Tilly demurred, but, intellectual democrat that he was, he bowed to our more modest ambitions. But he was right. In this book, I take up the intellectual challenge of extending our approach in *Dynamics* to the most contentious politics of all: war. I hope to show that the advent of war is sometimes driven by social movements; that movements often affect the conduct of war and sometimes change its directions; and that wars often trigger the rise and expansion of movements in their wake. I also wanted to understand the relations between war and contention in the global war on terror mounted by the Bush administration in the wake of the bombings of September 11, 2001.

I quickly found that many scholars knew much more about the constitutional issues surrounding that war than I did. If I had a contribution to make, it would be as a comparativist who claimed to know something about contentious politics in the United States and Western Europe and could use these comparisons to learn about our contemporary conundrum. That explains the unconventional architecture of the book. In part 1, I explore these relationships in three historical cases: revolutionary France, the United States during the Civil War and Reconstruction, and Italy from World War One to fascism. In part 2, I turn to war, states, and contention in the United States. The radically new phenomenon of the twenty-first century, I will argue, is not that national movements episodically go to war against other states but that states wage war against transnational movements, with profound implications for domestic liberties and for the international alignments that I turn to in part 3.

This takes me to the third origin of the book: contemporary politics. Observing the aggressive response of the Bush administration to the tragedy of September 11, 2001, I worried that my country was in danger of abandoning its devotion to the democratic rights that have expanded through two centuries of struggle. As they pursued the criminals who took thousands of lives on that day, Bush and his government seemed indifferent to the rights of Americans and hostile to those of foreigners. True, the excesses of the Bush-Cheney regime had receded by the time I began this book in 2008. But under the "liberal" government of Barack Obama, the American state is still abusing rights in the name of security and continues its warlike behavior across the globe. I wanted to understand whether the first decade of the twenty-first century was a temporary cycle of emergency rule or reflected the growth of a permanent international state of emergency. I also wanted to know how hard it would be for Americans to roll back a set of policies that were becoming ingrained in their country's domestic and foreign practice. Those are the origins of this book.

Introduction

Readers of the *New York Times* awoke on March 2, 2014, to find an alarming headline:

Ukraine Mobilizes Reserve Troops, Threatening War

A day after the Russian Parliament granted President Vladimir V. Putin broad authority to use military force in response to the political upheaval in Ukraine that dislodged a Kremlin ally and installed a new, staunchly pro-Western government, the Ukrainian government in Kiev threatened war if Russian sent troops further into Ukraine. . . . What began three months ago as a protest against the Ukrainian government has now turned into a big-power confrontation reminiscent of the Cold War and a significant challenge to international agreements on the sanctity of the borders of the post-Soviet nations.[1]

What was happening here? In November 2013, a protest movement had erupted in the Ukrainian capital against President Victor Yanukovych's decision to cancel a long-planned agreement between his economically strapped country and the European Union. Yanukovich had been persuaded—his enemies would say "bought"—by Russian President Vladimir Putin to draw back from Europe by the inducement of a $15 billion loan if his country joined a Russian-led trade group. European leaders responded that if Yanukovych accepted the Russian offer, all bets were off for a Ukrainian link to the European Union. Western Ukrainians—including most of the residents of Kiev, the capital—were outraged by Yanukovych's move. The protesters in Kiev soon occupied the Maidan (the central square of the city), evoking the Ukrainian Orange Revolution of 2004 (Beissinger 2011). They called, first, for the association of Ukraine with Europe and, then, for an end to corruption and increasingly demanded that the president resign.

Those protesters were largely peaceful, but their demonstrations soon "turned violent"—that is to say, the regime's riot police turned on them, using snipers to pick off protesters in the streets, killing eighty-four, and arresting hundreds. Outrage at the regime's overreaction spread around the country and across Europe, and the Maidan occupation fell into a pattern of barricade building, police charges, occupation of government buildings, speeches by opposition politicians, and government warnings of fascist infiltration. What had begun as a largely peaceful protest movement rapidly militarized, with groups of young "hundreds" donning helmets and gas masks and carrying improvised shields against the increasingly ineffective, but no less brutal, police.

As the confrontations escalated, international actors mobilized on one side or the other. In Europe, French, German, and Polish envoys brokered a compromise that would save Yanukovych's face but give the protesters the link to the European Union they wanted; in the East, Russian President Putin offered Ukraine a downpayment on his promised loan and urged Yanukovych to stand fast against the protesters. The Russians grudgingly agreed to the European compromise proposal, but suddenly, as quickly as he had canceled the original EU association deal, Yanukovych disappeared, only to reappear again in the Russian-speaking part of Ukraine and then in the Russian Federation, claiming to have been overthrown by a *coup d'état*. While the Maidan occupiers cheered jubilantly, opposition politicians set up a provisional government, accused Yanukovych of mass killings, and threatened to take him to the International Criminal Court. In Washington, President Barak Obama and Secretary of State John Kerry cheered the advent of the provisional government; in Brussels, EU Foreign Commissioner Catherine Ashton spoke cautiously of a major injection of cash to bolster the Ukrainian economy.

The ebullience surrounding Yanukovich's fall was soon eclipsed by what happened in the Crimean peninsula of Ukraine between February 28 and March 2. On those days, armed men in uniforms bearing no insignias began to appear at key points in the Crimea, an area that had been part of Russia since the time of Catherine the Great but had been handed to Ukraine in 1954 by Nikita Krushchev, Communist Party chief, when the region was still part of the of Soviet Union (see map I-1). The peninsula was heavily peopled by Russian speakers and was the home of the Russian Black Sea fleet. Slowly at first and then increasingly insistently, Russian-looking armed forces surrounded Ukrainian military facilities in the region, took over the Parliament, and occupied the Kerch ferry crossing between the Crimea and Russia. The identity of these forces became clear when the newly appointed prime minister of the Crimea called for Russian intervention to protect the citizens of the region against armed attacks. Russian armored vehicles soon rolled across the border as the Russian Duma declared it to be the duty of Russia to protect Russian-speaking civilians from attacks it claimed were coming from "fascists, nationalists, and anti-semites" directed from Kiev. A full-scale military intervention, allied with internal pro-Russian demonstrations, was underway. On March 16, the takeover was certified by a full-scale plebiscite on the attachment of the Crimea to Russia, which a large majority of Crimean voters supported.

In the wake of these events, Western observers saw the Russian takeover as the worst foreign policy crisis since the Cold War. In Brussels, the European Union and the North Atlantic Treaty Organization (NATO) fulminated that the attack violated the 1994 Russian commitment to respect Ukrainian territorial integrity. In Washington, President Obama warned Putin that his country was risking international isolation and economic sanctions, while in Moscow the state-controlled press and the Kremlin propaganda machine revved up patriotic fervor to support the annexation of the Crimea. A wave of domestic contention against a weak and corrupt state had brought about the collapse of its government, triggered an

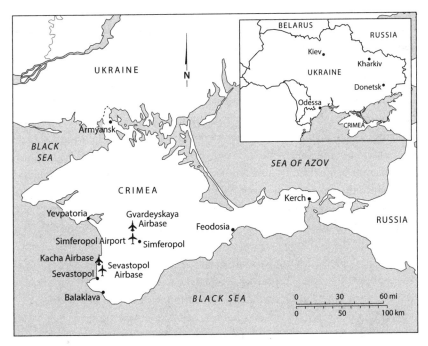

MAP I.1. Ukraine, Crimea, and the Kerch connection to Russia. BBC News, http://www.bbc.com/world-europe-26414600, accessed March 3, 2014.

internal countermovement, and led to a military takeover by a neighboring state. But given the physical isolation of the Crimea from the West, the lightning success of the Russian takeover, and the unwillingness of Western capitals to commit themselves to its defense, Putin's coup was soon accepted as a fait accompli. As we now know, the tug-of-war between Ukraine and Russia did not end with the annexation of the Crimea—and neither did the role of contentious action (see the conclusions to this book).[2]

The events in Ukraine after November 2013 have a number of lessons for students of war, states, and contention:

Contention triggers military crises, but crises instigate more contention. It was the popular occupation of the Maidan that triggered the collapse of the Yanukovich government and the Russian takeover of Crimea, but that takeover produced its own wave of contention in eastern Ukraine. As thinly disguised Russian troops infiltrated into the Crimea, pro-Russian nationalists occupied government buildings in Donestk and Luhansk and Russian nationalists urged Putin to go deeper into Ukraine.

History really matters. The headlines focused on the stalwart protesters, the brutal police, the fallen president, and the Russian invaders, but none of these events can be understood without recalling the historical precedents. Since the time of Catherine the Great, who wrested it from the Ottomans, Russians considered the Crimea part of their empire, an attachment that continued under the Soviets and has remained alive, despite the treaty granting the Crimea to Ukraine in 1994. As for the Ukrainians, their memories are equally long, but they were mainly inspired by bitter memories of Joseph Stalin's purges, by the great famine caused by collectivization, and by the Orange Revolution of 2004.

Be careful what you wish for. The determined protesters in the main square of Kiev, the Russian leaders who tried to quash their rebellion, the separatists who founded the "People's Republics" of Donetsk and Luhansk, and the new Ukrainian government all thought they knew what they wanted: the first wanted to get rid of a corrupt elite, the second wanted to bring Ukraine back into a reassembled Russian empire, the third wanted to rejoin that empire, and the fourth thought it could quash the separatists without risking further Russian intervention. But the occupation of the Maidan triggered a series of responses that no one could have wanted. Faced with police teargas and snipers' bullets, the enthusiastic young protesters on the Maidan gave way to militarized "hundreds" with questionable democratic credentials; the Russian-speaking nationalists of Eastern Ukraine brought down the savage repression of the Ukrainian army and its volunteer allies. As for Vladimir Putin and his allies, the ultimate result of their invasion was to place Russia back in an isolated status it had escaped two decades before and to throw the listless Russian economy into a recession; and the Ukrainian government found itself facing the armed might of Russia.

In times of crisis, the line between internal contention and international conflict grows thin. Who would have thought in November 2013 that four months later the Ukrainian president would flee his country and that Russian tanks would cross the Kerch straits into the Crimea? Or that, in response to the pro-Western protests in Kiev, a countermovement would arise in eastern Ukraine calling for secession and attachment to Russia? Domestic contention, state response, and international conflict were causally linked, as they will be in all the episodes in this book.

This Book

The events in Ukraine and Russia in late 2013 and early 2014 were both dramatic and unexpected, but the conjunction of internal contention, state collapse, and war, or the threat of war, is not as rare as observers at the time thought. In this book, I argue, on the contrary, that social movements, and contentious politics in general, play an important role in three war-related processes: mobilization for war, war-making, and political conflict in war's wake. In this book, I show that political contention sometimes entices states to go to war but sometimes works to prevent war; I examine how contentious politics influences war-making, sometimes instilling patriotism in citizen armies and sometimes assuring defeat by passive or active resistance; and I examine how contention at war's end sometimes strengthens opportunities for movements, sometimes leads to change in regimes, and sometimes helps movements to overturn them.

In the book, I also argue that war and preparations for war have complicated effects on rights. Scholars have long puzzled about the relationships between war and rights, as though they were examining a simple mechanism with two moving parts; they have missed the vital role of contentious politics in mediating between war and rights. Sometimes war constricts rights, but sometimes not. Sometimes contention encourages the state to expand its power, but sometimes not. Sometimes contention turns the rule of law upside down, but sometimes it helps to advance it. Some kinds of rights—such as women's rights in the 1920s—are advanced by war, while others—such as civil liberties—are often reduced. To understand the relationships between war and rights, we need to add contention to the formula.

To do so, we need to understand how states deploy two forms of power, which intersect differently with contentious politics. Authoritarian states exercise control largely through despotic means—I call this *hierarchical power*. In contrast, more liberal states use a combination of repression and what Michael Mann (1987) calls *infrastructural power*, which controls civil society from within. This form of power has the contradictory effect of constraining contention and of opening the state to efforts by civil society actors, who can use their access to power to gain resources but who can also use it to challenge the state's policies.

The intersection of war-making and internal contention has long had a profound effect on the state, as I show in the historical chapters in part 1; it has also profoundly shaped the contemporary national security state in the United States, as I show in part 2. In addition, globalization and internationalization have produced a new kind of war—between states and movements—that is changing the connections among war, states, and contention in fundamental ways.

In chapter 1, I lay out the concepts and hypotheses that I advance throughout the book. In part 1, I focus on the role of war and contention in three historical episodes of state-building: France, the United States, and Italy. Readers may wonder why I chose these three episodes for extended analysis. The choices were partly personal (I read the languages of these states and have some familiarity with their histories) but mainly theoretical. The French case shows how war, revolution, and internal contention created a radically new kind of state; the U.S. Civil War shows how a country strong in civil society but weak in central power evolved through war-making into a modern Leviathan with close ties to business; and the Italian case shows how war produced a new fascist movement that created a radically new form of state. The three cases together show the three main ways in which contentious politics intersects with war and state-building.

In part 2, I focus on the growth of the national security state in the United States and contention against it from World War One to the War on Terror. I argue that the combination of hierarchical and infrastructural power has produced a pattern of rule by law that shifts periodically between permissive and repressive reactions to protest. The culmination of this pattern is found in the crystallization of the national security state in the second half of the twentieth century and in its expansion into an international state of emergency in the early twenty-first century.

In part 3, I present evidence that the new forms of warfare experienced since the end of the Cold War have challenged Western states' dedication to rights and exposed the contradictions in liberal internationalism. In the conclusion, I return to the comparative-historical framework of chapter 1, asking whether the "new wars" of the twenty-first century are merely an intensification of earlier trends or war-making against transnational clandestine violent movements has initiated a new wave of global contention. I also briefly apply the approach to four nationalist movements after World War Two to explore how well it "travels."

I draw on three main literatures: international relations, comparative-historical analysis, and contentious politics. From international relations theory, I take the insight that different kinds of war produce different state responses and that globalization and internationalization have produced what amounts to a new form of warfare. But, unlike that tradition, I focus here mainly on the domestic processes surrounding this new form of warfare. From comparative-historical studies, I take its attention to the structural foundations of war and contention, and the key distinction between hierarchical and infrastructural power (Mann 1987). But, in contrast to that largely structuralist tradition, I emphasize the processes of war's initiation, war-making, and what happens to the state in war's wake. From the contentious politics tradition, I take the examination of anti-war movements, but I extend that tradition to examine civil society support for war-making and for political contention, in general.

The method I use in this book is comparative analyses of extended episodes of war-making—briefly in the case of the three historical studies and more intensively in the case of the United States in the late twentieth and early twenty-first centuries. I draw on historical monographs, original materials, and—in the case of the United States in the contemporary period—on personal interviews with activists.

If the book has a special contribution to offer, it is to integrate the study of contentious politics, war-making, and state-building. Internal contention, I argue, is often responsible for bringing on wars; it often affects how wars are fought and how states gain resources and opportunities for war-making; and it sometimes changes the nature of the state in war's wake. In turn, contention is deeply affected by warfare and its domestic expressions. Charles Tilly (1992a) argued that, while states make war, war also makes states. To his axiom, I add the codicil: "When states make war, this changes internal contention and thus the nature of the future state." But this is not a simple story of civil society heroes resisting aggression from state villains; the paradox is that the same civil societies that sometimes produce resistance to war and state expansion also provide states with the infrastructural power to mobilize society and suppress resistance.

These are big claims, and if I am not to descend into generalities, the book's scope will have to be limited in time, space, and subject matter. I have limited it in time to wars since the French Revolution; in space to the Atlantic/European world, France, Italy, Great Britain, and the United States; and in subject matter to major conflicts in the histories of those nations. I also give little attention to the traditional subject of war studies—the interactions among war-making states.

There are precedents for examining a few states in comparative-historical perspective to unearth general mechanisms and processes. Barrington Moore (1966) carried out extended analyses of modern state-building to focus on the role of revolutions in the political process. Theda Skocpol (1979) compared three great revolutions—all of them leading to war—and the kind of states they produced. Michael Mann (1987) disaggregated the sources of power into hierarchical and infrastructural forms, a distinction that helps us in understanding war and contention in the United States. Tilly (1975, 1985, 1992a) teaches that intensive analysis of the processes and mechanisms of historical change can tell us a great deal about general historical trends and theoretical questions relating war to state-building. The book is offered to readers who are as concerned as I am about the negative effects of the long wars of the early twenty-first century, but it is also for scholars who, I hope, will examine war and state-building in the light of contention. My hope is that it will also help us understand the explosion of contention in the early twenty-first century.

STUDYING WAR, STATES, AND CONTENTION

In 1659, toward the end of the Puritan Revolution, army officers sent Parliament a petition demanding an increase in the military budget. The members of Parliament (MPs) refused to act on their demand and voted a ban on soldiers holding meetings without government permission. In response, troops entered London, where they encamped until a new rump parliament was called. Richard Cromwell, the successor to the Puritan Commonwealth his father had founded, was too weak to deal with the army's actions and was forced to resign. When he eventually slunk off to France, the heir of the Stuart line, Charles II, awaiting his chance in Holland, returned in temporary glory. The Puritan Revolution was over.

It was in this atmosphere that Samuel Pepys, master diarist, sent a description of the melee he had witnessed outside Westminster between City apprentices and soldiers to his patron, Lord Edward Montague (Tomalin 2002, 74–75). On December 5, the apprentices brought a petition calling for "the removal of the army from their streets, so that 'a rising was expected last night, and many indeed have been the affronts offered from the apprentices to the Red-Coats of late.'" The government responded with a proclamation prohibiting "the contriving or Subscribing of any such petitions or papers for the future" (quoted in Tomalin 2002, 74–75). In response to the threat of the apprentices, many more soldiers, foot and horse, were sent to the City:

> The shops were shut, the people hooted at the soldiers. . . . boys flung stones, tiles, turnips &c. . . . some they disarmed and kicked, others

abused the horses with stones and rubbish they flung at them. . . . in some places the apprentices would get a football (it being a hard frost) and drive it among the soldiers on purpose, and they either darst not (or prudently would not) interrupt them; in fine, many soldiers were hurt with stones, and one I see was very near having his brains knocked out with a brickbat flung from the top of an house at him. On the other side, the soldiers proclaimed the proclamation against any subscriptions, which the boys shouted at in contempt, which some could not bear but let fly their muskets and killed in several places. . . . (Pepys to Edward Montagu, December 6, 1659)[1]

Readers may think it odd to begin a book on war, states, and contention in the modern world with a brief conflict between apprentices and soldiers in early modern England. But Pepy's story reveals the factors that were already linking war-making, state-building, and contention in the seventeenth century. Consider what was happening in the story:

- *the army* attempted to militarize the Puritan Commonwealth;
- *the government* was asked to raise taxes to keep it afloat and satisfy the army's needs;
- *Parliament*, with an eye on its members' financial interests, was reluctant to vote these taxes; and, finally,
- *political contention* between the apprentices and the soldiers forced Parliament to give way to the army over financing the state's ability to make war.

The story also suggests how a state's center of hierarchical power—the military—clashed in times of tension with the MPs in Parliament and with politics in the street—both of which tried, unsuccessfully, to rein in the army. It also tells us how contentious politics—in the clash between the apprentices and the army and between the army and Parliament—was the spur for a major change in the emerging English state (Porter 1994, 83). And, finally, it hints at the future development of what I call the *national security state*, the employment of emergency measures against contentious actors in times of war or domestic turbulence.

This time, it was the army that won, setting back the constitutional monarchy for three decades. But another war, brought on by the Catholic convictions of the returned monarch, spurred Parliament to bring Protestant William and Mary to England in a Glorious Revolution that established Parliament's power and sent the army to the barracks (Brewer 1990). Yet, when we remember the Puritan Revolution, we tend to think of religion and neglect the intersections among war, state-building, and domestic contention that led to these changes. Those are the relationships that I set out to examine in this book.

One reason for this gap in our understanding is that we tend to see war in isolation from domestic contention. "Traditionally," notes Mary Dudziak, "this distortion has been tolerated because wars end" (2010, 4). But *do* wars end quite so neatly? England was almost constantly at war from the Civil War that began in 1640 until the end of the Commonwealth, and these wars were accompanied by almost constant internal struggle. Following the French revolution, the new state was at war almost uninterruptedly from 1792 until Napoleon's defeat. And the United States was at war for more years than it was at peace through much of the nineteenth century.

Not only that. Since the Spanish-American war of 1898, U.S. wars have become ever longer. While the war against the Spanish lasted for one year, Americans fought for two years in World War One; for four in World War Two; for thirteen from the beginning of involvement in Vietnam to the evacuation of the last G.I.s from Saigon; and for nine in Iraq, twelve in Afghanistan, and thirteen in the War on Terror since 2001. If we consider the Cold War as a real war, which in terms of military mobilization it certainly was (Griffin 2013, 67–68; Hogan 1998, 60), the average length of U.S. wars becomes even longer. "In the twenty-first century," Dudziak continues, "we find ourselves in an era in which wartime—the war on terror—seems to have no endpoint. . . . how can we end a wartime when war doesn't come to an end?" (2010, 4).

Why is it important that wars have grown longer over time? One reason is that it has given enormous power to what President Dwight Eisenhower called "the military-industrial complex" (Weiss 2014). Another is that it created a national security state whose grip on civil society was only heightened by the events on September 11, 2001 (Posner and Vermeule 2005). But a third, less obvious reason is that the longer wartime lasts, the more likely it is to overlap with "normal" politics and thus to reshape domestic contention.

In part 1 of this book, I will show that movements have long been involved in aiding and abetting war-making, in mobilizing citizens to support—or to oppose—the government, and in profiting from political opportunities that arise in war's wake. In part 2, we will see that in the late twentieth and early twenty-first centuries social movements have become major players in episodes of war. Indeed, these *composite wars* have pitted movements against states in sequences of interaction, repression, and sometimes open warfare. And increasingly, movements have crossed borders to escape repression and in pursuit of their claims. In response, states have learned to use international institutions to pursue them, as I will show in part 3. Intranational, transnational, and international conflicts have become increasingly imbricated in the long wars of the late twentieth and early twenty-first centuries.

If movements are so deeply imbricated with war-making and with changes in the state, we might expect to find a rich literature on the relations among war, state-building, and contentious politics. Alas, we do not. Students of international relations have seldom investigated the relations between domestic and international conflict; students of domestic politics give little attention to the effect of war on contentious politics; and although there is a rich literature on antiwar movements among scholars of movements, these almost never examine how movements lead to war, how movements support war-making, and how war affects contention in war's wake. This book sets out to fill that gap.

Relations between war and state-building have received more attention than the relations between war and movements. Charles Tilly, whose historical work on the origins of the Western state was the inspiration for this book (1985, 1992a), found resistance to war in the form of tax revolts, anticonscription riots, and refusals to house soldiers or provide armies with subsistence. Modern states, he argued, were born when elites fought neighbors over territory. To do so, they hired civil servants and professional soldiers and extracted resources from their citizens. Extraction, the quartering of soldiers, and the occupation of borderlands led massively to contention: "The organizational structures of the first national states to form [i.e., in Europe]," writes Tilly, "took shape mainly as a consequence of struggles between would-be rulers and the people they were trying to rule" (1992a, 206–7).

Extracting resources from the populace led to conflicts that could be resolved in only one of two ways: by becoming a coercion-rich state that subjected people to harsher internal rule or by according them privileges that became the sources of citizenship (Tilly 1992c; see also Tilly 1986, 2004). Those privileges gave citizens the protection they needed to produce war materiel and the political resources they could use to engage in contention. War, for Tilly, was not only the origin of state-building, but of citizenship, and in the grudging extension of rights to citizens lay the origins of contentious politics. But not even Tilly did more than gesture at the complex and shifting relations among war, state-building, and contentious politics.

In this book, I attempt to fill this gap. Drawing on three scholarly traditions—social movements and contentious politics, comparative-historical analysis, and international relations, I will show that war and contention are inextricably related to one another and that both of these intersect with state-building and state transformation.

Social Movements and Contentious Politics

The major actors in contentious politics are social movements—"collective challenges, based on common purposes and solidarities, in sustained interaction with elites, opponents, and authorities" (Tarrow 2011b, 9).[2] Movements arose in conjunction with the consolidated national state and spread across the globe alongside imperialism, mass literacy, and industrialization (Tilly 1984). Movements have long had a close relationship to war-making through nationalism, civil war, guerilla insurgencies, and antiwar campaigns. Each of these variants has given rise to its own scholarly literature, often with little connection to the others, but all are part of a broader relational field I call contentious politics.

By *contentious politics* I mean episodic, public, collective interaction among makers of claims and their objects when at least one government is a claimant, an object of claims, or a party to the claims and the claims would, if realized, affect the position of a least one of the claimants (McAdam, Tarrow, and Tilly 2001, 5). It might be objected that all forms of politics include contention, but this is actually untrue; processes such as financial exchange, licensing, celebrating, and passing routine legislative enactments are part of politics but are not normally contentious. Congressional debates and elections are contentious all right, but they are not nonroutine.

It might also be thought that *contentious politics* is another term for social movements, when it actually refers to the field of interaction among collective actors or those who represent them, whether they are social movements or not. The term does include movements, but it also includes contention between striking workers and their employers, insurgent armed forces and their governments, the contestants in civil wars, and revolutionary coalitions and the states they strive to overthrow. The distinction is important because it is often actors other than movements that support war-making, such as the U.S. civil society groups that rallied around entry into World War One; oppose it, such as the Italian Socialist Party that did so in the same period; or the military or police, such as the Royal Ulster Constabulary (RUC) that supported the Protestant side against Catholic insurgents in the Northern Irish "Troubles" (see chapter 5). More important, as we will see, movements, parties, and institutions intersect in conflicts leading to war, during wartime, and in war's wake.

Contentious actors sometimes use conventional means—such as the filibuster in the U.S. Senate—but more often their tactics are transgressive, employing combinations of conventional, disruptive, and violent forms of action on behalf of new or evolving social actors (McAdam, Tarrow, and Tilly 2001, chap. 2). At one end of this vast spectrum of contention are forms of action that engage contenders regularly with authorities, such as public interest groups and lobbies, whereas at the opposite extreme—and conceptually overlapping with war—are violent forms such as terrorism, revolutions, and civil wars. Figure 1.1 lays out a scheme of the forms of contention we will encounter in this study and their proximity to the boundaries of two key dimensions of contention: its typical duration and its degree of conventionality or violence.

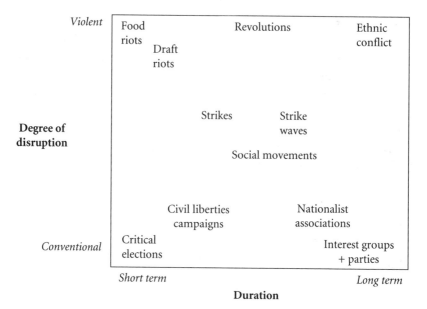

FIGURE 1.1   A descriptive typology of the forms of war-related contentious politics in this book.

Figure 1.1 is not intended to exhaustively catalog all forms of contentious action but, instead, to help us to think about the relationships among the concepts in the book. First, it ranges from very brief forms (e.g., the draft riots during the U.S. Civil War) to long-term forms (e.g., the Italian Nationalist Associations that preceded and helped to trigger the country's intervention in World War One); second, it ranges from largely peaceful forms (e.g., elections) to the most violent forms (e.g., revolutions, civil wars, and terrorism); third, movements are more likely to be conventional or disruptive than violent, although they can become violent when engaged with countermovements or the forces of order; and fourth, whereas some of these forms (e.g., elections and riots) have definite organizational formats, others can last for decades with a variety of formats.

Finally, the forms of contentious action we will see in this study are not mutually exclusive. An antiwar movement can produce riots, protest campaigns, petitions, or peace lobbies; social movements can empower a revolution but also engage in legal mobilization; and revolutions, civil wars, and terrorism are frequently commingled. For example. movements sometimes encompass shorter-term strikes and protests, but they often endure for decades and become deeply embedded in state-society relations. Movements often intersect with parties—for example, in the "party in the street" that opposed the Iraq War (Heaney and Rojas 2015). In at least two of the cases we will examine—the French Revolution and fascist Italy—movements became movement-states, which are more likely to go war than are most others.

Will we find a historical progression from lesser forms of contention to greater ones as states grew larger and wars became more deadly? It is logical to think that as wars and the states that fought them expanded so did their forms of domestic contention. But contention over war-making has also become more institutionalized. For example, opposition to the U.S. War on Terror has taken three major forms: an antiwar movement in the street, legal mobilization from human rights lawyers, and the opposition of civil society groups. Moreover, the once-clear lines among forms of armed conflict—interstate wars, extra-state wars, and intrastate wars—have become blurred, and in many countries, the ordinary forms of contention have merged with more violent forms. Technical changes in war-making have, of course, assisted this process, but most important, I will argue, are the processes of globalization and internationalization that have expanded contention across borders since the end of World War Two.

In this book, I will show that political contention has become imbricated with war-making in three important ways: (1) in mobilization for war, sometimes working to prevent war but more often enticing states to go to war; (2) in war-making, sometimes instilling patriotism in citizen armies and sometimes assuring defeat by passive or active resistance; and (3) in war's wake, when political opportunities open up to change the direction of states and sometimes to overturn them.

Movements often take advantage of the chaos of war to mobilize on behalf of their claims. Some of these movements, such as women's suffrage, had nothing to do with war, whereas others, such as draft resistance and antiwar movements, were spurred by the war itself. Such contention, or its threat, is the immediate cause of the adoption of the elements of emergency powers that have been institutionalized in the national security state. It has also brought out the tension between two kinds of state power: hierarchical power and infrastructural power. This takes us to the second source of this book—the comparative sociological analysis of states and contention.

War and States in Comparative-Historical Studies

From the 1960s on, scholars working in the tradition of comparative-historical studies began to investigate the role of war in state-building and state transformation. This tradition was spawned by the seminal work of scholars such as John Giddens (1985), Margaret Levi (1988, 1997), Michael Mann (1988), Barrington

Moore Jr. (1966), Theda Skocpol (1979), and especially Charles Tilly. While this book draws on the contributions of many of these scholars, it follows most closely the teachings of Tilly, especially in his 1992 book on war and state-building, *Capital, Contention and European States*, and the work of Mann in his book series *The Sources of Social Power* (1986, 1993, 2012, and 2013) and articles (1987).

Tilly's work inspired a generation of scholars—mainly in political science—who extended, criticized, and reinforced his findings about the importance of war in state-building. These writers explored how war impacted states in venues as disparate as early modern Europe (Ertman 1997; Spruyt 1994, te Brake 1998), Latin America (Centeno 2002), Africa (Herbst 2000), the United States (Bensel 1991), Southeast Asia (Callahan 2003), and in the Third World in general (Taylor and Botea 2008). Their studies have added greatly to our knowledge of the war–state-building nexus, but few gave concerted attention to the relationships among political contention, war, and state-building.[3]

Part of the problem was that few scholars working in this tradition resolved the question of the autonomy of the state vis-à-vis social forces. Tilly defines the state as "an organization which controls the population occupying a definite territory . . . insofar as (1) it is differentiated from other organizations operating in the same territory; (2) it is autonomous, (3) it is centralized; and (4) its divisions are formally coordinated with one another" (1975, 70).[4] Others, such as Nicos Poulantzas (1975), saw the state as the arena, the condensation, the crystallization, the summation of social relations within its territories, but hedge on its active or autonomous role. Still others, such as Samuel Finer (1975), focused on the growth of military power, seeing society as little more than an object of statecraft. Few have tried to bring together the bottom-up tradition of Marxism with the top-down tradition of statists such as Finer. Part of the uncertainty is because these theorists see state power overwhelmingly as "despotic power" (Mann 1987), eliding the increasing capacity of modern states to organize power *within* civil society—what Mann calls "infrastructural power" (1987; see later in the chapter).

Despotic power grows in wartime. As Europeans were creating the modern state, Immanuel Kant wrote that "as long as states apply all their resources to their vain and violent schemes of expansion . . . no progress (towards civil republicanism) can be expected" (1991, 4). Similarly, at the dawn of the U.S. republic, James Madison warned, "Of all the enemies to public liberty war is, perhaps, the most to be dreaded, because it comprises and develops the germ of every other" (1795 [1865], 491–92). Historians and sociologists have been no less pessimistic about the impact of war on rights; Bruce Porter concluded that "A government at war is a juggernaut of centralization determined to crush any internal opposition that impedes the mobilization of militarily vital resources" (1994, xv). Similarly, Anthony Giddens concluded that "the garrison-state emerges in a garrisonised world, in which resort to the threat or use of organized violence is more-or-less chronically present" (1985, 245).

Legal theorists and political scientists have also given great attention to the expansion of despotic power in wartime. Carl Schmitt, in a series of works that presaged national socialism, reduced state sovereignty to the discretion of the ruler. "Sovereign is he who decides on the exception," he wrote (Schmitt 2005, 5). Schmitt's theories were based on the notion that politics is a struggle between enemies, with the prime enemy being those who oppose the ruler's designs. In recent decades, and especially after the expansion of executive power in wartime in the United States, Schmitt's theories have been subjected to increasing exposure and criticism.[5]

Political scientists have been no less concerned at the threat of state aggrandizement in wartime. The term *garrison state* was coined by Harold Lasswell (1941, 1998) before World War Two when he observed the implications of Japan's bombing of Chinese cities.[6] A third theorist of exceptional powers was Clinton Rossiter. Generalizing from the Civil War experience, and in contrast with Lasswell, Rossiter (1963) argued in favor of dictatorial power during emergencies.[7]

Michael Mann (1987 disaggregated the forms and logics of state power with direct relevance to the relationship among states, war-making and contention. Surveying world history up to the present day, Mann (2012, 6–14) divided the sources of power into political, military, economic, and ideological forms. He also divided state power into two types: despotic power, "the power of the elite itself over civil society," and infrastructural power, "the power of the state to penetrate and centrally coordinate the activities of civil society through its own infrastructure" (1987, 114).[8] Other scholars, such as Linda Weiss (2014), Dan Slater (2010), and Desmond King and Robert Lieberman (2008), used a similar concept to describe modern political economies.[9] By broadening Mann's concept of despotic to hierarchical power, this distinction will prove especially pregnant in understanding how different states responded to the strains of war. The key to understanding the growth of the American state in wartime is its combination of hierarchical and infrastructural power, as I will argue in part 2 of this book.

Domestic Conflict in International Relations

The third tradition that this study draws on is from international relations and relates to the role of domestic conflict in wartime. Jack Levy and William Thompson define *war* as "sustained, coordinated violence between political organizations" (2011, 3). The only variation on that convention in this book is that the terms *civil war* and *revolution* are seen as referring to forms of contentious politics as well as to forms of war-making. *Terrorism* I define, with Donatella della Porta, as "clandestine political violence" because the usual definition of the term *terrorism* has become so broad as to be almost useless (della Porta 2013; see also Tilly 2003).

International relations theorists have long recognized that wars are not simply contests between states but emerge from, are fought out within, and sometimes transform domestic politics (Stein and Russett 1980; Kier and Krebs 2010a). For example, there are now important literatures on diversionary wars,[10] external support for civil wars (Checkel 2013; Jenne 2006), wars and democracy (Kier and Krebs 2010b; Reiter and Stam 2002), and revolutionary warfare (Walt 1996). But international relations scholars have been slower to connect the forms of domestic contention to international conflict (Kier and Krebs 2010a, 1). This is in part because of the specialization that divides their field from the study of domestic politics, but it is also because they are understandably more concerned with the destructiveness of major wars than with the role of domestic contention (ibid.; see also Rasler and Thompson 1989).[11]

The form of domestic contention that has interested international relations scholars most are revolutions because they so often lead to international conflict (Walt 1996). The English Revolution began when Charles I tried to bypass Parliament to gain revenues for war against France; the French monarchy fell so deeply into debt during the Seven Years and American wars that it was forced to call an Estates General, which led to the 1789 revolution; Italy's intervention in World War One was driven by internal contention as it weakened the state, producing greater contention and the fascist revolution; and Russian losses in World War One so "discredited tsarist rule, encouraged military defections, and made the state's vulnerability patent" that the revolutions of 1917 followed (Tilly 1992a, 186). With globalization and internationalization, revolutions have become ever more likely to lead to international conflict. Stephen Walt points out that "states that undergo a 'revolutionary' regime change are nearly twice as likely to be involved in war as are states that emerge from an 'evolutionary political process'" (1996, 1).[12]

Why do revolutions so often lead to war? Walt argues that mutual misperception between revolutionary states and their neighbors is partly responsible for revolutionary wars (ibid., 4–5). But there is a more structural reason for the linkage between revolutions and external war. In the course of the cycles of domestic conflict that often follow revolutionary breakthroughs, the suppression of domestic enemies easily transforms into external war-making as they are identified with the enemy abroad, as conflict with domestic opponents militarizes, as their foreign allies step in to assist them against the revolutionary regime, and as the language of warfare percolates from domestic to international politics.

International relations scholars have recently become interested in terrorism, not only because terrorist actions are often launched from abroad but because of the growing tendency—especially after September 11, 2001—for terrorist movements to diffuse across borders (Sageman 2004). Much of the work in this field has a strong public policy bent, relies disproportionately on government—especially U.S. government—sources (della Porta 2013, chap. 1), and underplays the connections between clandestine violence and domestic politics. In chapter 5, I argue that terrorism is one—but not the only—form of the "new wars"; I will use the term *composite wars* because they challenge the traditional distinction between international and domestic contention. The term also makes clear that both insurgents and states use a combination of conventional and unconventional means.

International relations scholars have traditionally divided armed conflict into three types: interstate wars, extra-state wars, and civil wars. Among the first, wars between great powers have attracted the most attention (Rasler and Thompson 1989). But great-power wars have become rarer over time—decreasing from thirty-four in the sixteenth century to seventeen in the eighteenth century to fifteen in the twentieth century (Levy 1983). As the number of great-power wars have declined, war has become ever more lethal; in the warlike eighteenth century 4 million people were killed in wars, in the nineteenth century 8 million were slaughtered, and in the twentieth century 115 million died in battle, not counting the millions of civilians who perished in that century's wars. "Those numbers" Tilly concludes, "translate into death rates per thousand population of about 5 for the eighteenth century, 6 for the nineteenth century, and 46—eight or nine times as high—for the twentieth" (1992a, 67).

As interstate wars declined in number, global exploration, empire-building, and conquest led to an increase in extra-state wars. Beginning in the sixteenth century, Western states "discovered" the less-developed parts of the world, conquered their "natives," and fought over their territories. Once established, these empire builders spent decades putting down rebellions and expanding and protecting their borders. Only at the end of the two world wars did the thrust of imperialism ebb, and with it the extra-state wars of the imperial powers. Moreover, with the threat of nuclear annihilation looming above them after 1945, the great powers no longer dared to engage in major wars either, at least with one another.

As the great powers began to loosen their grip, their armies, which had more or less kept the peace among hostile populations, began to retire to the metropole. The result was that the weak states that emerged from colonization faced frequent internal wars. Groups that had formally been "minorities" within empire-created borders rebelled against the successor states as they discovered themselves to be "nations." Moreover, the elite group that emerged most powerfully from colonialism was the military, which soon shed itself of parliamentary trappings and engaged in coups and other forms of internal strife. The ultimate result was that, as the number of interstate and extra-state wars declined, domestic conflict in ex-colonial states has become militarized and the number of civil wars, insurgencies, and guerilla wars increased.

Just as domestic politics can lead to war, war-making exacerbates domestic conflict. It does so by increasing the power and prestige of military officers, providing domestic actors with arms and the experience to use them, and transferring forms of organization learned in war into civil conflict. We will see in chapter 4 how their experience in the trenches of World War One furnished Mussolini's *squadristi* with the resources to seize power. More recently, the Afghan war against the Soviet occupation led the United States to supply the *mujahaddin* with both personal and small arms, weapons that they then used for internal and transnational war.

Although states dominated war-making in the eighteenth and nineteenth centuries, war is no longer the monopoly of states. First in colonial conflicts in Burma, Indochina, and Algeria; then in conflicts between Israel and the Palestinian militants; next in the development of armed groups opposing Soviet rule in Afghanistan; and most recently in the Middle East in general—war is no longer the monopoly of states. A basic question in the twenty-first century is how the entry of nonstate transnational actors on the scene of war-making affects the nature of war, its connections to domestic politics, and the rights of combatants.

Five Intersecting Questions

The object of this book is to understand how war-making, state-building, and contention intersect. But readers who expect to find single deductive answer to this question will be disappointed; so varied are the forms of war-making, the types of contention intersecting with warfare, and the kinds of state involved that there is no bumper sticker for the questions that this book takes on. But there are recurrent processes connecting contention to war and state-building that this book examines. Five basic questions emerge from the various episodes I will examine:

- How does war-making produce state-building, and what are their joint effects on rights and citizen contention?
- How do states control contention in times of war?
- How do states interact with civil society in wartime?
- How does war affect contention in the wake of war?
- How does war affect the future relationship between states and contention?

Answers to these questions can be proposed only at the end of the book, but it will be helpful here to lay out the conceptual tools that will help to confront them.

War-Making, State-Building, and Citizenship

It was Tilly (1975, 1985, 1992a) who argued that war and preparations for war were at the origin of the modern state and that this joint process eventually produced citizens and citizen rights. In a fusillade of books and articles, he examined the relationships among war, state-building, and rights. Unlike Lasswell and Rossiter, who focused on the repression of rights in the short run, Tilly focused on the long-term role of war in creating and expanding rights. "I think," he wrote, "that citizenship rights came into being because relatively organized members of the general population bargained with state authorities for several centuries." Citizens and states, he reasoned,

- first bargained over the means of war and
- then bargained over enforceable claims that would serve their interests outside the area of war,
- that in turn helped to enlarge states' obligations to their citizens—which Tilly, somewhat unusually, called "protection."[13]

These processes, Tilly argues, created an intimate connection between war-making and state-building: "States," as he famously wrote, "make war, but war makes states" (1975, 42).

Rulers have always needed financial resources to go to war. Sometimes they pressured banks and wealthy individuals to provide support; sometimes they extracted them from those they conquered; but increasingly, they drew on the contributions of taxpayers, great and small. As is well known, the need for war financing gave the English Parliament leverage against the monarchy and ultimately led to its growth into the center of the British Constitution (Brewer 1990). But financing wars was at the heart of conflicts between kings and people throughout history, no less in the American colonies than in the monarchies of Europe. Transferring or withholding war financing was the origin of both the demands of citizens for rights and their resistance to central power.

It was not only the extraction of resources to pay for wars that pitted citizens against their states. Resistance to the quartering of soldiers, to conscription, and to war itself periodically mobilized citizen resistance to war-bent rulers. These episodes of contention ranged from low-level malingering and draft evasion to the draft riots of the U.S. Civil War to the revolt of an entire region—the *Vendée*—against conscription for the French revolutionary wars. It was only in the twentieth century that organized peace movements developed against war-making. Some of these were opposed to war in general; others were opposed to particular wars, such as the draft resistance movement against the Vietnam War; and others mobilized against the threat of war.[14] To Tilly's aphorism that "war made states and states make war," we might add the corollary that "war and states make movements" and that movements engaging in contention with states extracted the rights of citizenship and invented new forms of contentious politics that endured in war's wake.

How States Control Contention in Times of War

In the episodes in this book, as each state went to war, different forms of states of exception—the French *état de siège*, the U.S. suspension of *habeus corpus*, and the Italian use of *pieni poteri*—were instituted. Whether these states of exception are "a zone of anomie in which . . . all legal determinations are deactivated" (Agamben 2005, 50) or partial exceptions to continuing constitutional government, as Rossiter suggests, is one of the fundamental questions I examine in this book. A key question is whether exceptional powers take similar or different forms during different conflicts to control different kinds of contenders.

In her work on what she calls "the international state of emergency," Kim Lane Scheppele found a strikingly similar sequence of institutional and policy responses in a large number of states of emergency, a sequence she calls "the emergency script" (2010, 134–44):

- *Executive centralization.* In the first step, power is centralized—usually when parliaments are already weak or self-destructive.
- *Militarization.* Once the other branches have been marginalized, the next step is the militarization of the use of executive power.
- *Procedural shortcuts.* Once power is firmly in the hands of the executive and the military is positioned as the key responder to the threat, new bodies of state are established and old bodies that used to provide procedural checks are bypassed or neutralized.
- *Putting people in their places.* Regimes of preventive detention are set up and popular demonstrations are banned.
- *Inversion of speech protection.* Formerly protected speech is criminalized, newspapers are closed or nationalized, and censorship is instituted; in France, the flourishing of new newspapers that followed 1789 was progressively choked off as opposition newspapers were closed down and an official press was used to proselytize for the war and condemn opponents as traitors.
- *Reversal of transparency.* Government actions are blanketed in secrecy; legal decrees, detentions, and even trials are kept secret; state officials hide behind anonymity; and surveillance increases.

- *Anticipatory violence.* Typical emergencies in their later stages deploy disproportionate violence against real or imagined opponents; in France, the definition of *aristocrats* was gradually broadened to mean opponents of the regime, and eventually all political opponents of the regime were designated as counterrevolutionaries.
- *Lingering powers.* Emergency powers often last well beyond the threat that called them into being; this is the process that we today call the "ratchet effect."

We will return to Scheppele's emergency script in each of the cases of armed conflict we examine. In chapter 10, we also examine her hypothesis that the emergency script has internationalized in the years following 9/11. We will see that the type of war that a state engages in affects how and how much it represses dissent. Although large-scale warfare produces a tendency to increase domestic control, mass mobilization for war can create incentives for the state to gain popular support by relaxing coercion (Andreski 1954). Small wars are less likely to trigger repression of domestic contention, but much depends on how these wars are framed—as transformative wars or as restorative wars (Krebs 2009). The advent of highly professionalized war-making, often using "contractors" (i.e., mercenaries) instead of citizens, may be reversing the tendency Stanislav Andreski saw for large-scale wars to produce citizen mobilization (Avant 2010).

How Do States Interact with Civil Society in Wartime?

Whereas traditional coercive states impressed their subjects into war-making, modern warfare requires greater and broader citizen mobilization. We can see this difference by comparing the changes in mobilization in tsarist Russia and its Soviet successor state. While the tsars were satisfied impressing their serfs into their armies for years, Stalin mobilized the entire society to fight off the Nazi invader using the symbols of great Russian nationalism. Liberal states are even more inclined to use consensus mobilization rather than constraint, using symbols of patriotism, liberalism, and the defense of freedom to do so. With the American and French revolutions, the need to muster overwhelming military force led leaders to mobilize citizens around the symbols of republican purpose. This was the origin of the citizen army and of a corresponding revolution in war-making that eventually involved entire populations (Kestnbaum 2002). This is where we first begin to find the importance of infrastructural power: it was at this stage that states began to regard the legitimation of war-making and the allocation of benefits to those who supported the war effort as important in war-making.

Citizen groups sometimes oppose going to war, but as we will see, they are more likely to support their leaders, at least at the outset of conflict. As states impose higher taxes, armies suffer defeats, and the body bags return from the front, enthusiasm for war dampens. Movements develop in reaction to these costs but also against the constriction of rights that almost always occurs when states go to war. In the Vietnam years in the United States, a cycle developed from opposition to the war, to illegal government behavior, to a movement against spying and in favor of rights that reached into the heart of Congress. We will see a similar cycle in chapter 9 in the movements triggered by the war in Iraq.

How Does War Affect Contention in War's Wake?

What happens to states and contention when wars end? Aaron Friedberg (2000) assures us that the expansion of state emergency powers are rolled back at war's end. This was also Rossiter's (1963) belief, based on his study of the Civil War and other U.S. emergencies. But rolling back governmental powers is easier to do with government spending or the size of armies—the variables that Friedberg studied—than with the emergency script that Scheppele describes. More worrying than the imposition of controls during wartime is when the temporary wartime measures of control slide into permanent restrictions of rights. We do not need to believe that leaders deliberately use the extension of controls to achieve despotic power in war's wake; competition for votes, bureaucratic inertia, the desire of intelligence officials to keep doing what they were doing, and public support for the repression of "subversives"—all these are forms of "the ratchet effect" that we will find in war's wake.

Ratchet effects can be temporal, as an executive takes on more and more powers over time, or they can be horizontal, as increases in power migrate from one government agency to another, or they can even be transnational, as they cross national borders (Scheppele 2006). Ratchets are generally statist; that is, they expand the extent and power of the state. But two legal scholars, Eric Posner and Adrian Vermeule (2005), also argue that here can also be a libertarian ratchet following periods of state expansion. Although social movements are frequently throttled by statist ratchets, libertarian ratchets, they argue, can create new rights that respond to social movements' demands—for example, the successful demand for women's suffrage that followed World War One.

Posner and Vermeule's major example of a libertarian ratchet came after the Vietnam War, when both Watergate and the uncovering of the FBI's illegal counterintelligence programs (COINTELPROs) led to legislative and judicial reforms against government overreach (see chapter 6). But states are never permanently hamstrung by the peacetime rollbacks of their wartime actions. As new states of emergency develop, rulers can develop new instruments of surveillance and control that sidestep the libertarian reforms of the last postwar period. Chapter 8 will show how the American state expanded both its hierarchical and its infrastructural powers in the decade following 9/11.

What can citizens do in response to the continuation of wartime measures in the wake of war? This is where contentious politics comes in. Although the mass of the citizenry usually demobilizes when wars end, citizen activism is the only recourse when—often in the name of liberty—citizens' and human rights are threatened by states using their wartime power in war's wake. But this depends on the presence of civil society actors dedicated to other peoples' rights against governments that have just emerged from war. As we will see in Chapter 9, both traditional and innovative forms of contention developed in resistance to the overreach of the Bush and Obama administrations.

How Does War Affect the Relationships between States and Contention in the Future?

As we have seen, many theorists have shown how war constrains contention. They are not wrong, but they tend to assume that state power is uniformly what Mann called "despotic power" and I call hierarchical power. This tends to occlude a second form of power—infrastructural power—that is especially typical of modern states. When a despotic state goes to war, it uses the instruments of state power—the military, the police, and rule by states of exception—to control its citizens. But modern states have instruments that go beyond emergency powers—infrastructural powers—that operate within civil society. Issuing propaganda in favor of the war; allotting defense contracts, mobilizing civil society groups; denigrating opponents; and, perhaps most important, wrapping the project of war-making in the myth of legitimacy—these strategies are all tools that are used through the state's infrastructural power. When a state is infrastructurally strong, it "allows for the possibility that the state itself is a mere instrument of forces within civil society" (Mann 1987, 115).

In this book, we will encounter different combinations of hierarchical and infrastructural power as states control contention in times of war. A state that is hierarchically strong can be infrastructurally weak—for example, Italy when it intervened in World War One. Conversely, a state that is hierarchically weak can be infrastructurally strong—for example, the North at the outset of the U.S. Civil War. Whereas hierarchical power leaves citizen groups with little recourse between malingering and revolution to oppose war-making states, infrastructural power works in two directions: it provides the state with ties within society to gain support for war-making, and it also provides opportunities and resources

TABLE 1.1   A Mannian typology of types and degrees of power at the outset of war in the four cases in this book

HIERARCHICAL POWER	INFRASTRUCTURAL POWER	
	LOW	HIGH
Low	France (1791)	United States (1861)
High	Italy (1914)	United States (2001)

Source: Mann 1987.

for civil society groups to gain advantages and to oppose their government's wars and impositions of citizen rights. Table 1.1 lays out a rough grid of the combinations of hierarchical and infrastructural power at the outset of war in the four states we will examine.

War not only triggers cycles of contention in the immediate wake of war; it also produces new forms of contention, changes the relative power position of different social actors, legitimates or de-legitimates the elite, and can produce new actors who emerge from the war with new or strengthened resources. Workers who were disciplined by industrial policies; soldiers who return from the war with military experience and, sometimes, resentment at their losses; financial capitalists who have gained economic leverage over the state and experience dealing with state officials; women who have sacrificed for the war effort and hope to make gains from the nation's gratitude—these are some of the structural changes brought about by war that can have profound effects on the future state.

Globalization and Internationalization

Thus far, I have treated war, states, and contention as if they were framed by domestic boundaries, and, with respect to the cases I deal with in part 1, this seems a fair limitation. However, in part 2 I deal with the wars of the late twentieth and the beginning of the twenty-first centuries, when not only had the nature of war changed but two major processes made states more porous and movements more transnational: globalization and internationalization.

I define *globalization*, with Robert Keohane (2002, 194), as the increasing volume and speed of flows of capital and goods, information and ideas, and people and forces that connect actors between countries. This definition has the virtue of parsimony and also allows us to see globalization as a process that varies over time. Students of collective action have mainly seen it as the source of conventional nongovernmental organizations (NGOs) that operate transnationally, but it has enabled the growth of clandestine violent networks as well.

Internationalization means the increasing network of links among state actors and between states and international institutions. It provides an opportunity structure for actors previously confined to domestic spaces, fosters the diffusion of political-economic policies, a shift in scale from the national to the international level, and the internalization of international issues. International institutions and alignments also provide frames for domestic contention (Hironaka 2005, 22). Internationalization goes beyond interstate relations to include increased vertical ties between states and international institutions and the infrastructural links of nonstate associations and movements within the matrix of states and institutions (Tarrow 2005). This expansion of the concept will help us to see contentious politics as not only moving across boundaries but providing resources for shifting the scale of conflict from the local to the regional and international levels.

As globalization and internationalization have expanded, they have produced new opportunities for transnational actors. New actors increasingly accessed global frames of meaning, learned new forms of contention from others' examples, saw them as relevant to their own situations, and formed transnational alignments with others with whom they identified (della Porta and Tarrow 2005). This means that when we turn to war and contention in the twenty-first century, we are no longer dealing only with domestic forms of contention but with transnational coalitions. We are dealing with something else as well, with what Scheppele calls the international state of emergency. Internationalization has provided state actors with mechanisms, institutions, and treaties for dealing with the transnational actors who threaten their interests (see chapter 10).

Conclusions

This chapter has merely raised the issues that will be examined once we turn to the episodes we will examine in this book. Underlying them all is a question that we will turn to in the conclusion: What is the long-term effect of the interaction of war and contention on the development of modern states?

A simple but inadequate conclusion would be that because war is violent and liberal constitutional states seek peaceful solutions to social conflict, war-making and liberal states have been opposites since the French and American revolutions. That is correct as long as we focus only on illiberal goals. But since the French and American revolutions, the liberal creed has often been used to justify military efforts, both to mobilize armies and to gain the support of civilian populations. To some extent, these legitimating efforts are cheap talk. But no ideological justification is mere superstructure; states that exercise their power though infrastructural means are obliged to engage with their citizens. Many of the reforms we take for granted today—the citizen army, women's suffrage, and the welfare state—were spurred by war, preparations for war, and contention in war's wake (Starr 2007, 2010).

But all these eventualities assume that states and their citizens are fully in control of their common fate. That may have been true in the nineteenth and twentieth centuries, but in the new century, both the forms of power and the means of contending against them are no longer limited to the nation-state. As Mann argued in the last volume of his *Sources of Social Power* (2013), globalization is extending the range of state power and leading citizens beyond their boundaries to contest it. But globalization and internationalization have expanded the means of war and contention too. As in the past, but with a wider range, war is the cauldron in which states and citizens experiment with new forms of power and new modes of contention. What is different is that the line between war and peace is no longer clear and that both the forms of contention and their repression are increasingly global and international.

But these are complex matters, and they continue to evolve in the second decade of the new century. Before we can turn to them, it is important to establish how war, state-building, and internal contention intersected in earlier periods of history. We begin with the French Revolution, in which both modern war and the modern state began to take their contemporary shape. We then turn to the U.S. Civil War—the first industrial war—in which domestic contention transformed into violent conflict, which in turn spurred both an antiwar movement and a radical Republican Party that expanded both freedom and the Constitution. We turn, finally, to the impact of World War One on Italy, where the world's first fascist movement gave rise to a new model of authoritarianism and to the world's first totalitarian state. Our consideration of these three classical wars and their relations to state-building and contention will lay the groundwork for a more sustained encounter with war, states, and contention in the United States.

Part I

WAR AND MOVEMENTS IN THE BUILDING OF NEW STATES

2

A MOVEMENT-STATE GOES TO WAR

France, 1789–1799

In December 1791, Jacques Pierre Brissot de Warville, a leading member of the Girondin faction of the new revolutionary elite, told the Jacobin Club, "A people that has just won its liberty after ten centuries of slavery, needs a war in order to assure its consolidation (quoted in Walt 1996, 66). Brissot was not just talking about a thirst for war; France was in a state of emergency caused by both external threat and internal contention. In the west and south, insurgencies were erupting; on the borders, exiled nobles were urging France's monarchical neighbors to attack the new state; and since August, the Parisian crowd had been urging the Assembly ever more forcefully to liquidate its enemies. The crowd's anger was stoked by the flight of the king and queen and their apparent plotting with France's neighbors to overthrow the new regime. "Domestic politics," observes Walt, "now erupted and soon drove Europe over the brink" (ibid). From 1792 until Napoleon Bonaparate's defeat and exile in 1815, France was at war with its neighbors almost continuously (Bell 2007; Bertaud 1988; Blanning 1986).

Was Brissot's call to action no more than a cynical ploy to displace the conflicts within the revolution onto foreign adventures? Or an uncontrollable spiral of conflict fed by uncertainty by both France and its neighbors? Or the inexorable result of the desire to create an ideological utopia? None of these answers takes account of the political process within the new revolutionary state. As Stephen Walt writes, "A second cause of war [alongside the hostility of France's neighbors] was the struggle for power in France" (1996, 64).

Although the French could not have known this in 1789, they were building a powerful movement-based state, constructed on the basis of the hierarchical power they had inherited from the Old Regime and on a new kind of power—infrastructural power—that emerged from the conflicts within the revolution. The French revolutionaries were successful in making war because they could draw on both the habits of centralization and on the power of a movement for change in the name of liberty. The two together produced the world's first powerful emergency state.

This was not at all obvious at first. In April 1792, French troops crossed the border into Belgium to attack a superior Austrian army, soon to be joined by Prussia (Walt 1996, 74–75; Blanning 1986, chap. 4). The army—like the French state—was in disarray, made up partly of professional soldiers inherited from the Old Regime and partly of raw recruits who lacked discipline and training (Bertaud 1988, 63–79). After nearly three years of revolution, the state had lost much of its hierarchical power, and its new leaders had not yet succeeded in penetrating the society they had precariously conquered. The early results were catastrophic; the inexperienced French troops "broke and ran at their first encounter with the Austrian forces," a general was murdered by his own troops, and the remaining officers "declared an offensive impossible and refused to move" (Walt 1996, 75).

Yet, within a remarkably brief period, the republicans reorganized the army, integrated its professional and conscripted sectors (Bertaud 1988, chap. 4), pushed back the invaders, and conquered half of Europe. They overthrew the crowned heads of Italy and Spain, triggered revolutions in the Low Countries, and created a ring of dependent republican governments around the hexagon (Palmer 1964, chaps. 3, 6, 9–14). They did this, in part, by organizing a *levée en masse* that brought hundreds of thousands of citizen-soldiers under the colors, inventing the model of the citizen-army in the process (Bertaud 1988, chap. 5; Kestnbaum 2002). By the time Napoleon took power in 1799, what had begun as a rag-tag army of national defense had evolved into an army of imperial expansion. The French republicans invented total warfare (Bell 2007), but they created something else as well—a state that combined militant nationalism with direct rule and the state's penetration of society.

Histories of the revolutionary decade frequently focus on the aggressive expansionism behind the French achievement (Blanning 1986, chap. 4). What is often obscured is that it succeeded in large part because the French republicans were the first in history to demonstrate the military potential of mobilizing a democratic movement through centralized control. But that decade also revealed the dangers in such a dynamic; as the new state developed, the liberal sentiments of the early revolutionaries were ground down between the threat of internal counter-revolution and the pressures of external conflict. A democratic movement-state at war gave rise to the first modern consolidated state. But it also reversed the rights granted to the French under its first constitution-like document—the Declaration of the Rights of Man and the Citizen.

The Politics of a Movement-State

Four political processes brought France its extraordinary military successes—violence, radicalization, provisioning, and state-building—along with contentious politics. But these processes also produced a transition from the liberal constitutionalism of the new state's founding to the system of mobilization into which it developed. All four emerged in response to war and intersected with contentious politics within the revolution.

Violence, Peripheral and Central

No revolution is ever entirely peaceful, but in France each phase of the revolution triggered new and interacting forms of violence, ranging from unorganized *jacqueries* (peasant riots) to organized urban *journées* (days of rioting), such as the "revolution of August 10th" that led to the end of the constitutional monarchy, and to insurrections and counter-revolution in the west (Tilly 1964). Critics have often collapsed all these forms of violence into the Terror. But there are three things wrong with this highly condensed image:

First, violence was an important facet of French politics and society long before the revolution. Jean-Clément Martin (2006) has vividly demonstrated the violence of everyday life in prerevolutionary France, alongside the deliberate violence of the state's punishment of criminal behavior. The guillotine, we often forget, was invented to replace the viciously violent practices of the Old Regime's executioners, who had made sure that suspects were brutally tortured before they were killed.

Second, after 1789 violence was pervasive, many-sided, and in large part undirected. "The country," according to Martin, "thus enters into a veritable state of civil war, unified by the cleavage that develops between the revolution and the counter-revolution. Religious, social, regional and cultural antagonisms combined as authority dissolved and both legality and legitimacy were placed on the agenda" (ibid., 12). The effect of this widespread violence was to create a climate of uncertainty and suspicion on all sides and assured that the new regimes' leaders felt themselves assailed on all sides (Kaplan 1982).

Third, as in many civil wars, violence was both central and ideological (what Stathis Kalyvas [2003] calls Schmittian violence) and peripheral and personal (what he calls Hobbesian violence). The preoccupation of most historians with the Terror has focused attention only on centralized violence and obscured the enormous amount of violence in the periphery, much of it caused by the private settling of scores, by brigandage, and by self-appointed vigilantes doing the revolution's work at the grassroots. Violence was more of a process than a policy.

Radicalization

Interacting with, but not reducible to, the spiral of widely diffused violence were the ideological conflicts between warring parties that triggered each change in regime. Simplifying radically, we can summarize these cleavages with Tilly (1993, 165):

May 1789–July 1789	Crown versus Third Estate
1791	Beginning of the civil war
June 1792–January 1793	Crown versus revolutionary regime
March 1793–December 1793	Vendée rebellion; Jacobins versus Girondists, Federalists
August 1799–November 1799	Directory versus royalists versus Bonaparte

These episodes were not divided into neat stages, as observers such as Crane Brinton (1965) thought, but overlapped and interacted. "Within each of these periods," writes Tilly, "France experienced not one but a succession of revolutionary situations, as control of the central apparatus shifted, coalitions formed among their opponents, the segments of state power controlled by the opposition changed and popular support for various contending factions fluctuated" (1993, 165–66).

In the Vendée region, for example, insurgency erupted first over the government's insistence that priests sign a loyalty oath to the regime, then over forced conscription, and throughout over land seizures before it ripened into full-scale civil war (Martin 1998). When the army was sent to put down the insurgency in the west, the brutality of the external war was transferred to France's home territory (Bell 2007, chap. 5). Entire cities, such as Lyon, Toulon, and Marseille, were for a time under rebel control and had to be conquered by full-scale military invasions.

Even as insurgencies were defeated, widespread brigandage marked the second half of the revolutionary decade, leading the Directory to expand the extraordinary powers that had been developed to deal with counter-revolution to much of the country (Saint-Bonnet 2001; Le Gal 2005). Rural violence, at first triggered by peasant assaults on the landed estates, spread to grain seizures, anti-tax protests, and conscription riots. These rebellions within the revolution lacked the consistency of the counter-revolution in the west but were more widespread and continued throughout the revolutionary decade, taking on a Paris-versus-the-provinces character that led the regime to respond with the same kind of measures it had used against the enemies of the regime.

The Provisioning Crisis

During the Old Regime, one of the primary tasks of the monarchy was to regulate the price of bread and assure an adequate supply of flour to the cities—especially to Paris (Kaplan 1984). The revolution exacerbated the problem as estates were invaded, roads became dangerous, and the central state lost the power to control prices and the food supply. In the course of 1793, popular pressure forced the republicans to pass two measures to control prices: the decree of July 26, which banned the hoarding of commodities, and the law of September 29, which fixed a "general maximum" of prices (Martineau 1989, 128).

Contention interacted with dearth. The crowds that surged into the Legislative Assembly in January 1792 and into the Convention in September 1793 were not only calling for death to counter-revolutionaries but for bread at a fair price (ibid., 127). It was the demand of the *sans-culottes* for cheap and reliable food that led, in September 1793, to the imposition of the general maximum and led the Convention to send a revolutionary "army" to the provinces to assure grain supplies and punish hoarders (Cobb 1987). The combination of pressure from the Parisian street, the Jacobins' ability to exploit it, and the fear of starvation combined to produce the atmosphere of crisis that brought the Jacobins to power and made commercial speculation a crime for which the radicals in the Assembly demanded the death penalty (ibid., 130–31).

State-Building

The revolutionaries were engaged in a serious, prolonged, and arduous process of state-building from the beginning (Bell 2007, 92). "A new state apparatus was being built," write Pierre Lascoumes and Pierrette Poncela, " and its personnel saw themselves with the particular responsibility of defending the security and the credibility of the institutions and of political practice" (1989, 98–99). As Tocqueville famously argued, the revolutionaries did not invent a centralized state out of whole cloth. Napoleon, he argued, invented little that was new, simply picking up on and refining the centralization inherited from the Old Regime

(Tocqueville 1955, 202). His memorable phrase is "that since '89 the administrative system has always stood firm amid the debacles of political systems. There might be dynastic changes and alterations in the structure of the state machine, but the course of day-to-day affairs was neither interrupted nor deflected" (ibid.).

As in many of his other claims, Tocqueville was half right. Napoleon did inherit a centralized administrative structure, but it was one that the revolution had built. The Old Regime was never as centralized as Tocqueville claims. The revolutionaries swept the traditional provinces from the map, replacing them with uniform *départements*, districts, cantons, and communes and applied direct rule to many regions for the first time. Their reforms raised the status of some provincial cities while lowering that of significant others (Lepetit 1988); they transferred local power from provincial elites to patriot coalitions and replaced many of these with more reliable administrators; and they stripped away the tissue of ancient liberties and exemptions that many localities had enjoyed for centuries (Tilly 1993, 168).

The revolutionaries also created a new system of justice, reining in the hated judges, rewriting the judicial code, and establishing rule of law. Based on a law of 1790 reorganizing the judiciary, a new penal code was created, regularizing and standardizing criminal law. As Pierre Lascoumes and Pierrette Poncela write, "The modern penal code was developed more to enable participation in the new political order than to ratify civilian contracts. Its major aim was not the protection of goods or people but of institutions, and new republican and older values" (1989, 74).

Defending a state-in-the-making from its internal and external enemies was at the heart of the new penal code. In their content analysis of the Code of 1791, Lascoumes and Poncela pinpoint the overwhelming importance of protecting "political interests" in the thinking of the Constituent Assembly. Of the 224 articles in the Code, 43.6 percent were concerned with protecting political interests, 35.5 percent were classified as "natural morality," 8.2 percent were intended to protect economic interests, and only 12.7 percent aimed at defending "civil morality" (ibid., 101).

But the revolutionaries were not just building a state—they were building a *revolutionary* state, a mission that marked their debates from the beginning. In the deliberations of the Assembly, the lawlessness of the monarchy was a constant reminder to make the law supreme. Trial by jury was imported into the legal system and maintained even during the periods of greatest tension. Debates in the Assembly were marked by deep philosophical discussions about what a revolutionary state should look like; even the dress to be worn by different classes of civil servants was carefully studied, although never implemented (Hunt 1984). The revolutionary state was not only designed; it was performed.

Contentious Politics

Each of these processes—violence, radicalization, provisioning, and state-building—intersected with a confused and contradictory process of contention (Martin 2006, 81, 123–24):

- Although much of the violence was a sign that public order was breaking down, violence also broke out over provisioning, state-building, and political competition. The most visible violence took place in the periphery, where municipal and then regional revolts broke out over conscription, religion, taxes, and federalism versus centralization.
- Radicalization, which occurred mainly within institutional politics, was in part a response to and in part a spur to popular violence; in fact, there was a constant interaction between national and peripheral, Schmittian and Hobbesian violence (Martin 2006).
- Food riots were a traditional part of contentious politics, but the subsistence crises during the revolution inspired thousands of violent incidents across the country. The price of bread, and its suspected hoarding by counter-revolutionary forces, became a touchstone for revolutionary politics (Kaplan 1984).
- State-building triggered contention too, especially from people and localities that had been exempt from taxation in the past. "Resistance and counter-revolutionary action followed directly from the process by which the new state established direct rule," concludes Tilly (1993, 171).

War was not the inevitable result of these processes—the ambitions of France's neighbors to quash the revolutionary state had much to do with it. But it produced opportunities both for internal contention and for state expansion. War heightened the risks from internal violence and made it urgent to secure a reliable and affordable source of provisions. It reinforced the centralizing logic of the new state and created the justification for the creation of exceptional institutions and reshaped those that had been created in the heady days of 1789. To understand this state of exception, we must first understand those institutions, beginning with the primary constitutional document of the revolution—the Declaration of the Rights of Man.

From Constitutional Liberalism to Republican Defense

Rights were not a new idea to the heirs of the Old Regime. After all, it was in the name of defending their rights that the *parlements* of the Old Regime resisted the attempts of the monarchy to extract new taxes. But those rights were privileges that attached to particular individuals, groups, and corporations; the idea that there was a set of universal rights available to all men (women were another matter) resided mainly in the works of the physiocrats until the revolution began. These ideas were brought to the Constituent Assembly by a class of educated Frenchmen—men such as Pierre Samuel du Dupont de Nemours; Gilbert du Motier, the Marquis de Lafayette; and the Abbé Emmanuel Joseph Sièyes—who were steeped in the work of Enlightenment philosophers such as Hugo Grotius and Samuel von Pufendorf and were influenced by the republican ideas of the American founders (Gauchet 1989, 819; Wright 1993).

As one of its first acts, the Constituent Assembly that met in August 1789 passed the Declaration of the Rights of Man and the Citizen, granting rights that it claimed were not only "inalienable" but equal and secure (Rials 1988). The Declaration was a deliberate reaction against the use of secret and irrevocable *lettres de cachet* (condemnation without appeal, literally, by private seal of the king) (Le Gal 2012, 4–5). It was written along lines suggested by the English Bill of Rights, the declarations of the new American states, and the American Declaration of Independence (Badinter 1989, 16–17). But in its sweep and simplicity, it went much further than these documents. As Lynn Hunt writes, never once mentioning king, nobility, or church, it declared the "natural, inalienable and sacred rights of man" to be the foundation of any and all government (2007, 16).

The Declaration was not an isolated gesture in establishing rights. In a judicial act of 1790, the delegates established trial by jury—an institution that endured through the revolutionary decade (Brown 2006; Schnapper 1989). They followed this by abolishing primogeniture and the *lettres de cachet*. They established institutions for compulsory mediation to hear disputes between parents and children, granted rights to Jews and Protestants (Badinter 1989, 19–20), and (briefly) enfranchised men without property and lowered the age of majority from twenty-five to twenty-one. In 1794, their successors abolished slavery. When they framed the Constitution of 1791, they made the words of the Declaration its preamble (Rials 1982; Lascoumes, Poncella, and Lenoël 1989, 88–96). Even under the Convention and the Directory, the words of the Declaration continued to be raised as a banner proclaiming liberty as the goal of the revolution.

Words, of course, are one thing, and practice quite another. The Declaration was never made an organic part of the Constitution of 1791, as was the Bill of Rights in the U.S. Constitution. And although it was full of generous libertarian sentiments—including the right of revolt—nowhere did the framers buttress it with an organism to assure that the rights it elaborated would be protected. Their major preoccupation was with throttling the power of the king and establishing the absolute prominence of the law and the legislature (Glénard 2010; Rudelle 1993).

Article VI of the Declaration read⌐:

> The law is the expression of the general will. All citizens have the right to contribute, both personally or through their representatives, to its development. It must be the same for all, whether it protects or punishes. For its constituents, the law—expression of the general will—cannot be wrong.

The legalism of the constituents was perhaps the most durable inheritance of the revolution for French constitutional practice (Gauchet 1989, 827; Rudelle 1993). The Constitution of 1791—like the two that followed—was heavily Assembly-centric. The Assembly was to propose and pass the laws; the king had no more than a suspensive veto; and there was no judicial body to judge the constitutionality of the laws the Assembly passed (Glénard 2010). Although a *Tribunal de Cassation* (Court of Final Appeal) was created in 1790, that institution was conceived as tributary of the legislature and had no power to pass on the constitutionality of the laws it passed or even to interpret ordinary law (Articles 19–21; Halpérin 1987). When the legislature did not like the Tribunal's decisions, it could simply annul them (Halpérin 1987, 10).

Seen against the backdrop of monarchical discretion, this was a clear advance; but with respect to rights, it left the status of the Declaration more symbolic than real. Rights continued to be invoked—for example, by Jean-Antoine-Nicolas de Condorcet, when he justified putting the "finalities" of the laws over their "disposition" (1847–1849 [1968]; quoted in Saint-Bonnet 2001, 293). But, although the authority of the Declaration was repeatedly affirmed during the course of the revolution, war, internal insurgency, the provisioning crisis, and the demands of state-building led to increasing denials of rights in practice. In the words of Jean-Clément Martin, "The traditional language of rights is being assaulted by the upsurge of a new language based on threatening claims that declare legal a new social organization, a 'we' that makes demands and whose expression depends on emotion and metaphor" (2006, 81).

Although Article III of the Declaration established a broad concept of individual liberty, allowing individuals "to do anything that does not injure others," these limits were to be established through ordinary laws (Woloch 1994, 24). No constitutional court was created, either in the Constitution of 1791 or in its successors, to prevent the legislature's actions from abrogating principles inscribed in the Declaration. "Judicial power will be badly organized if the judge enjoys the dangerous privilege of interpreting the law or of adding to its stipulations," wrote one deputy (quoted by Gauchet 1995, 58; see also Ferrand 2010; Rials 1982, 17).

In the absence of judicial review, the Assembly, and then the Convention, could adjust its views on rights to the political needs of the moment. Listen to how Condorcet justified overriding the Constitution of 1791 when he saw the *patrie* in danger: "An irrevocable law that would prevent action when it is obviously necessary, and that would give the national will no means of expression when public safety demands it would be absurd" (1847–1849 [1968]; quoted in Saint-Bonnet 2001, 293). As a result, the stirring rights accorded French citizens by the Declaration were contradicted in fact as early as the constitutional monarchy, when the legislature was engaged in gaining control of the clergy and staunching the power of the king (1789–1792). The Republic, the Directory, the Consulate, and, of course, the Empire continued the practice, with the difference that the legislature had increasingly less power. In revolutionary France, something like a state of exception rapidly smothered the constitutionally vested rights that were proclaimed in the early years of the revolution. This led to the invention of emergency rule.

The Invention of Emergency Rule

War and contentious politics were the origin of the state of emergency. By 1793, France was in a constant state of armed conflict. It was against the threat of military defeat that the Committee of Public Safety was set up, newspapers critical of the revolution were closed down, and political disagreement began to be framed as treason (Lynn 1983, chap. 3). As institutions for administering wartime justice were created (Schnapper 1989), states of siege were expanded to broad swaths of the national territory (Le Gal 2011), and political opponents were put "outside the law" (de Mari 1991).

Between the heady rights-driven claims of 1789 and the ordered dictatorship of Napoleon, there was a red thread exposed by the changing language of the revolutionaries. At the beginning, citizenship talk was dominant, as the language of the Declaration reveals. Nowhere more than in the army was the new concept of citizenship expanded. "Jacobinism," writes Jean-Paul Bertaud, "instilled the principle of unity, its essential watchword. There were no more 'whites' and 'blues,' no more draftees and volunteers, no more Alsacians, Auvergnats, and Gascons, but only Frenchmen fighting in the cause of Liberty against aristocracy" (1988, 229).

But gradually, a new language came to dominate debate, producing a more threatening language of politics (Martin 2006, 81; Tarrow 2013a, chap. 2). Citizenship, proclaimed with such *élan* in the Declaration, was quickly surrounded by constraints in the Constitution of 1791 (Rials 1982, 8–9). Although the Constitution of 1793 expanded voting rights to all men living in France who had reached the age of twenty-one (ibid., 20), that constitution was never implemented and the distinction between "passive" and "active" citizens (based on taxes; ibid., 24) was reestablished in the Year III. Not only that—people under indictment, those who had been declared bankrupt, and those who could not show that their net worth equaled the local value of two hundred workdays were excluded from the vote (ibid., 9).

The first right to be curtailed was the right of association. The first move came quite early, in the *Loi martiale* ("martial law") of October 1789, banning what the Assembly called *attroupements* (which today would be called demonstrations). Then, in June 1791 the Assembly passed the famous Le Chapelier law, abolishing the corporations and refusing to allow "intermediate groupings between 'the general interest' and the 'particular interest' of each citizen." A law of August 1791 curtailed freedom of speech, punishing "voluntary calumnies against public functionaries . . . and all calumnies against private parties at their request" (Godechot 1968, 64).

The Jacobins had developed a network of societies across the country that both drew on an older associational tradition and brought together a new local elite from among the upper and middle classes. According to Michael Kennedy, from 19 cities in 1789, the clubs expanded to 213 in 1790 and to 833 in 1791 and 1792 (Kennedy 1982; Higonnet 1998). But, as the Jacobins shifted from organizing in civil society to government, their leaders began to close down other vibrant clubs that had debated the goals of the revolution before and after 1789; when they were defeated in 1793, their societies were repressed and the remaining members went underground. From then on, whichever group opposed the faction in power was branded enemies of the revolution.

Next to be modified was the system of military justice. A liberal law of October 1791 had allowed appeals from military tribunals to the *Tribunal de Cassation* in times of peace. In the same year, another law did away with the powers of military officials in "places of war" and limited these places to a carefully demarcated list of fortresses and fortified towns (Le Gal 2011). But after war was declared, a new law held that "the judgments of martial law courts, like those of military tribunals, would not be subject either to appeal or to cassation" (Halpérin 1987, 116). States of siege were proclaimed even far from the border, where there was either violence or the threat of violence (Le Gal 2005, 2011). At the same time, decrees passed by the Convention removed the right of a wide range of suspects to a jury trial (Brown 2006, 95–96; Schnapper 1989, 160–61). "When an ordinary criminal court sat without a jury or depended on the verdict of a 'special jury' chosen with political criteria it was called 'judging revolutionarily'" (Schnapper 1989, 161).

No category of people was more heavily sanctioned by the law than those who had gone into exile, including the ones who had returned. Three categories of exiles were targeted by an act of March 28, 1793: those who left France before July 1, 1789, and failed to return before May 9, 1792; those who could not prove continuous residence in France after the latter date; and those who moved to parts of the country occupied by the enemy. The penalty for emigration was perpetual banishment and the loss of all property, or *mort civique* ("civil degradation") (Simonin 2007, 28). Returned emigrants were to be sentenced to death, and the same penalty was applied to their accomplices (see the summary and statistics in Greer 1935,15–16, table 4). The term *exile* soon became a synonym for *enemy*.

Early military defeats led to fear that the revolution was in danger and caused the noose to be tightened on dissent (Godfrey 1951, 4). This was what led Georges Danton in March 1793 to propose the creation of a special revolutionary tribunal that would process indictments from both department officials and the Committee of Public Safety (ibid., 8–10). From December 1793 on, "representatives on mission" began to send suspects to this tribunal for indictment (Brown 2006, 996). After the June 10, 1794, *journée*, the law of 22 Prairial denied prisoners the right to employ counsel or to call witnesses in their defense and declared the death penalty the only possible outcome for defendants who were found guilty. In response to external war and internal contention, revolutionary France was inventing emergency rule.

Wars, Politics, and Citizenship

Why give so much attention to rights during a revolution that upended so much of the social structure? Wasn't the revolution, because it was dominated by the Terror, ideologically bound to abuse rights, as the revisionist school of French historiography would have it (Furet 1989; Gueniffley 2000)? The situation was actually far more complicated. Rights continued to matter to the French throughout the revolutionary decade, even as late as the Empire (Le Gal 2012). Why else would the elites have maintained the institution of elected juries in their regular court system even as they were judging suspects "revolutionarily" (Brown 2006, chap. 4; Hans and Germain 2011)? Or why give notorious terrorists jury trials after Maximilien de Robespierre's fall instead of condemning them summarily (Steinberg 2010, 2013)? Rights—or at least the legal forms of rights—mattered to the revolutionaries, even as they were putting people "outside the law."

The revolution did not transcend ordinary politics either. On the contrary, the elites were engaged in many of the processes typical of politics in ordinary times: building and reforming a state, provisioning cities, collecting taxes, passing thousands of laws and decrees, recruiting and maintaining an army, and electing deputies by local assemblies (Tilly 1993, 8). From the evidence we have, local elections were vigorously contested, and politics soon entered the army. Even Napoleon was a "political" general, using the tools of political propaganda to enhance his reputation and helping to advance "the dissolving of boundaries between politics and the military that characterized the age of total war" (Bell 2007, 132). What the revolution did change was the concept of the citizen, and that change was at the heart of both its destructive and its creative power.

From the beginning, citizenship was seen as an honor and was surrounded by performative rituals. The citizen who did not behave honorably could suffer civil degradation (Simonin 2007, 28). Civil degradation deprived the citizen of the exercise of his political rights. "By means of the new sentence of civil degradation, honor becomes an interest protected by law" (ibid., 57). Ceremonies of degradation were integrated into the penal code so as to "render visible the dignity of the revolutionary citizen" (ibid., 40; Martinage 1989, 117). Gradually at first, but with increasing intensity, the signs of citizenship—loyalty, honor, even costume (Hunt 1984)—marked the bad citizen from the good one, in some cases leading to persecution and even execution.

It was not sufficient to simply not disobey the law; the bad citizen, we learn from Article VII of the Declaration of Rights and Duties of the Year III, was "one who, without openly infringing laws, can evade them without the need for either cunning or skill" (de Mari 1991). "From the start of the first uprisings in the West," writes Bernard Schnapper, "a decree of March 19, 1793, outlawed the rebels. . . . As for those who were captured carrying arms, they appeared before military commissions and all procedural timetables were cut short" (1989, 26). The practice of putting people "outside the law" allowed the revolutionaries to punish suspects by exceptional means while maintaining untouched the rights encapsulated in the Declaration and the Constitution.

Between March 1793 and 9 Thermidor in the Year II, Eric de Mari found that a total of almost 22,000 people were judged "outside the law," of whom more than half (13,048) were condemned to death. The largest proportions were found in the counter-revolutionary west and the insurrectionary southeast (11,234 and 8,541, respectively), but significant numbers were judged to be "outside the law" in the east and south as well. Table 2.1 reproduces de Mari's summary statistics for the number of people tried "outside the law," the number of condemnations to death, and Donald Greer's corresponding statistics on the number of executions during the Terror.

Greer's data show that "the Terror struck hardest in regions of civil war in the West," in the south, and the southwest, where there were manifestations of counter-revolution second only in importance to the conflagrations of the Vendée and the Rhône Valley (Greer 1935, 40). It was also intense in the border

TABLE 2.1   Judgments and death sentences for citizens "outside the law" in revolutionary France, from March 19, 1793, to Thermidor year II [1795], by region

REGION	NUMBER JUDGED OUTSIDE THE LAW	NUMBER CONDEMNED TO DEATH	NUMBER EXECUTED (GREER DATA)
Paris region	99	13	27
Northwest	377	241	268
North	210	56	551
Center	482	53	134
East	1,144	133	133
South	1,118	462	434
Southwest	1,220	440	457
Southeast	5,915	3,109	3,158
West	11,234	8,541	8,674
Total	21,799	13,048	13,946

Sources: de Mari 1991; Greer 1935.

departments, where "the Jacobins regarded the Terror as a defense of the frontiers" (ibid, 40–41). Maps 2.1 and 2.2, drawn from Greer's analysis, reveal the close territorial connections among war, insurgency, and repressive violence. But extraordinary justice also turned on brigands and ordinary criminals. The brigand bands were a challenge to the state because they combined crime and politics, social resistance and the threat of counter-revolution. Long after Robespierre and the Jacobins fell, the state continued what amounted to a state of emergency.

Whether we regard the Terror as a system, as Furet (1981) and his followers do, or as an aggregate of partially centralized and partially peripheral violence, as contemporary scholars do (Martin 2006), state violence was only one element in the development of a state of permanent emergency. This was in part because France remained at war, with only a brief interlude, until Napoleon fell and in part because intermovement conflict and ordinary brigandage created as much disorder as insurrection did.

We can see this best when we look at the rise and growth of states of siege during the revolutionary decade. Technically, the state of siege means the transfer of the maintenance of public order from civil to military authority. It was traditionally employed only in *places de guerre et postes militarires* ("places of war and military posts") "when these places and posts were in a state of siege."[1] But between 1791 and the Consulate, there was what we today would call a "ratchet effect"; that is, the concept of the state of siege was extended from places of

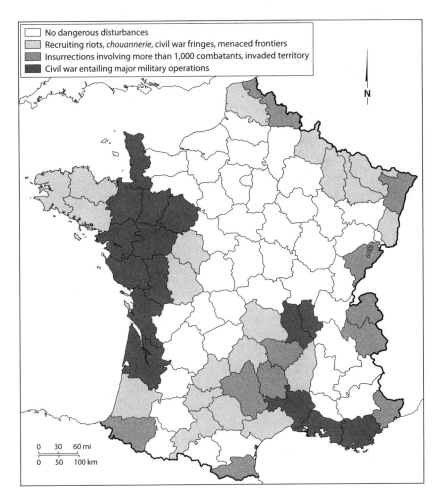

No dangerous disturbances
Recruiting riots, *chouannerie*, civil war fringes, menaced frontiers
Insurrections involving more than 1,000 combatants, invaded territory
Civil war entailing major military operations

N

0   30   60 mi
0   50   100 km

MAP 2.1   The geographical incidence of the counterrevolution in France. Greer 1935, frontispiece 1.

war to any part of the country that authorities saw as threatened by insurgency, counter-revolution, or ordinary violence and brigandage (Le Gal 2005)—the so-called *état de siège fictive* ("fictitious state of siege"). Of course, areas where the counter-revolution erupted were also more likely to be those in which states of siege were declared, but the use of states of siege was much more widespread (the correlation between the two is only 0.045). In fact, more than twice as many states of siege were declared during the Directory (1795–1799), when the Jacobins were no longer in power, than during the Terror (Le Gal 2011, 591–93). Figure 2.1,

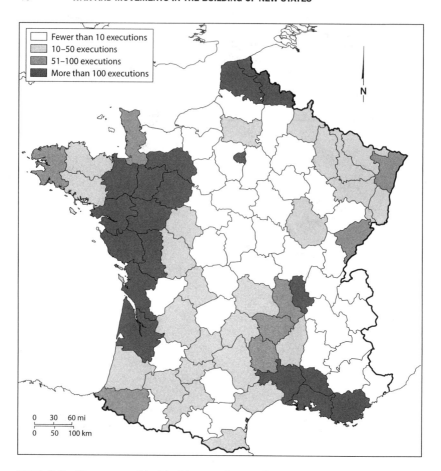

MAP 2.2 The geographical incidence of executions in France, March 1793–May 1795. Greer 1935, frontispiece 2.

drawn from Sébastien Le Gal's work, shows how the number of declarations of states of siege grew after the fall of Robespierre.

It would be a mistake to put this eighteenth-century revolutionary state in the same category as the genocidal regime of Adolf Hitler or the Gulag state of Josef Stalin. First, much of the killing was aimed at a genuine counter-revolution, as in the Vendée; second, the state of siege was used as often against ordinary brigandage as against rebellion; and, third, France was at war during most of the period in which exceptional measures were employed. If there is a parallel to be found in these measures, it is with the states of exception that contemporary liberal states have used during wartime.

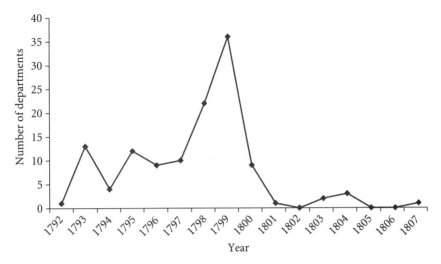

FIGURE 2.1 Departments in a state of siege, 1792–1807. Analyzed by the author from Le Gal 2011, app.

The Birth of the Emergency Script

In chapter 1, I laid out the model of the emergency script, which Kim Scheppele (2006) developed on the basis of her database of twentieth-century episodes of emergency rule. What is most striking about Scheppele's emergency script is how closely it fits the sequence of responses to internal contention and foreign war two centuries earlier in the French revolutionary state.

Centralization. Territorial centralization was one of the first administrative acts of the Constituent Assembly, but control of the periphery continued to be tightened over the course of the revolutionary decade (Godechot 1968). The legalism of the framers and their desire to weaken the judiciary and the executive left power centralized in the Convention and, within the Convention, in its two most important committees (Woloch 1994, 42). When the Jacobin Convention fell, power remained centralized in the Directorate, the Consulate, and, of course, the Empire (ibid., 46–51). But the "vacuity of power" that the evacuation of executive and judicial power produced (Martin 2006, 123–24) led to the next stage in the emergency script—militarization.

Militarization. Once the other civilian branches had been marginalized, the next step was the militarization of executive and judicial power. First, the legions of Parisians who were sent out to the provinces to police provisioning, under the label *armées révolutionnaires*, became instruments of political policing (Godechot 1968, 354–55). The officers who declared local states of siege became essentially local dictators. At the same time, the revolution invented a new and important French figure—the political general. "They typified, and helped to advance the dissolving of boundaries between politics and the military" (Bell 2007, 132; Bertaud 1988, 267). A growing militarization of politics resulted from the inability of the political institutions to cope with the challenges of ending the revolution.

Procedural shortcuts. Once the military was positioned as the key responder to the threat, new state bodies were established and old ones that used to provide procedural checks were bypassed or neutralized. We see this in the creation of revolutionary tribunals and in the gradual emasculation of the jury system. The Revolutionary Tribunal short-circuited the regular courts and the jury system, and military commissions increasingly took over the management of public order (Bertaud 1988, 201, 329; Schnapper 1989).

Putting people in their places. The next step in Scheppele's emergency script is the setting up of regimes of preventive detention and the banning of popular demonstrations. In France, the protections of the civil law were progressively removed from suspects who were placed "outside the law." Priests who refused to sign the Civil Constitution of the Clergy were forced into exile, and people who showed insufficient patriotism or "honor" suffered indignity or worse (Simonin 2007). Many suspected enemies of the regime were exiled, others perished on the guillotine, and many thousands died in the repression of the counter-revolution.

Inversion of speech protection. The next step in Scheppele's emergency script is the criminalization of formerly protected speech, the closure or nationalization of the press, and the institutionalization of censorship. In France, the flourishing newspaper world that followed 1789 was progressively choked off as opposition papers were closed down and an official press was used to proselytize for the war and condemn opponents as traitors. Press freedom was essentially quashed by March 1793, except for the press of the regime, which was used to diffuse patriotic propaganda to the troops (Godechot 1968, 348–49; Bertaud 1988; Lynn 1983).

Reversal of transparency. The Law of Suspects allowed local committees to make arrests on suspicion of disloyalty, federalism, or support for monarchy without reference to the ordinary courts (Godechot 1968, 378–79) When the Revolutionary Tribunal was created in March 1793, its judgments were made irreversible within twenty-four hours, without recourse (ibid., 381). The Consulate passed decrees and informed the legislative chambers only afterward about what they had done. And, of course, Napoleon passed decrees without reference to the rubber-stamp legislature.

Anticipatory violence. In France, mass violence in the west took thousands of lives indiscriminately in areas that were thought to be susceptible to rebellion. The definition of *aristocrats* was gradually broadened to mean all opponents of the regime. Eventually all political opponents were designated as counter-revolutionaries and punished through summary justice.

Lingering powers. In France, the state of exception, despite being seen as a necessary exception to the rule of law, became the basis of a massive expansion of rule *by* law, as in contemporary authoritarian systems and, occasionally, in liberal democratic systems too (see chapter 6). From the suppression of counter-revolutionaries, there was an extension of states of siege to communities and departments where brigands and ordinary criminals were taking advantage of the chaos of war and rebellion. The French never used the term *emergency rule*, but it is still true in France today that radical centralization takes the name of its inventors—Jacobinism.

Conclusions

We should not exaggerate the permanent damage to rights and contention in the wake of the revolution. In the short term, of course, most of the rights enunciated in the Declaration of the Rights of Man were honored in the breach. The republicans closed down the revolutionary clubs that had flourished after 1789, they put people "outside the law," and they transformed the state of siege from an instrument for the defense of border strongholds to a general method of military rule. These moves toward exceptional rule during the revolution were hardened into a hierarchical state under the Empire.

But in the long term, the Declaration inspired both French and international constitutional development to an astonishing degree. "For nearly two centuries," concludes Lynn Hunt," despite the controversy provoked by the French Revolution, the Declaration of the Rights of Man and Citizen incarnated the promise of universal human rights" (2007, 17). The document became a universal symbolic expression for states—even hierarchical states—that recognize the reciprocal power of civil society. Hierarchical and infrastructural power have continued to concatenate in the history of modern states.

Nor was contentious politics permanently stifled by the heritage of the centralized state. Post-revolutionary French history is rich with cycles of both peaceful and violent protest. The French practically invented the peaceful demonstration (Favre 1990), expanded the use of the barricade from the defense of neighborhoods to an instrument of revolutionary organization (Traugott 2010), and continue today to vigorously employ contentious politics. But, unlike contention in the United States, which remained mainly local, contention in France rapidly gravitated to the national level, where it was met by a strong and hierarchical state that snuffed out early efforts to govern society from within.

We will find differences among the emergency scripts that grew up during the French Revolution and the other cases in this book. For one thing, the French revolutionaries had no models to follow as they fashioned responses to simultaneous internal and external emergencies. For another, there was not sufficient unity in the revolutionary class for it to "plan" its responses—these came about through conjunctural interactions among war, internal dissention, state-building, and political conflict.

But as we will see, such interactions and adaptations are present in our other cases as well: in President Abraham Lincoln's at first narrow and then general suspension of *habeas corpus* during the U.S. Civil War; in the Italian state's expansion of house arrest into the sweeping use of internal exile; and in the expansion of the war powers of the U.S. president to carry out illegal surveillance, torture, and targeted killings in the years after 9/11.

Most important, the French case shows that, because of its weakness, a new revolutionary state is more likely to rely on hierarchical than on infrastructural power. This pattern was repeated and intensified in the fascist, national socialist, and Soviet revolutions, with this difference: the French revolutionary state was empowered by an ideology of liberalism, a doctrine that, once in place, allows the state to make war with the backing of its citizens, as we will see in the next case of war, state-building, and contention.

3

A MOVEMENT MAKES WAR
Civil War and Reconstruction

Civil Wars have a complex effect on state-building because they are at the same time forms of warfare and episodes of contention.[1] This raises thorny questions about the use of state judicial and police powers to restrain opponents, who are, at the same time, enemies and citizens, and about what happens to them in war's wake. The U.S. Civil War was especially complex in these respects. It was fought by a party—the Republican Party—that was uncommitted to ending slavery at the outset of the war but was transformed by the war into a movement-party that brought about a quasi-revolution (Ackerman 1998). That revolution extended citizenship to black Americans, liberalized the Constitution with three Reconstruction amendments, strengthened the state, and forged an alliance between the state and capital that has lasted to the present day. In the course of the war and during Reconstruction, the Union grappled with the problem of the rights of citizens and enemies in ways that would remain a thorny issue, as we will see in part 2. Citizenship, the Constitution, the state, and its relation to society were all transformed by the Civil War and Reconstruction.

This chapter begins with the interaction between social movements and institutional politics in the antebellum period. It then turns to the war and to how it brought Lincoln and the Republicans around to a position close to that of abolitionism but also affected how the government dealt with opponents. It closes with an analysis of the postwar period as a long episode of movement-countermovement interaction. In the process, we will ask how the Civil War reshaped the American state and its relation to civil society. Although these changes would not become clear until years later, the groundwork was laid in the contentious politics of the 1850s and in the Civil War and Reconstruction.

The Contentious Politics of the 1850s

So many contentious events marked the decade preceding the Civil War that it is difficult to know where to begin: with the Fugitive Slave Act, the conflict over "bleeding Kansas," the caning of Senator Charles Sumner on the floor of the U.S. Senate, John Brown's attack on the Harper's Ferry arsenal, the Lincoln–Douglas debates before the 1858 senatorial election, the *Dred Scott* Supreme Court decision, or its devastating aftermath. Less remembered, but archetypical of all that was happening, was the collapse of the balance rule in Congress that had maintained slave and free states in an uneasy equilibrium since 1820. The balance rule was at the same time the glue that kept the congressional parties from disintegrating and the cork that kept popular passions over slavery from exploding.

The Congressional Balance Rule

Barry Weingast (1998, 2002) has analyzed both that agreement and its breakdown, beginning with the admission of California as a free state at the beginning of the decade.[2] But the compromise was much older, going back to the first major congressional conflict over slavery triggered by whether Missouri should be admitted to the Union as a slave or a free state in 1820; the conflict was resolved by an agreement to balance its admission as a slave state with Maine's admission as a free one. This produced an agreement that the entry of each free state into the Union was to be balanced, either immediately or soon afterward, by the entry of a slave state. As Weingast (1998, 151; 2002, 56) argues, the arrangement kept contention over slavery at bay for another thirty years. While the slave states had only about 40 percent of the seats in the House, their nearly equal representation in the Senate and the pro-slavery Democrats' nearly complete domination of the presidency from Jackson's election in 1828 ensured that antislavery legislation could never be successfully passed.[3]

But that agreement was both imperfect and fragile, not only because it was easily broken by defecting politicians seeking electoral advantage but because structural and demographic changes were increasingly reinforcing the underlying cleavage between North and South. The result was that an assertive new actor—the nonslavery West—tilted the balance between the North and South and helped to create an interregional coalition—the Republican Party—that defeated the South in the elections of 1860.

To understand how contention was prevented from boiling over until the 1850s, we need to remember, first, that the authors of the federal Constitution had compromised on the issue of slavery, banning the slave trade after 1810 but leaving its regulation in the hands of the states—which was essentially a way of saying that the South could continue to profit from its peculiar institution. Second, the Constitution contained a three-fifths voting rule that held, for purposes of the apportionment of congressional seats, that unfree individuals would be allotted three-fifths the weight of free individuals. Third, Article I, section 9 of the Constitution prohibited Congress from banning the slave trade before 1808; Article I, section 20 placed the control of labor contracts in the hands of the states; and Article 4, section 2 prevented slaves from gaining their freedom by escaping to the North. Finally, the Constitution allocated two Senate seats to every state, regardless of its population, ensuring that the less-populated southern states would have equal (or nearly equal) representation)in that chamber with the more populous northern states. While antislavery activists in the House periodically offered antislavery resolutions, equal representation in the Senate allowed southern senators to just as regularly block them. Only if the number of free states came to seriously outnumber the slave states in the Senate, or if other issues combined with slavery to bring North and West together, would the balance shift.

Why would northern politicians want to maintain the balance of slave and free states? The motives were largely electoral. Both the Democrats and Whigs had substantial representation in regions in which they were in the minority; allowing slavery to polarize the political debate would have risked the loss of enclaves of Whig voters in the South and of Democrats in the North, hurting both parties (Ransom 1989, 29–32; Silbey 1967). There was thus a partisan imperative to leave slavery in the hands of the states, one that underlay the balance rule and reinforced the institutional rules laid down by the Constitution. The equilibrium held until economic and demographic changes combined with electoral change to undermine it.

What Undermined the Balance Rule?

As immigration swelled the population of the North, both Northerners and immigrants began moving in droves to the fertile lands of the West. Canals and railroads soldered western economic interests to the North and its transatlantic ports, and the balance of population and economic dynamism between North and South began to shift (Ransom 1989, 131). Westward expansion, and the subsequent admission of new states to the Union, held the greatest potential for conflict, and everybody knew it. It was not simply that Northerners were not slaveholders; slavery in the West would threaten the livelihood of farmers seeking to make a living off the land with family labor. Conversely, as fear spread among Southerners that their region was losing parity, they looked to the creation of new slave states in the West to keep up with the North's expansion. Unless new slave states were created, the natural population dynamism of the North would undermine northern politicians' commitment to sustaining slavery (Weingast 2002).

While Congress was holding slavery at bay through the balance rule, the issue was growing increasingly intense in the country. Contention revolved around a number of issues: slavery in the District of Columbia, the guerrilla war between pro-slavery and antislavery factions on the frontier, the illegal movement of slaves across state boundaries, and the Fugitive Slave Act that Congress passed to stop it. The advent of the Republican Party in the mid-1850s was the electoral weight that upset the balance between Whigs and Democrats: although not all Republicans were opponents of slavery, their electoral presence in the North and West gave them incentives to unify around interests that the two regions shared.

The Republicans' political acumen and the errors of their opponents were the visible causes of Republican victory. In 1854, Illinois Democratic Senator Stephen A. Douglas attempted to build a national constituency for his presidential ambitions by pushing through Congress the Kansas-Nebraska Act. In the name of popular sovereignty, the act effectively repealed the Missouri Compromise by allowing the admission to the Union of new states with or without slavery, as their voters might decide.

Douglas's compromise was lethal to the Democratic Party in the North: "Nearly all [the antislavery forces] were quick to perceive the political opportunities it afforded and hastened to capitalize upon them" (Sewell 1976, 260). Even though they lost the presidential elections of 1856, the Republicans established themselves as an interregional party that could come to power with an antislavery platform. Then there were the abolitionists, who had nothing to do with Douglas's error or the Republicans' success; but, as often happens when contentious politics intrudes on institutional arrangements, an initially unpopular issue—the abolition of slavery—became the wedge that gave this unpopular movement new weight in the political system.

From Moral Abolition to Political Antislavery

Abolitionism was never more than a minority movement, derided for its utopianism and regarded as an irritant even in the North. Arising out of the same "second great awakening" as enthusiastic religion, temperance, sabbatarianism, women's rights, and anti-Masonry, the abolitionists were numerically weak, ideologically divided, and widely despised (Sewell 1976, 40). But abolitionism had an effect on politics in three indirect ways. First, it offered a language of sin and damnation to characterize an institution that most Americans had regarded as a form of property (Davis 1969; Foner 1995, chap. 3); second, it framed its argument in terms of national identity and draped it in the creedal rhetoric that resonated with many Americans; and third, it produced a generation of anti-slavery politicians, many of whom entered the surge parties of the 1840s and 1850s before gravitating into the Republican Party (Barnes 1957; Sewell 1976). Although the most famous moral abolitionist, William Lloyd Garrison, rejected politics for most of his career, by the 1850s antislavery had become a political persuasion in the party system, with the electoral potential to cut across the cozy lines of Whig and Democratic partisanship.

The evolution of antislavery from a movement of moral outrage to a form of political activism occurred gradually and unevenly. First came the lobbying and petition campaigns of the 1830s (Barnes 1957), then the formation of the Liberty and Free Soil parties (Sewell 1976, chaps. 1, 3), and finally the emergence in 1856 of a majority faction of the Republican Party. While moral abolitionists were isolated by their religious uprightness, antislavery activists worked within the party system, forging coalitions with moderate opponents of slavery and others whose interest in slavery was minimal. When the Republicans rose to national power with Lincoln's election, the abolitionists were still a minority within it, but war—and mobilization for war—gave their ideas influence well beyond their numbers.

From Structure to Action

Antislavery would have remained impotent had it not been for a broader set of changes in U.S. society. First, structural changes bound the North and West closer together and set them increasingly apart from the South (Weingast 2002, chap. 7); second, an identity shift in both regions contributed to the conflict's radicalization; and third, the brokering of a coalition among antislavery advocates, nativism, and western settlement undermined the foundations of the antebellum party system.

Structural Change

Between 1845 and 1854, just under 3 million people entered the United States—most of them from Ireland and Germany, many of them hard-drinking and urban

(Ransom 1989, 131). The majority settled in the North, driving down wages and inducing Northerners to move west, in a powerful economic-demographic vacancy chain of migration and replacement. The expansion of the West and its links to the North left the South, with its more static rural society, increasingly behind and culturally isolated. Not only did the population of North and West grow faster than that of the South, but most Westerners came from the nonslave states of the Northeast, sharing the region's Protestant background and spirit of enterprise. As the North expanded westward, "the Northern economy increasingly became integrated as more trade traveled along an east-west axis than along a north-south axis" (Weingast 1998, 184).

Identity Shift

If the demographic and economic changes of the 1840s and 1850s provided a structural foundation for political change, they also promoted the formation of new identities as antislavery activists came together with nonabolitionist Northerners and Westerners around a program of settling the West by "free men on free soil" (Sewell 1976, chap. 8). They mainly came from a generation of farmers and would-be farmers who looked with apprehension on the competitive drive of slaveholders from the South. Whatever they thought of African Americans—and many Westerners despised them—admitting slavery into the new states of the West would give Southerners economic advantages that the Northerners lacked. The direct result was the Free Soil Party, which became a reservoir of votes for the Republicans.

But "free soil" was more than the program of a party; it became the master frame of western politics, connecting those who entered politics as moral abolitionists with those whose major concern was blocking the creation of a slave-owning economy. From the former came the moral fervor that gave mid-century politics its apocalyptic air; from the latter came the complementary desire to keep slave agriculture—and African Americans—out of the West. As ties formed among political abolitionists, western farmers, and eastern merchants and Protestants, their societal vision and political identity broadened to the idea of free men employing free labor on free soil, opposing "slavery's illegitimate coercions and the condition of labor in the North" (Foner 1995, xxiii, 11; Sewell 1976, 293).

The conflicts of the 1850s produced a reaction in the South, one that was also wrapped in the language of the American creed. The southern states had long suppressed political and religious speech where slavery was concerned, including sermons by abolitionist preachers, and had censored the mail and the press. But as antislavery advocates trumpeted the virtues of free labor against the "slave power" of the South, Southerners responded with an image of Northerners as soulless, money-grubbing, and self-righteous, in contrast to their own civilization, built on the symbols of family, religion, and respect for the Constitution (Genovese 1992). As George Fredrickson observes, "It took the assault of the abolitionists . . . to force the practitioners of racial oppression to develop a theory that accorded with their behavior" (1971, 321).

Radicalization and Polarization

The disruptive effects of westward expansion on the party system were already evident in the 1854 congressional elections, when two new parties heavily represented in the West—the Know-Nothings and Free Soilers—burst on the political scene. Although neither party won a single Senate seat, between them they gained forty-three seats in the House, threatening the electoral balance between the Whigs and Democrats in that chamber. The Democrats regained their losses in the presidential election of 1856 (Ransom 1989, 137), but nativism, Free Soil, and antislavery combined to realign a party system that was already defunct by 1856. The result was sectional, ideological, and partisan radicalization, the breakdown of the balance rule, and polarization into rival sovereignties.

It was in "bleeding Kansas" that the Civil War was presaged with violent conflict. In that territory, northern small farmers and southern proponents of slavery had settled in the same areas (Fellman 1979, 289). Each camp maneuvered to gain an electoral majority that would turn the territory into either a slave or a free state when it entered the Union. In the unsettled conditions of the frontier, a ruthless guerilla proxy war between North and South broke out between the passage of the Kansas-Nebraska Act and the beginning of the Civil War.

By 1858, the realignment of U.S. politics along sectional lines was in place, as North and West formed a solid electoral majority for the Republicans, and the Democrats emerged more and more as a purely regional party (Poole and Rosenthal 1997, 99). Identity shift produced regional ideologies that caricatured and condemned each region in the eyes of the other; but what crystallized this process of radicalization and territorial polarization more than anything else was a decision of the U.S. Supreme Court.

Dred Scott

In December 1833, a doctor named John Emerson of St. Louis, Missouri, a slave state, received an army commission and reported for duty in Illinois, a free state.[4]

He took with him a slave, called Dred Scott, purchased from a certain Blow family, also of St. Louis.[5] After twelve years, Emerson returned to Missouri with his slave, his wife, and two daughters. When Emerson passed away in 1843, the ownership of the slave family passed to the wife, who eventually made her way east, where she turned over her affairs to her brother, John Sanford—the "Sanford" in the case of *Dred Scott v. Sanford*.

Scott, in 1846, went to the Missouri state court system with the claim that, because he had lived in a free state, he was a citizen and not a slave and had the right to be freed. The Missouri courts were divided on the issue, but in 1852, the state Supreme Court decided against him and returned him to slavery. At this point, the case attracted the attention of antislavery lawyers, who encouraged Scott to bring his suit to the U.S. Circuit Court in St. Louis. Again, he lost, but in 1856, his lawyers brought the case to the U.S. Supreme Court. In 1857, Justice Roger Taney wrote his momentous decision against Scott, triggering a national debate that polarized positions on slavery still further and helped to produce Lincoln's successful run for the presidency three years later.

Coming on the heels of the "bleeding Kansas" conflict, the de-aligning 1856 elections, and the abrogation of the Missouri Compromise, the case was widely expected to produce a solution to the slavery conundrum, and so it was greeted by incoming President James Buchanan in his inaugural address (Fehrenbacher 1978, 312–13, 473). Buchanan was a Pennsylvania Democrat who had been elected with southern votes and hoped to keep the South in the Union by supporting the expansion of slavery to the territories.[6] Taney's opinion for the Court signaled that decades of temporizing over slavery were over. For, rather than simply concluding that the Court lacked jurisdiction over a case involving state law, he chose to declare that African American descendants of slaves were not citizens under the Constitution. This meant that free blacks in the North—as well as escaped slaves—would be vulnerable to enslavement. Although the Declaration of Independence had declared that " 'all men are created equal," he averred, this applied only to white men. The decision meant that Congress had no power to prohibit slavery in the territories. It also had profound economic implications. If slavery could enter any state, North or South, then it would reduce the value of land in the West and of the investments of Northerners who had invested there.[7] "Any one of these conclusions would have sullied the Court's reputation," writes Christopher Eisgruber; "together, they were a disaster" (2009, 155).

Dred Scott inspired Southerners to push harder for the extension of slavery into the territories and convinced thoughtful Westerners that their future lay only in soldering the alliance with the North through the Republican Party (Fehrenbacher 1978, 417). It was at this point that the term *slave power* began to circulate widely in the press across the North and West.[8] No less passionate were the responses of the southern press, whose defense of slavery could now be wrapped in the legitimacy of the Constitution (Fehrenbacher 1978, 417, 451, 418). In response to the decision, several states modified their constitutions; in others, legislative battles were fought over the status of free blacks; and in national politics the approaching presidential election became a battle between the now-divided Democrats and a Republican interregional coalition whose members understood the political advantage that *Dred Scott* gave them. A national governing coalition and a new party system were born on the ruins of the balance rule and the political stupidity of the Supreme Court.

Coalition Formation

Abraham Lincoln embodied this coalition. A Westerner and, at best, a tepid antislavery advocate, his campaign against Douglas in the 1858 Illinois senatorial election revealed him to be an astute political strategist. In a series of campaign debates, Lincoln maneuvered his opponent into taking compromise positions that pleased neither his own party nor the Republicans. Douglas praised the sanctity of the *Dred Scott* Supreme Court decision, whereas Lincoln's strategy was to frame the decision as a provisional one that would need to be studied, modified, and possibly overruled by a new congressional majority (Fehrenbacher 1978, 455, 442).

By the 1860 election, the electoral weight of the Whigs had been whittled down to insignificance, the Democrats had split into northern and southern factions, and Lincoln—who won the nomination against William H. Seward of New York, an abolitionist—brought together a coalition of North and West, nativists, abolitionists, Free Soilers, Whigs, and northern Democrats. Although Lincoln was no abolitionist, Southerners read his election as the conquest of the party system by the antislavery faction. It was never so simple, however, and Lincoln did what he could to avoid war until southern militias made it impossible by surrounding and bombarding Fort Sumter (Goodheart 2011). With their chances of expanding slavery into the West blocked and a sectional party in control of both the presidency and Congress, the states of the lower South either had to bow to the Republican hegemony or secede.

War and Emancipation

Slavery had long been understood to be a prerogative of the states *in* the states; but the right of property in human beings was never recognized by most northern constitutional lawyers. Slavery may be local, advocates argued, but freedom is national (Oakes 2012, chap. 1). As long as the South remained in the Union, this tension remained largely theoretical and was argued out in the pages of the newspapers and on the floor of Congress; but once the South seceded and the Union government began to exert prerogatives it had never before claimed—for example, the draft, the blockade of southern ports, and the income tax—the national quality of freedom became more relevant than ever before.

Support for emancipation was never unanimous in the North, even among Republicans, and few Northerners had contemplated the possibility of equal rights and equal capacities for African Americans. Lincoln himself had seldom pronounced in favor of black rights, and in his first Inaugural Address, when he still had hopes of coaxing at least some southern states back into the Union, he denied an intention to despoil slave owners of their property. In November 1861, he even revoked an order by General John Frémont freeing the slaves in Missouri (Neely 1991, 34). If nothing else, Lincoln had to go easy on slavery or risk the Union losing the key border states: Delaware, Maryland, West Virginia, and Missouri.

As the big slave-owning states of the Deep South lined up their forces, they tried to leverage the hesitant border states into joining the secession. These states were a particular problem for the Republican government and for Lincoln. They had large numbers of slaves and slaveholders, and their strategic position between North and South made their support—or at least their neutrality—crucial for the survival of the Union. Convinced they were the key to victory, Lincoln could not afford to alienate them by emancipating the slaves. Map 3.1 makes clear why he was so cautious; the border states formed a band from east to west, from the precincts of Washington, D.C., to the frontier.

Contrabands

In May 1861, three escaped slaves crossed the James River to Fort Monroe, near Hampton, Virginia, asking the fort's new commander, Benjamin Butler, for their freedom. The Fugitive Slave Law and Lincoln's explicit policy of noninterference counseled returning the slaves to their master, but Butler decided to regard them as "contraband" and keep them safe in the fort, especially because they had revealed key military intelligence. When a Confederate officer politely asked for their return, Butler replied, "I mean to take Virginia at her word. . . . I am under no constitutional obligation to a foreign country, which Virginia now claims to be" (quoted in Goodheart 2011, 314). By the next week, escaped slaves were appearing at Fort Monroe almost hourly. The entire nation and the White House

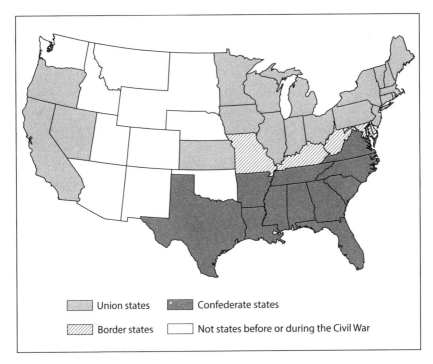

MAP 3.1 Union, Confederate, and border states at the outset of the U.S. Civil War. Union states include those admitted during the Civil War; border states are those with some slave-based agriculture that remained in the Union. http://en.wikipedia.org/wiki/Border_states_%28American_Civil_War%29. © CC BY-SA 3.0.

were soon engaged in a discussion of Butler's "contraband" argument, a term he might have employed only tongue-in-cheek.

As the war began to go badly, and as escaped slaves continued to cross Confederate lines, Lincoln was suddenly under pressure from his generals to clarify his initial policy of denying any intention to free the slaves. Slowly, he shifted 180 degrees to describe slavery as "a vast and far reaching disturbing element" (ibid., 321) in the nation's history, sounding more like a moral abolitionist than the savvy frontier politician he was. When he finally issued the Emancipation Proclamation, Northerners were already regarding Southerners not just as opponents but as enemies (Goodheart 2011).

In the course of the war, emancipation became the central issue of the Republican Party. When, in September 1862, Lincoln issued the Proclamation, there was widespread shock in the North. Why did he do so? Although the northern population was still divided on slavery, the president was under pressure by the hard-pressed and poorly led Union army to attack the southern economy by encouraging the slaves to lay down their tools. Emancipation began not as a policy but as a response to a military reality to which the president slowly adjusted.

Like much else in U.S. history, emancipation was dignified by the linkage between freeing the slaves and the American creed. "Four score and seven years ago," in the first sentence of the Gettysburg Address, did not hearken back to the Constitution—which had shamefully divided black people into fractions for purposes of allocating the vote to white people—but to the Declaration of Independence, which had seldom been invoked as a source of policy before. With the Emancipation Proclamation, Lincoln began the process that would transform abolitionism from an unpopular movement to the basis of the triumphant Republican Party's postwar program.

Emancipation, combined with military victory, lent the Republican Party a new and more stirring message. From a coalition of northern business, western farmers, and political antislavery advocates, it was infused with a new vision, especially after Lincoln's reelection in 1864. Henceforth there was no longer a sharp dividing line between moral abolitionism and political antislavery; the dominant faction in the governing party became the Radical Republicans. They were radical not only in their support for occupying and reforming the South but for their support for the cause in Congress as the war came to an end. This was the strategy that led to the passage of the Reconstruction amendments—the most substantial change in the U.S. Constitution since the founding (Ackerman 1998; Frank 2010).

Contention in the North

But antislavery had far from conquered the North, and as in the case of the French revolutionary period, the cleavages and conflicts of ordinary politics did not disappear because the country was engaged in a civil war. Immigrants, who were subject to the draft, could not easily understand why they should leave their jobs to fight for a cause they barely understood and often did not support; the border states, where slavery was a familiar (if not a dominant) institution, were especially incensed at a war that was threatening their territories.

In 1862, the Confederate army tried and failed to gain control of Missouri. What followed was an armed conflict between rebel guerillas and the Union army. Guerilla warfare was not new on the frontier, but, writes Mark Neely, it "constantly threatened to break down the customary distinction between soldiers and civilians" (1991, 47). At one point the commanding Union general, Thomas Ewing, wrote to his superiors, "About two-thirds of the families on the occupied farms of that region [i.e., western Missouri] are kin to the guerillas, and are actively and heartily engaged in feeding, clothing, and sustaining them" (quoted in ibid., 47). It was in Missouri that Union General Ulysses S. Grant first authorized the arrest of civilians and the taking of civilian hostages. But the draft, the need to support a national war effort, and residual racism created a remarkably contentious politics in the North as well. Some of this contention remained within institutional boundaries—especially as the Democratic Party began to revive. But some of it rolled out into the streets where it produced draft resistance, rioting, and the use of exceptional powers.

Partisan Conflict

When war broke out, the Democratic Party was split and deeply weakened. After all, the Democrats had divided along sectional lines in the elections of 1860, allowing Lincoln to be elected with only a plurality of the votes. As Joel Silbey writes, "Three conventions, two candidates for president, two rival national headquarters, two campaigns, and much virulent sniping characterized the party in 1860." In the Senate, the northern rump of the Democrats held only 14 seats to the Republicans' 31; in the House, they held 44 to the Republicans' 105 (Silbey 1977, 21, 51). It seemed for a time as if the war might give rise to inter-party solidarity.

The Democrats' first response to the advent of war was to wrap themselves in the Union flag. Some went so far as to join the Republican administration, others worked to reorganize the party in its reduced geographical bases while support-ing the war effort, and still others remained unreconciled to "black republi-canism" (Sewell 1976, chap. 13). For a time, Democrats called for a "no-party" government, and some, such as Stephen Douglas, former presidential candidate, even conferred with Lincoln about how to bring his party into open support of the government (Silbey 1977, 45).

Faced with the task of creating an army from scratch with a weak and de-centralized state and fighting a war that was threatening northern territory, the Republicans had little time for healing the wounds of party strife. In fact, they used their newly found power to pass legislation—such as the tariff and financial bills—that had little to do with the war but was anathema to the Democrats (Sil-bey 1977, 46–47). And they were not above using martial law "to screen eligible voters and influence results in favor of candidates who supported the Union war effort"; opposition newspapers were shut down, public assemblies were banned, and "in Maryland . . . a federal commander even stopped the sale of pictures of Confederate military officers and political leaders" (Bensel 1991,142).

And it was the Republicans' unwillingness to consider compromises to re-store the Union that raised the hackles of northern Democrats. They saw in the legislation of the Thirty-seventh Congress a prime example of what the Republicans were up to. The government's emancipation law for the District of Columbia and legislation to confiscate the property of Southerners in rebellion led to bitter criticisms on the part of Democratic leaders, "but they never held enough seats in either house to frustrate Republican legislation" (Neely 1991, 50–51).

As the war began to go badly, the Democrats shifted to a strategy of open opposition—if not to the war itself, then to what they saw as the president's pro-black policies and dictatorial methods (Silbey 1977, chap. 3). Their score in the 1862 election results increased their confidence that they could defeat Lincoln and bring the war to a close. Comparing the combined Democratic vote in the 1860 presidential elections with their total in the 1862 congressional elections, we can see that the Democrats lost votes in only three states; ran more or less evenly in three more; and gained votes, sometimes substantially, in nine others.[9] From that point on, they no longer hesitated to attack Republican "despotism." This was especially true as contention rose in the country, especially around the issue of conscription.

Opposition in the Streets

It was easy enough for Northerners to support the government when the isolated garrison at Fort Sumter was fired on by Confederate batteries, but the draft threatened costs for northern communities and stirred up resistance, especially among urban immigrants who could not understand why they should fight for southern slaves. The problem for the Union government was how to define opposition to the war: as the exercise of the rights of citizenship or as disloyalty and treason. A subsidiary question was how opponents of the war were to be judged: through the ordinary courts or through military justice. In some of the border areas, the capacity of the courts to function effectively was questionable, and in others, the war was raging and military officers could be forgiven for wanting swift justice to demonstrate the costs of resistance.

We tend to see the question today through the framing of the North, which won the war and whose antislavery goals most Americans would support. But to many, it seemed outrageous that a war that was ostensibly being fought in the name of expanding liberty was being staffed through measures that took power away from states and localities and centered it in a distant and heretofore absent central state. Military recruitment had previously been carried out at the state level, through the citizen militias provided for by the Constitution. But state and local voluntarism quickly proved inadequate for a long war, and in March 1863, after several false starts, the Union government resorted to the draft (Hyman

1975, 215). Conscription brought at once a move toward greater central power and a blurring of the lines between civil and military authority. Both to manage recruitment and to "apprehend soldiers and civilians for acts impeding or avoiding conscription and to punish them in military courts," a national system of district provost marshals was created. These officials were not above employing special agents, private detectives, and spies and calling on field commanders and state home-guard units for assistance in ferreting out malingerers (Hyman 1975, 215, 218, 194–95). National conscription both increased the strength of the central state and triggered riots in several states.

The draft riot in New York City showed that opposition to the draft could be violent—and could target free blacks (Hyman 1975, 169; McPherson 1988, 610–11). The four days of rioting left 105 people dead (Stone 2004, 91, 92). But New York was not alone. In Boston and Chicago, violence erupted between federal troops and mobs opposed to the draft. Mobs murdered two enrollment officers in Indiana, and the army had to send troops into Pennsylvania, Wisconsin, Ohio, and Indiana to restore order. Antidraft and antiblack violence erupted in Boston, Newark, Albany, Chicago, and Milwaukee. "Across the Union," writes J. Mathew Gallman, "sixty local provost marshals were wounded performing their duties" (1994, 148).

Conflict over conscription was greatest in the border states (Neely 1991, chap. 2). Lincoln responded with a policy of guarded, but increasing, recourse to the restriction of rights. At first, the writ of *habeas corpus* was suspended for narrow corridors and localities, but soon the army began to use military commissions to punish draft resisters and those who encouraged them. By 1863, entire regions of the North and West were under effective military government. "In 1861," writes Hyman, "there were not enough institutions or laws appropriate to cope with the danger which disloyalty posed" (1975, 169). This was the first experience in the country with something resembling an emergency script.

State-Building through Emergency Rule

The antebellum United States, in the terms made famous by Stephen Skowronek, was governed by a "state of courts and parties" (1982, chap. 1). If this now seems a bit exaggerated,[10] behind it lay the uneven local penetration of the national state to the grassroots and the stubborn resistance of the states and the Supreme Court to federal interference in state affairs. Apart from subduing Indians and fighting wars with Britain and Mexico, the federal government lacked a permanent apparatus with which to secure the frontier or assure internal order in times of emergency.[11] Only the Fugitive Slave Act of 1850 had created something resembling a national police force to capture and bring escaped slaves back to the South (Hyman 1975, 13).

The secession of a substantial part of the Union led to a rapid expansion of the national state into the northern economy and society. In 1861, the new and untried Republican administration had to rapidly fashion both a way to finance the war and an internal security policy, partly while Congress was out of session (Vladeck 2004, 166–67). It decided, with thin legal authority, to blockade southern ports, despite the fact that administration leaders insisted that the South was not, and could not be, a foreign power. State authority was centralized, administrative capacity was increased, troops were conscripted and liberties limited, railroads were subsidized and put under state control, securities trading was modernized, slaves were admitted as soldiers into the Union armies, southern property was confiscated, tariffs were set, and peace was negotiated (see Bensel 1991, 217, table 3.13). The mobilization of the resources needed to fight the world's first industrial war produced a major advance over the "state of courts and parties" (cf. Skowronek 1982). The first legal move with implications for how the war would affect the central state's authority had to do with commerce on the high seas; the second had to do with the president's suspension of the writ of *habeas corpus*. Both of these increased the power of the executive against the other branches of government and vis-à-vis the states and citizens.

Ships and Suspension of the Writ

When Union shops blockaded southern ports, the Supreme Court affirmed the constitutionality of the blockades in the famous *Prize Cases*, even though Congress had not yet declared war (Brandon 2005, 24).[12] The cases were doubly important because they showed how the federal government could combine international and local law to advance a policy that had little or no legal foundation. For the Court's majority, it was perfectly consistent to declare a blockade under international law while treating captured sailors as pirates or traitors under U.S. law. With the help of his wily secretary of state, William Seward, Lincoln "had discovered that the laws of war did not so much restrict his powers as augment it" (Witt 2012, 151).

But it was with respect to the war on the ground—and particularly the rights of those in the North and the border states who opposed the war—that Lincoln's government expanded the government's use of emergency powers. The Alien and Sedition Acts of 1798 had given a hint of how Congress might abridge rights when national emergencies threatened (Stone 2004, chap. 1). But that particular emergency never came, and with Thomas Jefferson's election in 1800, the issue of rights in wartime largely went to sleep. General Winfield Scott created military commissions during the Mexican War, but they were used to discipline U.S. troops who were accused of abusing civilians (Neely 1991, 40–41). It was through the suspension of the writ of *habeas corpus* and the use of military commissions to try civilians who opposed the Civil War that the government expanded the traditional boundaries of central state authority.

The writ of *habeas corpus* is the only common-law practice mentioned in the federal Constitution, and it is cautiously hedged about with the modifying clause "except in cases of rebellion or invasion [when] the public safety may require it" (Article I, section 9). This was a situation that—apart from the brief British invasion in 1812—faced the federal government only with secession. Moreover, that clause is found in the article dedicated to the powers and limitations of Congress—not in Article II, which enumerates the powers of the executive. This left in doubt whether the president, or the armed forces acting on presidential authority, could suspend *habeas corpus*. In any case, the federal government and the federal courts had little experience with either suspension of the writ, martial law, or the military commissions that usually accompanied it.[13] This suddenly changed in spring 1861, when the new administration took power. Resistance to the war appeared in Baltimore, Maryland, soon after Lincoln's inauguration, in April 1861.

Maryland was a slave state that had not seceded following Lincoln's election. But it was boiling over with anger at the prospect of a war against fellow slave states. When a secessionist mob attacked the Sixth Massachusetts Volunteers, who were attempting to reach Washington from Baltimore, and a pro-secession mayor ordered the destruction of the bridges connecting the city to the North, Lincoln suspended the writ and declared martial law on the "line" connecting Washington to the North (Stone 2004, 84–85; Hyman 1975, chap. 6).

On May 25, soldiers at Fort McHenry, basing their authority on Lincoln's suspension of the writ, arrested John Merriman, a secessionist who was suspected of having burned bridges and destroying telegraph lines leading to the city. Merriman filed a writ of *habeas corpus*, which the commandant of the fort, George Cadwalader, refused to honor (Hyman 1975, 84). When Chief Justice Taney, in whose circuit Baltimore lay, sent a U.S. marshal to serve the officer with the writ, he was refused entry to the fort. That led to the opinion that Taney, in his capacity as circuit court judge, wrote in the famous case of *Ex Parte Merriman*.[14]

Taney was hardly a defender of civil liberties. He was a Marylander, a slaveholder who had released his own slaves, but a fierce defender of states' rights—as we saw in his opinion in *Dred Scott*. Although not acting on behalf of the full Court, in *Merriman* he launched a full-throated rejection of the idea that the army, acting on behalf of the president, could arrest a civilian without benefit of trial or stating the evidence against him before a court. Although he did not miss any opportunity to swipe at both Cadwalader or Lincoln in his opinion, the core of Taney's decision was that the Constitution did not assign to the executive branch the power to suspend *habeas* and that this right inhered only to Congress. When he learned that the president not only claimed the right to suspend the writ but also the power to delegate it to a military officer, Taney argued,

> I certainly listened to it with some surprise, for I had supposed it to be one of those points of constitutional law upon which there was no difference of opinion, and that it was admitted on all hands, that the privilege of the writ could not be suspended, except by act of congress. . . . The clause of the constitution, which authorizes the suspension of the privilege of the writ of *habeas corpus*, is in the 9th section of the first article. This article is devoted to the legislative department of the United States, and has not the slightest reference to the executive department. (17 F. Cas 148)

Taney went even further. Evoking constitutional experts from Blackstone to Story, he argued that there was never a constitutional warrant either in England or the United States to usurp the power of the judiciary to decide if a prisoner was being legally held. If the president was delegating to military forces the right to supplant sitting courts, he maintained, then the military authority "has, by force of arms, thrust aside the judicial authorities and officers to whom the constitution has confided the power and duty of interpreting and administering the laws, and substituted a military government in its place, to be administered and executed by military officers" (*Ex Parte Merriaman*, 7 F.Cas., 152). Admitting that he had no force with which to enforce his order, Taney transmitted his opinion to the president "to determine what measures he will take to cause the civil process of the United States to be respected and enforced" (ibid., 153). Lincoln ignored both the decision and Taney's irony and extended the "line" on which *habeas* was suspended up the East Coast of the United States.

Merriman's arrest was only the first of a number of incidents in which army officers, acting with or without the prior consent of the executive, arrested civilians for impeding the war effort, for publishing antiwar editorials, and, in one famous case, for expressing opposition to the war in a public speech. But it was conscription, and the worry that not enough young men would step forward to fight, that tightened the government's noose around dissent. In July 1862, Lincoln issued a new and broader suspension of the writ. "The origin of this new habeas-corpus proclamation," writes Neely, "lay in the Militia Act of July 17, 1862, which empowered the secretary of war to draft for nine months the militiamen of states that failed to upgrade their militias" (Neely 1991, 52). This was a conscription law in all but name, and Lincoln issued the *habeas* proclamation to enforce it. It was only in 1863 that Lincoln sent to Congress the Habeas Corpus Suspension Act (12 State 755), which removed the separation-of-powers objection that Taney had raised in his Merriman opinion.

The period that followed marked what Neely calls "the lowest point for civil liberties in the North during the Civil War, and one of the lowest for civil liberties in all of American history" (1991, 53). It was not only the sweeping language of the proclamation that made it so draconian but the desperation of the government at its wartime defeats and the fact that there was no trained machinery in place to recruit conscripts in an orderly fashion. The judge advocate, Levi C. Turner, set loose "a horde of petty functionaries to decide without legal guidelines one of the highest matters of state: precisely who in this civil war was loyal or disloyal" (ibid., 54). An army of sheriffs, constables, and deputy sheriffs was set loose, with predictable abuses, to arrest those who tried to escape or who encouraged others to do so. Once imprisoned, these people might have no recourse to civil courts because the writ of *habeas corpus* had been suspended for any such person.

The Military Commissions

Given that the suspension of *habeas* was expanded on the eve of the 1862 election, it was widely suspected to have been carried out for political gain. The case that came closest to sustaining this argument was that of Clement Vallandigham, an ex–Democratic Party representative who was arrested for advocating in public that young men should refuse to serve in the army when called.[15] General Ambrose Burnside, who was in charge of the Ohio military district in which Vallandigham's speech was made and who had established himself as the arbiter of treasonable expression, arrested Vallandigham without asking Washington's approval (Stone 2004, 96–98). He was brought before a military commission the next day and charged with "publicly expressing . . . sympathy for those in arms against the government of the United States, and declaring disloyal sentiments and opinions with the object and purpose of weakening the power of the government in its efforts to suppress an unlawful rebellion" (quoted in ibid., 101). Vallandigham filed a petition for a writ of *habeas corpus* before Judge Humphrey H. Leavitt, who denied it in an opinion that read more like a speech defending the president than the attempt of a jurist to find the law (ibid., 103).

Judge Leavitt's opinion was as important for what it did not say as for what it did. It said that, in times of war and subversion, the ordinary guarantees of the Constitution should not be allowed to interfere with the prosecution of the war and that the courts lacked the expertise to judge the correct balance between civil liberties and military necessity (Stone 2004, 104). What the opinion did *not* deal with was the question of whether the Constitution allows military commissions to try civilians where the courts are open and functioning—as they were in Ohio in 1863. The most important civil liberties decision of the war, *Ex Parte Milligan*, which turned on that issue, would be decided only after the war was over. In the meantime, the war enormously expanded the categories of people who were subject to military justice to include army contractors, guerilla fighters, horse thieves, bridge-burners, and deserters and malingerers. More than half of the 4,271 recorded cases of military commissions trying civilians came from the border states of Missouri, Kentucky, and Maryland. In Missouri alone, there were over 1,900 trials by military commission—50 percent more than in the occupied Confederacy itself. Another 193 trials were held by military commission in Maryland, 200 in Kentucky, and 271 in the District of Columbia (Neely 1991, 167–75); in contrast, the numbers in the Northeast were insignificant.

Lincoln's defense of military commission trials—like his defense of the other restrictions on civil liberties imposed during the war—was that they would end at war's end. "But trials by military commission did not end with the war, and Americans never forgot them" (ibid., 175). They were used in the South during Reconstruction until they were struck down by the Supreme Court. In subsequent decades, they were used to try Native American leaders on the frontier. In the next century, they were excavated by Franklin D. Roosevelt to condemn German spies who were caught in New Jersey, and they were used again during the War on Terror by the George W. Bush and Barak Obama administrations (Witt 2012). The Civil War, which was fought more directly to expand freedom than any other war, was the fountainhead for the future emergency powers of the American state, both in war and in war's wake.

Although the suspension of *habeus* was most obvious for expanding the national state's hierarchical powers, it also expanded its infrastructural reach. Just as Lincoln's government was becoming more draconian in repressing the opponents of the war, the national state was becoming more actively engaged with civil society: using local sheriffs to enforce the draft, instituting an income tax, floating loans without the consent of Congress, and building railroads to the West. In terms of its social coalitional base, the ties it forged with financial capital in New York, Boston, and Philadelphia endured after the war, laying the foundation for what amounted to a new northern social base for the exercise of central state power (Bensel 1991).

In the short run, as occurs in most wartime situations, these interventionist moves strengthened the hand of the state in the economy. But, as occurred following World Wars One and Two, the state rapidly retreated from the economy in war's wake. Not only that—the influence that financial capital gained through its close ties with Lincoln's government endured as the presidency languished under Lincoln's successors and Congress became absorbed with the problems of Reconstruction and the settling of the West. Whereas the state's hierarchical power grew stronger during the war, its infrastructural power vis-à-vis capital declined in war's wake (Bensel 1991).

After the Revolution

Taken together, the Civil War and Reconstruction were a revolutionary series of events. Black emancipation ended the world's largest system of slavery; the Reconstruction amendments had a long-term liberalizing effect on the Constitution; and, as long as it lasted, black political participation was both widespread and effective. But the period was also a complex mixture of movement-countermovement struggle, the making and retracting of rights, military occupation, and the ultimate fall of black political power. Its unusual quality was revealed symbolically by its two most dramatic events: (1) the assassination of one president and the impeachment of another, and (2) the passage of the Thirteenth, Fourteenth, and Fifteenth amendments, which freed the slaves, gave African American men citizenship and voting rights, and laid the foundations for the modern concept of due process of law. Nothing like either of these had occurred before, and although assassination attempts followed apace, there would not be an impeachment of a president until 1997 with the impeachment of Bill Clinton by another Republican-dominated Congress (Chafetz 2010).

Contention over Reconstruction

Reconstruction was highly political from the start. Created by the Republican majority in Congress, it prescribed continued congressional control over the South through the Command of the Army Act. This was intended to assure Republican control and oppose the pacifying plans of the new president, Andrew Johnson, who had already tried to quash Congress's moves in the direction of racial equality. With sweeping determination, Congress passed the three Reconstruction amendments, made citizens of former slaves, gave them the (theoretical) right to vote, and created the bare bones of a welfare system. But all this was done with political ruthlessness; the Republicans packed the Supreme Court to wreak their will on the president and impeached him when he stood in the way of their projects. Even as it created new rights, Congress expanded the reach and power of the American central state.

The re-admission of the former slave states to the Union was entangled with the struggle to pass the Reconstruction amendments. As long as Lincoln was alive, re-admission to the Union was handled as a military matter, with provisional governors appointed by Washington and antebellum constitutions reestablished, leaving the issue of black suffrage for the future. But once Lincoln was gone, the question of re-admitting the former Confederate states became entangled with the struggle for extending the vote to the former slaves. This was the problem the Republican-led Congress had to solve against the opposition of a hostile president. "Before the states could be legitimately allowed to return to the fold," argues Bruce Ackerman, "The Nation must extend its protection to these black men and women, guaranteeing their rights as American citizens" (1998, 181).

The issue had already appeared in the debate over the passage of the Thirteenth Amendment. But Congress passed that amendment before the southern states were re-admitted to the Union; the real clash came with the debate over ratification of the Fourteenth Amendment, when the Republicans were willing to do almost anything to achieve the ratification they wanted. "Not only did their Fourteenth Amendment guarantee all blacks the privileges and immunities of citizens of the United States; it gave them the right to claim citizenship in any state they wished—including the right to vote" (Ackerman 1998, 134–59, 164). Before it was over, the debate over the amendment led to the politicization of the occupation, the radicalization of constitutional debate in Washington, and the impeachment of President Johnson when he tried to oppose the Republicans' designs. In the end, only their victory in the 1866 congressional elections allowed the Republicans to pass the amendment on their own terms.

The problem of black suffrage fed into partisan politics. When Republicans looked at the electoral future of the South, blacks were the only large voting bloc they could count on. Hence, the issue of the rights of the former slaves was seen as crucial to the future of the Republican party's national support. Reconstruction took place in a still-hostile region under military control in which white vigilantes and black militias were both active. It was unlikely that northern officers who had just fought a ruthless war and faced a restive white population and a dependent mass of ex-slaves would be tender about civil liberties. Military commissions were one of the tools employed to pacify white southern opposition to Reconstruction.

Ex Parte Milligan

An early postwar Supreme Court case dating from the military trial of an Indiana Democratic politician revealed just how political Reconstruction would be. In 1864, Lambden P. Milligan, who was involved in an intrigue with a disloyal organization, The Sons of Liberty, was arrested and tried by a military commission and sentenced to hang. In ringing tones, a bare majority of the Court denied that the scope of rights varies in times of war: "The Constitution of the United States is a law for rulers and people, equally in war and peace, and covers with the shield of its protection all classes of men, at all times, and under all circumstances. No doctrine, involving more pernicious consequences, was ever invented by the wit of man than that any of its provisions can be suspended during any of the great exigencies of government" (*Ex Parte Milligan*, 71 U.S. [4 Wall.] 2 [1866], 120–21).[16]

Most constitutional lawyers have read *Milligan* as a case about civil liberties in time of war. But this was not true at the time: the army was using military commissions in the South to try white Southerners who were fighting against emancipation. When the *Milligan* decision came down, both the Republicans and the northern press saw it as a challenge to Reconstruction. Thaddeus Stevens, a Radical Republican, called it "perhaps not as infamous as the Dred Scott decision," but "far more dangerous in its operation upon the lives and liberties of the loyal men of this country" because it has "taken away every protection in every one of these rebel States from every loyal man, black or white, who resides there" (Palmer and Ochoa 1998, 211–12). Denying military commissions the power to try civilians, it appeared to Republicans, would shackle Reconstruction authorities from restraining the white militias that were opposing military rule and attacking black freemen who were attempting to establish their rights.

Reducing Black Voting Rights

The political aim of Republican intransigence in the South was to create, in the black population, a solid electoral constituency. Creating such a constituency may have seemed easy at first. After all, Congress had banned ex-Confederate officers from serving in the Senate, the military was officiating over elections, and the former slaves were not lacking in political resources. Former black soldiers, many of whom had become activists, the black churches, and a system of political clubs called the Union Leagues, first developed during the war to promote northern electoral mobilization could serve as an electoral machine for Republican candidates (Valelly 2004, 33). Not only that—at war's end a significant number of free blacks had come South to work in the Freedman's Bureau and in the network of schools and welfare agencies created by Reconstruction. These were the core of the future black social elite of the region.

For a time, the new black voters and the delegates they elected met the Republicans' expectations. By 1867, the Bureau of the Census reported, between 85 and 100 percent of adult black males in Florida, Georgia, Mississippi, the Carolinas, Alabama, Louisiana, Texas, and Virginia had registered to vote (Valelly 2004, 33). Almost all voted for Republican candidates, many coming from among their own race (ibid., 77). But the end of Reconstruction and the determined resistance of the white power structure destroyed black voting power, both in the state legislatures and in Congress. In 1876, there were 162 black state legislators and members of the House of Representatives; by 1878, this number had been cut in half, and by 1890, there were only a handful remaining.

Much of the work of reducing black voting power was done by a combination of electoral chicanery, poll taxes, and literacy requirements (ibid., chap. 3); some was accomplished by outright intimidation and repression. But there were factors in the country at large that contributed to its collapse as well. By the 1870s, the North was sick of the financial and moral burden of administering Reconstruction, factionalism had weakened the Republican organizations in the South, and the courts were unwilling or unable to protect black voting rights. In the disputed presidential election of 1876, a deal was struck allowing the Republican candidate, Rutherford B. Hayes, to enter the White House in return for his agreement to end Reconstruction. This began of a period of white southern ascendency in Congress that lasted through the New Deal and the Fair Deal (Katznelson 2013).

It is hard to escape the conclusion that the Republicans had lost heart in their project to create a great biracial, cross-regional electoral coalition. The original decision was based on their desire to add the South—through the agency of the emancipated black electorate—to their electoral buttresses in the North and West. But once southern white intransigence had begun to whittle away black rights and northern voters had wearied of the costs of Reconstruction, the Republicans realized that they could build a national coalition on the basis of a pro-business, pro-farmer coalition of Northerners and Westerners.

As Republican fervor for black electoral power collapsed, a gradual process of disenfranchisement began to produce Democratic electoral victories, first in the South and then nationally. When the Republicans regained control of national politics at the turn of the twentieth century, they took no action to reinstate black voting rights. Why not, asks Valelly, and he answers, "the black-white, North-South coalition of 1867–1868 was supplanted by a new *white-white* North-West coalition. . . . The enormous growth of the Republican Party in the late 1890s outside the South substituted for lost black voters at the margin" (2004, 135).

The abandonment of southern black voters took on deeper importance given the future role of the Supreme Court in interpreting the Fourteenth Amendment in ways that left African Americans in a position that was, in some ways, "worse than slavery" (Oshinsky 1996). The nadir, of course, came in the case of *Plessy v. Ferguson* (163 U.S. 537), in which the Court held that whites and blacks could be separated by facilities that were "separate but equal." "Negro suffrage," wrote W. E. B. Du Bois, "ended a civil war by beginning a race feud" (2005, 52).[17] But closer to the grassroots, "black codes," poll taxes, and outright intimidation and violence ended the dream that emancipation would bring equality to the former slave population.

None of this negates the profoundly revolutionary implications of Reconstruction for U.S. society. It liberated millions of people from the status of property and, in the Reconstruction amendments, gave future generations the tools with which to establish their rights. Moreover, the Republicans retained a commitment to constitutional forms and chose to operate through party competition. Of course, to achieve their liberalizing aims, the Republicans were drawn into an act of constitutional slight-of-hand to pass the Reconstruction amendments. In contrast to the French republicans' treatment of the Declaration of the Rights of Man, their actions did not lead to a permanent abridgement of the Constitution. But the way Reconstruction was implemented left the way open for the resurgent white power structure to wipe away many of the gains of emancipation.

Conclusions

The Civil War left a complex heritage for state-building, for the armed forces, and for the future of contentious politics and rights in wartime. First, with regard to the development of the American state, the war enhanced the size, the centrality, and the reach of the federal government in both military and in civilian terms. But this was not only true of hierarchical power; the need to fight the first industrialized war enhanced the position of financial capital and increased its power within the state (Bensel 1991). The North did not fight the Civil War to benefit capital, nor did northern capital finance the war to save the Union; nevertheless, the alliance struck between the two left financial capital in a much stronger position than before the war—strong enough to become the most powerful force in postwar policymaking and to control the state's infrastructural power for generations to come.

Second, with regard to the armed forces, although conscription ended with the end of the war and soldiers were henceforth mainly employed on the frontier, it was now a truly *national* army, one that could be mobilized more rapidly, used more efficiently, and turned more easily to the repression of contention than the scattered militias that Lincoln found on coming to power. But there was an irony. Because the economic growth of the North provided plenty of employment for ambitious young men in the decades following the war, the officer corps drew on the one region of the country where industry was slow to develop—the South. Southern officers would henceforth lead the army that had left their region in waste and would impress on it their particular racial ethos. It is thus no accident that the armed forces did not begin to be integrated racially until the end of World War Two (Kryder 2000).

Third, with respect to contentious politics, the war was not the direct product of abolitionism but of a sectional conflict in which slavery was only one element. The abolitionists had been a despised minority in much of the North at the outset of the war, and Lincoln himself certainly had no intention of threatening the institution of slavery in the South. But the Civil War was a crucible of radicalization and polarization that led to the adoption of the abolitionist program by the president and the Republicans. The removal of the southern states from Congress and the incentives of war-making gave the Union government the ability to make "freedom national" (Oakes 2012), adopting the goals, if not the rhetoric, of the abolitionists. Once that occurred, the Republicans emerged as a movement-party, one that would use its dominance of Congress to pass the Reconstruction amendments—the most thorough-going democratization of the U.S. Constitution since the founding.

Finally, with regard to rights in wartime, the Civil War and Reconstruction etched something resembling Scheppele's emergency script into the practice of American war-making. Remember her argument from chapter 1? Emergencies, in Scheppele's account, produce a centralization of power, a partial militarization of the state, the creation of irregular forms of policing and policymaking, "putting people in their place," anticipatory violence, and a ratchet effect (Scheppele 2006, 2010). The Civil War showed few signs of anticipatory violence and remarkably little control of the press or elections, and much of the machinery of social control was abandoned at the end of Reconstruction. But both the war and Reconstruction produced a much more determined use of the suspension of *habeas corpus* and of military commissions than had been true before the war. These would remain, in Justice Robert H. Jackson's later words, "like a loaded weapon ready for the hand of any authority that brings forward a plausible claim of an urgent need" (*Koramatsu v. U.S.* 323 U.S. (1944) 259).

The story of contention and state-building during the Civil War and Reconstruction raises a question that we have already seen in the French Revolution: What, if any, is the relationship between liberalism and the restriction of rights? The French revolutionaries continued to think of themselves as defending liberty even as they put citizens "outside the law." We may well think that the suppression of *habeas corpus* and the use of military commissions during the Civil War were short-lived responses to an emergency; indeed, before he was killed, Lincoln showed every sign of wishing to reverse them. But what of the Republicans' use of military commissions in the South after the war and their "making" of elections to create rights for the freed slaves? And what of the use of military commissions to punish rebellious Native Americans later on? What is the relationship between liberal goals and illiberal means of achieving them? We will reencounter this question throughout the remainder of this book.

A WAR MAKES MOVEMENTS

The Strange Death of Illiberal Italy

The outcomes of the French Revolution and the U.S. Civil War were largely progressive. But many wars are followed by reactionary results—as in Italy and Germany after World War One. In both countries, international changes, structural factors, and the rise of new extremist movements concatenated in the collapse of budding democracies and descent into authoritarian rule. Can these outcomes be explained by the international conjuncture after World War One, by deep structural flaws, or by what was happening in domestic politics?

Of structural factors in Italy, there were plenty—starting with the weakness of its Liberal state and its industrial economy when it emerged from World War One (Einaudi 1933; Lipset 1960; Moore 1966); the international factors were too many to count—including the failure of the government to achieve its war aims in the Treaty of Versailles and the impact of the Russian revolution. Together these contributed to the failure of an already weak and divided political class and to the rise of both outraged irredentism and to left-wing hopes that the Italian working class could "do as they did in Russia."

Both structural factors and international events were critical, but as explanations, they elide the critical role of contentious interaction in the country's descent into authoritarianism. Mussolini was no uniformed clown, strutting on the stage of Italian politics like a *commedia d'ell'arte* performer and many thought the Socialist and Communist parties constituted a serious threat of revolution. Those parties' verbal pyrotechnics far outstripped their practical capacities, but Mussolini was something else. Building on the resentments of the war and on the availability of disheartened veterans and anxious landowners, the future dictator built something new: a militia-like social movement that combined elements of leftist populism with extreme nationalism and anticommunism that provided a model for populist leaders for generations to come.

The Italian state was also profoundly changed by the war. Not only did the government and the military take on a directive role in the economy they had never had before but civil liberties were profoundly restricted and even the welfare state was reformed—if only to limit the politicization of the masses (Procacci 2013, chap. 3). But the deepest changes were political: the center-left and center-right Liberals who had dominated the political class before the war were delegitimated by wartime devastation and postwar disappointments; the Socialist party, which had been moving steadily toward social democracy before the war, was both split and taken over by its "maximalist" faction; and a new and ruthless fascist party emerged from veterans' dissatisfactions and landowners' fears and gained power in the span of three turbulent years of social conflict.

How the war and the period of social conflict that followed produced the world's first fascist movement is the main subject of this chapter. I begin the chapter with Italy's structural foundations; I then turn to the illiberalism of the Liberal state and to the effect of the war on that state's collapse. I return, finally, to the originality of the fascist movement. I show that it was the interaction among war, contention, and the state's strong hierarchical power and infrastructural weakness that led to fascism.

The Historical-Structural Foundations

The puzzle of Italian fascism is that, although the Italian state was profoundly illiberal, it was democratizing, at least in a formal sense, both before and after World War One (Farneti 1978). Italy's Historic Right had defined the political community extremely narrowly when it consolidated power in 1871. In that year, only 2.3 percent of the adult male population was given the vote. Frightened of both Catholic and working-class dissent, only in 1882 did Parliament extend the suffrage but, even then, to only 7 percent of adult males. Alberto Aquarone points out that this was not much lower than the suffrage in other European countries (2003, 260–61), but there were differences. First, in much of the country the vote was managed by the provincial prefects; second, it was heavily corrupted—at least in the South—through local clientele networks (Salvemini 1955); and third, after Agostino Depretis became prime minister in 1876, its effects were vitiated by parliamentary transformism (*trasformismo*)——the practice of transforming

elected deputies from the opposition to supporters of the government by promises of patronage (Mack Smith 1959, 107–17).

But after a period of particularly vicious repression during the last decade of
the nineteenth century, democratization began to take hold. Led by the Liberal
prime minister, Giovanni Giolitti, the reformists expanded the vote to almost the
entire male electorate in 1913, although a second ballot penalized the growing
Partito Socialista Italiano (PSI; Socialist Party).[1] Giolitti began to build welfare
institutions and to encourage the country's budding cooperative movement and
trade unions (Riley 2010). Although he never succeeded in coopting the rapidly
growing PSI, the country was going through an industrial takeoff that seemed to
promise future prosperity (Salamone 1960).

These were major changes, but Giolitti lacked a well-organized centrist party
to back up his policies. His fall from power, and his replacement by the conservative nationalist, Antonio Salandra, reversed many of his policies. Italy's entry into
World War One gave Salandra the opportunity to crack down on opponents—
in particular, on the antiwar leadership of the PSI. Sidney Sonnino, his foreign
minister, even claimed that the only alternative to revolution was to go to war.[2]
The effects of the suffrage reform were neutralized until the war's end, and the
working class was placed under military control. But in the year after the end of
the war, manhood suffrage and proportional representation were both conceded
to adult males and the PSI—under a new maximalist leadership—emerged as the
country's largest party. By 1919, a wave of new and inexperienced voters—many
of them Socialist and others Catholics—entered a political system riven with
deep structural and political cleavages.

A Country of Cleavages

What were these cleavages? First, of course, was the deep division between North
and South.[3] The former, despite remaining pockets of backwardness, was rapidly
industrializing, and much of its agriculture—particularly in the Po Valley—was
commercialized (Aquarone 1981, chap. 1). It produced some remarkably modern industrial centers and a Socialist-led working class that appeared—especially
under Giolitti—to be on its way to full social citizenship (Salamone 1960; Corner
2002, 278). Northern Italy's civil society was rapidly developing, with a network
of cooperatives, agrarian leagues, unions, and employers' associations (Putnam
1993; Riley 2010; Cardoza 1979, 1982).

In contrast, apart from a few enclaves of industrialization around Naples
and Palermo, the South remained largely agrarian, and most of its agriculture
was divided between large and unproductive landholdings owned by absentee

landlords (the *latifundie*) and small handkerchiefs of land tilled by peasants with unstable tenure.[4] Its politics were dominated by local notables, and the region was linked to national politics through clientele chains that were more personalistic than ideological. In contrast to the North, where party identification was beginning to crystallize and party organizations were taking root at the grassroots (Putnam 1993), southern voters were mobilized into shifting voting blocs through *trasformismo* and *clientelismo*. Table 4.1 compares the proportions of the active population employed in agriculture, industry, and services soon after unification and in the decade preceding World War One and the active percentage of the population in the country's two major regions.

Second, although most of the Italian population was Catholic, the liberal elite—which had liquidated the Papal State in 1871—was only nominally so, and much of central Italy, the Socialists, and part of the Liberal political class were anticlerical. Until the turn of the twentieth century, Catholics were banned by papal decree from participating in national politics. It was the clerical-secular split that made the Liberals so reluctant to expand the suffrage because they believed that, if given the vote, the peasants would vote heavily for Catholic candidates. As the papacy reluctantly lifted the ban on Catholics' participation in politics, Catholic political action began to appear in the early twentieth century through the Gentiloni Pact, which made it possible for a newly formed Popular Party to seek votes from across the class structure (Kalyvas 1996). The political system reflected these structural cleavages.

But this account leaves out two crucial factors. First, although Italians referred to their system as "the Liberal state," it was not into a liberal system that these forces lurched at the turn of the twentieth century. Italy's was a deeply illiberal system with highly centralized institutions, uncontrolled police powers, and a judicial system that was both deeply politicized and dependent on the executive (Meniconi 2013). The most important cleavages were political, and many of them were embedded in—and not between—the major political forces. After

TABLE 4.1 Occupational distribution in Italy by region, sector, and active population, 1871 and 1911 (%)

	1871		1911	
SECTOR	NORTH	SOUTH	NORTH	SOUTH
Agriculture	34.8	28.6	26.0	26.4
Industry	12.2	12.8	14.7	9.5
Services	10.9	11.8	8.8	7.6
Total active	57.9	53.2	49.5	43.5

Sources: Associazione per lo sviluppo dell'industria nel Mezzogiorno 1961, 50; Istituto Centrale di Statistica, 1966, 3: 28–39.

Giolitti's bold move toward progressive capitalism in the first decade of the twentieth century, Italy's leaders entered World War One unprepared for modern warfare and then proved unable to meet the demands of the social movements triggered by the war. But these weaknesses were not simply conjunctural; they went back to the origins of the unified state.

The Origins of the Liberal State

On his appointment as governor of Naples after the defeat of the Bourbon monarchy in 1860, Luigi Carlo Farini, a Piedmontese Liberal, wrote to the interior minister in Turin of his frustration at having to deal with the turbulent reality of the southern provinces:[5]

> I have only three hundred *carabinieri* to deal with thirty thousand thieves. . . . I have entire districts in the hands of brigands and no soldiers to send there. I have one hundred thousand petitioners around me and [Giuseppe] Garibaldi's followers growling . . . and you think I can create a system of civil laws and manage the annexation? (Luigi Carlo Farini to Minister Minghetti, November 1860)[6]

Farini's complaint about Naples reveals the recurring problem that Italian elites would face over the next sixty years: managing a society that had not "made" its own revolution. Italy's was a passive revolution in which large sectors of the population were not involved or to which they were positively hostile.[7] But the story also shows why the constitution of the new state would be both centralized and illiberal; it was born during a raging insurgency and a continual state of emergency.

Born in Contention

After unification, the Piedmontese soon faced continual contention, fed by a combination of Bourbon loyalists, papal-financed guerillas, Republicans who were angry that the revolution had been taken over by a royal conquest, and ordinary peasants attempting to use the fall of the Bourbons to wrest control of the land from the landholders (Molfese 1964). The new rulers tried to dismiss the violence as "brigandage," but it was a virtual civil war. At its height, at least thirty-nine guerilla bands were identified in Basilicata, the poorest of the southern regions, alone (Davis 1988, 182–86).

But unrest was not limited to the South. "The development of the new state took place in the following decades against the constant challenge of social unrest and new forms of political opposition" (ibid., 187). Each stage in the consolidation of control triggered new outbreaks of protest, from the extension of Piedmontese free-trade principles to the rest of the country, to the annexation of the Papal States, to conflicts over conscription and taxation, to the formation of clandestine associations inspired by Mazzinian republicanism (ibid., 186–94). But the most dangerous new tendency was anarchism, which spread from Naples, where Mikhail Bakunin had spent the winter of 1865–1866, to central and southern Italy.

After the defeat of the Paris Commune of 1871, internationalist anarchist associations formed throughout the country, gaining support among the middle class, artisans, and workers, especially in the Romagna, where papal rule had left a deep tradition of anticlericalism and radicalism (ibid., 194–95). Anarchism also found a following among the marble workers of Massa and Carrara, among building workers in Rome, and among southern and Sicilian peasants. Insurrections in Bologna, Benevento, and Caserta in the 1870s convinced the government that it was facing a widespread conspiracy that combined revolutionary internationalists, Bourbon legitimists, and criminal elements (ibid., 197).

Like many leaders of states born in civil strife, Italy's new leaders chose to centralize the state administration and to institutionalize repression through a largely unchecked police force and a politicized judiciary. Every time contention threatened to get out of hand, emergency powers and martial law were declared. More permanently, it produced a judiciary that lacked independence from the executive, an army that was repeatedly used to repress civilians, and an inability to distinguish between ordinary protest and real rebellion.

Hierarchical Power and Its Discontents

Nothing could seem more antithetical to the material conditions of the new state than the creation of a centralized administrative state. The Piedmontese-led government inherited a peninsula and the two main islands that were divided among eight major and minor states, each with its own administrative and judicial traditions (Romanelli 1995). The *Statuto* (the Piedmontese constitution of 1848), which was applied to the entire country in 1861, was full of liberal sentiments, and Count Camillo Benso di Cavour, the first prime minister of the unified state, seems to have favored a federal system. But given the threat of internal subversion in the South and elsewhere, it was not irrational for the country's new leadership to choose a centralized administrative model. As Aquarone writes, "the fundamental question was not to secure the bases for as broad a participation in public life as possible, but rather to guarantee the survival of the unified constitutional state—if necessary, even against the will of the majority, if only provisionally" (2003, 264–65).

But there were costs, and they were not insignificant ones; centralization meant, in effect, that the same class of Piedmontese moderates who had "made" Italy would govern the peninsula from the North. Many local and regional officials were purged by the new leadership, and others were reduced to implementing laws passed by the northerners. It also meant that once-dominant capital cities such as Naples, Florence, and Milan were reduced to the status of provincial capitals, leading to resentment and, at times, revolt. And it meant, finally, that rules of liberal political economy developed in Piedmont would be applied to the rest of the country, snuffing out infant industries in some regions of the South.

But centralization was imperfect from the start. First, the same class that made the political *Risorgimento* became the administrators of the new state (Melis 1995, 194). Some ministries were barely present in the provinces, while others had vast peripheral outcoppings. This meant that—in contrast to the French prefectoral system, from which it was adapted—it was the political system that offered the most useful route for local interests to reach the central state (Cassese 1974; Melis 1995, 196; Tarrow 1977). The state was hierarchical, but power was concentrated nowhere in the administration.

Agents of Repression

As in the rest of Europe, World War One tightened controls on civil liberties in Italy, but the state that entered the war was already highly illiberal. The legislation that governed the administration of justice and policing was the product of the emergency powers conferred on the Piedmontese government during the War of 1859 (Davis 1988, 211).[8] Both the criminal code and police regulations contravened the liberties guaranteed by the Piedmontese *Statuto* (Merlini 1995). "The freedoms which the law of Liberal Italy conceded with one hand were deliberately either revoked or made discretional with another" (Davis 1988, 212; see also Rodotà 1995).

The magistracy was politicized from the outset (Neppi Modona 1973), and the institution of the *pubblico ministero* (roughly "public prosecutor") created a class of judicial officials who reported directly to the interior minister (Guarnieri 1995, 371–72; Rodotà 1995, 311). The higher magistrates came predominantly from the upper bourgeoisie and "the regime was indifferent to the idea of judicial control of the constitutionality of the laws" (Guarnieri 1995, 372; Rodotà 1995, 325). Each time rebellion arose or threatened to break out, emergency laws or decrees rode roughshod over the high-minded articles written into the *Statuto*.

As for the police, they were conceived more as an instrument to protect the state than one designed to defend public order (della Porta and Reiter 1998). No single police force was created by the new regime: the *questori, pretori, carabinieri,* and ordinary police of the *pubblica sicurezza* were granted separate and partially overlapping powers, creating a confusion of jurisdictions (Davis 1988, chap. 8; Guarnieri 1995, 373–77). Vagrants, idlers, and the unemployed were regarded as inherently suspicious. By the late 1870s, between 3,000 and 4,500 individuals a year were subject to *ammonizione* (warnings) in Milan alone, and possibly as many as 100,000 a year in the country as a whole (Davis 1988, 222).

More serious than the *ammonizione* was the power of *domicilio coatto* (house arrest) exercised by the police. This empowered them to enforce house arrests and curfews in specific places, often far from people's homes. *Domicilio coatto* was first employed after the anarchist rising in the Romagna in 1874, but it eventually became "an instrument of standard policing. When it was used in combination with the *ammonizione*, it offered the police a comprehensive system of detention that remained outside the criminal law and its procedures" (ibid., 223). In the 1880s, a system of penal colonies was added to these tools, making it possible to put people away for long terms without their cases being processed by a magistrate, even when evidence of a criminal offense was lacking (ibid., 224).

This system of police powers was expanded in the 1890s, when, in response to uprisings in both Sicily and Milan, Prime Minister Francesco Crispi introduced a new set of emergency regulations that empowered the police to impose house arrest on "all dangerous persons convicted of crimes against public order or which involve the use of explosive substances as well as all those who have made manifest their intention of committing such crimes against the social order," that is, anticipatory detention. These instruments produced "a real and proper penal subsystem independent in substance from the regular courts and run by the police" that could be used for the wholesale arrest of suspected anarchists, socialists and other suspected subversives (Guarnieri 1995, 379).

As if this were not enough to undermine the liberal claims of the *Statuto*, a succession of "special laws" were passed during periods of tension—against brigandage, highway robbery, and anarchism. Freedom of the press was suspended four times, and freedom of association was temporarily liquidated by a royal decree in 1899 (Cassese 2010, 53–57). As for freedom of speech, it was never formally sanctioned, but it survived uneasily in a situation in which "political propaganda could be forbidden when it was judged to be against the law or encouraging people to disobey the law" (ibid., 53–58).

The army was regularly used to suppress civil disorder. "More than in any other European country," writes Aquarone, "the Italian ruling class assigned a primary role in the maintenance of public order to the military" (1981, 108). Between 1861 and the turn of the twentieth century, the government made use of the state of siege ten times, followed by the transfer of the powers of ordinary courts to military commissions (Violante 1976, 494–503). During the rolling crisis of the

1890s, states of siege and military rule were established in Sicily and along the Tuscan/Ligurian coast, in Milan, and in other big cities (Guarnieri 1995, 379–80). In Milan, a military attack on supposed protesters in a monastery led to over one hundred deaths with more than fifty wounded (Aquarone 1981, 147).

It was in the crisis of the 1890s that the country barely escaped moving in an authoritarian direction (ibid., 145–49). It was only due to an improvement in the economic situation, the availability of a moderate coalition under the leadership of Giolitti, and the determined opposition of a coalition of left-wing parties that an authoritarian inversion was avoided (ibid., 152–77). But the Italian state's powers of social control were both harsh and divided—a contradiction that sharpened during the war and made it easy for an adventurer such as Mussolini to destroy his enemies and take power in war's wake. Before turning to those changes, we need to understand the period that came closest to putting Italy on a path to democracy—the age of Giolitti—and its failures.

Giolitti, Socialism, and Nationalism

At the turn of the twentieth century, Italy went through a period of rapid industrial expansion (ibid., 21–23). While agriculture continued to contribute half of the gross domestic product, there was also a rapid increase in the production of grain and a rationalization of production in the Po Valley (ibid., chap. 1; Zangheri 1960). But despite these signs of economic takeoff, relations between management and workers—both in industry and in agriculture—remained patrimonial at best and more often exploitative. It was the solid alliance among conservative landowners, aggressive industrial managers, and right-wing politicians that Giovanni Giolitti, in his long period of political supremacy, aimed at combatting. He largely succeeded as long as he remained in power, but his attempt to cooperate with "subversive" Socialists and trade unionists was too much for Italy's conservative elites, and a new nationalist coalition came to power in 1914, plunging the country into a war that was neither necessary nor adequately prepared for.

The Normalization of Contention

The progressive governments under Giolitti (1901–1914) liberalized industrial relations, expanded the suffrage, nationalized the communications and transportation systems, and returned the country to constitutional norms after the exceptional rule of the late 1890s (Aquarone 1981, 2003; Salamone 1960). Giolitti's major success was to moderate class conflict by recognizing the legitimacy of collective bargaining, curbing the arbitrary power of management, and passing a number of social and economic laws that began to create links between the state and civil society (Aquarone 1981, chap. 3). His rule also limited the arbitrary repression of dissidence. Under Giolitti, the state of siege was employed only after the massive earthquake in Messina and Reggio Calabria in 1908 (Violante 1976) and the prefects, although still retaining their role in assuring public order, began to take on the mediation of industrial disputes in the country's rapidly expanding industrial sector (Procacci 2006). This was the beginning of constructing the kind of infrastructural power that Italy had lacked when prefects, police, and magistrates regarded the lower classes with suspicion.

There was a negative side to Giolitti's long domination of Italian politics. Although he came out of the administration, he shifted positions with the political winds, moving out of office each time the seat of government became too hot, and involving the country in a war in Libya, in part to expand his majority. And while he governed as a modernizer in the North, his tactics in managing the South grew out of the nineteenth-century practice of *trasformismo* (Salvemini, Bucci, and Arfé 2000). Even Giolitti's signal successes—reversing the trend toward authoritarianism at the end of the 1890s and creating links to the working class—were only partial.

Worker and Peasant Socialism

Beginning in the 1890s, two new forms of working-class organization began to develop in the countryside and the cities. The first was the combination of *federazioni di mestiere* (occupational groupings) and *camere di lavoro* (workers' chambers). The former were typical of trade union organizations throughout the West, but the latter—locally organized transoccupational centers for the coordination and the stimulation of collective action for both industrial workers and farmworkers—were almost unique to Italy. Together, they soldered local solidarity around strikers and gave strikes a potentially political character (Aquarone 1981, 49).

The second distinctive factor of Italian labor organization was its strength in the countryside. Largely following the geography of the capitalization of agriculture, farmworkers' leagues began to develop at the same time as other workers' organizations. This was not only the result of the growth of commercial farming but of the close connections between the peasant movement and the PSI (ibid., 51). We can see the growing strength and the combativeness of Italian farmworkers from the strike statistics collected by Lorenzo Bordogna and Giancarlo Provasi in Figure 4.1.[9]

Figure 4.1 reveals two important features of Italian collective action before the end of the Liberal period. First, the number of days lost to strikes per

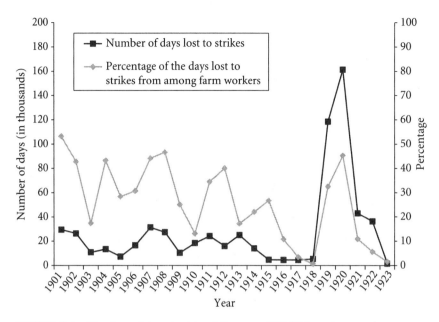

FIGURE 4.1 Number of days lost to strikes per 100,000 workers and percentage of the total among farmworkers, 1901–1923. Data from Bordogna and Provasi 1979, 188–89, 234.

100,000 workers fell during the first years of *giolittismo*, only to increase again in 1907–1908 and again in the years before Italy's entry in the war. Strikes dropped radically during the war due to wartime restrictions but rose astronomically afterward. The figure shows a high variability in the number of strike days lost over the two decades following the turn of the twentieth century. This was due not only to economic cycles but to political cycles as well. Second, the proportion of farmworker strikes among the total was strikingly high, ranging from over 53 percent of the total strikes in 1901 to 6 percent when fascism took power in 1922. In a volatile labor market, farmworker protest was the most volatile of all.

How can we explain the high level of combativeness of this young labor movement and its rapid fluctuations from one year to the next? Three reasons can be advanced. First, because the farm sector was an important part of the labor movement, the variations in weather and productivity affected strike volatility. Second, the variations in political repression due to changes in governance affected the willingness of workers and peasants to engage in collective action. Third, the combativeness of the countryside came from the mass of proletarianized farmworkers in the Po Valley, which would play a key role in the coming of fascism, as we will see later.

There was a constant in Italian contention through the 1890s and the first decades of the new century: the steady growth of the PSI. Founded in 1892 by a miscellaneous group of socialist and working-class groups, PSI membership expanded rapidly after the turn of the twentieth century (Aquarone 1981), drawing in members from outside the working class. This breadth of support gave the party a leading role on the left wing of Parliament but also in defending liberal values against the repressive assaults of right-wing governments. Table 4.2 shows the steady growth of electoral socialism, both before and after the key electoral reform of 1913.

Table 4.2 shows something else as well.—the spectacular growth of political Catholicism after 1900 and especially after the war, when the new Popular Party appeared (Kalyvas 1996). Gaining the support of one-fifth of the electorate, many of them rural Catholics with no previous voting experience, the new party's leader, Don Luigi Sturzo, a Sicilian priest, tried to occupy the center of the political spectrum. This would have made possible a bipolar party system pitting center-left Socialists against center-right Catholics (much like what occurred after World War Two) had it not been for the intrusion of a new political force in Italian politics— right-wing nationalism that found its outlet in intervention in World War One.

Enter Nationalism

The fear of Socialist workers began to produce a conservative reaction against Giolitti, and the war gave the historic right the opportunity to impose a more conservative regime (Corner 2002, 291). Intervention in the war was seen as an

TABLE 4.2 Percentage of votes and number of parliamentary seats for the Italian Socialists and Catholics [*Partito popolare*] in national elections, 1895–1921

	ITALIAN SOCIALIST PARTY		CATHOLICS		
ELECTION YEAR	VOTES (%)	NUMBER OF SEATS	VOTES (%)	NUMBER OF SEATS	TOTAL VOTERS
1895	2.95	15	—	—	1,251,000
1897	2.95	15	—	—	1,241,486
1900	6.50	33	—	—	1,497,970
1904	5.70	29	0.59	3	1,593,886
1909	7.40	39	3.80	26	1,903,687
1913	10.10	68	4.50	34	5,100,615
1919	34.40	203	20.50	100	5,793,507
1921	30.00	153	20.40	108	6,708,141

Source: The general source for this period is Piretti 1996.

opportunity to gain territory in Italy's northeast but also as a chance to divest Italy of the last twenty years of progressive politics and policy under Giolitti under the banner of national security. The idea of leaders such as Antonio Salandra and Sidney Sonnino was not only to assert Italy's role internationally but "to advance the power of a conservative bloc of forces, which—reinforced by a victorious war—would liquidate the Giolittian center-left experience" (Rochat 1976, 166).

But the historic right was not alone in pushing Italy toward an active military role. Since the 1880s, politicians such as Francesco Crispi had been convinced that Italy's future lay in colonial expansion. It was during his tenure as prime minister that the ill-fated Ethiopian adventure was attempted—and failed. In 1911–1912, a second sortie into Africa was attempted, this time against the remnant of the Ottoman Empire in Libya, with greater success. But the Libyan War produced few benefits and created a thirst for expansion that created a new fracture in Italian politics between the pacifists, who wanted to stay out of the impending conflict in Europe, and those who saw the increasing tension between France and Britain, on the one hand, and Germany and Austria, on the other, as an opportunity for expansion.

But on whose side should Italy intervene in the war? On the side of its traditional ally, France, or on the side of Germany and Austria-Hungary in the Triple Alliance? The political class was divided, not only over intervention versus neutrality but also over which of these two coalitions to join. The center-right was divided between the followers of Giolitti, who opposed entry into the war, and those of Salandra and Vittorio Emanuele Orlando, who pushed for it; the left was divided too, with Democrats and Republicans supporting intervention on the side of the liberal powers.

Money and agents flooded into Italy from both sides to push the decision one way or the other. In the end, Salandra, who had succeeded Giolitti as prime minister, threw in his lot with France and Britain, probably because there was more territory to be gained by defeating Austria-Hungary than by the defeat of the Western allies. Besides, entering the war on the side of the West would allow Salandra to gain the support of many Democrats and Republicans, who could see the war as a mission to expand democracy against the autocratic powers of Central Europe. Thus, to the deep structural cleavages between North and South, capital and labor, and left and right, a political cleavage was added—between pacifists and interventionists, not only between the parties but within them (ibid., 168). Rather than entering the war with a unified political class, as the British, French, Germans, and Austrians had done a year earlier, Italy went to war with a political class that was split along both political-social and foreign policy–military lines. These cleavages split the prewar governing parties and left

TABLE 4.3   The intersection of left-right and prowar–antiwar cleavages in Italy on the eve of World War One

	LEFT	RIGHT
Interventionists	Democrats	Right-wing Liberals
	Social Reformists	Right Catholics
	Independent Socialists	Nationalists
Neutralists	Socialists	Giolittian Liberals
	Left Catholics	

Source: Farneti 1978, 9.

a hollowed-out center that none of the postwar parties were able to fill. Table 4.3 shows the extent of political polarization on the eve of the war.

The Italian Emergency Script

Entering the war gave Salandra the space to ride roughshod over his opponents. He did this, in part, by using the tools his predecessors had employed during the turbulent 1890s but also by imposing new forms of military control over industry. The former powers were exercised against the entire population and the press, whereas the latter centered on exactly the groups whose support the government needed—the industrial working class. The result was that, when industrial conflict exploded at war's end, it would have a strong political component against a state that had not only taken the country into a devastating war but had suppressed the working class in doing so.

Repressive Justice

A state of siege and military tribunals constituted the central core of the decrees used by the Salandra-Sonnino government from the moment Italy entered the war (Procacci 2006). But Salandra's government went well beyond his predecessors, taking over all the functions of the legislative branch and legislating by decree, without consulting Parliament. "Both the years of neutrality and of the war were years of almost total suspension of the constitution," concluded Giuseppe Maranini, conservative constitutionalist. "The government governed by decree, even in passing tax legislation, with a Parliament that was mainly closed, and not consulted even when it was in session" (1967, 248).

In the event, the war was long, drawn-out, and went badly. If anything, it strengthened the conviction of the lower classes that the elites were both corrupt and incompetent (Lussu 2000). This was not only because soldiers were thrown senselessly against the better-armed and better-led Austrian armies but because the state of exception hit the lower classes far harder than the rich or the middle class. The police power of the prefects was increased, press censorship was re-imposed, mail was opened, people were prosecuted for suspicion of serious and indirect betrayal, the use of informants was widespread, and political activists were sent to prison or into internal exile (Procacci 2013, chap. 3). Military decrees substituted for civilian legislation, military judges substituted for civilian ones, and the military was given direct control of the management of war zones, in-cluding all the industrial areas of the country. Rather than mobilizing the popu-lation around liberal goals, as the French and British governments were doing, in Italy hierarchical power was intensified down to the basic units of production in the factories (Procacci 2006; Kier 2010; Rochat 1976).[10]

Italy was not alone in experiencing the strains of war on its institutions. In all five of the major Western and Central European powers–Great Britain, France, Germany, Austria-Hungary, and Italy—states of exception were applied, parlia-ments were closed or partially closed, the executive gained extensive powers, siz-able portions of the law and administration were militarized, and civil rights and liberties were reduced (Procacci 2009, 2011). But the Italian situation was unusual in three main respects. First, as we have seen, the liberalism of Italy's Liberal state was fragile, had been frequently reversed, and was never completely accepted by the right. "Although the structure of the state was a democracy—or at least, an authoritarian democracy—the absence of a unanimous consensus of the political forces about going to war justified the choice of coercion right from the beginning of the conflict" (Procacci 2011, 12).

Second, the other belligerents—with the exception of Russia—entered the war with their legitimacy largely intact and with a high degree of consensus on the justice of going to war; Italy did not. As table 4.2 shows, on the traditional divisions between left and right a new division was superimposed between inter-ventionists and neutralists, dividing the political class into pacifist and interven-tionist factions—even on the left.

Third, the Italian state was ill-prepared for industrial warfare and lacked the infrastructural power to mobilize its civilian population. There were material shortages everywhere, but only in Italy and Russia were there severe food short-ages from the beginning of the hostilities. The combination of antiwar protest, industrial conflict, and food protests led military authorities to impose repressive measures everywhere. But nowhere was repression as harsh or as systematic as it was in the factories. Military control gave management the tool it had long urged to discipline the workforce.

The Emergency Script in the Factories

There were four wartime practices used to control the working class that helped radicalize it in the immediate postwar years but also laid the groundwork for the authoritarian inversion that followed: the militarization of production, the roll-back of Giolitti's industrial relations reforms, heightened labor repression, and the direct involvement of the state in industrial production:

First, soon after entering the war, Italy created a new bureaucracy, the *Mobilitazione industriale* (IM), to direct its industrial mobilization (Kier 2010).[11] "The appointment of military officers to run IM signaled Italy's militarization of the working class" (ibid., 145). As the war progressed, however, the IM actually became more oriented to arbitrating industrial disputes than to repression (Tomassini 1992, 181–82).

Second, Giolitti's labor reforms were quickly rolled back. Wages were frozen at prewar levels, strikes were banned, and arbitration boards set wages and working conditions (ibid.). Workers suspected of union activity could lose their draft exemptions, and large areas of the country were removed from civilian jurisdiction and placed in a virtual state of siege (ibid.).

Third, labor repression was heightened. "In fact," concludes Elizabeth Kier, "Italy's coercive strategy more closely resembled its autocratic adversaries than its democratic allies" (2010, 147). Workers could be sent to the front for absenteeism, and attempts to organize in the factory were treated as subversion. As a result of the presence of the state in the factories, strikes were politicized, a tendency that continued after the war (Tilly 1992b, 593).

It was inevitable, therefore, that the war would both heighten social tensions and add to the polarization of the party system. "Labor," writes Kier, "had been unused to dealing with the state to protect its interests, and this new— and repressive—contact radicalized labor's demands, fueled its alienation from the state and created an unprecedented level of class solidarity" (2010, 151; see also Procacci 1992). One result was the factory council movement that ripened into the occupation of the factories after the war (Spriano 1975). Another was the explosion of membership in both the unions and the PSI at war's end. And yet another was the creation of an insurrectionary atmosphere and the illusion among many sectors of the working class—and the terrified bourgeoisie—that revolution was the only answer.

Social tensions were not limited to the factories. Many peasants had profited from the high prices for grain that the army's needs assured. But as thousands of their sons—ill-equipped and poorly led—perished in the snows of the Dolomites, there was a scarcity of labor in the countryside, putting a strain on those who remained, especially on women and old people. Not only that—many land-owning peasants were encouraged by the wartime rise in food prices to take out loans to expand their plots (Sereni 1956). Others were encouraged by government promises to believe that land would be distributed to soldiers returning from the front. When the demand for food went down at war's end and the peasants learned that the government promises of land reform were illusory, the results were catastrophic. Just as the Liberal center imploded and the Socialists were split over the war, a wave of contention simultaneously appeared in both city and countryside.

The Cycle of Contention in War's Wake

"Ends of wars bring fateful times," writes Charles Tilly (1992b, 587) of World War One.[12] In Italy, this was true both in the party system and in the country at large. The splits in the political class had been partly suppressed and partly papered over during the war years, but they reemerged in the first postwar elections in 1919. This was the first election in which lower-class voters were allowed to vote. Catholic voters flowed into the new Popular Party of Don Luigi Sturzo; the PSI was taken over by its maximalist faction and radicalized by the Russian Revolution and the appearance of communist competitors; and the war produced the opportunity for a new and more ruthless actor to appear in the cities and countryside of north-central Italy—Mussolini's fascist movement.

The polarization of the party system was fed by an enormous release of pent-up resentment in the society. Despite the fact that Italy had been nominally victorious, at the end of the war "large parts of the Italian population, civilian and combatant alike, greeted the final victory with repeated denunciations of the war effort and derisive attacks on its consequences, despite enormous sacrifices" (Corner and Procacci 1997, 223). A cycle of contention began in the factories of the north-central region, but it rapidly spread to the countryside and the farmworkers.

Even before the war ended, antiwar, antistate, and anticapitalist resentment came together in a massive insurrection in Turin in August 1917. But it was only at war's end that mobilization reached its height in both the city and countryside. Over the next two years—the *biennio rosso* ("red two years") of 1919–1920—the number of days lost to striking rose dramatically from 464,000 in 1913 to almost 1.5 million in 1919 and to 1.9 million in 1920 (Franzosi 1997).

The strikes not only increased in number; they took on a new and more aggressive form in the occupation of factories, beginning in Turin in 1920 and spreading throughout the North (Spriano 1975). The occupations made it impossible for employers to shut striking workers out of the factories and difficult for the government to combat their actions without wholesale invasions of the factory premises. Even the Socialist-aligned Confederazione Generale del Lavoro (CGL) was of two minds about the occupations, providing verbal support for the occupiers but failing to call the general strike that would have been the only way to exert leverage on the government.

More important was the spread of militancy from the cities to the countryside. As workers were occupying factories, there were massive farmworkers' strikes in the Po Valley (see figure 4.1). Whereas in 1913 fewer than 80,000 agricultural workers had gone on strike, in 1919 the number rose to almost 500,000 and to over a million in 1920. To many observers, and certainly to the conservative press, Italy in these years appeared to be headed for something like what had happened in Russia in 1917.

But despite these widespread protests, the Italy of 1919–1920 was far from ready for revolution (Corner 1975, chap. 5). Indeed, by late 1920, the wave of industrial and rural protest had peaked; the major effect of the *biennio rosso* was to terrorize landowners in the countryside and to align them with much of the middle class in the cities (Farneti 1978, 12–16). By 1921, the number of days lost to strikes had been cut by more than half. Fascism arose as the wave of left-wing protest began to decline.

Polarization followed the wave of radicalization. The renewed militancy of the working class had the result of allying the middle and upper classes of city and countryside against the fear of an Italian version of the October Revolution. The economic dislocations of the war and the labor agitations that followed produced such uncertainty in urban propertied groups that the traditional cleavages between country and city, and industry and agriculture, were temporarily bridged. "Salaried [agricultural] workers and small peasants and industrial workers," writes Paolo Farneti, "were aligned on one side, small and large property and business owners on the other." This created what Farneti calls "a coalition of property and acquisition" (1978, 16) in the cities and countryside of north-central Italy arrayed against a coalition of workers, poor peasants, and farmworkers.

The Dissolution of the Party System

Both disillusionment at the outcome of the war and the realignment of class forces coincided with the change to a proportional electoral system in 1919. This meant that the political spectrum—already polarized before the war—became more so afterward. The number of parliamentary seats won by the moderate opposition—Republicans, Radicals, reformist Socialists, and Giolittian liberals—fell from 310 seats in 1913 to 214 in 1919, giving them insufficient seats to form a governing coalition. The Catholic Popular Party increased its seats by over 200 percent between the two elections, but its historic enmity with both the Social-ists and Liberals made a clerical-secular coalition impossible to imagine. On the right, the parties that had supported intervention in the war were crushed, falling from seventy seats to twenty-three, and two smaller interventionist groups—the Democrats and Constitutional Democrats—disappeared altogether (ibid., 10).

With this realignment, none of the theoretically possible governing coalitions had sufficient support to form a government. Giolitti tried, and failed, to put together a cross-party coalition of the kind he had led before the war. Between 1918 and 1921, four other prime ministers took office, but none lasted more than a few months. The hollowing out of the traditional party system left space for a sequential polarization, beginning with the cycle of contention from the left and ending with a reactive cycle of violence on the right.

As social conflict intensified and the political class proved incapable of man-aging it, support grew for fascism among conservative groups in city and coun-tryside, along with returned veterans, disenchanted trade unionists, and the sons of small farm owners. Fascism, which began as a populist movement appealing mainly to demobilized soldiers, found support among urban business groups and landowners in the Po Valley. Mussolini also gained the support of the small peasant owners who had acquired or expanded their landholdings during the war when food prices were high and easy credit available. At war's end, when prices dropped, many were unable to meet their payments on the mortgages taken out during the war. Large landowners were able to gather many of these small farmers into the *fasci* that attacked Socialist sections and chambers of labor in 1920 and 1921 (Corner 1975). While the left-wing organizations mobilized thousands of day laborers, and the Catholic unions organized tenant farmers and sharecroppers, the bulk of *coltivitori diretti* (small land-owning farmers) fell under the control of *gruppi combattentistici*—Mussolini's rolling squads of toughs and ex-soldiers (Sereni 1956, 14).

The Phasing of Collective Action

All episodes of mobilization are cyclical, some longer and more intense than others. As they decline, they leave disillusionment and disorganization in their wake (della Porta and Tarrow 1986). In Italy, the wave of left-wing mobilization had peaked by the end of 1920—exactly when Mussolini's *fasci* were providing a mass basis for disillusioned returning servicemen and peasant farmers. By the time fascist assaults on Socialist sections and chambers of labor began, left-wing urban mobilization was collapsing. A wave of largely unsuccessful strikes, cul-minating in the occupation of the factories, had revealed the rifts between the workers and the verbal revolutionism of the Socialists (Spriano 1975). As fascist violence escalated, left-wing mobilization was already in decline. Membership in the CGL, which had exploded toward the end of the war (Procacci 1992, 165–66), declined to less than one-fifth of its 1920 total in 1922 and to one-tenth of that by 1923. This facilitated Mussolini's task immensely; the provincial bullies on whom his movement relied would have been less courageous against a fully mobilized class enemy.

The sympathy of the forces of law and order provided political opportunities to the *fasci* too. Never friendly to the left, the police and the military had grown accustomed to imposing industrial discipline during the war and now stood by as Socialist headquarters and chambers of labor were torched (Rochat 1967, 1973; Mondini 2006). The courts were also useless because most jurists were unsympathetic to left-wing agitators who had been breaking the law since the war (Neppi Modona 1969). Most important, it was the support of the large landowners *(agrari)* that provided much of the manpower, the financing, and even the vehicles that the violent *squadristi* of the fascist movement used to attack Socialist and union headquarters (Corner 1975).

War, the State, and Contention

Explanations for a political system's descent into authoritarianism that focus on a single mechanism—structural cleavage, international events, or war—are always unsatisfactory. In this chapter, I have argued that, while Italy's deep social cleavages lay at the origin of the failure of the Liberal state, and the international environment was certainly important in leading the elite to intervene in the war and encouraging the Left to think Italy was ready for a Red October, it was the undemocratic nature of that state that stunted the integration of the working class and led to its radicalization.

Entry into the war was a response to what were seen as international opportunities, but it was also a way to re-impose discipline on the working class and prevent revolution by a weak state that lacked rooting in society (Rusconi 2014). In Mann's terms, we can say that the new state developed through "despotic power" but failed to develop the infrastructural power that could gain it the support of the lower classes. The war deepened these imbalances, militarizing the economy but failing to mobilize society on behalf of the government's war aims. Whereas countries such as Great Britain used a combination of infrastructural and hierarchical power to gain consent for the war, Italian elites relied almost entirely on constraint.

The war profoundly increased the role of the state in the economy, involving industrialists and technical personnel in wartime administration (Melis 1988).

It is not too much of a stretch to find the precedents for Mussolini's corporate state in the role of the state in the economy during the war (Maier 1975, chap. 5; Hintze 1975). It also affected the welfare state, but its most deeply-felt impact was on the civil liberties of workers, peasants, and soldiers. These factors triggered a radicalization of the left—especially in the countryside—which in turn produced a right-wing backlash of upper-class landowners and small peasants, which provided an opportunity for Mussolini at war's end.

Of course, the fascist regime introduced its own repressive laws and police practices that went well beyond what the Liberal elites had used during the war. For example, under the Unified Text for Public Security of 1926, people could be sent into internal exile for ordinary crimes. Soon after, a special tribunal was set up for the defense of the state to avoid the ordinary court system, which was considered too tepid for the Fascists (Neppi Modona 1973; Meniconi 2013). Among Mussolini's *fascistissimo* (very fascist) decrees were those that limited freedom of speech and association; reinforced the power of the executive; eliminated trade union rights; substituted elections with plebiscites; and increased control over the press, association, and expression. The police were reformed as well; after several experiments with mixed militia and professional police forces, in 1930 the Organization for the Vigilance and Repression of Antifascism (OVRA) was created (Amato 1967a; Aquarone 1965; Cassese 2010; Tosatti 1997).

But Mussolini invented little that was truly new (Cassese 2010); much of the fascist state's repressive architecture was adapted from that of its predecessor and from wartime practices of social control (Aquarone 1965, 238; Cassese 2010). For example, the unified text of public security of 1926 expanded the *domicilio coatto* and the *ammonizione* from the language of the law of 1894 (Amato 1967b; Aquarone 1965, 98; Cassese 2010, 35). The fascist special tribunal was the direct heir of the extraordinary military commissions of the past, made up of military officers and basing its peacetime decisions on the military penal code in wartime (Violante 1976, 522–23).The restriction of freedom of the press had predecessors too—in the 1859, 1866, 1894, and 1898 decrees that censored the press in response to the contentious episodes of those years (Cassese 2010, 49). As for policing, "the fascist regime expanded the already rich variety of the police forces" (ibid., 63). The OVRA itself was prefigured by the creation, during the war, of a Central Office of Investigations (Tosatti 1997, 233).

The new regime did not introduce radical change in the administrative structures either but intensified security practices that had become familiar from wartime measures. The *fascistissime* laws revived and extended both the letter and the spirit of the wartime emergency script restricting civil liberties—suppression of press freedom, closing down associations, and limitations of freedom of speech and opinion (Procacci 2006). Although the decrees that created a wartime state of emergency were revoked at war's end and Parliament returned to its central position, the policing of strikes remained in place.

The war, its mismanagement, and the government's inept controls created a profound antiparty and antisystem mentality among the Italian public, providing a mass base for Mussolini's *fasci* and covert support for his movement by the officer class and the police. From the revolutionary syndicalists to the idealist intellectuals around the journals *La Voce* and *L'Unità*, to the Nationalists, and the Catholic *popolari*, there was a profound alienation from a state that had led the country into a disastrous war and from its humiliating results (Sergio 2002). No small part of the success of Mussolini was to tap into this antipolitical alienation. But Mussolini also invented a new type of movement in the shape of a militia, using the demagogic tools of antiparty rhetoric to create a "superparty" (Scoppola, in ibid., xv).

It was the war that provided Mussolini with the raw materials to build this party/militia (Gentile 1989). Hundreds of thousands of soldiers and thousands of officers returned from the front to a society whose internal equilibrium had been unhinged by the war. Many fascist recruits were the sons of large landowners; others were the sons of peasants who had bought land during the war and could not pay their mortgages in war's wake; and still others had been syndicalists or socialist maximalists who saw the parliamentary state as incapable and corrupt. The real heritage of Mussolini lay in bringing the form of the militia into the political system and infusing a political party with the mission of a movement. That innovation would surface again in the more ruthless and more tragic national socialist revolution in Germany a decade later.

Part II
ENDLESS WARS

FROM STATIST WARS TO COMPOSITE CONFLICTS

In the episodes described in part 1, domestic contention intersected with war and state-building in three major ways: mobilizing for war, war-making, and contention arising in war's wake.

The French revolutionary wars were begun by a social movement struggling to establish a republican government against the hostility of surrounding states as well as against violent internal opposition. The state that emerged never lost its movement tendencies. The model of the citizen-army that it produced diffused across Europe, combining a strong professional ethic with a penchant for the nationalization of the masses and a tendency to authoritarianism. Opposition took the shape of a regional and religious countermovement in the West that was suppressed with the same ruthlessness that the republicans used against their foreign enemies. The success of French arms both at home and abroad was in part due to the invention of the citizen army, in part on instilling militant nationalism into French society and in part on the innovation of the consolidated national state.

The U.S. Civil War grew out of territorial contention over slavery. It pitted agrarian, slaveholding states against a political movement that combined a devotion to free labor with the defense of the Union. Here, too, there was an antiwar movement, one that took the form of opposition to the draft, riots against African Americans, and opposition by the Democratic Party. That movement failed, in part, because of its association with southern secession but also because the Union government created emergency institutions to defeat it. The war led Lincoln and the Republican Party to embrace the goals of the abolitionist movement and laid the foundations for a more centralized state and an economic Yankee Leviathan.

In Italy, the revolutionary transition from the Liberal state to its authoritarian successor was the result of widespread contention between left and right. World War One was opposed by the opposition parties and by a substantial part of the political class. The war shattered the country's political party system; led to postwar social conflict that was tantamount to civil war; and opened space for Mussolini's fascist movement, which turned the country's illiberal institutions in an authoritarian direction. This strengthened the state enormously and suppressed its socialist and communist opposition, but it left a heritage of fear of central authority that dogs the country's politics today. Just as significant, the war produced a new type of militarized movement that spread rapidly across Europe.

The episodes in part 1 show how different combinations of hierarchical and infrastructural power intersected with contentious politics in time of war. The French republicans came into office when both types of power were at their nadir. Attacks both at home and abroad and internal conflicts in the political class led to a massive expansion of hierarchical power, usually summarized as the Terror; but it also created peripheral violence and short-circuited the construction of citizen rights.

The U.S. Republican Party came into office in a country rich in infrastructural and poor in hierarchical power, but the Civil War shifted the balance toward greater centralized power while creating close and permanent links between the state and capital.

The Italian government went to war in 1915 with a determination to increase hierarchical power and snuff out the ties between the state and the working class that had been laid by Giolitti in the previous decade.

The episodes in part 1 also showed that rights are compromised whenever states go to war. In the French Revolution, suspected enemies of the revolution were put "outside the law"; in the U.S. Civil War, antiwar activists were tried by military commission and *habeas corpus* was suspended; and in Italy during World War One, labor rights were abridged and states of siege were declared in broad swaths of the country.

The wars we have examined were similar in three important ways. First, they all created successively greater forms of emergency power. The French created the first version of the emergency script, the Americans tried civilians in military courts, and the Italians extended the practices of emergency rule they had used against brigands and rebels to put the military in control of the factories. Second, all three innovated the mechanisms of warfare and state control. The French invented the citizen army and used it against internal rebellions and to create an empire; the Americans employed the draft for the first time and left behind the tradition of citizen militias that had been inherited from their revolution; and the Italians extended military rule to the factories, both to fuel the war effort and to discipline the working class. Third, there was a clear demarcation between the external and the domestic aspects of each of these wars. Although some social movements had loose ties with foreign states, they were domestically rooted and foreign influences on them were largely absent or secondary.

The wars of the end of the twentieth century and the beginning of the twenty-first are different from these wars in three important ways. Globalization and internationalization, added to innovations in military technology, have led to fundamental differences in how wars are fought, how states respond to them, and the corresponding changes in domestic contention. From early post-war conflicts over decolonization, to the Troubles in Northern Ireland and the clandestine armed movements of the 1970s, to the spread of Islamist radicalism across the globe, the traditional distinction among interstate, intrastate, and extra-state wars has given way to what I call composite conflicts. These are wars in which both nonstate and state actors employ a variety of conventional and unconventional means; in which the laws of war are either ignored or twisted out of shape; and in which the distinction between transnational and domestic contention becomes blurred or, in some cases, is totally effaced. This chapter explicates the concept of composite wars, outlines their diffusion in the global North, and focuses on one of them—the conflict in Northern Ireland—to show that the American wars of the twenty-first century are not sui generis.

Transnational Movements, Porous States, and Composite Conflicts

Between 1945 and the end of the twentieth century, there was a change in the balance of the three classical types of warfare recognized by scholars: interstate wars, extra-state wars, and civil wars. Drawing on the work of the Correlates of War program, table 5.1 demonstrates that there was a dramatic trend from interstate and extra-state wars to intrastate war-making. Although civil wars declined after the turn of the twenty-first century, events in Libya, Egypt, and especially Syria suggest that this was probably a temporary reversal of the longer-term shift from interstate and extra-state to civil wars.

However, the most significant trend in war-making since the end of World War Two—and especially since the end of the Cold War—was not a change in the balance among these three historical forms of war but the addition of a new form—wars of social movements against states. In briefest form, wars have become less formal, they more frequently involve irregular combatants, and they

TABLE 5.1 Number of wars of different types involving at least a thousand
death and total killed in civil wars, 1900–2007

DECADE	EXTRA-STATE WARS	INTERSTATE WARS	CIVIL WARS	DEATHS IN CIVIL WARS	
				NUMBER	PERCENTAGE
1900–1909	16	18	11	45,330	18.7
1910–1919	9	43	25	963,460	9.7
1920–1929	9	4	22	175,100	68.2
1930–1939	4	25	12	992,335	14.4
1940–1949	6	31	13	1,393,357	10.2
1950–1959	6	29	12	63,351	6.2
1960–1969	2	22	35	189,265	15.0
1970–1979	7	30	53	350,428	70.4
1980–1989	2	10	40	280,334	17.4
1990–1999	2	33	71	150,628	44.4
2000–2007	18	10	26	42,115	58.8
Total	81	255	320	4,645,703	13.0

Source: Data from Sarkees and Wayman, "COW Wars v. 4.0, 1816–2007," 2010, http://www.correlatesofwar.org/COW2%20Data/WarData_NEW/WarList_NEW.html.

are more likely to drag on for years—often for decades (Crane and Reisner 2011; Hironaka 2005; Kaldor 2006; Murray and Mansoor 2012). At the same time, states have become more porous, have become more open to the forces of globalization, and form increasingly close international links. And an increasing proportion of the movements involved in armed conflict are transnational.

The most influential account of the new wars of the late twentieth century is that of Mary Kaldor. In her 2006 book, *New and Old Wars*, Kaldor observes that these new wars were both severe and enduring, but she also points to several new factors: the growing privatization of violence amid the decline of state power and legitimacy (2006, 6); the centrality of identity politics "in contrast to the geo-political or ideological goals of earlier wars" (ibid., 7); war-makers' changed mode of warfare and organization (ibid., 8); and the hybrid nature of the combatants that make war against states.[1]

These encounters have multiplied in the decades since the end of World War Two, but the adjective *new* is somewhat deceptive.[2] After all, the properties that Kaldor attributed to the new wars could already be found in popular resistance to the French occupation in Spain in the early 1800s; in the struggle between insurrectionary anarchism and various European states in the late nineteenth century (Alimi, Demetriou, and Bosi, forthcoming); in the insurgency against the U.S. occupation of Cuba and the Philippines after the Spanish-American

War (Witt 2012); and in the wars of nationalist movements against the returning colonial powers after World War Two. In Burma, Malaya, Indonesia, and
especially in Indochina and Algeria, the returning British, Dutch, and French
colonial powers were met with movement-led insurgencies that had many of
the attributes of Kaldor's new wars and were fought by compounds of regular
troops and irregular forces (Murray and Mansoor 2012; see also the conclusions
to this book).

What is most notable about these new wars is that they were fought by states
against movements, with both sides employing irregular forms of warfare. This
has led many analysts of these wars to refer to them as "asymmetric." Asymmetric warfare refers to conflict in which one actor possesses notably weaker
material capabilities than another, leading that actor to employ unconventional means and to partially substitute political for battlefield strategies (Mack
1975). What the term leaves ambiguous is that—in response to unconventional
threats—state responses to the nonstate actor's threats are also unconventional,
and often illegal. Employing agents provocateurs, creating or financing rival nonstate groups, attacking civilian targets, and torturing and killing suspects off the
battlefield—these were the kinds of responses that states developed against clandestine political actors who used asymmetric tactics to advance their claims. For
this reason, I prefer the term *composite conflicts* to designate conflicts in which
both state and nonstate actors use a combination of conventional and unconventional forms of action.

Confrontations between nonstate actors and regular armed forces most often
begin with contentious politics and turn into armed struggle when protesters' claims are met by repression. Their small numbers makes it hard for these
movements to succeed using classical social movement performances—marches,
demonstrations, petitions, and elections. The state's attempts to defeat them
lead them to go underground, where they employ the only strategy open to
them—organized violence (della Porta 2013; della Porta and Tarrow 1986). This
does not mean that violence is never employed before these groups go underground but that—in place of spontaneous mass violence—underground groups
are more likely to employ planned attacks by small groups of militants who are
organized separately from the movement's public face (Seidman 2001).

Kaldor's (2006, 2–4) thesis about new wars has proven prescient for the wars
of the twenty-first century in another sense as well—the transnational connections of the movements she studied and their capacity to operate both within and
across state borders. These features, of course, have much to do with the growing
technical capacity of nonstate actors to engage in armed contact, but they are also
the products of globalization and internationalization.[3] The joint effect of these
two processes has been to make states more porous and, therefore, more open

to penetration by transnational actors (Katzenstein 2005; Smith and Johnston, 2002; Tarrow 2005).

A vast and optimistic literature greeted the early growth of transnational movements and NGOs in the 1990s. Most of these groups—such as the human rights, women's, and environmental organizations—were liberal in their policies and Western in orientation.[4] But at the same time, a new family of aggressive movements began to mobilize across transnational space. Often rooted in nationalist or religious/ethnic identities—less often on appeals to class—they used the mobility offered by globalization and the increasing porosity of states to organize across borders. Croatian nationalists in Australia and Canada, extreme orthodox Jews in New York and Israel, and, increasingly, Islamist militants with roots in the Middle East and Western Europe took advantage to their transnational connections to challenge target states and other actors, using a combination of political and military actions (Tarrow 2005, chap. 3).

These new movements engaged in spirals of interactive violence with the states they attacked. First, there was a process of mutual radicalization that led to underground organization. Second, this was followed by a process of encapsulation, assuring that the underground group would isolate itself from potentially moderating allies. Third, in response to clandestine violence, there was an adoption of emergency measures by the government, including the use of torture and violence against civilians. Finally, desperate for allies and looking for more vulnerable targets, some of these underground movements became transnational.

The advent of these new movements raises thorny theoretical and historical questions: First, are they the products of the negative side of globalization and, therefore, limited to the countries of the global South? Second, what is their implication for the boundaries between domestic contention and war-making? Third, what is their implication for civil liberties, both of foreigners and citizens, in the states they target? We saw in part 1 that social movements played crucial roles in Western states' mobilization for war, in war-making, and in war's wake. What we are seeing now is a family of movements that are not quite armies but that engage in forms of conflict with states that combine political and military actions and transcend national boundaries.

Composite Conflicts in the Global North

The rise of violent extremist movements in Africa and the Middle East led many Western commentators to see these movements as the products of the losing side of globalization.[5] In those regions, responding to the collapse of colonial empires and to the weakness of successor states, guerilla insurgencies and civil wars erupted and endured for years. In places such as Algeria, Indochina, and South Africa, irregular forces fought colonial or racially restrictive states with a combination of social movement activism and armed force. In the 1990s in both Africa and in the Balkans, ruthless internal wars accompanied the collapse of existing states or their degeneration into warlord states. These states responded with a combination of political, military, conventional, and unconventional tactics, often employing attacks on civilians and torture against assailants.

But in many places in the global North too, a combination of social movement activism, spirals of interactive violence, and violent clandestine movements led states to adopt reciprocal policies that verged on internal war-making and threatened civil liberties. In figure 5.1, which draws on the calculations of Jan Oskar Engene, we can see that in eighteen Western European countries between the 1950s and the end of the twentieth century there were major cycles of violence in which underground movements used armed struggle.[6]

Engene's data indicate that a total of 7,743 significant episodes of political violence were recorded in these countries, coming from almost 100 violent groups and resulting in 2,777 deaths.[7] Among these conflicts, five stand out for the extent of organized violence, the number of armed groups involved, the number of deaths from political violence, and the degree of militarization and emergency rule that their target states used against them: the United Kingdom, especially Northern Ireland; France and Algeria; Italy; Spain, predominantly in the

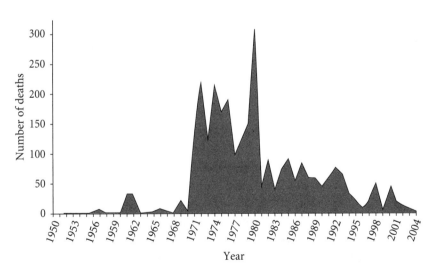

FIGURE 5.1 Annual accumulated death toll in Europe resulting from internal terrorist attacks, 1950–2004. Courtesy of Jan Oskar Engene from the TWEED data set, http://folk.uib.no/sspje/tweed.htm.

TABLE 5.2 Organized clandestine violence in five Western European countries and degree of militarization and emergency rule, 1950–2004

COUNTRY/ REGION	NUMBER OF ARMED GROUPS	MAIN IDENTITY OF ARMED GROUPS	NUMBER OF ACTS OF POLITICAL VIOLENCE	NUMBER OF DEATHS	PERCENTAGE OF VICTIMS IN WESTERN EUROPE	DEGREE OF MILITARY INVOLVEMENT	LEVEL OF EMERGENCY RULE
United Kingdom/ Northern Ireland	20	Catholic and Protestant	2,996	1,489	38.7	Total, after direct rule	Very high
France/ Algeria	41	OAS and separatist	2,573	145	33.2	Very high	Very high
Spain/ Basque country	32	Separatist	754	650	9.7	High	High
Italy	24	Extreme left and extreme right	555	298	7.2	Intermittent	Moderate
Germany	10	Extreme left	276	97	3.6	Absent	Low
Total	127	—	7,743	2,777	92.4	—	—

Sources: Statistics from Engene 2004. Estimates of state responses to terrorism from della Porta 2013 and Donahue 2008.

Notes: OAS, Organisation de l'armée secrète.

Basque country; and Germany. Table 5.2 summarizes five characteristics of these conflicts from Engene's data: the number of armed groups and their identities, the numbers of recorded acts of violence, the number of deaths from these events, the victims as a percentage of the victims in Western Europe, and the levels of military involvement and a rough estimate of the degree of emergency rule.

The Emerging Pattern of Composite Conflicts

Three major factors in the table 5.2 show that composite conflicts are not limited to the losers in globalization. Each of the five countries in table 5.2 were either established parliamentary democracies or—as in the case of post-Franco Spain—on a shaky route to liberal democracy when the insurgency exploded. Second, their liberal traditions did not prevent these states from responding to armed conflict with emergency rule and the containment of civil liberties; on the contrary, as in the United States after 9/11, their liberal traditions sometimes provided a cultural—or creedal—justification for the use of force against illiberal enemies. All of them, to some degree, militarized the conflict with their assailants and curtailed the civil liberties of their citizens. Third, to some degree, these conflicts were all transnationally embedded, from the cross-border and trans-Atlantic ties of the Irish nationalists to the transfer of the Organisation de l'armée secrète (OAS; Organization of the Secret Army) from Algeria to France itself, to the ties between the Spanish and French Basques and the weaker transnational ties of the Italian and German extreme left movements.

These same properties appeared in the 1990s as a new family of Islamist movements developed among radicalized Muslims, both in the global North and in the Middle East, that eventually engaged the most powerful liberal state in the global North—the United States, which responded to its attackers with the same combination of conventional and unconventional, legal and illegal measures as the states in table 5.2. As we will see in chapter 10, the United States also mobilized its considerable international weight to construct a system of legal and illegal methods to capture the killers of 9/11 and "associated groups."

Of course, each of these movements had particular features. Although all were aimed primarily at national states, some—such as the Northern Irish nationalists and the Italian extremist groups—also targeted opposing groups. In Corsica and in Basque country, they were based on ethnic/regional identities; in Germany and Italy they were based on extreme left-wing and fascist ideologies. Territorial politics were also common in these struggles. The Basque Euskadi Ta Askatasuna (ETA) and the Corsican independence movement fought for separation from Madrid and Paris, while the French OAS fought to keep Algeria French.

In each of these countries, some parts of the movement went underground, while others remained as its public face, and still others moved into institutional politics (della Porta 2013, chap. 2; Tarrow 1989; Gupta 2013). Radicalization of part of the movements was followed by the militarization of the state's response and by its adoption of emergency powers, sometimes, as in France and Northern Ireland, through the use of special courts and preventive detention; sometimes, as in Germany, through legislation; and often, as in Northern Ireland and Algeria, through the use of torture. Civil liberties—both of the combatants and of ordinary citizens—were an invariable victim of these composite conflicts, leaving a heritage of emergency measures that have been surprisingly durable.

Table 5.2 has no pretense of statistical representation; but note the rough correlation between the degree of lethality of the violence experienced and the degree of militarization and level of emergency rule that states adopted to combat it. Note also that in three of them—the conflict in Northern Ireland with the Irish Republican Army (IRA), the conflict over Algeria in France, and the conflict in the Spanish Basque country—there were cross-border ties. Finally, the country with the longest colonial history—Great Britain in Northern Ireland—combined a militaristic with a political response and employed unconventional as well as conventional means.[8] A rapid look at this conflict will illustrate the archetypical features of these northern "composite conflicts," prior to introducing the wars of the United States in the next chapters.

The Longest Composite Conflict

Although they are often studied sui generis, the Northern Irish Troubles were archetypical of the new wars of the late twentieth century, but like many of these conflicts, its roots went back for decades, if not for centuries.[9] Irish Catholics had been fighting against British rule since the French sent an expeditionary force to the island in 1798, which led to the Acts of Union, soldering the island to the United Kingdom and to the Protestant ascendancy (McGarry and O'Leary 1995, 332).

But it was World War One that gave Irish nationalists an opportunity to organize a full-scale insurrection against British rule. The Easter Rising of 1916 was the start of a downward spiral in Anglo-Irish relations and its suppression destroyed all hope of a peaceful solution. At war's end, the British agreed to divide the island into the mainly Catholic Irish Republic and the majority-Protestant five counties of the North in 1920. But this left northern Catholics divided from their co-religionists in the South.

The Northern Irish–British conflict was largely national, but the post–World War Two era was a growth period for international agreements and saw an extension of the Geneva Conventions to include protections for nonstate actors. However, precisely because they feared that it could be applied to Northern Ireland, the British government refused to ratify that protocol (Campbell and Connolly 2012, 18). As Prime Minister Margaret Thatcher once put it, Northern Ireland is "part of the United Kingdom as much as my constituency is" (Neumann 2003, 20). By insisting on the domestic nature of the Northern Irish conflict, the British avoided international involvement in its resolution, but their use of extraordinary measures to combat it—including the use of paramilitary mobs, the invasion of civilian neighborhoods, and the abuse of prisoners—was a continuation of its unconventional methods against nationalist movements in Southeast Asia at the end of World War Two. There was a period of border violence in the 1950s, but the modern phase of the conflict erupted only in the late 1960s (Engene 2004, 114–15) in the form of a civil rights movement, strongly influenced by the success of the black rights movement in the United States. But from the beginning it had both a public face, in the form of the Sinn Féin, and an underground wing, the IRA. The movement split in 1969, when its "Provisional" wing (PIRA) hived off and radicalized after the British killed a group of unarmed demonstrators on Bloody Sunday 1972 (Maney 2006).

After allowing the Protestant authorities to attempt to contain the violence for a time, the British government, under a Labour administration, tried to respond with reforms; this was followed by a Tory government that insisted on a law-and-order approach. This resulted in British troops being directly involved in the repression of Catholic nationalists and on assaults on civil liberties. Direct rule from London was imposed in 1972, followed by the transfer to the province of General Frank Kitson, who applied the counterinsurgency approach he had learned in repressing the Malayan and Kenyan insurgencies, which included the sponsorship of a clandestine countermovement.[10]

Like the French in Algeria, although the British regarded Ulster as an integral part of the United Kingdom, they were not above using preventive detention, special courts, disruptive quasi-mobs, and torture against their opponents. But the civil liberties of ordinary citizens were also deeply affected, especially those of Catholics, who the British army suspected of sympathy for the IRA. After the IRA split, the struggle spread to England, where a number of spectacular bombings brought home to the government that the conflict could not be contained by repressive means alone. It ended only with a cease-fire with the Provisionals in 1994 and the negotiation of the Good Friday Agreement brokered by the United States four years later.

Four characteristics of the Northern Irish Troubles marked them as an archetypical composite conflict: mutual radicalization, encapsulation, the adoption of emergency measures by the government, and trans/internationalization.

- Each move by Catholics, Protestants, or the British army seemed to radicalize the other side and led inexorably from a series of violent protests to a state of civil war (Ruane and Todd 1996, 1).
- The more repressive the government's tactics became, the deeper the militants dug into their own subcultures (della Porta 2013, chap. 5).
- The repression was particularly brutal because the enemy was a nonstate actor against whom the government felt no obligation to follow legal niceties or the Geneva conventions (Donahue 2008, 49–50).
- Although the struggle took place mainly on Irish soil, it was both transnational and international (Hanagan 1998; Bigo 1992, 40; Laffan 2002; Maney 2000).

Of course, the Northern Irish conflict had a number of particularities—beginning from what was, in retrospect, the fatal division of the island into north and south in 1920, leaving a Catholic minority trapped in the north under a Protestant hegemony. As in the new wars studied by Kaldor, there was a widespread privatization of violence; identity politics were central to the conflict; it involved both political and military, conventional and unconventional modes of conflict; and the movements involved were hybrid, with above-ground political groups engaged in conventional political conflict while clandestine groups engaged in armed struggle (Gupta 2007). In that sense, it was a precursor of the composite conflicts of the early twenty-first century, many of which are organized around religious/national cleavages, have a transnational base, evoke emergency measures from the states they attack, and are extremely difficult to defeat.

This takes us to the most important composite conflict of the new century—the U.S. global War on Terror and the two conventional wars it spawned. Americans saw the attacks by al Qaeda on the United States as something radically new, with its roots in the 1990s. But what has happened since September 11, 2001, was not sui generis and is not limited to movements arising in the global South. It was a conflict in which both sides used a combination of political and military tactics and crossed the boundary from the recognized laws of war.

Al Qaeda and the American Way of War

Americans like to think of themselves as a peace-loving people, insulated from the wars of Europe and Asia by two oceans, and more determined to make progress through enterprise than through conquest. But Americans have been involved in one form of military conflict or another since the founding. Of course, for a large number of these years, Americans were engaged "only" in suppressing Indian tribes, gaining territory, or engaging in police actions, leaving little trace on the international system. But as Mark Brandon concludes, "Military action has been such a substantial part of the history of the nation that it is not unfair to characterize the United States as a warrior state" (2005, 11).

The majority of these conflicts were "small wars": the suppression of Native Americans (39 years), external policing activities (105 years), and the occupation of other countries (51 years). Clearly, not all these years of war-making were as significant as others. But, as Ronald Krebs (2009) has argued, even limited wars can have profound effects on a nation's political culture, its state structure, and its policies. Table 5.3 calculates the years of U.S. military engagement from evidence that Brandon (2005) has gathered and codes them for the type of military engagement they involved.

A major feature of this history is that U.S. wars have grown longer; Americans fought for one year in the war against the Spanish in 1899, for two years in Europe in World War One, for four years in Europe and Asia in World War Two, for thirteen years from the beginning of U.S. involvement in Vietnam to the

TABLE 5.3 Number of U.S. military actions and number of years by type of conflict

TYPE OF CONFLICT	NUMBER OF ACTIONS	NUMBER OF YEARS
Internal suppressions[a]	15	39
External police actions	28	105
Seizures/occupations of territory[b]	16	51
Internal wars/revolutions	2	12
Undeclared foreign wars	13	71
Declared foreign wars	6	21
Total	70	299

Source: Data from Brandon 2005, 30–35. Brandon labels his list as "significant military conflicts of the United States." The original sources appear on p. 35.

[a] Includes only one nonnative internal suppression—the Whiskey Rebellion in 1791.

[b] Includes only occupation of territories outside of North America and does not include western expansion.

evacuation of the last Americans in 1975, for nine years in Iraq, for twelve years in Operation Enduring Freedom in Afghanistan, and since 2001 in the ongoing War on Terror. And if we consider the Cold War as a real war, which in terms of military mobilization it certainly was (Griffin 2013, 67–68; Hogan 1998, 60), the number of years U.S. wars have lasted grows even longer. As U.S. wars have grown longer, they overlap more and more with domestic politics and—as a result—with contentious politics (Dudziak 2010).

How has a nation that sees itself as peace-loving spent so many years at war without fomenting major episodes of contention among its citizens? A first answer—but one that is historically inaccurate—is that Americans never choose to go to war but only react to external threats. A second answer—that U.S. wars are consensual—is only partially true; as we will see, both World War Two and the Korean War were supported by the majority of its citizens. But as we have already seen, not all U.S. wars have been so consensual; there was considerable contention during the Civil War. In the next chapter, we will examine how two modern U.S. wars, World War One and the Vietnam War, gave rise to deep contestation.

This takes us to the third answer to the question about Americans' willingness to support war-making. Since the beginning of the twentieth century, U.S. conflicts have been invariably framed as wars to defend freedom—even the Spanish-American War, which Americans often forget was followed by the brutal repression of the Philippine independence movement. This deeply embedded creedal conviction was deployed to defeat those who contested the government's war-making plans.

As we will see in the next chapter, in most of twentieth-century U.S. wars, the combination of creedal arguments and emergency rule was relatively uncomplicated. After all, it was not unreasonable to think that the Prussian kaiser, the Nazis, or the international communist movement were threats both to freedom and to the United States. But the war that President George W. Bush launched against Islamist radicalism in the years after the September 11 bombings was different: there was no state-led threat on which to focus the American creed; no mass mobilization of citizens or conscripted soldiers; and, however dangerous its militants were to individual Americans or to U.S. allies in the Middle East, no one could believe al Qaeda was capable of defeating the United States. A major effort of framing was mounted to convince Americans that an all-out war against such an enemy would be worthwhile and would fit within the American creed.

There was a second difficulty for U.S. decision makers. Because the al Qaeda movement was not a state and its militants were organized into clandestine networks that could shift easily across borders, they would be impossible to defeat using classical military means. And because al Qaeda was unconstrained by the laws of war, U.S. leaders saw no need to abide by those laws themselves. This meant that, as the liberal creed was mobilized to convince the nation that it needed to go to war to defend freedom, illiberal means were mobilized to fight a war that could not be won on the battlefield.

How the U.S. government tried to reconcile the American liberal creed with emergency rule in the wars it launched in the first decade of the twenty-first century—and with what consequences for the state and domestic contention—is the central question of part 2. Before we turn to it, however, the briefest examination of this new enemy will be useful. Both in scientific research and in popular culture, the movement nature of al Qaeda has been obscured by a terrorist paradigm, and it has been conflated in the American imagination with the last two state enemies the United States faced. This has obscured that al Qaeda behaves, thinks of itself as, and responds to pressures as a social movement.

Al Qaeda as a Social Movement

Since the 1990s, and especially after the September 11 attacks, a terrorism industry has developed among Western academics, research organizations, and government agencies. "The years since 1990," writes Donatella della Porta, "saw a rise in research funds, as well as in the number of books published with 'terrorism' in their titles. . . . After 9/11 a new book on terrorism was published every six hours, whereas scientific articles on the topic tripled between 2001 and 2002" (2013, 11). Although much of this work was minutely well informed, much of it was influenced by the concerns of policymakers and was "deeply enmeshed in the actual practices of counterterrorism." To the extent that this work had a theoretical basis, it was in security studies, "a field focused at least in part on counterinsurgency" (della Porta 2013, 12). Al Qaeda has many of the same properties as the PIRA, the Basque ETA, the French OAS, and the Italian Red Brigades. Yet few scholars—at least in the United States—drew on the body of comparative knowledge we possess about clandestine social movements and the composite wars they waged in the late twentieth century when examining the threat to the United States.[11]

Of course, like other movement organizations, the groups that fall under the rubric of radical Islamism have a number of particularities. First, to an unusual extent, they have employed a radically innovative form of conflict—the suicide bombing (Hafez 2007). Second, they attacked states but had no clear project for the formation of an alternative state—only a vague project for the return of the Caliphate. Third, as they were repressed by authoritarian states in the Middle East, they shifted the targets of their attacks to the United States and European countries. That meant that they could be defeated only through the international cooperation of governments and police forces, with consequences that we will see in chapter 10.

But, despite these particularities, radical Islamism resembles the movements sketched earlier in a number of respects. First, it was radicalized by its organizations' struggles against their target regimes (Hafez and Wiktorowicz 2004; Alimi, Bosi, and Demetriou 2012). Second, like those movements, the number of their militants is remarkably small (Kurzman 2011). Third, they are organized through loose networks rather than as a hierarchical organizations (Sageman 2004; Pedahzur and Perliger 2006), which made them difficult to trace and even more difficult to defeat. Fourth, like many other movements that are organized in this way, they represent a broad spectrum of groups and factions—many of them in conflict with each other. And, finally, they have grown profoundly transnational—indeed, some would even say even "deterritorialized" (della Porta 2013, 64).

Civil Liberties in Composite Conflicts

Radical Islamism has been framed as "foreign," both in popular responses to its outrages and in scientific discourse. This has helped the targeted governments justify moving along a pathway from ordinary policing to an emergency script, much like what we saw in the British response to the IRA in Northern Ireland. Not only in the Middle East, where repressive states have long employed brutal tactics against Islamist groups but in the liberal states of Western Europe and the United States as well, state responses to this volatile and violent movement have approached the edges of legality and, at times, crossed that boundary into criminality.

As we will see in the next chapters, even as they solemnly cite the authority of international law, Western states have cooperated in the practices of indefinite detention, special courts, militarization, extraordinary rendition, and torture against suspects picked up on the battlefields of Afghanistan, Iraq, and elsewhere. This is not only because these movements are violent, difficult to detect and repress, and "foreign"; it is also because, as nonstates, their status under the international laws of war is ambiguous. Although civil libertarians have made a vigorous argument that nonstate actors have basic procedural rights, like the British government in Northern Ireland, the United States after 9/11 has been unwilling to concede that the al Qaeda and Taliban detainees swept up—often by bounty hunters not on the field of battle—are covered by the Geneva conventions (Crane and Reisner 2011).

As many critics—some of them dedicated opponents of terrorism—have noted, the constriction of the rights of opponents during wartime has a tendency to last beyond wartime and to extend to broader sectors of the population. This is especially true in conflicts in which the violent repertoire of tactics by clandestine movements is responded to by the states they attack with equally violent actions: the organization of countermovements, quasi-mobs, and agents provocateurs; the use of abusive interrogation techniques; and the extension of extraordinary surveillance to the broader public in the belief that casting a wider net will turn up the enemies of the state.

Even before the passage of the USA Patriot Act, as we will see, a secret presidential order charged the National Security Agency with sweeping up billions of private communications of both foreigners and Americans; and that act targeted not only the criminals of 9/11 but international terrorism in general. More broadly, immigrants became more suspect, and in apparent isolation from the War on Terror, became subject to increasing surveillance and deportation. We will turn to this tendency to a ratchet effect on civil liberties in the conclusions of this book. Composite conflicts not only engage states in spirals of interactive violence with their attackers; they trigger a ratchet effect that expands both the hierarchical and infrastructural power of the state and threatens civil liberties in general.

Conclusions

Readers may wonder why this chapter has mentioned the United States and the massacres it suffered in 2001 only in passing. The short answer is that the rest of this book will center on the U.S. War on Terror and on its implications for the

American state and for contentious politics. But there is a more important reason. It has become routine in the United States and elsewhere in the West to declare that the attacks on the World Trade Center and the Pentagon were unique. For example, even in 2014, an analysis of Google.com for the joint search terms *9/11* and *everything changed* yielded over 26 million hits.

But *did* everything change after 9/11? We have already seen that some of the features of the emergency script written to defeat violent clandestine actors could already be found in Western Europe from the 1960s through the 1980s. In the rest of this book, I examine how the United States responded to those events. But I will also show that this response was built on foundations that go back to the end of World War Two and to the Vietnam War: to the creation of the national security state and to the use of infrastructural power to assure popular support for the government's efforts.

Some things, of course, did change after 9/11. In the rest of this book we will see an extension of both the hierarchical and infrastructural power of the American state; a tendency to slide from the rule *of* law to rule *by* law; an expanded use of the media to maintain public support for war-making; the engagement of vast sectors of the U.S. economy in the business of national security; and, with respect to contentious politics, the incapacity of traditional antiwar and legal strategies to shift the state significantly away from its policies. Americans did not so much roll back liberal constitutionalism as reshape it around the requisites of fighting a conflict that was more intense but no different in kind than the composite conflicts fought by other states against other clandestine movements.

6

WARS AT HOME, 1917–1975

On March 7, 1971, when the Nixon administration expanded its war in Southeast Asia from Vietnam to Cambodia, mobilizations were held across the country. Apart from their size and geographical spread, these mobilizations were no different than the mass demonstrations that had become central to American contention since the early 1960s (Tilly and Tarrow 2007, 12–16). But when a small group calling itself the Citizens' Commission to Investigate the FBI broke into a modest Federal Bureau of Investigation (FBI) headquarters in Media, Pennsylvania, this event unleashed what would become the biggest scandal of J. Edgar Hoover's long reign at the agency (Medsger 2013).

None of the activists who broke into the FBI headquarters had a history of such desperate activities, although several had been involved in protests that ended with draft-card burnings. But, frustrated at the failure of the mass antiwar protest to roll back the war, they came to the decision that the only way to reveal the lengths to which the government had gone to shut down opposition was to expose the FBI's undercover programs. They did not know that among the trove of documents the break-in would expose was one word—COINTELPRO. COINTELPRO was the codename for a series of illegal FBI programs to disrupt and infiltrate groups of which FBI Director J. Edgar Hoover disapproved. Its exposure tore off the cover on the FBI's secret war on U.S. dissidents, and not only the antiwar movement.

The identity of the burglars was not discovered until many years later, when the statute of limitations had already expired. But along with the "Pentagon Papers" and the Watergate scandal, the information that emerged from the Media break-in helped expose Hoover's crimes, producing the most important policy outcome of the antiwar movement: the Church Committee investigations that led to the congressional oversight of intelligence gathering. When the break-in became widely known, one of the burglars, John Raines, said, "It looks like we're terribly reckless people. But there was absolutely no one in Washington—senators, congressmen, even the president—who dared hold J. Edgar Hoover to accountability."[1] Civil society had won a small victory against government overreach.

Why begin a chapter that surveys U.S. wars, protests against them, and the repression of protest with this tiny group's effort to expose the FBI, when there were far more numerous protests and more significant events, such as the release of the "Pentagon Papers" or the Watergate break-in, occurring around the war in Indochina? The first reason is that it shows how far the Cold War and the Vietnam War had expanded the American state's surveillance and suppression[2] of dissent long before 9/11. The second reason is that it demonstrates how small groups of individuals, using innovative repertoires of protest, can have as much or more impact on government surveillance than mass protests—a lesson that will appear again in the opposition to the Bush and Obama administrations' excesses. And the third reason is that it shows that protest often has an indirect effect on policy, for it was not until five years after the Media break-in that Congress—which was mainly supine as the Lyndon Johnson and Richard Nixon administrations ran roughshod over Americans' rights (Ely 1993, chap. 3)—tried to roll back the government's anticonstitutional actions.

This chapter begins with the first major U.S. intervention in a global war, in 1917, and its effects on the repression of dissent. I then look briefly at World War Two, when there was very little dissent but a great deal of suppression, before turning to the birth of the national security state after that war. I close with an analysis of the interaction of war and contention during the war in Indochina. The chapter will show that the American way of war and the reactions to it began long before the beginning of the War on Terror.

Global War, Antiwar Movements, and Domestic Repression

Less than two decades after winning the Spanish-American War, the United States was embroiled in the first global war—World War One. But its global nature was not the only thing new about that war. Like the Civil War, it was fought on an industrial scale, but with infinitely more death and destruction; unlike that war, it was fought on the home front through an organized attempt to mobilize public opinion. And, more than any U.S. war before or since, it led to the repression of dissident opinions—especially from the recent wave of U.S. immigrants. It was only well after the war ended that a movement to defend civil liberties and changes in the jurisprudence of the Supreme Court would roll back the assaults on rights that marked the Woodrow Wilson administration's waging of the war at home.

Preparations for the U.S. entry into the war were swift and dramatic. From a military establishment of about 165,000 in 1914, the army and navy grew to 2.9 million by 1918. Most of these soldiers went back to civilian life quickly after the war, but the armed forces in 1921 remained over 40 percent larger than they had been before the war. More surprising, the civilian establishment remained over 70 percent higher than it had been before the war.[3] War permanently increased the size of both the U.S. military and the civilian state.

More important than the rapid growth of the armed forces was the political impact of entering a global war. General John Pershing's expeditionary force may have done no more than put a finger on the scale of a war that the Western allies were already winning, but in the American imagination, it was the force of American arms, American ingenuity, and American determination that spelled the doom of the Central Powers. The rapid end of the war after the doughboys arrived in France, and the crushing economic effect of the war on U.S. allies, also increased the prestige of the United States in Europe, and especially of its president, Woodrow Wilson. When Wilson landed in Genoa in spring 1919, he was greeted by crowds of admirers (Mazower 2012, 155), and it was clear that no postwar settlement could be signed that the United States did not support.

It was not evident when the United States entered the war that it would leave it with such a heightened reputation. Indeed, Wilson had fought the 1916 election campaign on a platform of staying out of war, and when he changed his mind, it was against considerable antiwar sentiment. On the right, isolationist currents were strong, on the left, anarchist and socialist activists were enraged that Wilson had gone back on his word to keep the country out of the war, and German American groups were made uneasy by the strong strain of nationalism that the war unleashed in the American public.

Not only to counter the claims of these antiwar forces but also to mobilize a lukewarm public, the administration launched a major propaganda campaign in favor of intervention. The United States would not only come to the assistance of the besieged Western democracies; it would "make the world safe for democracy." Speaking to a joint session of Congress on April 2, 1917, Wilson said, "A steadfast concert for peace can never be maintained except by a partnership of democratic nations. . . . It must be a league of honor, a partnership of opinion. Intrigue would eat its vitals away. . . . Only free peoples can hold their purpose and their honor

steady to a common end and prefer the interests of mankind to any narrow interest of their own."[4]

As was often the case for this son of a Presbyterian minister, Wilson's tone
was stirring and optimistic, and he spoke feelingly of solidarity with the Western
democracies. The speech carefully denied any animus against the German people
or against Germany's allies. But there were intimations of a hard hand at home,
as when he alerted German Americans against disloyalty and cited evidence to
Congress that there were spies active on U.S. territory. The message combined
missionary fervor with imperial calculation, as indicated by the parallels Wilson
saw between the Monroe Doctrine (which had established U.S. hegemony in the
hemisphere in the previous century) and the future League of Nations. "I am proposing," he wrote, "that the nations should with one accord adopt the doctrine of
President Monroe as the doctrine of the world." "Only free peoples can hold their
purpose and honor steady to a common end and prefer the interests of mankind
to any narrow interests of their own" (quoted in Mazower 2012, 124–25).

The Antiwar Movement and Its Suppression

Wilson's invocation of international solidarity, democracy, and freedom carried
over into the public relations campaign that the administration waged throughout the war. The Department of Justice spared no effort to create an "'outraged
public' in order to arouse Americans to enlist, contribute money, and make the
many other sacrifices war demands" (Stone 2004,153). Under George Creel, a
journalist, Wilson created a public-private Committee on Public Information
that fostered a mood of fear, anger, and rabid patriotism (Vaughn 1980). Civil
libertarians have focused on the repressive actions of the administration both
during and after the war; probably just as important was the combination of
an official pro-war propaganda campaign and a privately organized civil society
movement in favor of the war.

Infrastructural Power and National Security

The government did not rely on hierarchical power alone to back its intervention
in World War One.[5] At the same time as Wilson was singing the praises of a war
"to make the world safe for democracy," support for the war was being stoked by
a spectrum of civil society groups. What is most interesting about these groups
was that they bridged what scholars often see as two distinct strands in American
political culture: support for the Constitution and support for national security.
"In April 1917," writes Aziz Rana, "the same month as the U.S.'s entry into World

War One, a recently formed group, the National Association for Constitutional Government (NACG) published the first issue of *Constitutional Review*" (forthcoming, 13). Founded by David Jane Hill, former ambassador to Germany and president of the University of Rochester, and supported by such luminaries as Nicholas Murray Butler, president of Columbia University; James Beck, future solicitor general; and Charles Warren, Pulitzer Prize–winning constitutional scholar, the organization called for a massive educational campaign to defend the Constitution and the government it had established from assault.

At the same time, a number of groups supported the goal of defending national security. The American Defense Society, the American Protective League, the Knights of Liberty, the National Security League, the Constitutional Liberty League, the American Legion, and the Sentinels of the Republic emerged as supporters, in civil society, of the government's pro-war propaganda campaign. As might be suspected, they were backed financially and politically by some parts of the business community, particularly by wealthy donors in New York City (ibid., 15–16). But they also established branches across the country, alongside less savory groups such as the Ku Klux Klan.

Although Americans now tend to think of constitutional commitment as a check on executive excess, the NACG and other constitutionalist groups were intertwined with a plethora of groups calling for enhanced national security. Indeed, writes Rana, "Constitutionalists at the time overwhelmingly saw devotion to the document as of a piece with calls for the heightened militarization of collective life" (ibid., 14). For example, Hill was not only the founder of the NACG but served as honorary vice president of the American Defense Society and spoke routinely on behalf of the National Security League—two groups that strongly supported the war effort; Butler was not only a contributor to the NACG's *Constitutional Review* but a member of the executive committee of the National Security League; Beck and Warren were also heavily involved with the league. "Given this overlap of membership and ideological goals," writs Rana, "it is hardly surprising that pro-Constitution and pro-security organizations often worked together on joint initiatives and even formed umbrella groups to coordinate their efforts, like the 1922 establishment of the Sentinels of the Republic" (ibid, 15–16). These groups provided a powerful infrastructural support for the domestic war politics of the Wilson administration. Their program included the use of educational campaigns, the enforcement of cultural assimilation and homogeneity—including the predecessor of the English-only movement—and the creation of a security apparatus "to root out individuals and groups deemed enemies of the Constitution" (ibid., 29).

Against whom were these campaigns directed? The interesting thing about the overlap between government propaganda and constitutional nationalism was that while the United States was preparing for war against an aggressively imperial opponent—the Central Powers—the campaign targeted the Kaiser's sworn enemies, who came from the immigrant groups who had fled authoritarian rule. Between 1865 and 1914, over 20 million immigrants entered the country, mainly from southern and eastern Europe, most of them poor and some bringing radical politics with them from Europe. Others were radicalized in the sweatshops, mines, and railways where they found jobs in the booming U.S. economy. A good proportion swelled the ranks of the radical social left that was instinctively against a war that many considered a conflict in the interests of capitalist elites. These antiwar groups included, among others, the Socialist Party, the Industrial Workers of the World, the Women's International League for Peace and Freedom, the Women's Peace Party, the National Civil Liberties Bureau, the Fellowship of Reconciliation, the Anti-Enlistment League, and the American Friends Service Committee (Heaney and Rojas 2015).

In reaction to the antiwar movement, and with Congress's support, the administration launched a series of policies repressing free speech and assembly. The results were ominous for immigrants and other leftists: the Espionage Act (1917), the Trading with the Enemy Act (1917), and the Sedition Act (1918). These laws "provided the legal infrastructure for a massive federal assault on speech, dissent, and immigrant rights." Throughout the war, the words *alien* and *sedition* reappeared in the American political lexicon, citizen vigilante groups were encouraged to root out subversives, and control of the mails was used to strangle dissent (Stone 2004, chap. 3).

What was the left doing in response to this avalanche of patriotism? Faced with a combination of patriotic gore, private vigilantism, and state repression, a few radical groups took up violence. This led to scattered attacks during the war and culminated in the bombing of the home of Attorney General Mitchell Palmer in 1919 (ibid., 220). The outrage that this move generated contributed to the infamous Red Scare that followed and to the rounding up and deportation of several thousand foreign-born radicals and the practical liquidation of the social left, which would not recover until the Great Depression in 1929.

The Creation of a Libertarian Left

The campaign of the Wilson administration and of constitutionalist/patriotic groups to throttle dissent had an unexpected effect—the spillover of the antiwar movement into a civil libertarian left.[6] Civil liberties were not a major feature of the left—or of any other major group in the United States—in the early part of the century. In fact, until the 1920s, the term almost never appears in books in the United States, as we can see from the NGram analysis of Google

Books in figure 6.1. The figure illustrates the striking newness of the development of a libertarian left after World War One through the growing presence in American culture of the term *civil liberties*. [7]

Under pressure of the government's increasing suppression of dissent, Roger Baldwin and Chrystal Eastman, internationalists, shifted their focus from antiwar agitation to challenging Espionage Act prosecutions and violence against dissidents, and offered legal support to people charged with disloyal speech (ibid., 183). This was the origin of the organization we know today as the American Civil Liberties Union (ACLU) and of the left libertarian current in American political culture (see chapter 9). "Civil liberties," writes John Fabian Witt, "emerged as the solution to the dilemma of internationalists in wartime" (2007, 193). But the ACLU remained a small and struggling organization in the 1920s, and as often occurs in the history of contentious politics, the recognition of the need to protect civil liberties in wartime began among academic and judicial elites.

Compare the Supreme Court's decision in *Abrams v. United States* (250 U.S. 616) in 1919 with later decisions of the same court. A group of Jewish leftists had been arrested by military police during the war for diffusing antiwar literature and were convicted under the Sedition Act. The tenor of the wartime climate is best communicated by the language of the judge, Henry DeLamar Clayton. Speaking of the defendants, he said, "The only thing they know how to raise is hell, and to direct it against the government of the United States" (quoted in Stone 2004, 206). Speaking for the Supreme Court in its review of Clayton's decision, Justice John H. Clarke summarily rejected the defendants' First Amendment argument, with Justices Oliver Wendell Holmes and Louis Brandeis famously dissenting (ibid.).

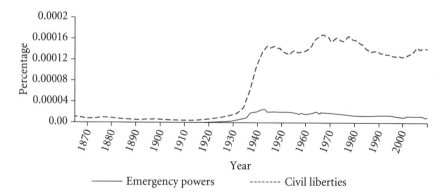

FIGURE 6.1   A Google NGram analysis of the appearance of *civil liberties* and *emergency powers* in books in American English, 1865–2008.

By the 1920s, the mood began to change. In 1920, a group of law professors and distinguished attorneys published a report on the illegal practices of the Justice Department; in the same year, a district court judge in Massachusetts ordered the release of twenty aliens who were being held for deportation because of their membership in the Communist Party (Stone 2004, 225); Congress repealed the Sedition Act; and in 1924, Attorney General Harlan Fiske Stone ended the FBI surveillance of political radicals (ibid, 230). These reversals support the views of Geoffrey Stone that there are sometimes "redemptions" of civil liberties in war's wake (ibid., 236–40). But the rollback of repressive legislation came slowly, and only when the fog of war had lifted. But how durable would this turn toward the defense of civil liberties prove to be? And how would the next U.S. involvement in global warfare affect the treatment of aliens and citizens of foreign origin? World War Two would demonstrate that the rollback of emergency rule that occurred in the wake of World War One was far from established.

Repression without Contention

The advent of World War Two brought a reenactment of the Espionage Act—this time in peacetime. In 1940, Congress also passed the Alien Registration (Smith) Act, which required resident aliens to register; made it easier to deport them; and forbade anyone from advocating, abetting, or advising the overthrow of any government in the United States by force or violence (ibid., 251). Even before the attack on Pearl Harbor, Representative Martin Dies (D-Texas) created the House Un-American Activities Committee (HUAC), with the ambition of exposing alleged communist influences in the New Deal. "Anticipating the conduct of Joseph McCarthy a decade later, Dies repeatedly attacked members of the Roosevelt Administration, especially Secretary of the Interior Harold Ickes and Secretary of Labor Frances Perkins, whom he accused of having 'radical associates'" (ibid., 246).

Other members of Congress chastised Attorney General Frank Murphy for failing to prosecute un-American activities with sufficient vigor. But as long as the country was not at war, there were still enough New Dealers in the administration to hold off the most aggressive calls for the repression of "subversives." Even so, Francis Biddle, who became attorney general after Murphy, was forced to urge civil libertarians to "be more realistic and to recognize that limitations of civil liberties might be necessary" should the nation go to war (ibid., 255). After Adolf Hitler invaded the Soviet Union in June 1940, the communists emerged as whole-hearted opponents of fascism, and it was against the pro-Nazi Right that the Sedition Act was employed (ibid., 272–75). But pro-German sentiment was limited and these were "retail" attacks on particular suspects whose loyalty was in question. It was only when Japan attacked Pearl Harbor that a "wholesale" assault on an entire population group was launched.

Internment

Two months after the devastating attack on Pearl Harbor, President Roosevelt authorized the army to designate "military areas" from which "any or all persons may be excluded." As Geoffrey Stone observes, "Although the words 'Japanese' or 'Japanese American' never appeared in the order, it was understood, unconstitutionally, to apply only to persons of Japanese ancestry" (ibid., 286). In two key cases, *Hirabayashi v. United States* (320 U.S. 81 [1943]) and *Korematsu v. United States* (323 U.S. 214 [1944]), the Court upheld the constitutionality of a curfew for Japanese residents and the conviction of a Japanese American for evading internment. After a period of being forced to live in miserable temporary facilities, 120,000 individuals—both citizens and resident aliens, adults and children—were forced to leave their homes in California, Washington, Oregon, and Arizona for concentration camps in isolated areas of the West.

No charges were ever brought against any of these individuals. There were no hearings and no law of the United States or any state was ever cited as authority for their incarceration. Using the same logic that the Supreme Court had used in the Civil War *Prize Cases*, the Court upheld the exclusion of ethnic Japanese in the *Korematsu* case and upheld a curfew in *Hirabayashi*, with the theory that a state of war gave the president the power to do essentially whatever he wanted.[8] "All this was done even though there was not a *single* documented act of espionage, sabotage, or treasonable activity committed by an American citizen of Japanese descent or by a Japanese national residing on the West Coast" (ibid., 286).

For once, it was not the FBI that sought the internment of "dangerous" aliens, and Attorney General Biddle strongly opposed the policy (ibid., 293). Instead, the pressure for moving Japanese and Japanese Americans from the West Coast came from California legislators, from Attorney General Earl Warren, and from citizens' groups—many of whose economic interests would be helped by it—for Japanese exclusion from urban areas on the West Coast: "The American Legion, the Native Sons and Daughters of the Golden West, the Western Growers' Protective Association, the California Farm Bureau Federation, the Chamber of Commerce of Los Angeles, and all the West Coast newspapers, including the liberal *Los Angeles Daily News*, cried out for a prompt evacuation of Japanese aliens and citizens alike" (ibid., 294).

Stoked by the regional press, there was widespread support in public opinion for the internment of both Japanese and Japanese Americans. In March 1942, a NORC survey found that 93 percent of Americans polled supported the policy of moving Japanese aliens away from the Pacific coast and 59 percent supported the same policy for Americans of Japanese origin (Berinsky 2009, 149–50). But what seems to have been most important in FDR's decision was not public opinion but the views of the military. In a classified report full of inaccuracies and insinuations, General John DeWitt, the army commander on the West Coast, argued strongly for Japanese and Japanese American internment (Stone 2004, 290; Tushnet 2005, 129–30).). But it was the president who signed the executive order in the face of the Fifth Amendment's guarantee of due process and the Sixth Amendment's guarantee of fair trials, which aimed at forbidding detention without a trial and conviction.[9]

The shameful chapter of Japanese and Japanese American internment was reexamined after the Cold War, and symbolic recompense was offered to its victims. At the celebration of the bicentennial of the revolution in 1976, President Gerald Ford issued a proclamation acknowledging that the executive order to intern the Japanese was "wrong." Seven years later, a congressional commission issued a report concluding that internment was the result of "race prejudice, war hysteria and a failure of political leadership" (quoted in Stone 2004, 306). Also in the 1980s, the *Hirabayashi* and *Korematsu* cases were reviewed by federal courts, which found serious and deliberate deceit in General DeWitt's final report and in the government's presentation of the evidence to the Supreme Court (ibid.). And in 1988, President Ronald Reagan signed an act that officially declared Japanese internment "a grave injustice" that was "carried out without adequate security reasons" (Stone 2004, 307).

But if the internment of an entire population group was evidence of the repression of which the government was capable, it is worth remembering that it was carried out in the shadow of Pearl Harbor, when Americans were terrorized by the possibility of another "sneak attack." The redemptive acts of Congress, the Court, and two presidents seems to have been genuine, and no future administration appears to have seriously called for anything like internment again.

It was after the United States and its allies had vanquished the Axis Powers that there was a return to domestic suppression, but it took very different forms than mass internment. From the beginning of the Cold War on, both hierarchical power, through the development of a national security bureaucracy, and infrastructural power, through the mobilization of civil society, combined to contain the supposed threat of domestic communism. And although the Cold War began not long after the defeat of the Axis forces, it was the Korean War that set in place the structure of what I call "embedded militarism."

Embedded Militarism

"When scholars work to fit the Cold War into the model of traditional wartimes, they obscure the crucial and continuing way a state structure was built," writes Mary Dudziak (2010, 93. "The Cold War," writes John Hart Ely "has bequeathed America a number of legacies—a sense of permanent emergency; a consequent condition of continuous large-scale military preparation; covert military operations of a sort we never ran or sponsored before; the infectious attitude of secrecy, even dishonesty, toward the American people that such operations necessarily involve us in; the ruinous borrowing required to finance it all" (1993, ix).

But the Cold War also bequeathed the U.S. economy with something else—what Noam Chomsky (1993) called "military Keynesianism." In the wake of World War Two, when a drawdown of the U.S. economy might have been expected to create unemployment and contention—as we saw in Italy—a renewal of military spending was injected into the U.S. economy, supported largely by relatively invisible deficit spending rather than by politically unpalatable tax increases (Flores-Macias and Kreps 2013). The Cold War was popular both because it pumped money into the U.S. economy and because of a collaborative effort of the state and civil society actors to popularize it and stigmatize its enemies.

The most visible change was the growth in the "peacetime" military. Although the number of men and women at arms declined dramatically from over 12 million people when the war ended to 3 million two years later, and Harry Truman failed to gain support for the universal military training he sought (Hogan 1998), the Selective Service Act in 1948 increased the number of people under arms to 3.6 million by 1952, at the height of the Korean mobilization. The numbers declined somewhat when that war ended, but by 1955, there were still almost 3 million men and women in the armed forces. Figure 6.2 traces the annual size of the military establishment from 1940, when the wartime draft began, to 1955, when the world had settled into a long and grueling state of semi-war.

The increasing number of men and women under arms was accompanied by a dramatic increase in military spending, despite the attempts of congressional Republicans to return to a balanced budget at war's end (ibid., chap. 3). In their book, Karen Rasler and William Thompson calculate post–World War Two military spending as a proportion of the gross national product (GNP) and find that it rose rapidly during the Korean War and remained at roughly the same proportion of GNP until the 1970s (Rasler and Thompson 1989, 147–49). In contrast to Britain and France, where military spending rose in the early Cold War but then declined, U.S. military spending never returned to anything like prewar levels (ibid., 209).

Alongside the growth of the "peacetime" army and of the military budget, there was an increasing militarization of the state, but it did not take the form

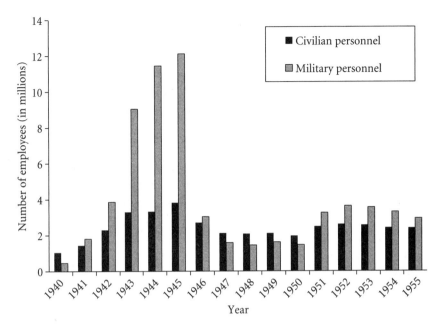

FIGURE 6.2   World War Two and early Cold War numbers of civilian and military personnel. The category "civilian personnel" consists of the number of employees in the federal government; "military personnel" consists of the number of uniformed personnel on active duty. U.S. Bureau of the Census 1965, 710, 736–37.

that Harold Lasswell had feared. Rather than generals taking over civil administration, it grew through the accretion of new agencies of national security around the mainline federal departments. The National Security Act of 1947 created the Office of the Secretary of Defense, the Joint Chiefs of Staff, the National Security Council (NSC), the Central Intelligence Agency (CIA), the National Security Resources Board (NSRB), a munitions board, a war council, and a research and development board. These expansions "altered the architectural face of the federal government" (Hogan 1998, 65).

The Cold War military buildup also created a new relationship between the American state and private enterprise. Aaron Friedberg (2000) discerned a return to a prewar-size state in the years after World War Two, but his conception of state power was more suited to despotic regimes than to the combination of hierarchical and infrastructural power typical of the United States. As Linda Weiss writes, "the power of modern industrial states is infrastructural, not despotic"; U.S. antistatism is very real, but rather than curtailing state capacity, "antistatist impulses have channeled it along particular paths—effectively reshaping the nature of state power expansion, rather than simply restricting it" (2014, 17). What happened after World War Two was the national security state's "close entwinement with nonstate actors and the private sector and its spawning of innovation-driven hybrids" (ibid.).

As the national security state expanded and the Cold War hardened, "a new breed of professionals in foreign and military affairs" who had left the private sector for government service during the war stayed on at war's end (Hogan 1998). These nonelected experts would prove essential in leading Truman—a Midwesterner with essentially no foreign policy experience—to adopt the strategy of containment. This strategy—constructed as a short-term response to what was seen as the Soviet threat to Europe and the Mediterranean—turned into a long-term global strategic posture, to the dismay of George Kennan, who had coined the term with a much narrower goal.

True, containment was founded against a very real threat to Europe and the Mediterranean. But the internal communist threat to Greece was quickly quashed, and Turkey was never seriously threatened. But, once constructed, the strategy of containment was "protracted for another thirty-five years for reasons largely internal to the United States, rather than in response to external pressures and perils" (Craig and Logevall 2009, 4). Domestic politics—and especially the elite-structured "othering" of foreign and domestic opponents—became the central cleavage in public opinion and remained there for the next three decades (Berinsky 2009). What began as a strategic response to a specific geopolitical threat became a standing commitment that eroded the boundary between peace and war and created a permanent state of war.

The Permanent State of War

The pre–Pearl Harbor political order had recognized a sharp distinction between the powers of government in wartime and in peacetime. With the onset of the Cold War, that distinction began to erode (Hogan 1998, 12; Dudziak 2010, chap. 3). "Secretary of State Dean Acheson and others argued that the Cold War was 'in fact a real war,' against a nation that was determined to achieve 'world domination'" (Hogan 1998, 70). With his "Truman Doctrine" speech of 1947, the president solidified the country's war fever and made it a permanent part of American political discourse. By the onset of the Korean War, he was casting the Cold War as "a permanent struggle of global proportions" (quoted in ibid., 71).

On June 24, 1950, North Korean forces crossed the thirty-eighth parallel, beginning a sweeping conquest of U.S. ally, South Korea. The attack was as daring as it was unexpected. The North Koreans were acting on their misperception that the United States did not consider the Korean peninsula strategically important and almost overwhelmed the South Korean army before the U.S. army could organize a counterattack (Cumings 1981; Zelizer 2010, 99). The shock was equivalent to the one that would shatter Americans' self-confidence in 2001, and—like that shock—it gave the president and his administration enormous leeway to expand the power of the executive state.

The Expansion of Presidential War Power

The U.S. military response to the Korean invasion was decisive, but President Truman labeled the action a United Nations "police action" in support of the Republic of Korea. On June 26, he announced that the UN Security Council "had acted to order a withdrawal of the invading forces to positions north of the 38th parallel and that . . . the United States will vigorously support the effort of the Council to terminate this serious breach of the peace" (quoted in Fisher 2004, 97; see also Zelizer 2010, 100). This was the first of many efforts to internationalize U.S. military efforts. But despite its internationalist framing, the Korean War was the product of the nascent national security state that was already in place in 1950.

Four government documents fostered the idea that peace and war would no longer be airtight compartments:[10] (1) the internal telegram sent by George Kennan, at the time chargé d'affaires in Moscow, to the State Department in February 1946, launching the strategy of containment; (2) an internal report by Clark Clifford and George Elsey, Truman aides, warning of the Soviet Union's military buildup, of its alliances with other communist parties, and its expansionary policies in Europe and the Mediterranean; (3) Truman's response to the retreat of Great Britain from the Mediterranean in the speech to Congress in 1947, extending the Monroe Doctrine to Europe and asking Congress to provide massive funding to Greece and Turkey to oppose Soviet expansion; and (4) a document produced by the NSC, NSC-68, in the wake of the communist victory in China and the first Soviet test of an atomic bomb. These four documents of early postwar history not only warned of the gravity of the Soviet threat and called for its containment but built on the assumption that "a new era of total war had dawned on the United States" (Hogan 1998, 12).

Yet there was something odd about this heightened state of alarm and readiness. Except for Korea, the Cold War was more a state of mind than an armed conflict with a beginning, a middle, and an end (Dudziak 2010, 68). Fed by a generalized fear that began with the dropping of the atom bomb on Japan at the end of the war, "It did not take long," writes Ira Katznelson, "for anxiety about the bomb to supplant the festive mood that dominated the late summer of 1945. Nor did it take long for a new climate of fear, with the bomb as its original impetus, to engender a crusading national security state" (2013, 410). "American citizens were summoned once again to 'wage a war against the emergency,' but an emergency dissimilar both from the kind Franklin Roosevelt had announced on his first Inauguration Day and from the time-bound emergency of World War Two" (ibid., 409). The heightened state of emergency may be the reason why there was so little antiwar activism against the Korea War.

The Steel Seizure Case

Of course, ordinary contention did not end because the United States was once again sending troops abroad; the trade unions, although they were held back by the newly passed Taft-Hartley Act, still had some of the militancy they had gained during the union-friendly New Deal. In early 1952, when negotiations for a pay raise failed with the nation's steelmakers, the United Steelworkers voted to begin a major strike against the industry. Fearing that a pay raise would increase inflation and that a stoppage would hurt the war effort, Truman wrote an executive order "nationalizing" the industry under the president's inherent powers. But Congress had already considered amending the Taft-Hartley Act to give the president the power to seize the nation's steel mills in times of emergency and rejected it. Allowing the president to ignore the declared will of Congress was a step too far for the Supreme Court, even in wartime. On June 12, 1952, by a 6–3 decision, the Court held that that the commander-in-chief's authority to prosecute a foreign war does not empower him to seize private property to resolve a domestic labor dispute. "This is a job for the Nation's lawmakers," Justice Hugo Black wrote, "not for its military authorities" (*Youngstown Sheet and Tube Co. v. Sawyer* 343 U.S. 579 [1952]).

It was not because of Black's majority opinion that the steel seizure case was historic but because of the concurring opinion of Justice Robert Jackson, who sharply distinguished presidential decisions in which Congress has not issued defining legislation from those in which it has. In the latter case, Jackson reasoned, presidential power is at its nadir.[11] This was a sound constitutional decision that had an unanticipated consequence; in future wars, presidents who claimed discretionary powers to which Congress had expressed clear opposition would henceforth resort to secret executive orders to evade congressional scrutiny. It was for this reason that President Bush, in October 2001, would charge the National Security Agency (NSA) with beginning a program of mass surveillance in secret (see chapter 7).

In the meantime, the Cold War and the Korean War created a hegemonic discourse that entered deeply into civil society; reshaped public opinion into an us-versus-them mentality previously found only in wartime (Westad 2005); and constricted political contention into a bipolar contest between good and evil, patriotic Americans against domestic communists, socialists, and "fellow-travelers." In the absence of a hot war, military preparedness, expanding budgets, and the draft were justified by an implied threat against U.S. interests that never came. In the absence of actual armed conflict, this would be easier to accomplish if civil society could be mobilized behind an ideology of national security.

The Cold War National Security State

Gaining support for the Cold War was relatively easy from one sector of American society—those who ran and profited from security-related industry. Far more than in any previous war, the Cold War led to a permanent soldering between the state and war-related businesses. The linkage took a variety of forms, ranging from short-term contracts to longer-term contractual relations, to what Linda Weiss calls "hybridization." She summarizes, "Through an extensive array of private-public alliances and innovation hybrids, technology development programs and investment funds, the United States has created not a liberal, but a hybrid political economy—one that is shaped by a national security state deeply entwined with the commercial sector" (2014, 195).

Congress, although it never ceased to rail about the need for a balanced budget, grudgingly appropriated funds for war materiel. Faced by the new avalanche of administrative agencies and managers created around national security, congressional leaders reorganized its committee system (Hogan 1998, 4–5), creating constituencies dependent on defense spending and on defense-related technology. Although members of Congress might rant and rave about the growth of the federal budget, through committee memberships and support for local industries, Congress became a willing partner in the growth of the national security state.

Deeply concerned about the power of this "iron triangle,"[12] Truman's successor, Dwight D. Eisenhower, complained about the conjunction of an immense military establishment and the growth of a large arms industry. After two terms in office, the retiring president warned that:

> The total influence—economic, political, even spiritual—is felt in every city, every statehouse, every office of the federal government. We recognize the imperative need for this development. Yet we must not fail to comprehend its grave implications. Our toil, resources and livelihood are all involved; so is the very structure of our society. In the councils of government, we must guard against the acquisition of unwarranted

influence, whether sought or unsought, by the military–industrial complex.[13]

Yet it was under the Eisenhower administration that the trend toward the creation of a hybrid public-private political economy shaped around the needs of national security was solidified (Weiss 2014, 28, 33). Although the rate of growth in public-private collaboration slowed down after the Korean War (ibid., 189), the patterns that were established under Eisenhower endured—even under the self-declared "small-government" Reagan administration in the 1980s (ibid., 41). But political-economic hybridization on its own would not have created a constituency for the Cold War. Preparing a war-weary public for a drawn-out strenuous dual with the Soviet Union would require a broader reach into civil society than economic ties between the state and industry.

Mobilizing Infrastructural Support

In war's wake, public opinion routinely rejects the sacrifices that citizens will willingly make in wartime. This trend was worrisome to the NSC, which warned in its NSC-68 document that "a large measure of sacrifice and discipline will be demanded of the American people," "who would be asked to give up some of the benefits which they have come to associate with their freedoms" (quoted in Hogan 1998, 17). To gain support for these sacrifices, the country would need to believe passionately in the seriousness of the threat from the Soviet Union and on the primary role of the United States in opposing it. A public relations campaign redolent of the Committee on Public Information in World War One, but much more widespread, was launched alongside the defense spending and higher taxes to support it.

The bellicose rhetoric coming out of the Soviet Union in the years after the war provided plenty of material with which to stoke patriotism. But in the absence of a real war, the public would need to be convinced that the sacrifices it was being asked to make were justified. This led to a growth of government propaganda, which became permanent and professional and was aimed at a stratum of opinion leaders (Brewer 2009, 142–45). But it also led to alliances with civil society groups to make sure that Americans appreciated the freedoms they enjoyed. From 1947 on, the country was awash in a wave of patriotic rhetoric, public festivals, and anti-Soviet propaganda. As social scientists trumpeted the virtues of the U.S. pluralistic society, civil society groups were mobilized against the threat of totalitarian communism.

Even before the Cold War began, a group of movie-industry employees launched the Motion Picture Alliance for the Preservation of American Ideals

(MPA). "These anti-Communists," writes John Sbardellati, "detected an insidious plot to infiltrate the nation's influential institutions, Hollywood being among the most important of these, given its ability to reach the masses" (2012, 70–72). The MPA regarded the movie industry as a powerful shaper of national politics and culture, vulnerable to the inroads of communist writers, authors, and directors and left unprotected by the blindness or indifference of the producers. To this end, the MPA launched a *Screen Guide*—written in part by screen writer and future libertarian guru, Ayn Rand—to guide the studios in defending against communist infiltration. The *Guide* warned against the dangers of criticizing Americanism, of praising collectivist values, of producing political films, and of hiring personnel who would advance the communist cause (ibid, 94–100).

Hollywood producers were not easily swayed by Rand's guide, but the FBI certainly was. The bureau "wholly adopted the MPA's *Screen Guide*, using it as an ideological tool to determine the subversive nature of a number of motion pictures" (ibid., 96–97). The FBI also seems to have relied on informants from the MPA for intelligence on motion pictures and on communists who were in their sights as the HUAC got into gear.[14] One such informant eventually rose to become governor of California and later president of the United States.

Not only the MPA, but the American Legion joined in the anticommunist Hollywood Cold War. The Legion played an active role in clearing those tainted by communist connections and provided the workers needed to picket allegedly subversive films. For example, the Legion warned its members to beware of *Salt of the Earth*, a film about the plight of a mine strike by Hispanic workers, which had been written by blacklisted writers (ibid., 186). Across the country, the Legion threatened to picket any theater that screened the film.

As some civil society groups mobilized against the threat of internal subversion, others organized to remind Americans of the virtues of the system they lived under. Archetypical was the cross-country tour of the Freedom Train, "a travelling archive of historic documents that visited more than three hundred cities between September 1947 and January 1949" (Hogan 1998, 426). The effort was the result of a carefully organized campaign by political leaders who represented the "official culture" of the postwar period. It was supported by the government, by movie studios, and by the Advertising Council. It led to the creation of the American Heritage Foundation to direct and support the project.

The Freedom Train's travels kicked off in Philadelphia to celebrate the 160th anniversary of the Constitution.[15] Wherever it went, it culminated a week of citizenship training called Rededication Week, orchestrated by local elites with assistance from the foundation. Its progress across the country was accompanied by a film called "Our American Heritage," by an illustrated booklet produced by *Look* magazine, and by articles contributed by *Reader's Digest* illustrating the growth of free institutions in England and the United States (Hogan 1998, 428–29). "The government and private elites behind the Heritage Foundation " writes Hogan, "used the Freedom Train to construct a national identity that was more ideal than real, in part by appealing to a traditional cultural narrative that celebrated consensus and triumphs at the expense of divisions and failures" (ibid., 430). Although it was framed more as "we are wonderful" than as an attack on anyone else, it helped to mobilize public opinion against what was increasingly framed as "the threat to our liberties."

Public opinion during the early Cold War was strongly anticommunist. In the most systematic surveys carried out during the early Cold War years, Samuel Stouffer reported that 68 percent of a national cross-section of the public would be unwilling to allow an "admitted Communist" to make a speech in their communities, 66 percent favored removing a book written by such a person from the public library, 90 percent favored getting communists out of defense plants, and 91 percent were willing to fire a communist from a high school teaching position (Stouffer 1955, 40). Community leaders were somewhat more tolerant, but only a bare majority of local elites interviewed by Stouffer would allow communists to speak publicly or have a book available in public libraries, and just as many would have fired communists from defense plants or high school teaching positions (ibid).

Of course, visceral anticommunism was difficult to disentangle from intolerance in general, and Stouffer's surveys showed that majorities of Americans at the time were intolerant of nonconformity of any sort.[16] But there was a special level of hostility to communism, less because of the threat of espionage or sabotage than because of fear that it would infect Americans. "I think that there is danger," said one of Stouffer's respondents, a junior high school teacher in Washington, D.C., "because Communists try to undermine our ideals, our ways of thinking" (ibid., 157–58).

The American national security state was created, in part, by expanding the federal state structure, by creating a system of "governed interdependence" with private industry, and by overselling the foreign threat, which ricocheted back into public opinion and delegitimized those who would question its buildup (Griffin 2013, 66). But the growth of the national security state was also driven by domestic politics. "The public may be directly influenced by some dramatic events, such as Pearl Harbor and 9/11," writes Adam Berinsky; but—as in the domestic arena—"public opinion is primarily structured by the ebb and flow of partisan and group-based political conflict" (2009, 5, 7). From the end of World War Two, politics was strongly structured around the cleavage between "us" and "them" and the suppression of communist and other left-wing and liberal causes. This meant that, even after the tensions of the Cold War began to abate, the fear of domestic communism continued to roil American politics and to constrict civil liberties.

The Constriction of Civil Liberties

Popular memory tends to identify the Cold War anticommunist crusade with Senator Joseph McCarthy in the early 1950s, but it actually began soon after World War Two among congressional Republicans anxious to end the long hegemony of the Democratic Party over national politics. The first to launch the theme were Republican candidates in the 1946 congressional election (Zelizer 2010, 66). Attacking the Truman administration for being "soft on communism," candidates such as Richard Nixon took control of the House and Senate for the first time since 1932. But there was soon a migration of domestic anticommunism from the Republicans to the Democrats. Even figures close to Roosevelt, such as Bernard Baruch, Wall Street financier, warned, "Our enemies are to be found abroad *and at home*" (quoted in ibid., 69, emphasis added).

The 1946 Republican electoral victory marked the beginning of a repeated back-and-forth spiral of competition for anticommunist ground that social movement theorists call the "radical flank effect" (Gupta 2013; Haines 1984). When right-wing Republicans in opposition attacked "communists in government," the Democrats in power responded with a more moderate version of their opponents' demands for greater surveillance. In March 1947, Truman issued Executive Order 9835—the Loyalty Oath—giving the government the power to investigate government employees for association with totalitarian or communist groups. Truman thought the communist domestic threat was minimal, but, according to his aide, Clark Clifford, he was planning to run in 1948 and had to recognize it (Zelizer 2010, 67–68).

Truman's loyalty oath program gave Congress the opportunity to get into the anticommunist business, with a number of separate committees launching investigations, most notoriously the HUAC, which took the federal government, the labor movement, educational institutions, and Hollywood as its targets (Stone 2004, 354–66). It offered a political opportunity for demagogues like McCarthy to create his own witch hunt for subversives in government without the legal guarantees that the government program prescribed. Although McCarthy was eventually censured by Congress, in May 1953 Eisenhower created a new criterion for dismissal from government employment—taking the constitutional Fifth Amendment privilege against self-incrimination opened federal employees to certainty of dismissal (ibid., 351). The law, it seemed, could be used against the Constitution.

The result was predictable—a witch-hunt atmosphere that seeped from the public sector into private employment; from Washington, D.C., to Hollywood; and from government to university loyalty oaths. Hollywood executives and self-promoting missionaries such as Ronald Reagan leapt to condemn and blacklist communists in the entertainment industry; liberal groups, like the Americans for Democratic Action, fell in line with the anticommunist mood of the moment (Keller 1989; Sbardellati 2012); progressive unions began to exclude communist organizers from their ranks; and a network of anticommunist intellectual groups began to populate the public sphere (Hogan 1998, chap. 10). Even supposedly objective social scientists, such as Stouffer, aimed their work at defeating the "Communist conspiracy" (1955, 13).

The reach of the Red Scare was enormous, but its results were insignificant. During the years 1947–1953, more than 4.7 million individuals were investigated. About 1 percent of these inquiries turned up enough information to trigger full investigations. Of these, about 8,000 led to the filing of formal charges, of which more than 90 percent were cleared. This left roughly five hundred individuals who received discharges, of which the Civil Service Commission overturned about one-third (Stone 2004, 348).

The indirect effects of the scare were more severe. Thousands of U.S. citizens, terrified of being investigated because of their past or present political opinions, retreated from public life—and some from U.S. soil. "Because of the ambiguity of the very concept of 'disloyalty,' and the highly secretive nature of the process, no federal employee—or *prospective* federal employee—could consider herself exempt from the danger of investigation," writes Geoffrey Stone; "The loyalty program created a pervasive system of being 'watched'" (ibid., 349–50). A few brave civil libertarians protested against being forced to sign loyalty oaths, but many more left academia or suppressed their progressive or liberal views.

The courts were quick to support these anticommunist programs. Under the Smith Act, the government in 1949 indicted a group of leading communists for advocating the violent overthrow of the government. In *Dennis v. United States* (341 U.S. 494 [1951]), the Supreme Court substituted a new and more restrictive limit on free speech than the "clear and present danger" criterion that had guided its decisions on speech since the days of Justices Holmes and Brandeis. *Dennis* became for a time the standard of judicial holdings restricting free speech and free association.

The new doctrine also gave a hunting license to the FBI. The bureau began to investigate opinions, which it took as a proxy for behavior, often based only on information gathered from anonymous informants. Individuals who were interrogated by the FBI were often asked questions that had nothing to do with communism or with their purported association with the Communist Party (Stone

2004, 346). Although still acting like a domestic intelligence bureau, the loyalty program gave the FBI a foundation to expand into a political police force and, ultimately, into the core of an independent security state (Keller 1989).

Even as the Soviet Union's control over its satellites began to disintegrate and the U.S. Communist Party was collapsing, the FBI expanded its investigations of subversion. In 1956, the FBI created its first COINTELPRO, a program designed to investigate, infiltrate, and disrupt the Communist Party (Davis 1997, chap. 1; Keller 1989, chap. 5). But the witch hunt had a ratchet effect, spreading beyond registered communists; a second COINTELPRO, targeting the (anticommunist) Socialist Workers' Party, was created in 1961; a third targeted radical right-wing organizations, notably the Ku Klux Klan; and a fourth targeted radical black militants. The term *extremist* now began to enter the FBI's lexicon, instead of the narrower terms *communist* or *subversive* (Keller 1989, 130). Even homosexuals and lesbians suffered from a "lavender witch hunt" that began with the claim that such "deviants" were susceptible to being blackmailed by communist agents.[17]

There was also a trickle-down effect of the anticommunist crusade. Informed and trained by federal government officials, state and local governments, and even local school districts, picked up where Congress and the FBI left off, leaving little recourse for radicals and dissidents except to change their residence or leave the country. The entire balance of American politics began to shift to the right, in large part through the destruction of the left and of liberals' fear of being tarred with the brush of communism (Craig and Logevall 2009). Even progressive groups such as the ACLU and Americans for Democratic Action—fearing being tarred with the brush of leftism—began to trim their support for liberal causes.

The nuclear arms race was one of the two areas of public debate that was partially sheltered from the Cold War hysteria. Led by such traditional peace organizations as the World Federalists, the Quakers, and the Women's International League for Peace and Freedom, a small but sturdy pacifist movement was active throughout the Cold War. They were eventually joined by new groups, such as the Federation of Atomic Scientists, who knew better than most what were the dangers of a nuclear future. Many of these groups came together in the Committee for a Sane Nuclear Policy (SANE) in 1957 (Katz 1974). But in the atmosphere of rabid anticommunism of the 1950s, even a mild proposal for a test ban treaty was attacked as following the communist line (ibid, 20).

The other progressive movement that flourished in the 1950s was civil rights, but, ironically, its success in influencing government was connected to the Cold War. We often think of the civil rights movement as beginning in the "liberal" 1960s, but some of its greatest successes came in the heart of the Cold War, driven partly by the gains that African Americans had made as they moved out of the Jim Crow South and partly by the government's foreign policy goal of demonstrating the superiority of American freedom. It was unthinkable to both Truman and Eisenhower that the United States would act as the defender of freedom against the communist menace while continuing to oppress African Americans within its shores (Dudziak 2000; McAdam 1998). But while foreign affairs spurred the expansion of civil rights to African Americans, the domestic political climate fueled a Red Scare that constricted civil liberties in general (Dudziak 2010, 84–85).

The passion for rooting out communists cooled in the 1960s and 1970s, even as the Cold War continued. The reason was that repression was never a direct effect of the level of international threat but was bound up with the struggle for political advantage in domestic politics (Dudziak 2010, 90–92). Even as the Supreme Court returned to a posture more protective of civil liberties, the Cold War left a heritage of domestic repression similar to the constitutional nationalism we saw during and after World War One. As late as the mid-1960s, Americans were still often writing about constitutional loyalty, as they had in the years following World War One.[18]

Worship of the Constitution—so vividly impressed on the American landscape by cultural artifacts such as the Freedom Train—began to decline as the containment doctrine of the 1940s and 1950s expanded into the domino theory used to justify the Vietnam War and as the body bags began to return from Southeast Asia. It was at this point that contention around civil rights and in the universities began to spill over into a broad-based antiwar movement (McAdam 1988, 173–78, 188–89). But the secret face of the national security state was far from dead, and it permitted both a clandestine strategy of the FBI to spread to other parts of the government and a ruthless White House to fashion a strategy of repression that threatened not only the antiwar movement but the Constitution itself.

The Antiwar Movement

The U.S. involvement in Southeast Asia went back to 1950, when the Truman administration decided to assist the French in their effort to regain control of their former colony (Kahin 1986, chap. 1).[19] With the French defeat in 1954, the Eisenhower administration decided to create and sustain a noncommunist bastion in South Vietnam with an "advisory" U.S. military role (Logevall 2001, 86). In 1961, the newly installed John F. Kennedy administration decided to increase the number of U.S. military advisers there to 9,000 (Herring 1979, 86). By 1964, there were 16,000 U.S. "advisors" in Southeast Asia, a figure that President Johnson soon raised to 23,000 (ibid., 116). A year later, Johnson decided to send another 40,000 ground troops to Vietnam, and this began a process of escalation that would not be reversed until the war had been thoroughly Americanized. "Johnson," writes George C. Herring, "took the nation into war in Vietnam by indirection and dissimulation" (ibid., 133).

Johnson, of course, had inherited the presidency when John F. Kennedy was assassinated, and he worried that the Republican Party would attack him in the 1964 presidential election if he decided to negotiate a way out of Vietnam. But, even after winning that election by a landslide, he ignored the advice of his politically astute vice president, Hubert Humphrey, who wrote him in February 1965 that "the American people find it hard to understand why we risk World War III by enlarging a war under terms we found unacceptable 12 years ago in Korea, particularly since the chances of success are slimmer" (quoted in Logevall 2012, 126).

The Vietnam War was the product of the incremental growth of the national security state that was launched in the late 1940s and expanded institutionally through the 1950s. Campbell Craig and Frederik Logevall put this succinctly: "America's Cold War changed shape after 1950. It became a global campaign, much more ideologically charged, far more expensive . . . and a substantially greater factor in the lives of Americans" (2009, 127). The particular trajectory of the escalation of the Vietnam War was not inevitable but grew out of the embedded militarism of the national security state.

Some students of the Vietnam War see it as a tragic misadventure that could have been avoided had another president, less uncertain about his legitimacy, been in power in Washington. But the war was the result of ideological, institutional, and domestic political factors that grew out of the national security state as it developed after World War Two:

First, the war encapsulated the ideology that had developed since Woodrow Wilson took the country into World War One that the U.S. was the world's bastion of freedom, which included a superior attitude toward the country's allies; Americans thought of their intervention in Southeast Asia as different from that of others—for example, the French, who were looked down on for fighting to retain their colonial empire (Logevall 2012, 707). The very malleability of the American creed, as Joseph Margulies (2013) teaches, made it a powerful discursive instrument in justifying a war in Southeast Asia.

Second, intervention was buttressed by the institutions that had been created or expanded in the early Cold War. Consider the FBI. Under its politically astute director, J. Edgar Hoover, it enjoyed dependable support from the press—even the liberal press (Keller 1989, 53–55). In the 1950s and 1960s, a long-running TV series, *The FBI*, portrayed the bureau in extremely favorable terms that were vetted by Hoover's associate Cartha de Loach. As late as 1965, 84 percent of the public had a "highly favorable" opinion of the FBI in a Gallup poll. "To the American people," writes William Keller, "the FBI was the defender of freedom, the guardian of the American way, and J. Edgar Hoover was a living legend and authentic folk hero (ibid., 114).

Third, attitudes toward the war were embedded in partisan politics. This can be seen from a succession of public opinion polls that were taken between 1964 and 1972. As long as Johnson held the presidency, Democrats were roughly 10 percent more likely to support the war than were Republicans. "Only when the office passed to Nixon," writes Adam Berinsky, "did their levels of support drop below that of Republicans" (see figure 6.3). Partisan cues played a crucial role in structuring opinion toward the war (Berinsky 2009, 111, 119).

The New Antiwar Contention

Scholars of social movements have given great attention to three major sectors of mass protest in the United States in the 1960s: civil rights, the student movement,

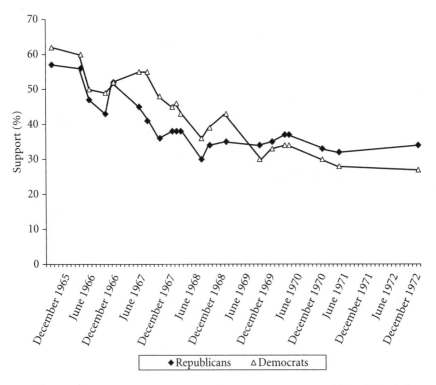

FIGURE 6.3 Partisan trends in support for the Vietnam War, 1965–1972. Gallup Poll data from Berinsky 2009, 119. Reproduced courtesy of the author, and the University of Chicago, © 2009 by the University of Chicago. All rights reserved.

and the antiwar movement. These sectors were never fully independent—they were part of what activists called *the* movement, drew on overlapping audiences, and gained strength and experience from each other. In particular, the antiwar movement drew on models of militancy and on experienced activists from the civil rights and student organizations of the earlier part of the decade. But it also drew on more traditional sources of pacifism, radicalism, and antiracism.

The movement was also able to draw on public disillusionment with the war as well as on general discontent with the government. It mobilized a wave of demonstrations that began soon after the Gulf of Tonkin Resolution, which continued—with a temporary pause for the 1968 election campaign—until 1972, when the Nixon administration had already moved toward withdrawal. Figure 6.4, drawing on the Dynamics of Collective Action data set, tracks the trajectory of antiwar protests marked by various phases of the war in Southeast Asia.

Although it is the sheer magnitude of the movement that leaps out from the data in figure 6.4, it was the intensity of the protests and the qualitative innovations of the organizers that attracted the media and disconcerted authorities. These consisted of the following:

- The formation of coalitions among liberal and progressive groups that would normally have had little contact with one another.
- The presence of scientists and representatives of mainstream religious groups among the protesters.

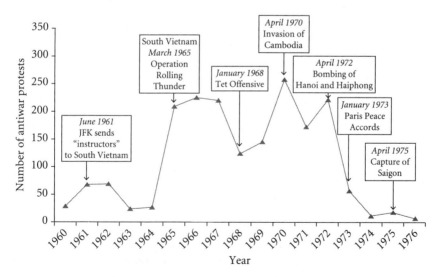

FIGURE 6.4 U.S. Vietnam War engagement and the number of antiwar protests, 1960–1976. Dynamics of Collective Action data, 2009, http://www.stanford.edu/group/collectiveaction/cgi-bin/drupal/. Courtesy of Sarah Soule.

- The mounting of major "days" of protest labeled "moratoria," such as the October 15, 1968, Moratorium that attracted thousands of participants.
- Theatrical performances like the teach-ins, the public burning of draft cards, and the 1967 "levitation" of the Pentagon.
- The co-occurrence of organized violence from minorities like the Weathermen with the mass peaceful protest from national coalitions.

Public opinion toward the movement was always divided, and it became actively hostile after the 1968 Chicago Democratic Party Convention. But even as the movement radicalized and the media turned hostile to it, public opinion began to shift away from support for the war. Support had been 55 percent in a NORC survey in summer 1965 and 60 percent in a Gallup poll of July 1965 (Berinsky 2009, 21). But as the military commitment and costs of the war began to grow, public support began to drop, settling at 30 percent in 1968 and rising only minimally between then and the 1973 U.S. departure from Vietnam (ibid., 20–21).

Opposition to the war diffused into disillusionment with the American state in general, particularly among a sector of the public—young people—who had been politicized by the civil rights and student movements and were subject to the draft. "The decline in trust from the 1960s to the 1970s was fueled by citizens' reactions to the war in Vietnam, Watergate, and civil rights initiatives," write Margaret Levi and Laura Stoker (2000, 475), political scientists. The escalation of the war, its increasing human and political costs, and the growing evidence that the public had been deceived quickly eroded the support Johnson had extracted from Congress under the pretext of the Tonkin Gulf affair.

The Johnson and Nixon administrations both made determined efforts to paint the war in positive terms, but as the body bags returning from Vietnam multiplied, the cost of the war became harder to suppress. This was especially true because a new actor—television—made it harder for the government to influence public opinion than in the 1950s. During the early Cold War, the press had been a willing partner in the government's anticommunist stance. But it lacked the breadth and immediacy of the visual media that would develop during the civil rights movement. The televised spectacle of police attacking young black demonstrators with hoses and attack dogs created a new role for the media—representing and framing social movements for the public. As Todd Gitlin writes, "In the late twentieth century, political movements feel called upon to rely on large-scale communications in order to *matter*, to say who they are and what they intend to publics they want to sway" (1980, 3).

As public outrage grew and successive administrations continued to escalate the war, contention grew more radical and even, at times, violent. Most of the early antiwar protesters were moderate to liberal and focused most of their energies on the atomic bomb (Katz 1974). But in the wake of the civil rights movement, and faced with the gathering escalation of the war in Southeast Asia, more radical groups began to mobilize against the war as well. These groups first came together in 1965 in large-scale public protests against the war.

The media were quick to respond. As Gitlin writes; "With the SDS [Students for a Democratic Society] March on Washington on April 17, 1965, student antiwar protest . . . became big news" (1980, 27). At first fascinated by the newness of the movement, by its innovative tactics and by its flamboyant language, the press soon began to frame it with themes that would stick to it, even as it grew much larger and attracted support from groups that did not share its radical goals. The turning point came with the violently repressed protests at the Democratic National Convention in Chicago in summer 1968.[20]

The media's increasingly negative image of the movement was in part a response to the image of long-haired protesters burning draft cards and in part a spillover from the urban riots of the middle of the 1960s, when cities like Newark and Detroit erupted in civil strife. Even though the rioters were largely African American, and the people in the antiwar movement were mainly white, many Americans came to see antiwar protesters as inherently violent. For example, when the moderate liberal group SANE held an "overwhelmingly middle-class, middle-aged, middle-of-the-road march in Washington in November 1965," TV reporters and photographers zeroed in on the radical fringe of marchers (Katz 1974, 94).

But the media's attention to the antiwar movement was double-edged. On the one hand, the media framed the movement in violent terms that alienated much of mainstream opinion, but on the other, the media gave the movement great attention, lending antiwar protesters a degree of legitimacy. Legitimation grew as mainstream politicians, such as Senator William Fulbright (D-Arkansas), launched congressional hearings on the war (Zelizer 2010, 196). Although the Johnson administration was not above tarring the movement as under communist influence (ibid, 211), media images of police battering protesters evoked solidarity from college students around the country (Davis 1997, chap. 4). A major turning point was the killing of four students and the wounding of nine others by a National Guard detachment at Kent State University in May 1970.

Whether in response to public opinion, to the movement's actions, or to the growing human and financial costs of the war, political elites began to turn away from the war beginning with the first major escalation (Burstein and Freudenberg 1978; McAdam and Su 2002), especially after the bombing of Cambodia (Ely 1993). A series of congressional antiwar resolutions and the loss of congressional allies like Fulbright made clear to President Johnson that the war was both a military and a political disaster. His announcement that he would not run for reelection, and Vice President Humphrey's attempt to distinguish his position on the war from Johnson's, was not sufficient to persuade the electorate, and in January 1969, Richard Nixon and the Republican Party came to power on a platform of ending the war.

It was under Nixon that the national security state—now once again in the hands of its natural ally—began to expand its surveillance of civilians. The surveillance of U.S. citizens from World War One to the early Cold War was what we might accurately call "retail"—it was mostly aimed at individual communists and "fellow travelers," using the authority of the Smith and McCarran acts. But even as the courts began to nibble away at the restrictive legislation of the early Cold War, a more "wholesale" attack on civil liberties was being launched, both by the FBI and by the Departments of Justice and Defense[21]

From Retail to Wholesale Repression

FBI programs began to target antiwar protesters by adapting the Bureau's anti-communist COINTELPRO model. The new program, we now know, was run with complete autonomy from the Justice Department and the White House (Keller 1989, 175), with no oversight from either Congress or the courts. In contrast to the earlier ones, the New Left program was open-ended and used undefined tactics against broad targets. Field offices "were told to make every effort to depict 'the scurrilous and depraved nature of New Left activists.'" In internal memoranda, Hoover urged that "every avenue of possible embarrassment must be vigorously and enthusiastically explored" (quoted in Davis 1997, 47). The New Left COINTELPRO symbolized "an overall shift in the middle and late 1960s from protection of the liberal state toward the creation of a political police and ultimately an independent security state" (Keller, 189).[22]

In part to contest the tentacle-like grasp of Hoover over internal security and in part disturbed by the threat he saw in the urban disorders of the mid-1960s, Attorney General Ramsey Clark—a dedicated liberal—set up a new unit within the Department of Justice, the Interdivisional Intelligence Unit (IDIU). Under Assistant Attorney General John Doar, the IDIU not only gathered data from U.S. attorneys and other sources on potential sources of urban revolt but tapped into the vast databases that had been created to administer President Johnson's Great Society welfare programs (Scott 2013, chap. 2). The IDIU communications center maintained a direct link with the White House, the army's Directorate for Civil Disturbances, the U.S. attorney for Washington, D.C., and a number of police departments in the capital area. It "provided Clark with an alternative intelligence source and analytic team to the FBI" (ibid., 45), but it also increased the number and variety of federal agencies collecting data on Americans.

The same was true of the Pentagon's domestic surveillance activities. Ignoring the 1878 Posse Comitatus Act, which prohibited the use of the military for law enforcement, following the Detroit riots the army developed a vast domestic surveillance program (Scott 2013, chap. 3). Known as the CONUS (Continental U.S.) Intelligence Branch, a computerized hub was created to link eight different military intelligence groups under the command of Lieutenant General William Yarborough, who had commanded counterintelligence operations in Germany during the height of the Cold War. Yarborough believed that there were "outside influences" aiding Americans who protested against the war and brought in a generation of army officers to gather intelligence to predict social upheaval. "These officers," writes Katherine Scott, "practiced Cold War counterintelligence methods honed in Berlin, Saigon, and Seoul—use of spies, disinformation campaigns, and electronic and technological surveillance . . ." (2013, 53). Coached by armed forces personnel, "State and local police borrowed from the Pentagon's war toolkit" and received weapons from the Pentagon through the Law Enforcement Assistance Administration (ibid., 57).

Johnson's resentment at the opposition to the war had been muted by his liberal connections and by the fact that the intelligence agencies found no evidence that the antiwar movement was infiltrated by communists. But this had no credit with his successor, Richard Nixon, who came to the presidency with a long history of domestic anticommunism and whose personality left him susceptible to conspiracy theories. Encouraged by Hoover to believe that critics of the war were subversives and panicked by increasing congressional defection from support for the war, Nixon ordered the intelligence agencies "to prove the relationship" (Griffin 2013, 130), and when they failed to do so, he created his own private intelligence agency within the White House. This was the origin of the illegal infiltration of left-wing and antiwar organizations, the bugging of the office of Daniel Ellsberg, the "Pentagon Papers" whistleblower, and, ultimately, the Watergate break-in.

Nixon's tapes reveal both his state of mind at the time and his determination to break the law to defeat his political enemies. Speaking to Attorney General John Mitchell, he demanded, "I want you to shake up these (unintelligible) up around here. Now you do it. Shake them up. Get them off their goddamn dead asses and say now that isn't what you should be talking about. We're up against an enemy, a conspiracy. They're using any means. We are going to use any means. Is that clear?" (quoted in ibid., 143). In the name of fighting a war that his predecessor had described as part of the fight to defend the free world from totalitarianism, Nixon "turned the capacities of the intelligence agencies built up during the post-1945 period to use against foreign powers inward against American citizens" (ibid., 121).

Rollback

The corruption of the U.S. constitutional system during the Vietnam years was never systematic or complete. As early as 1966, Johnson had signed the Freedom of Information Act (FOIA), giving legal support to the public's right to request government information. In the Privacy Act of 1974, the Sunshine Act of 1976, and the Foreign Intelligence Surveillance Act (FISA) of 1978, reformers in Congress tried to bend back the executive's power to surveil citizens, collect information in secret, and leave the public ignorant of its domestic intelligence activities (Scott 2013, 6–7). Not only that—as the FBI and the Nixon administration were throttling free speech and eroding Americans' privacy, the Court's 1969 decision in *Brandenburg v. Ohio* overturned *Dennis* (Stone 2004, 531–23). Even Congress, which had voted a virtual authorization for war in the Tonkin Gulf Resolution, vigorously opposed the secret Cambodian incursion when it came to light in 1970 (Ely 1993).

In the 1970s, there was a widespread rollback of the government's surveillance and of its illegal disruption of dissenters.

- In 1971, the army announced that it was banning the collection of information about individuals and organizations "unaffiliated" with the military, except when "essential to the military mission and destroying material it had previously gathered" (Stone 2004, 496).
- In 1973, angered at Nixon's incursions into Cambodia without informing it, Congress passed the War Powers Resolution over the president's veto.
- In 1976, President Gerald Ford prohibited the CIA from using electronic or physical surveillance to collect information on the domestic activities of Americans and banned the NSA from intercepting communications within, from, or to the United States.
- After Hoover passed away, Clarence Kelly, the new FBI director, apologized for FBI abuses, asserting that they must "never be repeated" (ibid.).
- In the same year, Attorney General Edward Levi imposed limitations on the FBI's investigative activities.

The Church Committee, which was convened in the wake of the Media burglary and the Watergate break-in, was the most shining exhibit for the theory that American democracy periodically redeems itself following wartime abuses against civil liberties. We will turn in the next chapters to the question of how durable these post-Watergate reforms turned out to be. For now, there is a more immediate question: How much of this rollback can be attributed to the self-correcting mechanism of the American creed and how much was the result of actual contention against the abuses of the previous decades?

Looking back at the protests of the 1960s, Doug McAdam and Yang Su (2002) find some support for the hypothesis that antiwar protests were responsible for the passage of congressional resolutions against the war. In fact, they find that highly disruptive protests simultaneously increased pro-peace voting in Congress while depressing the pace of congressional actions. Paradoxically, these were the same protests—violent ones or protests that triggered violent repression—that increased public hostility to the antiwar movement. In general, it is difficult to establish a direct relationship between antiwar activism and public policy change.

But like many social movement scholars, McAdam and Su specify the antiwar movement mainly through the numbers of public protests—which mainly meant set-piece demonstrations in public squares—eliding other forms of protest activity that may have been equally or more important. The public burning of draft cards, the presence of Vietnam veterans at peace demonstrations, even the "levitation" of the Pentagon were surprising and innovative performances that caught the attention—if not the approval—of the media. Much like the civil rights movement studied by McAdam (1983) in the previous decade, each attempt by the government to repress contention led the movement against the war to adopt new and more challenging forms of contention.

Three broader forms of contention that went beyond public protest events were important in rolling back the abuse of rights during the Vietnam War and would prove important in future conflicts.

First, the reports of journalists and the publication of government documents detailing the failures and abuses of the war made clear that there were people inside the state who were willing to use their access to classified materials to challenge the government's credibility. Of these, by far the most spectacular was the "Pentagon Papers," the Defense Department's secret history of U.S. decision making during the war prior to 1967, released by Daniel Ellsberg. Published in the *New York Times* and the *Washington Post*, the Pentagon's own history "directly contradicted the official myth of America as a reluctant intervener in Vietnam's affairs" and revealed that the government had "systematically deceived its own people about its behavior and intentions" (DeBenedetti 1990, 314–15).[23] The "Pentagon Papers" may have done more to damage the credibility of the government's prosecution of the war than all the protests that were mounted over the length of the war.

Second, what we might wish to call counterintelligence operations, most spectacularly the break-in of a Philadelphia-area FBI office (Medsger 2013), uncovered evidence of the Bureau's illegal activities. The Citizens' Commission to Investigate the FBI first passed the documents it found on to two members of Congress, Parren Mitchell (D-Maryland) and George McGovern (D-South Dakota), before releasing them to the *New York Times*, the *Washington Post*, and the *Los Angeles Times* (Davis 1997, 10–14). When he saw them, Carl Stern, NBC journalist, demanded that still more documents be released. When the Justice Department refused to do so, Stern's lawyers filed a civil action in U.S. District Court and a U.S. district judge decided that the documents should be released (ibid., 16–17). It was in the light of these documents and the emerging Watergate drama that the Church Committee was created.

Third, although the energy of the antiwar movement eroded as the war wound down and militant members of the movement—such as the Weathermen—moved into armed struggle, a second-generation movement against the excesses of the surveillance state developed out of the antiwar movement. This was not a classical social movement, marked by public protests and overheated rhetoric, but a quiet coalition of "good government activists, investigative journalists, elected officials, and public interest groups" who worked both inside and outside Congress to make the reform of the national security state possible (Scott 2013, 183). Some of their efforts—such as the FOIA and the creation of permanent congressional intelligence committees—survived into new attempts to roll back executive expansion; others—such as FISA—have been bent out of recognition (see chapter 7); and still others have been made irrelevant by the march of technology and the ability of the government to employ it without changing the law (see chapter 9). After four decades in which executive power grew and civil liberties were abused, the end of the Vietnam decade brought a scaling back of executive power and a revival of concern for civil liberties. In these reversals, contentious politics played a key role.

Conclusions

This chapter will have succeeded if it has demonstrated evidence for four claims:

- From World War One onward, there has been a determined use of hierarchical power to construct a national security state, bolstered by an intimate connection between the federal government and security-based industry, and a widespread use of infrastructural power to gain support of war-making.
- There was opposition to almost all these wars, but contention was almost always contained, controlled, and repressed. The one exception was

opposition to the Vietnam War, when the government went well beyond its traditional mechanisms of engaging and mobilizing the citizens to launch a concerted attack on privacy and civil liberties.

- The Vietnam War in particular shows that war offers domestic incentives to leaders and their opponents to go around the law to prosecute dissent and suppress opponents.
- But the Vietnam War also shows that determined citizens and elites, when they are under pressure to support an unpopular war, can be remarkably innovative in the forms of contention they devise.

As we will see in the next three chapters, elites determined to go to war can find new ways to evade reforms created to control their actions in the previous war. This forces civil society activists to search for new and more ingenious means of opposing emergency rule. In response, activists engage in the kinds of mass protests we have seen in the movement against the Vietnam War, but they also invent new repertoires of contention, both against and within the state's infrastructural power.

THE WAR AT HOME, 2001–2013

Three factors changed fundamentally between the conflicts examined in chapter 6 and the U.S. wars of the early twenty-first century. First, these wars both lasted longer than past conflicts and bled into one another in a conflict that combined conventional war-making with a war against Islamist radicalism. Second, the American state had grown more powerful but at the same time was more porous. Third, the enemy that triggered this series of wars looked more like a transnational social movement than a state enemy, making the enemy both more elusive and making ignoring the laws of war more tempting in dealing with it. To respond to these interlaced dilemmas, the American state deployed both hierarchical and infrastructural power to defeat this elusive enemy and create consensus at home.

In comparison to the composite conflicts sketched in chapter 5, the U.S. global War on Terror had several special features: a homeland security system that invaded Americans' privacy more than ever before, an expanded use of the media to create and maintain support for war-making, and the extended use of emergency powers—many of them digital—to detect and deal with alien enemies (Cole 2003). In general terms, the crisis of 9/11 allowed a president who represented a minority of the electorate and his administration to gain the power to construct a system of emergency powers.

These powers and the responses to them in the United States will be investigated in detail in this and the next two chapters. This chapter examines how the global War on Terror was constructed by the first administration of George W.

Bush and Richard Cheney, and how the rule of law was transformed into rule *by* law to justify the administration's ambitions. I focus on how the wars following 9/11 were framed by the government, on the role of the media in communicating that construction to the public, and on how government lawyers tried to reshape the law. In chapter 8, I turn to the implications for the American state of its enduring wars, and in chapter 9, I examine resistance to the wars in domestic politics in the streets, in civil society, and in the courts. In chapter 10, I turn to the international spinoffs of these policies and their effects on the institutions that were born under the star of liberal internationalism.

Creating an Atmosphere for Illegality

The major problem—but also the major opportunity—for U.S. leaders after 9/11 was that the enemy was a nonstate actor that was largely unknown to the majority of the population. This created a diffuse sense of threat that engendered public distrust, both in general and toward Arab Americans. "Years out from 9/11," write Jennifer Merolla and Elizabeth Zechmeister, "32 percent of the public thought U.S. Muslims are more loyal to Islam than [to] the United States, 19 percent thought U.S. Muslims condone violence, and 54 percent were worried about radicals within the U.S. Muslim community" (2009, 10–11). More startling still, the proportion of Americans with unfavorable attitudes toward Islam grew from 39 percent in October 2001 to 49 percent in 2010 (Margulies 2013, 141). These negative views increased most rapidly among those who were sympathetic to Bush's policies, 85 percent of whom held a negative view of Muslims by 2010 (ibid., 144). The unknown nature of the enemy and the growing antipathy toward Muslims facilitated a radical centralization of power in the executive and the illegal policies it followed.

These policies were facilitated by the fact that al Qaeda was not a state.[1] This had legal, cultural, and political implications.

Legally, the nonstate nature of the movement gave the administration enormous latitude in how it dealt with captured militants.[2] The Bush administration claimed that the Geneva Conventions did not apply to these belligerents because they were "unlawful" combatants. By extension, it was argued, the Geneva conventions did not apply to the Taliban either because its fighters were agents of a failed state. International lawyers would fight over these designations for years, but in the atmosphere of rage and angst over 9/11, such fine distinctions escaped most Americans. In the meantime, the United States rounded up thousands of detainees—many of them bought from warlords in Afghanistan.

Culturally, the nonstate nature of the movement made it hard to encompass in the American imagination. Americans know what to make of a state that is dangerous—even evil; but mysterious bearded foreigners hiding in caves in the mountains of Afghanistan and Pakistan were much harder to comprehend in the American creed (Margulies 2013). This made it easier for the government to treat suspects as if they had no rights at all.

Politically, for the first time in its history, the United States faced an adversary that was geographically dispersed, lacked an institutional presence, and was driven by a mentality more like that of a social movement than a state. To complicate matters, al Qaeda was a *transnational* movement, with a structure based on widely dispersed networks that could not easily be attacked, a guiding frame that was world-historical rather than policy oriented and a tactical repertoire that ranged from the conventional to the extremely violent. In al Qaeda, U.S. decision makers faced an opponent who was foreign in every sense of the word.

This foreignness created uncertainty; uncertainty fostered fear; and fear created ambiguities, overlapping jurisdictions, and confusion. But it also gave the administration enormous discretion in how to treat the al Qaeda and Taliban detainees. After 9/11, the Bush administration fashioned policies of questionable legality and—in the name of rooting out the common enemy—undertook a war in Iraq that was illegal under international law and created even more enemies. The infinitely expandable term *homeland security*, adopted as an official mantra after 9/11, helped the administration to justify its actions even when these actions were far from home.

Homeland Insecurity

The term *homeland security* first appeared in a proposal by a group of strategic thinkers calling themselves the Catastrophic Terrorism Study Group (Carter, Deutsch, and Zelikow 1998).[3] The group's report criticized the dispersion of domestic and foreign intelligence efforts that had contributed to the failure to detect either the 1993 attack on the World Trade Center or the 1998 bombing of the U.S. embassies in Kenya and Tanzania. The report called for bridging what its authors called the "law enforcement/national security divide" (ibid., 80). It presaged a shift in strategic attention from foreign states to nonstate actors, to the concealment of weapons development, and to unconventional deployments. It also called for the involvement of the private sector in the government's intelligence apparatus (see chapter 8) and a global expansion of U.S. efforts to seek out the sources and the agents of terrorism. Most important was the team's effort to signal to the government that "the threat of catastrophic terrorism spans the globe, defying ready classification as solely foreign or domestic" (ibid, 81).

The advent of 9/11 was dramatic evidence that the Study Group's fears were well founded. In the reflection and self-reflection that followed, many of its ideas for reorganizing the national security system reappeared. But, in the wake of the tragedy, the most important reaction was the sense of threat: threat to the government, to the armed forces, and, especially to the "homeland" (a term that first appears in the Study Group's rhetoric).[4] Underlying all the government's policy responses to 9/11 was the idea that the homeland was in peril and that Americans needed to be kept safe from the threat from outside.

Although there were plenty of reasons for Americans to feel threatened after 9/11, the sense of threat radiated outward from the administration. Assistant Attorney General Jack Goldsmith wrote that "It is hard to overstate the impact that the incessant waves of threat reports have on the judgment of people inside the executive branch who are responsible for protecting American lives" (2007, 72). Administration figures "never tired in propagandizing the threat of terrorism and the need to battle it" (Nacos, Bloch-Elkon, and Shapiro 2011, 43). Defense Secretary Donald Rumsfeld instructed his staff to keep terrorism alive as an issue.[5] The system of colored threat levels showed how easy it was to manipulate public opinion in a period of fear and uncertainty. These warnings were changed so often that they eventually became the butt of ridicule on late-night television (ibid., 31). Some administration figures were called on the carpet for not buying into the threat narrative more urgently.[6]

In surveys beginning in 2001, when voters were asked how worried they were about being victims of terrorism, the "combined worry" category of voters rose to 50 percent after 9/11 and never went below 45 percent as late as 2005 (Merolla and Zechmeister 2009, 6–7). Although public fear of terrorist attacks declined in the immediate aftermath of 9/11, it continued at a high level in the years that followed (Nacos, Bloch-Elkon, and Shapiro 2011, 52). As Brigitte Nacos and her collaborators note, although the number of those who were concerned with the fear of terrorism "a great deal" gave way to those who were "somewhat concerned," "Around the seventh anniversary of the 9/11 attacks, three of five Americans still expressed such concerns"; "very few people thought that major terrorist attacks were 'not likely at all' in the future" (ibid, 443).

Fear of terrorism even cropped up in the administration's response to Hurricane Katrina in 2005. Amid the human devastation that followed the natural disaster, the U.S. Northern Command reminded commanders who had been sent to the region that "The real world terrorist threat still exists and to remain vigilant. . . . Remain aware of potential terrorist and extremist threats and continue to report suspicious activity" (reported in Arkin 2013, 75). After Katrina, David Addington, Vice President Cheney's chief-of-staff, seemed more worried about the possibility of an insurrection than about the massive human tragedy occurring on the Gulf Coast (reported in ibid., 62).

The pervasive sense of insecurity made it easier for the administration to overcome the public's underlying skepticism about foreign military adventures and offered an opening to justify an attack on Iraq in 2003. If Saddam Hussein could somehow be linked to the bombers of the September 11 outrages, it would be easier to convince the public that the assault on Iraq was a defensive war. Three years after Vice President Cheney made the demonstrably false claim that there were ties between Osama bin Laden and the Iraqi dictator, 64 percent of the public still believed the fabrication (Bennett, Lawrence, and Livingston 2007, 22). The failure of the antiwar movement to stop the rush to war in late 2002 and early 2003 had much to do with the public's willingness to believe that Sadaam Hussein was somehow connected to the terrorists of 9/11 (see chapter 9).

Many of the administration's claims backing the attack on Iraq were based on specious or concocted evidence—such as the idea that the aluminum tubes observed from the air were meant to be used in producing weapons of mass destruction or the claim that Iraq had purchased "yellowcake" uranium in Africa for making nuclear weapons. The former claim was quietly dropped after CIA technicians shot it down, while the latter was punctured by Joseph Wilson, a former diplomat whose wife, Valerie Plame Wilson, was "outed" from her CIA position by the administration in retaliation for his exposure of the "yellowcake" lie. Plame later told the story of how she was paid back for her husband's exposure in a best-selling book (Wilson 2007).

The diffuse sense of threat created by 9/11 and manipulated by the administration also affected the outcomes of elections. The Bush-Cheney team fought the 2004 election, in part, based on their claim that they could do a better job of keeping the country safe from terrorism than John Kerry, once an antiwar activist. When a carefully orchestrated swiftboat campaign cast doubt on Kerry's war service and painted his antiwar activism on his return from Vietnam as tantamount to treason, he lost his early lead and was easily defeated by the Bush-Cheney team.[7] When Osama Bin Laden sent a threatening video message a few days before the election, both Attorney General John Ashcroft and Defense Secretary Rumsfeld leapt on it and tried to get Department of Homeland Security (DHS) Secretary Ridge to elevate the threat level. Troubled by this openly political ploy, Ridge asked himself, "Is this about security or politics?"[8] Whether security or politics, the ploy worked. "Exit polls and post-election surveys showed that Bush [in the 2004 election] benefited from voters most concerned with terrorism" (Nacos, Bloch-Elkon, and Shapiro 2011, 55).

Enemy Aliens

Support for civil liberties suffered serious erosion in these years. After a brief honeymoon period after 9/11 when Americans appeared to embrace traditional libertarian values, there was a decline in support for specific areas of civil liberties, which endured over time, even after the end of the Bush administration and the election of Barack Obama (Brooks and Manza 2013, 72–73). Survey work by Clem Brooks and Jeff Manza and secondary analyses by Joseph Margulies and Brigitte Nacos and her collaborators both show that, although attitudes toward the protection of civil liberties remained positive in the abstract, the decade following 9/11 saw a rise in hostility to Muslims, growing indifference to torture and to illegal detention, and even a decline of trust in general.[9] When the public was asked about specific issues such as the possible closure of Guantánamo, large majorities chose options limiting the rights of detainees (ibid., 65).

In the months after 9/11, hundreds of Arab Americans were summarily detained in places such as the Metropolitan Detention Center (MDC) in Brooklyn. Among the documented abuses, many of the men had their faces smashed into a wall where guards had pinned a t-shirt with a picture of an American flag and the words, "These colors don't run." Despite the fact that none of these men was ever charged with a terrorist offense, many were held in the MDC for eight months and some were deported on immigration charges.[10] But were the Bush administration's drumbeat of threat and its rush to war entirely responsible for the public's pliability? Between the administration's construction of 9/11 and the public's frightened reactions were the media.

The Media and the War on Terror

As many scholars of communication have shown, the Bush administration was alert to managing the news and to framing it so as to marginalize critics of its policies (Nacos, Bloch-Elkon, and Shapiro 2011). With the Iraqi insurgency growing, the government released figures claiming that 2003 "saw the lowest number of international terrorist attacks since 1969." The story was true as far as it went, but two academic analysts, Alan Kreuger and David Laitin, revealed that the alleged decline was actually the result of "a decline in non-significant events." The researchers found that, in the year following the attack on Iraq, more serious terrorist attacks had actually reached their highest level since 1982 (Kreuger and Laitin 2004, 1). At the same time, the administration coopted a good part of the press by "embedding" reporters with the invading force in Iraq.

The government's ability to manipulate the media in wartime is not automatic; it depends, among other things, on the news values of the media, on the cooperation of willing publishers and editors, and on the political context in which the news happens.

In terms of news values, the media are more inclined to give prominence to the onset of a crisis than to the crisis resolution. Each time the government raised the color alert from yellow to orange, the media allocated prominent lead segments to the story. But when the DHS announced that the threat of imminent attacks had declined, the media gave the story less prominent attention. Brigitte Nacos and her collaborators find that the national media allocated an average of 642 words to each "imminent" threat of terrorism but only 43 percent reported reductions of terror alerts. In addition, 100 percent of the announcements of terror alert increases were reported at the top of newscasts, but only 13 percent of announced reductions of terror alerts were reported (Nacos, Bloch-Elkon, and Shapiro 2011, 38–39).

In terms of compliant publishers and editors, the mainstream media depend on cooperation from government officials and are often loath to publish stories that are critical of its behavior. When the Bush administration made extravagant claims about the threat to the United States posed by Saddam Hussein, these claims were given front-page prominence by the press, but warnings about the unreliability of the evidence usually appeared on back pages. For example, in the run-up to the attack on Iraq, when the administration claimed that Sadaam Hussein was seeking materials for nuclear weapons, the story was covered in the *New York Times* with a lead article headlined "U.S. Says Hussein Intensified Quest for A-Bomb Parts." Five days later, when the *Times* discovered that the intelligence agencies were not convinced of these claims, the story appeared on the paper's inside pages.[11]

Media transmission of how the government frames the news is not automatic; it needs to be "indexed." As Lance Bennett and his collaborators write; "When prominent officials or institutions are in public conflict over an issue, the news gates of the mainstream American press typically open to admit a wider range of voices and viewpoints from society, including advocacy groups, interest organizations, policy experts, and members of communities" (Bennett, Lawrence, and Livingston 2007, 40). But when the official line is unopposed by other powerful actors, then the media "report much the same stories in the much the same terms, because they track the inside power game of Washington politics so closely" (ibid., 4). "Information that may challenge and even undermine official accounts of events is so often screened out of mainstream news unless there is an opposing official to be the champion who brings in the story" (ibid., 6).

But the most important "opposing official" in responding to the Bush administration's claims was missing. It was the Democratic Party, which was so intimidated by the horrors of 9/11 and so frightened by being labeled disloyal if it questioned official policy that it went along with the administration's framing. As Bennett and his collaborators observe, virtually all Democratic members of Congress were seriously compromised by "a series of consistently narrow strategic political calculations that cautioned against challenging an initially popular president who had wrapped himself and his war in the flag and every other high patriotic symbol" (ibid., 33). The result was that the press published unchallenged whatever official story emerged from the well-oiled media-management machine of the White House and the Department of Defense, at least at first. In the absence of a lively debate in the political class about what the government was doing, the news was framed in ways that turned the public's attention away from issues that should have concerned it.

Consider how the Abu Ghraib scandal was shaped by the government and indexed by the media. For a brief moment, the reports of torture in this prison in Iraq threatened to expose the widespread abuse of prisoners, which we now know was legitimated from above (ibid., chap. 3). The photos from the prison showed degrading treatment of prisoners, "including building pyramids with their naked bodies and leashing them like dogs; sexual humiliation . . . and brutality, such as threatening naked prisoners with unmuzzled dogs and posing, grinning, beside a prisoner's corpse" (ibid, 72–73).

Abu Ghraib might have led to the exposure of the harsh interrogation techniques that higher officials had approved, not only in Iraq but in Afghanistan, Guantánamo, and an archipelago of "dark sites" maintained by the CIA around the world. But at the request of the Pentagon, CBS news withheld the story for two weeks, giving the government time to frame it, minimize it as the result of "a few bad apples," and give the Pentagon time to investigate it internally. By the time the story aired, the administration had its story ready; Abu Ghraib was the result of isolated cases of mistreatment at the hands of a few low-level soldiers (ibid., 73).

It is no surprise that a government that was abusing detainees for the better part of two years would want to suppress information about its interrogation practices. What was more distressing was that most of the press ignored the growing evidence that the torture of prisoners was systematic and was authorized from above. After some hesitation, most of the press bought into the official story that the Abu Ghraib photos indicated nothing more than what President Bush called "disgraceful conduct by a few American troops, who dishonored our country and disregarded our values" (quoted in ibid.). Torture became a topic of public debate only in 2005 when respected Senator John McCain (R-Arizona), who had been tortured as a prisoner in Vietnam, launched a debate about the administration's policies. Only when opposition was legitimated by someone with the status of McCain did the press begin to index the practice as "torture."

Friendly critics, such as Jack Goldsmith, point to the few intrepid reporters who exposed the administration's illegal policies as part of what he calls "accountability journalism," "the idea that journalists should root out and explain the secret or unknown operations of powerful institutions so that citizens can hold these institutions to account for their actions" (Goldsmith 2012, chap. 3). Goldsmith is thinking of such actions as the exposure of the secret CIA's dark sites in 2005. Indeed, outposts such as the *Post*, the *New York Times*, and *The Guardian* stood out for their intrepid investigative reporting and their willingness to brave lawsuits or worse (see chapter 9). In the face of the general willingness of the media to buy into the government's lies, exaggerations, and omissions, they were rare outposts of journalistic integrity.

Given the veil of secrecy around the government's detention policies, the absence of a strong opposition voice, and the media's "indexing" the news around the administration's lines, there was little for a prospective social movement to go on. This may be one reason for the inability of the antiwar movement eighteen months later to stop the rush to war and for the collapse of that movement soon afterward (see chapter 9). In the absence of an active press and a vigorous opposition party, the opposition to the Bush administration's policies would have to await the actions of an unconventional minority of digital protesters long after the administration itself was gone (see chapter 9).

Writing an Emergency Script

There has been so much excellent work on the war, detention, and surveillance policies of the Bush administration that the best I can do here is summarize the work of others.

In their thoughtful book on public opinion since 9/11, Clem Brooks and Jeff Manza (2013, 28) offer a convenient summary of the policy changes that were made in the years following 9/11. The first act was the passage of the US Patriot Act of 2001, later amended and expanded in 2006, and renewed again in 2011 under the Obama administration.[12] The act's Section 215 was the foundation for the future expansion of the NSA's surveillance programs, which went well beyond the intentions of the legislators who had passed it. Indeed, when in 2013 Edward Snowden exposed the extent of the NSA's spying on Americans and others, Representative James Sensenbrenner (R-Wisconsin), who was deeply involved in crafting the Patriot Act, launched a legislative effort to revoke it.[13]

This was not the limit of the emergency script written by the administration after 9/11. It authorized of the CIA to seize suspected members of al Qaeda or associated organizations without seeking authorization from the countries where they were found and bring them to secret detention centers for interrogation; authorized the agency to assassinate members of al Qaeda and other terror organizations, again without seeking authorization from foreign governments; authorized expanded foreign and domestic surveillance by the intelligence agencies, including wiretapping and reading e-mail and other Internet communication without formal court authorization; secretly authorized the rendition of suspects to foreign states where they might be tortured or otherwise abused; authorized the use of "enhanced interrogation" techniques against terrorist suspects; adopted extensive new security requirements for airports, ports, and federal buildings; and encouraged the adoption of similar requirements by states, local governments, and other nations (see Scheppele 2006; see also chapter 9).

Underlying all these radical expansions of executive power was the Authorization for the Use of Military Force that was passed by Congress after 9/11.[14] That law granted to the president the power to use all necessary and appropriate force against al Qaeda and organizations responsible for the 9/11 attacks.

Guantánamo and the Military Commissions

The most visible expansion of the emergency script came quickly in the establishment of the U.S. military base at Guantánamo Bay, Cuba, as a holding location for suspected terrorists. This was justified as a technical and logistical move, but its real meaning was to place suspects in the power of the government but theoretically outside the jurisdiction of the U.S. courts.

Of all the administration's national security moves, this was the one that caused the most controversy. It was where Defense Secretary Rumsfelt claimed the government had placed "the worst of the worst"; where, at first, not even the names of the detainees were released; from where rumors of physical abuse and religious mistreatment soon leaked out; and where lawyers for the detainees were heavily restricted in access to their clients, who were denied access to the bases of their incarceration.[15] Given the breadth of the executive's definition of legitimate targets, Guantánamo was soon crammed with people who had little or nothing to do with al Qaeda and nothing at all to do with 9/11 (Ohlin 2015, 126). The administration extended this authority to "associated forces" of al Qaeda (ibid.). But although the term had no legal meaning and went well beyond the attackers of 9/11, it reappeared in the 2006 Military Commissions Act.[16] Guantánamo became the symbol of the fact that the administration was ratcheting up its campaign from al Qaeda and the Taliban to radical Islam in general.[17]

In line with its assertion that Guantánamo was outside the jurisdiction of U.S. courts, the administration set up a military commission system, offering the detainees no due process rights and heavily restricting their and their attorneys' access to the information on the basis of which they had been detained. Although national security was asserted as the reason for this restriction, it was at least as likely that the administration was holding a number of prisoners whose only crime had been being in the wrong place at the wrong time and that—were they to be put on trial under U.S. law—they would have been released because they had been tortured. Military commissions were seen as a solution to all these problems. The commissions would furnish the appearance of rule of law while using a simulacrum of the law.

But these commissions turned out to be an albatross around the administration's neck. A series of court cases made it clear that the administration could not simply create new institutions when it did not like the existing ones. The first case to come down from the Supreme Court was *Hamden v. Rumsfeld* (548 US 557) in 2006, in which the court ruled that the prisoners were entitled to the minimal protections of Common Article 3 of the Geneva Conventions. The administration responded by asking Congress to pass the Military Commissions Act of 2006, which prohibited prisoners who had been classified as enemy combatants or were awaiting hearings on their status from using *habeas corpus* to petition federal courts in challenges to their detention. In turn, this act was declared unconstitutional by the Court in the case of *Boumediene v. Bush* (553 US 723) in 2008, at which point the newly elected Obama administration revised the earlier act, providing somewhat greater procedural rights to the detainees.[18]

Even with the Obama era's softening, however, these were still "special courts," similar to the British Diplock Courts in Northern Ireland in all but name (Ni Aolain and Gross 2013). There was another similarity to the British emergency script as well—the use of torture as an instrument of interrogation. This was the most profound transformation of the rule of law into rule by law because it was theorized and authorized by lawyers in the heart of the institution that had been established to defend the rule of law—the U.S. Department of Justice.

From Rule of Law to Rule by Law

In the Vietnam War, the Nixon White House simply ignored both the law and the Constitution, as we have seen in the last chapter; but the Bush administration ruled *by* law. As Jens Ohlin writes, "When Bush ordered the creation of CIA black sites in Eastern Europe, he did it because government attorneys said that he could" (2015, 24–25). This was true in many aspects of the law on terror but most notoriously in the detention and treatment of prisoners. In March 2002, when the Inter-American Commission on Human Rights asked the administration to establish the legal status of detainees through a competent tribunal, the government claimed to be acting consistently with the Geneva Conventions (see chapter 10). Under cover of international law, the administration was planning to rule *by* law.

In the Bush administration's policies toward detention, the aim was not to narrow the range of prisoners' rights but to deprive them of all rights. The justifications for abuse were carefully plotted by a small group of lawyers in the Office of White House Counsel and the Department of Justice. As David Cole writes, "Justice Department lawyers wrote legal memos that authorized what should have been unthinkable, twisting the law to conform to what the CIA wanted to do, rather than instructing the CIA to conform its conduct to law" (2012, 54).

The first such memo was written by John Yoo and Patrick Philbin, in the Justice Department's Office of Legal Counsel (OLC).[19] In it, Yoo and Philbin did not address the question of the guilt or innocence of the prisoners who were about to arrive in Guantánamo but only the question of whether a federal court would have jurisdiction to receive a petition for a writ of *habeas corpus* on behalf of any of them. Yoo and Philbin relied on a well-known World War Two case, *Johnson v. Eisentrager* (339 U.S. 763, 1950), in which the Supreme Court had ruled that German nationals, caught in China toward the end of the war, did not have *habeas* rights in the federal court system. What Yoo and Philbin ignored in using *Eisentrager*, however, was that the Germans were citizens of a country then at war with the United States and were tried when China was an active theater of war. Moreover, they had received a trial before a military commission with rights that resembled those they would have enjoyed in the federal courts. Yet in a caricature of legal reasoning, Yoo and Philbin relied on *Eisentrager* to argue that Guantánamo in 2002 was legally equivalent to China and Germany in 1945 (Margulies 2006, 48–49).

The "jurisdiction memo" was struck down by the Supreme Court in the first important *habeas* case brought against the administration, *Rasul v. Bush* (542 U.S. 466), which was argued in 2004.[20] But in a second memo, written in early January, 2002, Yoo and Robert Delahaunty argued that the prisoners detained in Afghanistan did not enjoy the protections of the Third Geneva Convention because they were not identifiably prisoners of war; nor did they enjoy the protections of the Fourth Convention, which protects nonbelligerents because they were not "civilians" but "unlawful combatants."[21] Not only that—the government's lawyers ignored the practice, set out in Geneva III and followed by the U.S. army in Vietnam and as recently as the 1990 Gulf War, of resolving all doubtful cases about prisoner-of-war (POW) status when prisoners are taken through Article 5 tribunals.[22] Until then, prisoners were supposed to enjoy the fundamental rights of POWs. For Yoo and Delahaunty, the president, exercising his commander-in-chief and chief executive powers, could dispense with Article 5 hearings by declaring that there was no doubt about their status (Margulies 2006, 56–57).

Given that most of these detainees were not captured by U.S. troops but were swept up by bounty hunters in Afghanistan, most of them turned out to have little or no intelligence value. The same would turn out to be true in Iraq, where "Large quantities of detainees with little or no intelligence value swelled Abu Ghraib's population" (quoted in Danner 2004, 31).[23] The government's lawyers dismissed the statutory commitment to abide by the Geneva Conventions or the Convention Against Torture in its treatment of detainees. This amounted to "the frank declaration by the administration," in the face of both its international commitments and its domestic law, that in war "the law is really silent" (Margulies 2006, 58).

What does it mean to say that the law is silent? It would not take long to find out. On August 1, 2002, Yoo and Assistant Attorney General Jay Bybee sent the most notorious of the "torture memos" to Alberto Gonzales, counsel to the president.[24] Gonzales was concerned about whether the methods being employed in Guantánamo Bay would expose CIA interrogators to prosecution for the aggressive interrogation techniques they were using in what later emerged as dark sites for high-value prisoners. In a phrase that resounds sickeningly even today, they defined torture to include only such pain as is "equivalent in intensity to the pain accompanying serious physical injury, such as organ failure, impairment of bodily function, or even death" (see the Bybee memo, reprinted in Greenberg and Dratel 2005, 172). With so restrictive a definition of torture, it followed that most of what the CIA interrogators were doing could be classified as to no more than "enhanced interrogation."[25]

Diffusion from the Dark Sites

The administration's use of the law to justify torture began in the dark sites and diffused from there to Guantánamo, and from there to Afghanistan, and then to Iraq. In September, Guantánamo interrogators traveled to Fort Bragg, North Carolina, to get information from instructors who were training the armed forces to resist torture (the SERE [Survival, Evasion, Resistance, and Escape] program). A week later, "two Guantánamo behavioral scientists who had attended the Fort Bragg training drafted a memo proposing tougher interrogation techniques." In December, Secretary Rumsfeld signed a memo authorizing coercive techniques such as those described in the Yoo and Bybee memos to guide interrogators in Guantánamo. A copy of the Rumsfeld memo was then sent to Afghanistan, "where it continued to influence military interrogation practices long after it had been rescinded at Guantánamo. From there, the techniques made their way to Iraq." By March 2003, the OLC lawyers repeated to the Defense Department the legal opinions they had written to Gonzales for the CIA.[26] "The results were broadcast to the world on June 2004 in the Abu Ghraib photos" (Cole and Sands 2009, 16–17). Although they had been written narrowly to guide the CIA's treatment of the relatively small number of detainees held in the dark sites, the torture memos provided guidance that came to govern all interrogations in the War on Terror during the first Bush administration (Margulies 2006, 89).

The administration's legal memos purported to give the president the right to decide on the use of interrogation methods that Congress, in its 1994 statute implementing the Convention Against Torture, had banned. If the memos were allowed to stand, the president could also ignore the 1973 War Powers Resolution, a point that Yoo made in another memo of September 25, 2001.[27] They also ignored settled Supreme Court doctrine that the president could not act when Congress had deliberately expressed contrary views (*Youngstown Sheet and Tube Co. v. Sawyer*, 343 U.S. 579 [1952]).[28] In effect, the government lawyers claimed that once the president has invoked his commander-in-chief power, Congress's hands are tied and the Supreme Court has nothing to say about it.

Although these memos remained secret until they were released by the *Washington Post*, *Newsweek*, and the ACLU in 2005, Yoo, Bybee, and their collaborators did not go uncriticized. The most explosive reaction was that of Navy General Counsel Alberto Mora, whose memorandum criticizing the memos seethed with outrage. But after Rumsfeld rescinded his order, Mora's objections were whittled away by a working group of armed forces lawyers that was formed to work out interrogation guidelines.[29] Less volatile was the reaction of Jack Goldsmith when he became head of the OLC in October 2003. Goldsmith thought the Fourth Geneva Convention applied to native Iraqis, whether they were members of al Qaeda or any other terrorist group—although not to terrorists from foreign countries. "I also told [Attorney General] Ashcroft," Goldsmith remembers, "that violation of the Geneva Conventions in Iraq could be punishable under the domestic war crimes statute" (2007, 40–41).[30] Goldsmith eventually resigned over these differences.

After the 2002 memos became public and the Abu Ghraib abuses were exposed, Congress—led by Senator McCain—began to be restive with the administration's detention policies. But the OLC lawyers and the administration did not back down. Stephen Bradbury, who took over OLC in 2005, avoided the dismissive language of his 2002 predecessors but supported their conclusion that the techniques outlined in 2002 did not constitute torture. U.S. soldiers subjected to the SERE techniques in training, Bradbury assured his readers, "had not exhibited signs of severe physical pain or suffering or prolonged mental harm."[31] Meanwhile, Congress was working toward passing what became the Detainee Treatment Act of 2005.[32] But as Cole and Sands conclude, "even if Congress prevailed, the legal change would have no effect on the CIA's program" (2009, 31).

Is the distinction between rule of law and rule by law a distinction without a difference? I think not. First, rule by law convinces both decision makers and operatives that their illegal behavior is legally protected. An explicit motive of the OLC lawyers was to assure CIA interrogators that they would not be punished for their abuses. Second, engaging in rule by law provides a defense against the charge that they are breaking the law. Over time, and repeated often enough, this can create a "new normal," or at least a new content for long-legitimated symbols of the American creed (Margulies 2013). Finally, "legalizing" illegality draws opponents into the field of law, which is time-consuming, is expensive, and draws resources and energies away from other forms of contention, as we will see in chapter 9.

Afterword

On May 23, 2013, President Barack Obama spoke to the National Defense University at Fort McNair, near Washington, D.C. After greeting the audience, mostly made up of military officers, he recalled what had happened after September 11, 2001. "And so our nation went to war," he recalled. "We have now been at war for well over a decade. I won't review the full history. What is clear is that we quickly drove al Qaeda out of Afghanistan, but then shifted our focus and began a new war in Iraq. And this carried significant consequences for our fight against al Qaeda, our standing in the world, and—to this day—our interests in a vital region."

"Meanwhile," he continued, "we strengthened our defenses—hardening targets, tightening transportation security, giving law enforcement new tools to prevent terror. Most of these changes were sound. Some caused inconvenience. But some, like expanded surveillance, raised difficult questions about the balance that we strike between our interests in security and our values of privacy. And in some cases, I believe we compromised our basic values—by using torture to interrogate our enemies, and detaining individuals in a way that ran counter to the rule of law."[33]

It is ironic that, although he announced an end to prisoner abuse and the closure of the dark sites, Obama expanded the drone program that he had inherited from the Bush administration, killing many more people through this form of distant assassination than his predecessor had done. It is true that Congress stopped Obama and Eric Holder, his attorney general, from bringing detainees to the United States for trial by raising the political price for doing so; but the new president also maintained the practice of indefinite detention for prisoners who could not be convicted in court.

It is interesting that Obama, who was trying to put an end to the U.S. wars of the twenty-first century, should have turned so quickly to American "values." Values made a good rhetorical shift from the most illegal practices of the Bush administration, but this was a shift in rhetoric rather than in substance. Even the use of the law was not very different than the rule by law followed by Obama's predecessor, except for the rhetoric. "When President Obama ordered the targeted killing of an American citizen in Yemen," writes Jens Ohlin, "he did so only after the Justice Department said it was legal" (2015, 24–25).

Obama was not alone in invoking American values. When Americans think of the cataclysm that befell their country on September 11, 2001, they often turn to values: 9/11 "changed everything"; it was an event that caused the nation to "lose its values"; one that led to the insistence that "these values should not be changed"; or, alternatively, one that that led Americans to change their values in the name of saving them. Joseph Margulies observes, "When Americans come upon a social arrangement they want to preserve, they do not alter their behavior to fit their values; they alter their values to fit their behavior" (2013, ix–xi).

Who were the "Americans" who altered their values to fit their behavior? A terrorized public opinion did play a passive role in this shift. But as I have shown in this chapter, and as Secretary Ridge eventually realized, 9/11 was constructed by a White House and vice president's office that were determined to expand the power of what they regarded as "the unitary executive," and by a media establishment that—in the absence of challenging statements from an intimidated Democratic Party—indexed its coverage to jibe with the administration's message.

But the emergency script that was written after September 11, 2001, cannot be blamed entirely on an elite conspiracy. As we saw in chapter 6, the roots and the branches of the national security state go back to the end of World War Two and have expanded incrementally with each new security threat. Moreover, it is too simple to see the emergency practices that were installed after September 11 only as an expression of hierarchical power; a panoply of organizations and institutions were drawn into the administration's programs in a system of "governed interdependence," to adopt the useful term of Linda Weiss (2014), that allowed the government to use and expand its instruments of power into civil society. The effects of the U.S. wars of the early twenty-first century on its hierarchical and infrastructural power is the subject of the next chapter.

THE AMERICAN STATE OF TERROR

Twelve and a half years after 9/11, on January 22, 2014, the U.S. Justice Department filed a civil suit against a company that provides background security checks on prospective government employees and contractors.[1] According to the government's complaint, the U.S. Investigations Service (USIS) was estimated to have received $16 million in payouts from the federal government for at least 650,000 security clearances that were never carried out. The story would not have attracted much notice but for the fact that among the job candidates for whom false security clearances were filed were Edward Snowden, who would later make the largest whistleblower exposures in U.S. history, and Aaron Alexis, the technology contractor who killed twelve people at the Washington Navy Yard in September 2013.[2]

Leaving aside these ironies in the story, what does it tell us about war, state-building, and contention after September 11, 2001? At least three things immediately come to mind. First, the government was waging a new kind of war against a transnational nonstate actor—al Qaeda—that triggered a vast increase of recruitment into the national security state. Second, many of these new recruits did not go to work for the government proper but entered the para-state sector of security contractors—for example, Booz Allen Hamilton, the firm that Snowden worked for in Hawaii. Most of the personnel who were vetted by USIS (a private firm) work in the vast archipelago of security-related firms that have mushroomed in the years since 9/11. Third, this vast expansion of the state's infrastructural links with society opened opportunities for crime (as in the case of Aaron Alexis), for profit (as in the case of USIS), and for contention by citizens such as Edward Snowden who can use their links to the state to challenge its hegemony.

All wars increase the size and the scope of the state, but many of these increases are partially reversed in war's wake This is particularly true in countries such as the United States, with its strong antistate tradition (Friedberg 2000). But the growth of the 9/11 national security state came in the wake of a vast conservative movement to reduce the power of the state. "Government is not the solution," President Ronald Reagan famously said at his first inaugural address; "government is the problem."[3] The result of the contradiction between the growth of the national security state and the neoconservative antistate movement was that most of the growth of in national security recruitment following 9/11 came from outside the government.

In this chapter, I examine the paradox that, as the scope of the American state expanded in response to the threats exposed by 9/11, a good deal of state control leaked out through the state's relations with society. These trends have left the American "state of terror" more intrusive and less sensitive to civil liberties but also less coherent and more vulnerable to new forms of contention—such as the vast electronic whistleblowing of Edward Snowden. In chapter 9, I will examine the contributions of civil society groups to pushing back against government abuses. The national security state expanded enormously in the wake of 9/11, but its impact on civil society was contradictory. Although an immense national security sector was created on the margins of the state, it developed too rapidly and too chaotically for centralized control to be exerted over it.

There is a vast literature on the effects of the massacres of 9/11 and the wars that followed on the American state. Some observers see a fundamental threat to the Constitution in this expansion (Ackerman 2006; Arkin 2013; Fisher 2008); others find it a threat to democracy (Merolla and Zeichmeister 2009); and still others—less pessimistic—see a rollback following the government's excesses (Goldsmith 2012). This was not the first time that Americans wrestled with emergency rule in wartime. The Civil War, as we have seen, was truly regime-threatening and both expanded the scope of the state and impinged on civil liberties. Later wars created smaller emergencies—by which I mean armed conflicts in which the state was not threatened but leaders felt the need to command loyalty, restrict rights, and re-order the relations between the state and civil society. We saw such emergencies in World War One and in the Cold War. But 9/11 was special because the source of the emergency was an unseen and poorly understood transnational movement that could not be easily defeated with conventional means.

In their important book, *Law in Times of Crisis* (2006), Oren Gross and Fionnualla Ní Aoláin, lay out three ways that law can be shaped by emergencies: through accommodation, through "law for all seasons," and through "extra-legality." Although U.S. powerholders bent the law in the direction of their policies after 9/11, the law was actually *used* rather than swept aside, as we saw in the last chapter. This is an important distinction. When we read Carl Schmitt (1985) or Giorgio Agamben (2005), it would appear that all states at war follow what Gross and Ní Aoláin call "models of extra-legality" (2006, :chap. 3). But this assumes that state power is uniformly despotic—"the power of the elite itself *over* civil society" (Mann 1987, 114). In reality, however, modern states also exercise infrastructural power, which "denotes the power of the state to penetrate and centrally coordinate the activities of civil society through its own infrastructure" (ibid; see also Weiss 2006, 2014).

Most of the critics of the Bush administration's excesses focused on the growth in hierarchical power after 9/11. Indeed, there have been broad state intrusions on state and local powers, on congressional prerogatives, and on civil liberties after 9/11. But what these criticisms occlude is that there has also been a vast extension of the state into civil society. Engaged in profit-making activities, largely uncoordinated, a para-state sector has grown up around the government's security functions that is out of sight of ordinary citizens and beyond the capacity of the government to control. Legitimated by the ideology of neoliberalism and driven by war and insecurity, these relationships extend well beyond the traditional links between government and private associations (McConnell 1966) and even beyond the military-industrial complex that worried Eisenhower. The combination of hierarchical and infrastructural power, I argue, explains better than any single factor the capacity of the American state to carry on three interlinked wars during the first decade of the twenty-first century, to reduce the rights of citizens and foreigners, and to manipulate the rule of law.

But the same infrastructural power that enabled the state to mobilize civil society in wartime also encouraged a fragmentation of state structures and a confusion of jurisdictions. It also left opportunities for movements of opposition to the war, to the abuse of power, and to the surveillance of citizens to grow up within it (see chapter 9). In this chapter, I turn first to the expansion of hierarchical power, in particular the power of the state to surveil and monitor public and private behavior; then to the growth of "governed interdependence," both through the contracting out of crucial military functions and in the increasing role of private enterprise in national security; and, finally, to the expansion of surveillance, which has led to a crisis in the relations between the government and the electronic technology sector. The link between the war at home that we saw in the last chapter and the patterns of contention we will examine in chapter 9 was the expansion of the American state through this peculiar combination of hierarchical and infrastructural power.

Expanding Hierarchical Power

In the weeks and months following 9/11, a terrified administration and a compliant Congress adopted a sweeping set of policy changes that expanded the structure of the national security state. The first evidence that something was changing were heightened controls around the country's borders. For example, in the 2003 fiscal year, the budget for border security grew by over $2 billion, with a 29 percent increase in the budget of the Immigration and Naturalization Service (INS), a 26 percent increase for Customs and Border Security, and a major increase for the Coast Guard (Andreas 2003, 92). Thousands of new border police were hired, the formerly loose controls at the Canadian border were tightened, and a new fence began to creep along the U.S.-Mexican border. A side product was an increase in the control and expulsion of nondocumented immigrants, with the result that thousands of frightened Mexican workers were forced to return home.

Expanding Existing Agencies

Both the civilian establishment and the armed forces grew after 9/11. Civilian government employment rose from just over 2.7 million in the 2000 census to almost 2.9 million in 2010.[4] The mainline military did not grow nearly as rapidly, both because political pressures made it impossible to re-institute the draft and because Defense Secretary Rumsfeld believed in a small, highly mechanized force (Segal and Korb 2013). This meant that the wars in Iraq and Afghanistan would be fought by treating the reserves as part of total forces. By 2009, there were 1.3 million soldiers on active duty and another 1.1 million in the National Guard and the reserves (cited in Arkin 2013, 220).

The biggest changes were four. First, Secretary Rumsfeld implemented the theory that fewer, better-trained soldiers would fight more effectively than the larger forces that had gone into Iraq during the Gulf War of 1990. Rumsfeld was convinced that precision strike capabilities would allow the army to fight effectively with little loss of life (Mahnken 2013). Figure 8.1 graphs the relative numbers of the military and civilian personnel in Afghanistan and Iraq after 2001 and the number of private contractors from 2007 on. To satisfy Rumsfeld's productivity obsession, military personnel were forced to cycle in and out of dangerous overseas assignments—some of them two, three, or even four times (Segal and Korb 2013, 124).

Second, there was major growth in the number of civilian personnel in and around the military. The Defense Intelligence Agency grew from 7,500 civilian employees in 2002 to over 16,000 in 2010; the FBI's Joint Terrorism Task Forces grew from 35 to 106 units in the same period (Arkin 2013, 87); and the White

AFGHANISTAN

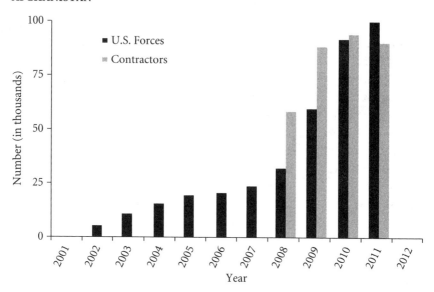

IRAQ

FIGURE 8.1 U.S. forces and military contractors in Afghanistan and Iraq, 2001–2011. Reliable statistics on the number of military contractors in Afghanistan and Iraq were not available until 2007. Private Security Monitor, Sié Chéou-Kang Center, University of Denver, 2014, http://psm.du.edu/national_regulation/united_states/index.html, accessed December 8, 2013.

House Military Office grew from about 800 employees before 9/11 to 2,500, backed by over 2,000 civilian contractors from more than a dozen private companies, by 2004 (ibid., 156–57).

Third, this growth was accompanied by a mushrooming federal budget for national security. By the end of the decade, the total appropriated to the National Intelligence Program—the umbrella organization that was supposed to coordinate all the nation's intelligence agencies—was $53.1 billion. But this figure does not include the military intelligence budget and probably understates the amount that was actually spent: A *Washington Post* article of 2009 estimated that the United States spent $75 billion over the previous year to finance worldwide intelligence operations.[5] Until the imposition of the "sequester" on government spending in 2012, this figure continued to grow.

Finally, the size and complexity of existing security agencies expanded enormously. This growth is best illustrated by changes in the FBI. After 9/11, the bureau established a new unit—the "Weapons of Mass Destruction Directorate—which combined law enforcement, intelligence analysis, and technical expertise" (Arkin 2013, 36). Within the bureau there now are seventy biological, chemical, radiological, and maritime technical teams to assist it in suspicious cases. In addition, "FBI WMD [weapons of mass destruction] coordinators work with biological, chemical, and nuclear specialists from state and local government—and the private sector—to keep abreast of scientific and technical developments that terrorists might exploit" (ibid., 139–41). This leaves aside the almost 200,000 employees in the DHS whose functions partially overlap with the FBI and those in the Defense Department's Military Assistance for Civil Disturbances (MACRIS) program (ibid., 104–5; Noftsinger, Newbold, and Wheeler 2007, chap. 5).

Creating New Organizations

The greatest area of growth after 9/11 was in the creation of new government organizations. In the last three months of 2001 alone, twenty-one new organizations were created, including the office that would become the DHS and the FBI's Foreign Terrorist Tracking Task Force. In 2002, another thirty-four organizations were created; in 2003, there were thirty-nine new organizations; in 2004, another thirty were either created or redirected to the terrorism mission; in 2005, twenty-seven more were created, followed by twenty-four in each of the next three years (Priest and Arkin 2011, 86). The most dramatic structural change was the creation of a new monster Cabinet-level department, the Department of Homeland Security, with its nearly 180,000 employees, drawn from part or all of twenty-two preexisting units of government, including the Coast Guard, the Secret Service, elements of the Department of Justice, the Internal Revenue Service, security guards at airports, and U.S. Customs (Ridge 2009, 131).[6]

The creation of the DHS reflected a combination of institutional tinkering and underlying fear. Drawing from other agencies, the new department was divided into four directorates—Border and Transportation Security, Emergency Preparedness and Response, Science and Technology, and Information Analysis and Infrastructure Protection—and given a mandate to encourage state and local governments in the fight against terrorism. It was also supposed to involve colleges and universities and the private sector in homeland security through grants to these institutions for innovative technologies and practices (Noftsinger, Newbold, and Wheeler 2007, 33–48). DHS Secretary Tom Ridge was particularly concerned to "turn American citizens into partners," "fully informed and prepared for anything" (2009, 72). Hierarchical power was to blend into infrastructural power.

The creation of the DHS complicated the problems of incoherence and overlapping jurisdictions that had permitted the 9/11 terrorists to enter the country. For example, when the department was asked to put together a plan to repress potential domestic terrorist attacks in the run-up to the Iraq invasion, the Department of Defense refused to cooperate (ibid., 140–41). When Hurricane Katrina hit the Gulf Coast, the DHS designated a political appointee with hardly any emergency management experience to lead the response. So incapable was DHS of responding to the Katrina disaster that the government was forced to bring in military contractors to help keep order and assist citizens who had lost their homes (Scahill 2007, chap. 18).

Even in as critical an area as the "threat levels" that DHS was supposed to announce, there was a lack of coordination. Brigitte Nacos, Yaeli Bloch-Elkon, and Robert Y. Shapiro (2011, 30) note that before Memorial Day 2003, while DHS Secretary Ridge was telling reporters there was no reason to raise the alert level, Attorney General Ashcroft was warning of an imminent threat to the country. As William Arkin sums up the confusion and institutional overlap created by this galloping growth after 9/11, "All of the now-too-familiar intelligence failures discovered on 9/11 recurred: parties not talking to each other, overclassification of information, limited distribution—and this despite billions invested in intelligence and information sharing, despite an entirely new homeland security apparatus . . ." (2013, 75).

The Surveillance State

In some respects, the wars of the twenty-first century advanced trends that were already underway since the beginning of the Cold War (Dudziak 2010). This is particularly true with respect to government surveillance, which was put on a wartime footing in the Cold War and began to expand with the advances in electronic communications in the 1980s and 1990s. The result was a classical ratchet effect. As Sandra Braman writes, "there is no longer the expectation that restrictions on civil liberties on the basis of national security concerns will be of short duration" (Braman 2006, 115). She continues, "the vast extension of surveillance to those whose activities are merely related to an ongoing investigation, as opposed to raising probable cause of actual involvement in illegal activity, have brought additional civil liberties under attack: freedom of association, privacy, the right to a fair trial, and access to government information" (ibid.).

Traditionally, if a citizen was going to be the subject of surveillance, the government would have to convince a judge that there was probable cause that either this individual or those he or she was in contact with were actually involved in illegal activity. But under the USA Patriot Act, hurriedly passed in the angst that followed 9/11, "Prior notice of a search is not required, nor documentation of any materials that might be taken" (Braman 2006, 133). The special Foreign Intelligence Surveillance Act (FISA) court that was established after the Watergate scandal was supposed to rein in government spying; but from the beginning, it almost never turned down the government's requests for broad search warrants. After 9/11, the Bush administration began to practice warrantless surveillance that was so extensive that it led one member of the court, Judge James Robertson, to resign.

Of course, the logic of the USA Patriot Act was to root out terrorists such as those who carried out the massacres of 9/11, and few would find this troubling. But the act was opaque in defining the criteria for who is a terrorist. Although a list of foreign terrorist organizations is published by the State Department and is frequently updated, the criteria for classifying these organizations as "terrorist" were never made clear and continually evolved. For example, under its criteria, charity organizations that donate funds to groups in the Middle East could be defined as aiding terrorism, and the basis for their classification need never be divulged. Individuals who find themselves on a government watchlist—even when they were placed on that list by mistake—can spend years attempting to find out why they were on the list. And once placed on one of these lists, these individuals find it virtually impossible to be removed from it.[7] In 2007, a government audit found that more than half of the 71,000 people then on the no-fly list had been placed there in error.

The Horizontal Ratchet

Much has been written about NSA surveillance practices. For now, it is enough to note what we might call a horizontal ratchet effect in the diffusion of post-9/11 U.S. government security practices. First, because search warrants no longer need to be tied to a particular individual or device, they could be national in scope.

Second, because information acquired through surveillance can be shared with law enforcement officials concerned with other criminal matters, the practice of issuing unsupported search warrants has migrated from terrorism to other criminal matters, such as drug enforcement and financial fraud. Finally, the Patriot Act quickly became a model for other legislative acts. For example, as early as 2005 the Electronic Privacy and Information Center found twelve statutes that were changed to permit greater surveillance of individual communications (ibid., 134).

The expansion of surveillance led to an alphabet soup of new and overlapping agencies and coordination committees cluttered with a bewildering variety of frequently changing mechanisms. These included a presidential Information Sharing Council, a Joint Intelligence Community Council, a Homeland Security Council, and numerous "fusion centers" to promote intelligence sharing at among federal, state, and local agencies (Smith 2010). They were intended to use police and intelligence resources to identify terrorist suspects, but once in place, their activities began to diffuse to the surveillance of domestic protesters. The inkblot spread of agencies responsible for surveillance, and its diffusion from terrorism to domestic contention, included state and local agencies and private security firms and contractors. The most worrying ratchet effect of the fusion centers appeared in 2011–2012, when the Occupy protests spread around the country. A Freedom of Information request by lawyers who represented Occupy participants turned up 4,000 pages of unclassified e-mails and reports from law enforcement officers, federal officials, security contactors, the military, and even a retail trade association. The surveillance of the Occupy movement by these various fusion centers appears to have overlapped with that conducted by FBI counterterrorism officials.[8]

The effect of 9/11 and the wars generated in its name expanded various forms of hierarchical power of the American state. But hierarchical power is not the only, or even the most powerful, form of the American state's power. The great advantage of the American state has always been that its links to its citizens go in both directions—upward and downward—even in times of war. It is an elusive power because it uses relationships that Americans—and those who study it—see as part of a *pluralistic* system. But the problematic property of pluralism is how easily its logic can be inverted.

Infrastructural Power and Governed Interdependence

Unlike centralized states such as France and Italy, the United States has never had a significant federal-state economic sector. Not even the New Deal created significant numbers of state enterprises, although the Tennessee Valley Authority came close. But from the beginning, the national security state leaned heavily on private firms and contractors, to the point that it is sometimes difficult to tell where government service ends and private enterprise begins. This was because of the enormous technological prowess of the private sector but also because the strength of antistatism in American political culture made it easier to justify contracts with the private sector than to increase the government's role in the economy (Friedberg 2000; Weiss 2014).

Many journalistic accounts have exposed the extent and dangers of the growth of the national security state, especially where intelligence (Priest and Arkin 2011) or military contracting (Shorrock 2008) are concerned. But the relationship between the government and private corporations goes well beyond military contracting; it extends into a dense web of institutionalized links to technologically producing firms that Linda Weiss has called "governed interdependence," in which the military is the central but far from the exclusive actor (Weiss 2014, 4). Beginning with occasional agreements and contracts after World War Two, the system expanded "towards a preference for hybrid organizational forms that merge public and private resources in distinctive an often intricate ways" (ibid., 7). The national security state continues to set the rules in this system, but "a government body works with or through private actors and entities to achieve its own objectives" (ibid., 15).

These public-private relationships expanded greatly in the years after 9/11. As Weiss writes, "Although security-oriented spending on S & T [science and technology] had already resumed by the late 1990s, the 'war on terror' provided new motivation and momentum for NSS [national security state]-led technology development—in fields including robotics (embedded in drones), biotechnology/biodefense, nanotechnology, cybersecurity, and renewable energy" (2014, 48). Figure 8.2 shows how national security state spending on research and development has expanded in six federal agencies between 1951 and 2008.[9]

Contract spending takes two main forms that are relevant to war-making: spending for military contractors—formerly known as mercenaries—who are employed for security, logistical, and other purposes in Iraq, Afghanistan, and elsewhere; and spending for intelligence firms that have taken over important sectors of national security. Although the former has gained the most glaring journalistic attention, it is the latter that seems to have taken on more fundamental functions in the national security state.

War by Other Means

Military outsourcing[10] has been an important part of the American security state since the first Gulf War, when the ratio of troops to contractors was roughly ten

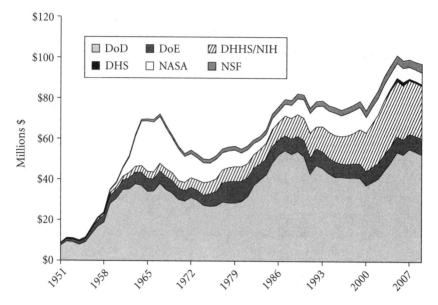

FIGURE 8.2 National security state spending on research and development by federal agency, 1951–2009 (in millions of 2005 dollars). DHHS/NIH, Department of Health and Human Services/National Institutes of Health; DHS, Department of Homeland Security; DoD, Department of Defense; DoE, Department of Energy; NASA, National Aeronautics and Space Administration; NSF, National Science Foundation. Weiss 2014, 49. Courtesy of the author and Cornell University Press.

to one (Avant and De Nevers 2013, 137). The Gulf War was organized in haste, after Saddam Hussein occupied Kuwait to gain control of its oil, thus the need for military contractors who could be quickly mobilized. However, the practice has since expanded all over the world, well beyond the U.S.-led wars in Iraq and Afghanistan. The further move to outsourcing was accelerated by three factors: the end of the Cold War; the Clinton presidency, and the growing Republican antistatism.

The end of the Cold War and the "peace benefit" it was supposed to bring are familiar causes for the rollback of government spending on the armed forces, but Clintonian centrism was equally important. After 1992, the new administration created a "public-private partnership to protect America's burgeoning cybercommunications sector" (ibid., 69). At the same time, the Republicans, who gained control of Congress in 1994, were calling for deep cuts in the federal workforce and for privatization of parts of the federal administration. But it took the addition of a new element—the pro-business obsession of Secretary of Defense Rumsfeld in 2001—to make Iraq and Afghanistan a "market for force" after 9/11 (Avant 2005; Singer 2003).

The election of President George W. Bush in 2000 brought Rumsfeld to the leadership of the military. He quickly published an article in *Foreign Affairs* calling for the transformation of the military (Rumsfeld 2002) and for a "small footprint" army that would be heavily dependent on sophisticated weapons systems, make increased use of special forces, emphasize covert actions, and rely heavily on the private sector. By spring 2007, writes Deborah Avant, there were between 130,000 and 170,000 military contractors in Iraq, "a number that matched or exceeded the number of U.S. troops" (2010, 245). As late as 2013, the Congressional Research Service reported that there were 108,000 private workers in Afghanistan, compared to the 65,700 U.S. troops who were stationed there.[11]

Much of this growth took place without adequate controls on either the number of contractors or the quality of the work they did, so no one knew what they were costing the taxpayers (Stanger 2009, chap. 2). When Congress finally got around to insisting on an accounting of the cost of these contracts, it showed a cumulative expenditure for equipment, supplies, and support services for contactors in 2002–2010 of at least $154 billion for the Department of Defense, $11 billion for the Department of State, and $7 billion for the U.S. Agency for International Development (USAID). Added to this was $5 billion in grants and cooperative agreements awarded by the Department of State and USAID. Figure 8.3 shows that cumulative spending on grants and contracts was roughly $177 billion through 2010 (Commission on Wartime Contracting in Iraq and Afghanistan 2011, 6). Needless to say, these figures do not include the funding for the NSA and the CIA.

Rumsfeld's model of a military with a smaller footprint created a goldmine for companies in the private military sector, many of them staffed by former military personnel (Scahill 2007). Much of this growth took place under the radar because the administration was very quiet about it and the press gave it little coverage, except when contractors were killed or killed others. In Iraq by the end of 2008, the ratio of troops to contactors was roughly one to one; in Afghanistan by September 2009, "contractors made up an estimated 62 percent of the U.S. presence in that country," and in 2010, there were still roughly 1.43 contractors for every American soldier in that theater (Avant and De Nevers 2013, 137). But it was not only in the deserts of Iraq and the mountains of Afghanistan that the U.S. government was outsourcing parts of the state; a similar process of privatization was taking place in intelligence centers and shopping malls surrounding Washington, D.C.

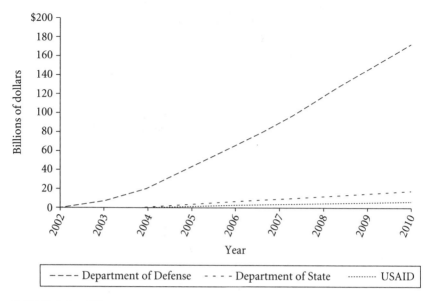

FIGURE 8.3 Military contracts and grants in Iraq, Afghanistan, Bahrain, Kuwait, and Qatar, 2001–2010. Commission on Wartime Contacting in Iraq and Afghanistan 2011, 6.

Privatizing National Security

The growth of government–private-sector intelligence cooperation goes back to the Eisenhower administration, when the Lockheed Corporation built the U-2 for the federal government's spying operations. By the 1960s, firms such as TRW, General Electric, Eastman Kodak, and Polaroid were building spy satellites, cameras, and reconnaissance aircraft for the government.[12] But it was not until the 1980s, driven by the desire to cut government spending and the Reagan revolution, that the outsourcing of government functions gained an ideological justification. In 1984, President Reagan appointed a commission, headed by Peter Grace, an industrialist, to "root out government inefficiency and the waste of taxpayer dollars." Over the four years in which it existed, the Grace Commission recommended closing dozens of government agencies or leasing them to the private sector (ibid., 81–82).

Reagan's privatization ideology proved more illusory than real. It was the Clinton administration's cuts in "unnecessary" governmental expenses, coinciding with the collapse of the Soviet Union, that created a strategic incentive to reduce expenditures in the public intelligence-defense complex. Hundreds—perhaps thousands—of well-trained government employees moved into the private sector. Yet there was still a need for intelligence, especially in the growing technology sector. During the Balkan wars, the gap began to be filled by private contractors, many of whom had served in the military and had retired to make much more money from the booming private security sector.

When the World Trade Center and the Pentagon were attacked in September 2001, the trend toward the partial privatization of government intelligence collection was already in motion. The serious failures in intelligence revealed by those attacks confronted the Bush administration with the need for security-cleared and experienced professionals with the skills and backgrounds to find the terrorists and prevent future attacks. But by now, writes Tim Shorrock, "it was too late: the people they needed immediately . . . were working in the private sector. . . . As a result, from 2001 on, Washington became a free-for-all for contractors" (2008, 113).

In *Spies for Sale*, a book that is much more serious than its title implies, Shorrock provides approximate data on the growth and the proportion of expenditures on intelligence contracting from the late 1990s on. In 1998, he discovered, intelligence agencies had spent $18 billion on contracts; by 2001, the figure had increased to almost $22 billion. In the two following years, contract spending for intelligence grew to $43.5 billion, where it remained for the next three years. In 2006, Shorrock reckons, the estimates were $43 billion and made up 70 percent of the estimated $60 billion that the government spent on intelligence (ibid., 19).[13]

The vast majority of contractors work quietly—indeed, secretly—around Washington, D.C. While researching their well-informed book, Dana Priest and William Arkin identified nearly 2,000 private companies involved with programs related to counterterrorism, homeland security, and intelligence (Priest and Arkin 2011, 86). Priest and Arkin found thousands of contractors working alongside military officers in shopping malls and office complexes around the capital. For example, more than 250 companies have a physical presence in and around Fort Meade, Maryland, where the NSA has its headquarters, (ibid., 74–75). This was hybridization with a vengeance (Weiss 2014, 147–49)!

The Washington area is not alone. Since 9/11, joint military-civilian clusters for collecting secret intelligence and carrying out surveillance have mushroomed around the country, for example, around the headquarters of NorthCom (the military's North American Command), which occupies a 140,000-square-foot structure outside Colorado Springs, Colorado, expanding by 20 percent after 9/11 (ibid., 110–12). After 9/11, the physical and demographic presence of the national security state spread like an inkblot across the American landscape.

The Vertical Ratchet Effect

The initiative for private-sector intelligence gathering also moved to the grassroots. After 9/11, many states and some cities began to collect intelligence information on their own (Sidel 2004, chap. 3). The most extensive programs were designed, with an assist from the FBI, by the New York City Police Department (NYPD), which included a program deceptively called "the Demographics Unit," which mapped Muslim communities, their mosques, and their businesses.[14] In 2014, under Bill de Blasio, the newly elected mayor, the NYPD shut down the unit, agreeing that working with community leaders in the Muslim community was a better way of identifying potential home-grown terrorists.[15]

For a time after 9/11, there were efforts to create a network of state-based data-mining systems. For example, a private Florida firm named Seisint created system called MATRIX (Multistate Anti-Terrorism Information Exchange) to make data more easily available to individual states (Sidel 2004, 58–64). MATRIX collected "government and criminal data from collaborating states and commercial databases to create detailed portraits of individuals," ranging from driver's licenses to criminal histories, addresses, and phone numbers to business associates. With a logic that presaged the bulk Internet- and phone-tracking strategy of the NSA uncovered by Snowden in 2013, the project's private managers promised prospective state partners that "[w]hen enough seemingly insignificant data is analyzed against billions of data elements, the invisible becomes 'visible'" (ibid, 58).

For a time, the DHS contributed support to this privately run, state-promoted project, but by the end of 2003, the local and national media began to publicize its perils and the government drew back. In spring 2004, reports Marc Sidel, "the ACLU and journalists uncovered evidence that Matrix's parent company, Seisint, had forwarded 120,000 names of suspected terrorists culled from its Matrix and other databases to federal and state authorities after September 11" (ibid., 63). The figure was difficult to credit for government officials, who had built their own databases. By 2005, the program had been closed down.[16]

The Perils of Infrastructural Power

There are many advantages to what Weiss calls "governed interdependence" between the government and the private sector, not least among them the technological spinoffs for the society as a whole (2014, chap. 2). But such spinoffs are not easy, time-saving, or inexpensive (ibid., chap. 8). Particularly in the military-intelligence complex that succeeded Eisenhower's military-industrial complex, there are special risks that go beyond the costs of hybridization that Weiss's account reveals. The most important is that the privatization of state functions is at best orthogonal to democratic accountability—and can even be antagonistic to it.

First, these companies not only serve the needs of the established intelligence agencies, which presumably know their business; they also work with the newly formed government agencies that were created in the wake of 9/11, which lacked the expertise and the experience to be able to tell what they were getting for their money. For example, the DHS, which subsidized the MATRIX program after 9/11, was staffed by inexperienced officials who were desperately looking around for sources of information to establish their agency's legitimacy. But even the Pentagon, under its wily Defense Secretary Rumsfeld, did not always know who was working for the various branches of the armed forces and what they were doing for their money. As Avant and Renee De Nevers observe, "The United States does not have the capacity to oversee these contracts successfully, and this failure has led to waste, fraud, and, particularly with regard to security contracts, abuse" (2013, 144).

To make things worse, after 9/11 the number of government personnel assigned to monitor contracts signed with private contractors was cut as the number of contracts exploded. This was, after all, an administration that believed in a small footprint. The same was true in the intelligence sector; as one former CIA analyst, John Gannon, told the Senate Judiciary Committee in 2006, the core problem in U.S. intelligence today "is that there is minimal executive branch supervision . . . and inadequate congressional oversight" of these contracting firms (quoted in Shorrock 2008, 136).

A third problem is that the existence of highly paid private firms able to hire people to perform tasks at salaries that the government cannot match has created resentment among both army and intelligence-agency personnel. Leaders of the intelligence community looked on with distress as well-trained analysts left government service for the private sector and then returned as contactors to do the same jobs for much higher salaries. A 2010 survey of Department of Defense personnel exposed a great deal of resentment, especially among lower-ranking and younger personnel, who were working alongside private contractors making much more [government] money than they were (Avant and De Nevers 2013, 142). Related to this, high-ranking officials who left the government for the private sector used their contacts in the executive branch and in Congress to lobby for contracts for their firms.[17]

In addition, when private firms carry out military or intelligence functions for the government, their underlying motivation is profit rather than accountability. It is not even easy to pin responsibility on individual firms for the behavior of their employees, as USIS discovered in the story that introduced this chapter (Avant 2005, 222). The profit motive is particularly irrelevant to national security in firms that contract to provide security, or even fight on the front lines, in Afghanistan and Iraq (Avant and De Nevers 2013, 143). The factors that made the citizen army effective—the combination of patriotism and solidarity—are less likely to motivate even former soldiers who are in it for the money (ibid., 140).

Most fundamental of all is the misfit between private security and the democratic political process. Whereas the military chain of command is ultimately responsible to civilian-elected leadership, private firms are not (Singer 2003, 215; Avant 2010). When we think of the mix of obligation and patriotism in the original concept of the citizen army, private contractors share neither one. As Allison Stanger writes, "Employees of private military firms answer neither to the U.S. military nor to the indigenous population they are involved in defending. They answer to the company that employs them" (2009, 90).

Conclusions

The observations I offer in this chapter suggest that there has been a fundamental—and contradictory—shift in the character of the American state since the bombings of the World Trade Center and the Pentagon in 2001. To summarize a complex series of developments that are not yet complete, there have been a growth in hierarchical power, growth in the complexity of the American state, and an increase in infrastructural power.

Remember Charles Tilly's argument about the impact of war-making on state-building? Although based on evidence from early modern Europe, Tilly's thesis applies to the American state in the wake of 9/11 in at least two senses. First, the American state has grown larger and its executive has grown bolder—especially in the surveillance of citizens; second, through horizontal and vertical ratchets, both private firms and the lower levels of government have become parts of the national security state in ways that have been extended to non-security areas of governance. Not only that: as the response to the riots following the shooting of a young black teenager by a policeman in Ferguson, Missouri, in 2014 showed, local police have been militarized by a major injection of national security expertise and arms given to state and local governments from the wars in Iraq and Afghanistan.[18]

As the chilling exposures on the reach of the surveillance state since 9/11 have shown, the hierarchical power of the central state has increased under both the Bush and Obama administrations. And although the more ruthless dark-side aspects of the Bush detention and abuse policies were moderated by his successor, both administrations have shown a penchant for interpreting the rule of law as rule *by* law. Congress has shown itself to be supine when faced by these moves, and although the Supreme Court reversed some of the most legally questionable policies, as we will see in the next chapter, the courts in general have not stood up for the rights of citizens or foreigners against an administration that has ruthlessly pushed for security over rights.

In addition, the growth in government agencies has increased the complexity of the American state, producing both confusion (as in the failure to control military contracting and the use made of military hardware by local police forces) and contradictory policies from different agencies of government (as in the debates over the color-coded threat alerts). The American state has gotten bigger but not necessarily more coherent; ruling by law instead of following the law has led the government to create new systems, such as the military commission system (see chapter 7), that work badly instead of relying on established institutions, such as the federal court system, that have been doing their work well for over two centuries.

There has also been an increase in the state's infrastructural power. After 9/11, an extensive external sector was created, both in the military and in intelligence work. In creating this system, the government reached deeply into civil society, subsidizing private firms, creating rich opportunities for national security lobbies, and outsourcing important parts of its military and intelligence functions to the private sector. This interpenetration has enabled the government to capture the profit motive of enormous numbers of citizens, but it also created a privatization of functions that now lie largely outside the control of the state.

Assuming that this account is accurate and the trend is not reversed, do these changes in the American state threaten democracy? Journalistic critics such as Arkin, Priest, and Shorrock certainly think so. Analysts of public policy have added systematic social science data to the investigative reporting of these journalists. Scholars of military affairs such as Deborah Avant and Peter Singer have revealed the lack of accountability of the private security firms. If published criticisms could roll back the expansion of the American state, there would be much less to worry about than current concerns exhibit.

Most worrying is Arkin's thesis that a clandestine state has grown up beneath the surface of the visible one. Arkin does not argue that the changes in the American state constitute a "Schmittian" state of exception buttressed by martial law. Such a turn would set off alarm bells in civil society, and not only on the liberal left. What is more invidious about his idea of a hidden state is that the thousands of defense contractors in the suburbs of Washington, the hundreds of technology companies in Silicon Valley, and the military contractors around the world do not think of themselves as subverting the Constitution. But cumulatively, their actions amount to an "American coup," the outcome of "mutual ignorance and manufactured complexity" (Arkin 2013, 10).

The central paradox in this expansion of the government's infrastructural power is that, although it provides the state with outposts in civil society, the power is so poorly controlled, so extensive, and so easily inhabited by individuals who are uncomfortable with the state's growing hegemony that it can both increase profit-making at the cost of the public and open space for resistance to the expanding state. The anecdote at the beginning of this chapter about the government's being billed for security checks that were never carried out is a representative example of the former; the extraordinary revelations about the government's surveillance that surfaced between 2011 and 2013 is the most glaring example of the latter. Only after the Snowden revelations in 2013 did Congress begin to bestir itself to examine how the NSA had managed to sweep up billons of phone records and did major Internet firms form a coalition to seek government surveillance reform.[19] As we will see in the next chapter, unconventional forms of contention have grown out of the state's infrastructural expansion.

CONTESTING HEGEMONY

In 2013, a virtual tornado hit the NSA in Ft. Meade, Virginia. A twenty-nine-year-old former government contractor, Edward Snowden, had downloaded a large number of government documents and passed some of them on to the press.[1] The Obama administration labeled Snowden a traitor, revoked his passport, and sought to have him arrested. With the government in hot pursuit, Snowden fled, first to Hong Kong and then, after trying to get to Ecuador, got stuck in Moscow, where he remained as an uneasy guest of the Russian government as this book went to press.[2]

Snowden's revelations not only demonstrated that the government was intruding on the private communications of U.S. citizens; it caused a crisis with some of the closest U.S. allies, such as Chancellor Angela Merkel of Germany, whose personal cellphone the NSA was tapping; the Brazilian government, whose state oil company, Petrobras, was hacked into; and even the British government, whose electronic spying organization, Government Communications Headquarters (GCHQ), was hand-in-glove with the agency. The exposure brought outrage from members of Congress, protests from around the world, and, perhaps for the first time, led members of the public to fear for their privacy.

The scandal exposed how far the American state's hierarchical power had expanded since 9/11. In fact, a FOIA request filed by *Al Jazeera* revealed an internal NSA document in which the agency invoked the events of that day to justify its electronic spying programs.[3] Ironically, Snowden's former job title was infrastructure analyst, which seems to have been NSA code to mean someone who looks for new ways of breaking into Internet and telephone traffic.[4] The crisis also showed how far the American state had expanded its use of infrastructural power in drawing on private resources to gather information.

It soon emerged that the NSA had been requiring the major U.S. electronic providers and phone companies to turn over their subscriber records through secret national security letters while the agency was secretly hacking into their communications through backdoors.[5] The FISA court had been signing off wholesale on the government's warrantless surveillance, and eventually the crisis led Congress to awaken from its long torpor where national security surveillance was concerned.[6] After a decade of court cases in which the government's mass surveillance could not be demonstrated by civil liberties groups because the courts denied that they had standing in the courts, Snowden decided to act.[7] He made contact with Glenn Greenwald, a journalist for *The Guardian*, and Laura Poitras, a documentary filmmaker, both of whom he hoped would be willing to release his findings. When some of his revelations were published in *The Guardian* and the *Washington Post*, they were picked up by wire services and newspapers around the world and immediately went viral on the Internet.[8]

Snowden's revelations soon triggered contentious public action. Twelve years to the day after the passage of the USA Patriot Act, protesters gathered on the Washington Mall to demonstrate against the government's electronic spying.[9] Evoking past civil rights marches, the protesters met in front of Union Station, marched to the mall, and demanded that the government "Stop Watching Us!" It brought together hundreds of thousands of citizens, both physically and connected from websites across the country; moreover, the organizing groups ranged across the ideological spectrum from civil liberties groups, such as the ACLU and The Bill of Rights Defense Committee, to groups normally associated with conservative causes, such as Freedom Works and the Libertarian Party.

Some of these groups were new. They had names such as Mozilla, the Electronic Frontier Foundation (EFF), the Electronic Privacy Information Center (EPIC), Freepress, and the Media Mobilizing Project (MMP). Following the rally, a coalition of the biggest tech companies met with Obama to protest the government's actions. The combination of left-leaning privacy groups, right-leaning libertarians, and the country's Internet giants was too much for President Obama; in January 2014, he was forced to go before the television cameras and confess to the government's electronic snooping and to set up a committee to advise him on reforming the agency.[10]

Snowden's actions not only used the Internet against the state; they expanded the range of contentious actors to groups whose primary activities depended on the Internet and had come to see in the government's surveillance programs a threat to individual and associational liberties. They demonstrate the expansion of contentious political action triggered by the wars of the twenty-first century and by the invasion of rights that those wars produced.

In the wake of 9/11, as we have seen, public opinion was largely immune to charges of government overreach; the Cheney wing of the Republican Party was making key decisions about surveillance, detainee treatment, and torture, and the administration was able to build on rage over 9/11 to support for the war in Iraq. Interestingly, there was no real pro-war movement to go into Iraq; the United States was simply anxious to punish someone for what had been done to it in 2001. But the immediate protests against the government's emergency rule most often failed and a legal mobilization against torture and illegal detention was stymied by the courts, the administration, and Congress. Only as the fear of attack dissipated and the longer-range potential of the government's actions became clearer could civil society groups organize effectively against the war and on behalf of rights.

Civil Society and Contentious Politics

"A persistent theme in American history," writes Jack Goldsmith, who served in the Bush administration, "is that "the rise of well-resourced advocacy groups that scrutinize government national security actions is one of the great accountability innovations of the last decade" (2012, 116). They are part of what Goldsmith sees as a neo-Madisonian "synopticon" consisting of Congress, the courts, the media, lawyers, and civil society groups reacting against government overreach to correct the constitutional balance. Writing from a different philosophical perspective than Goldsmith, David Cortright, long-time peace activist, examines the Vietnam antiwar movement, the disarmament campaign of the 1980s, and the worldwide mobilization against the war in Iraq and "traces the ways in which these movements were able to exert impact on U.S. and international policy (2014, 482). The first and the second campaigns had profound effects on U.S. war-making, the second campaign less so, but antiwar activists "played a key role in electing a president who carried out his campaign pledge to end the war" (ibid).

Goldsmith is correct that under the Obama administration there was a partial reversal of the worst excesses of the Bush years. But the civil society groups he lionizes would be surprised to learn that they were collaborating with Congress, the courts, and the media to restrain the government's abuses. In fact, as we saw in the last two chapters, few of these institutions were of the slightest use in defending the values of liberal democracy that Goldsmith sees at the heart of the American creed. On the contrary, the intelligence agencies went well beyond the tools that Congress had given them; Congress largely did the executive's bidding;

government lawyers ranged fast and loose over the law and used it to justify torture; the courts reneged on defending the rights that they had occasionally conceded; the media, with the exception of a few investigative journalists and their newspapers, since 9/11, largely acted as stenographers for the state.

This takes us to the mixed success of civil society groups in opposing war and its abuses in general. We will see in this chapter how few were their victories; how stubbornly the government fought them every step of the way; and how difficult it was for them to coordinate public protest, legal mobilization, and civil society activism in a country that had been traumatized by 9/11. If there was a neo-Madisonian "synopticon" it was in contentious struggle *against* the institutional actors that Goldsmith lionizes. But we will also see that groups large and small, those that specialize in civil liberties as well as groups with their own private interests, had indirect effects on government policy, which is why they continue to work to roll back the emergency script.

I examine the three main kinds of actors in this chapter, each of which used different mechanisms and entered the conflict at different times: the antiwar movement that led the mass protests against the Iraq war in 2002–2003; the legal groups that attempted to constrain the government's abuses in court; and the civil society activists who publicized these abuses and struggled to restrain the power of the state. These groups have used their access to the state's infrastructural power against the expansion of its hierarchical power. The major questions I raise in this chapter are whether and to what extent contentious politics can turn the tide against the abuse of the rule of law that we saw in chapter 7 and the national security state we examined in chapter 8.

There have been cycles of peace protest throughout U.S. history, and a permanent antiwar movement endured from World War One to the present day (Meyer 1993). But the first decade of the twenty-first century presented this movement with insoluble problems in mobilizing against central state hegemony. The country was genuinely terrorized by the attacks of 9/11; the government had launched the country into war while the public was still traumatized by those attacks; and the administration put in motion a determined campaign to shape public opinion and avoid the control of the courts and Congress. Yet hundreds of thousands of protesters did set out at some point to challenge hegemony. Where did they come from, and what happened to them later? The answers will tell us much about the strengths and limits of infrastructural power in the United States.

The Antiwar Movement Cycle

After the dramatic protest campaigns of the Vietnam War and the nuclear freeze movement of the early 1980s, the peace movement was in a period of abeyance

(Meyer 1990; Taylor 1989). Bogdan Vasi writes, "Starting from the mid-1980s, traditional peace SMOs [social movement organizations] had weakened such that by 1988 almost 60 percent of all SMOs were operating in some sort of affiliate relationship and only 14 percent of all SMOs were formally organized" (2006, 144).[11]

To understand the movement's resurgence, we need to go back to two years before September 11, 2001. After a decade in which many scholars thought social movements were becoming institutionalized (Meyer and Tarrow 1998), a wave of movements brought a new generation of activists onto the public scene against neoliberal globalization. Many of these had migrated from the environmental, feminist, gay and lesbian, and economic justice movements, in a process that David Meyer and Nancy Whittier (1994) call social movement spillover. They called themselves the global justice movement.

Although the new movement was transnational (della Porta and Tarrow 2005), the catalyst came from the United States. In Seattle in November 1999, a broad coalition of environmental and economic justice groups mounted colorful and contentious public performances against the World Trade Organization (WTO) meeting in that city. The campaign spread around the world and would be remembered and memorialized under the label "the Seattle model."[12] From Genoa to Göteborg, from Prague to Cancun, from Porto Alegre to Mumbai, there were efforts to repeat what had happened in the heart of world capitalism (della Porta. 2007; Smith 2008). Seattle, where the police temporarily lost control of the downtown area to an anarchist fringe among the protesters, became a model for future campaigns. Figure 9.1, taken from an analysis of an activist website from the Seattle area, shows how rapidly and how dramatically the global justice protest grew in Seattle both before and after the WTO meeting.

The data in figure 9.1 also show that, as the global justice campaign was collapsing, a new wave of protest—antiwar protest—was rapidly appearing. Eighteen months after the attacks on the World Trade Center, the Bush administration launched its war against Iraq. These plans were so openly signaled from fall 2002 that the antiwar movement had time to organize against them. On February 15, 2003, the largest peace demonstration in world history was mobilized against the plan to go to war. Many of the young people who were politicized against the WTO moved effortlessly into that movement. They joined activists from the social justice movement, the environmental movement, the labor movement, the antinuclear movement, the gay and lesbian rights movement, and the feminist movement and veterans of previous waves of peace protest (Gillham and Edwards 2003).

The events were coordinated and staged by an international network of movement organizations, most of which originated within the global justice movement (Walgrave, Rucht, and Van Aelst 2010) Although some of these protests

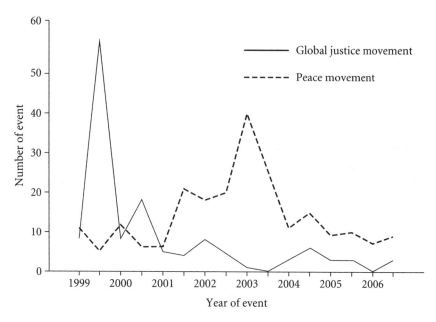

FIGURE 9.1 Number of planned protest events and meetings in the Seattle area, 1999–2006. Calculated from an online activist calendar, www.eatthestate. org, from the Seattle area, accessed September 2007.

were small in scale, others were enormous. In Rome, there were an estimated 3 million people assembled against the impending war, in Barcelona and London, more than a million, in Madrid, 800,000, in Melbourne and Sydney, 500,000, and in Paris, about 350,000. Most astonishing, in the heart of the American empire there were an estimated 1,500,000 protesters in the streets on that day, 500,000 of them in New York City alone (Verhulst 2010, 16–17).

From their eight-country survey of antiwar demonstrators on February 15, 2003, Stefaan Walgrave and Dieter Rucht and their collaborators showed that the campaign drew in part from university-educated, professional, and center-left citizens. But they were not overwhelmingly male (63 percent were female), not mainly young (43 percent were between forty-five and sixty-four years of age), and a bare majority had experience in previous peace demonstrations (56 percent overall). Indeed, in the eight countries studied by Walgrave and Rucht and their collaborators, an average of 31 percent had taken part in antiracism demonstrations, 24 percent in human rights protests, 42 percent in social justice campaigns, 20 percent in ecological protests, and 24 percent in the global justice movement (della Porta 2010, 127).

But by 2006, the antiwar movement had collapsed. How this happened was the result of both the result of the natural cycle of war-making—which leads to a "rally round the flag" effect once war breaks out—and from the effects of the electoral cycle that led many peace movement supporters to shift their activities from opposition to the war to support for the Democratic Party and the election campaign of Barack Obama.

Framing Antiwar Protest

When the Bush administration went to war despite the movement's efforts and in the face of broad international condemnation, as quickly as it arose the movement declined. A hybrid movement that came together in response to the Iraq War "spilled out" into grudging acquiescence, a shift into other movements, and a shift into ordinary politics (Hadden and Tarrow 2007). With so broad a spectrum of activists to appeal to, it was not surprising that the movement proved hard to hold together. Lynne Woehrle and her collaborators studied fifteen large peace organizations, ranging from the American Friends Service Committee to the feminist group Code Pink to ethnically based groups such as the Black Radical Congress, to the union-based United States Labor Against the War, and to more radical groups such as the War Resisters' League.[13] Diversity can sometimes be a positive factor for an emerging movement, but when slogans are as diverse as "the people united, will never be defeated," "peace is patriotic," "support our troops, bring them home now," or the more radical "no war for oil, stop the bombing, stop the war," this can muffle the cohesion of a movement (Woehrle, Coy, and Maney 2008, 3).

As Woehrle and her colleagues argue, leaders cannot frame their movements exactly as they wish; movement discourses "are reproduced, challenged, and transformed through an interactive, contested, and cumulative process of framing by multiple actors" (ibid., 6–7). Antiwar movements face a special burden in this respect. As Woehrle and her collaborators write, "During these historical moments when so much is uncertain and when ordinary people are often asked to risk so much, the dominant symbolic repertoire is the cupboard that gets opened first by policy makers; it is never bare and always well stocked. In addition, war itself offers an enormously powerful and potentially appealing symbolic terrain to all who are touched by it in any way" (ibid., 30).

During the first Gulf War and through the 1990s, U.S. peace organizations had "challenged nationalism more than they harnessed it." But after 9/11, peace protesters faced a special set of dilemmas: the nation had been wounded by a horrible and humiliating mass murder, they lacked influential allies, and the public supported the patriotic mood that enveloped the nation after 9/11.[14] But as we have seen, the mainstream media were soon in the grip of a carefully orchestrated government campaign to support the coming war, and opportunities for protest began to contract (Vasi 2006, 139). The result was that the peace movement was forced to try to "harness hegemony" rather than challenging it. American flags waved over most of the protest groups, and slogans insisted on the patriotic nature of avoiding going to war. Radical groups that sought to challenge the government's war efforts found themselves facing enhanced surveillance, media hostility or indifference, and even opposition from more moderate peace organizations. This was true even though the bulk of the activists were far from radical; many were in fact primarily identifiers with the Democratic Party and not with the peace movement, which helps to explain the movement's decline in the face of growing public opposition to the war.

The Party in the Street

For many years, social movements were seen as a form of collective behavior, a category of behavioral forms—including fads, crazes, panics, and crowds—that defined the unusual, the exotic, and the irrational in social life.[15] The 1960s gave a spur to the study of movements as normal forms of politics (McAdam and Tarrow 2013).This was true not only in the United States. Table 9.1 summarizes party-identification data and electoral results for activists surveyed in the eight countries in the Walgrave-Rucht survey. It shows that, among the demonstrators in all eight countries, there were high proportions of party identifiers, strong

TABLE 9.1   Party identifiers, voting in last national election, and support for center-left parties and green parties among surveyed anti–Iraq War protesters, February 2003 (%)

	UNITED STATES	UNITED KINGDOM	SPAIN	ITALY	NETHERLANDS	SWITZERLAND	BELGIUM	GERMANY
Party identifiers[a]	51	13	13	19	25	19	20	10
Voting in last national elections	91	(77/86)[b]	76	83	95	77	86	90
Supporting main center-left party[c]	65	(59/48)	57	49	19	79	24	39
Supporting green parties	33	(7/4)[b]	2	2	40	16	54	35

Source: Walgave and Rucht 2012, 207, 151, 152.

[a] *Party identifiers* is used here instead of the source's *party membership* to include the United States, where party membership is insignificant or absent.

[b] The original source divides the votes in the United Kingdom between England and Scotland but does not divide the percentages of party members.

[c] *Main center-left party* is used instead of the source's *social democrats* to include the U.S. Democrats.

electoral participation, and a significant number—especially in the United States—who identified with the institutional party of the center-left. This set up dilemmas for the peace movement, familiar from the movement past, between movement activists and party identities and between the strategy of challenging hegemony or the strategy of trying to harness it (Meyer 1990).

Connections to a major political party carried initial advantages for the antiwar movement, especially one that was challenging a government against an unpopular war (McAdam and Tarrow 2010). Parties provide activists with campaign experience, contacts with other activists, and support from shrewd party politicians. Like the anti–Vietnam War movement before it (Burstein and Freudenberg 1978) and the nuclear freeze movement of the 1980s (Meyer 1990, 224–25; Cortright 2014), the anti–Iraq War movement profited from the support of key Democratic Party leaders such as then Senator Barack Obama (D-Illinois), who made his reputation as a national figure in large part by taking up the banner of opposition to the war. In October 2002, Obama said that the war was a "cynical attempt" to shove "ideological agendas down our throats" and would distract from domestic problems such as poverty and health care.[16] Many antiwar activists would eventually campaign for Obama on the strength of what they took to be his antiwar position.

But the movement's connections to the Democratic Party also had a cost. Democratic Party leaders were less than comfortable at the prospect of cooperating with activists on their left. Second, Obama turned out to be much less of a principled antiwar candidate than he claimed, appointing Hillary Clinton—a hawk on the Iraq War—as secretary of state. Third, and most important, the election of a Democratic Congress in 2006 and a Democratic president two years later led many to drop out of movement activities altogether and turn to party politics (Hadden and Tarrow 2007). "After Obama's election," write Michael Heaney and Fabio Rojas, "the antiwar movement never again organized a protest with tens or hundreds of thousands of participants" (2015, 91). As figure 9.2, drawn from their study, shows, after the first half of the decade, when antiwar protests could draw crowds in the hundreds of thousands, there was a sharp decline in the scale of the antiwar movement's demonstrations.

The decline in support for the peace movement among Democratic activists after the political tide turned did not destroy the movement, but it did change its character. With less capacity to bring out large numbers of supporters and Democrats already engaged in the election campaign, the movement lost a great deal of its momentum, and with fewer Democratic supporters in the mix, there were proportionately more minor-party identifiers and a greater proportion of radicals (ibid., 154). Individuals with a stronger movement identity—those for

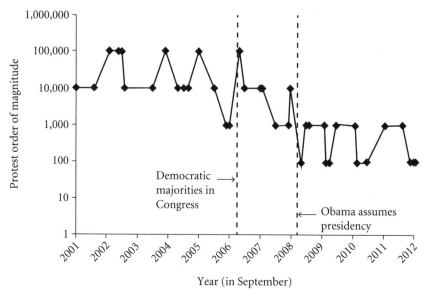

FIGURE 9.2   Size of national and nationally coordinated antiwar protests, 2002–2012. Heaney and Rojas 2015, app. D. I am grateful to the authors for allowing me to reproduce this data.

whom movement activism was core to their personal identities—increased or maintained their antiwar involvement (ibid., 158).

The Democratic Party was too much a part of the American system of institutions for strong party identifiers to remain active in a social movement that opposed the wars it was about to inherit, and the party itself was loath to vigorously oppose the war. As Democratic identifiers moved out of the movement, partisan and movement identities pulled activists in different directions, to the cost of the movement that had been launched with such broad support in the run-up to the Iraq War. Those who opposed the Bush administration's expanding agenda would have to look elsewhere than to the antiwar movement. Some thought they would find it within another pillar of the U.S. establishment—the legal profession.

Legal Mobilization

What can social movements do against a powerful state that manipulates the law for policy purposes? As the excesses of the Bush administration became evident in 2002 and 2003, a group of legal advocates began to use the legal process to oppose what they thought the government was doing. These were a skilled group of lawyers coming from the civil rights and anti–death penalty movements, but the problem of contesting the state's practice of rule *by* law is that it draws activists into legal conflicts that move at a snail's pace and are difficult to win against an administration with the tools of law and policy at its command, in the presence of a compliant Congress and of judges who are inclined to defer to the executive in times of war (Barkan 1984).[17]

Legal advocates cheered when, in a series of cases from 2004 to 2008, the Supreme Court gave the impression that it would guarantee a minimum of procedural rights for detainees in custody of the military.[18] When the *Boumediene v. Bush* (553 U.S. 723) decision came down in 2008, the Center for Constitutional Rights (CCR), which had been involved in the *habeas* cases from the beginning, wrote enthusiastically:

> In an historical decision, the Court unambiguously rejected the political branches' attempts to cut the federal courts out of the process. The Court had held that the Center's clients detained at Guantánamo have a constitutional right to file petitions for habeas corpus in U.S. federal court challenging the lawfulness of their detention.... We hope that the lower courts will quickly move to hold hearings in the 200-odd pending individual habeas corpus cases where detainees are challenging their indefinite detention without charges.[19]

But CCR's optimism was premature. The Supreme Court had granted the right but refused to describe its content, which allowed the lower courts to define that content extremely narrowly, which the Court allowed to stand. A district court judge had approved the *habeas* petition of Mohammed Al-Adahi, a Yemini national, but the D.C. Circuit Court of Appeals reversed that decision on the ground that the district court had held the government up to too high a standard of evidence. From *Al-adahi v. Obama* (613 F.3d 1102 [2010]) on, apart from seventeen Uighers who were released, only one detainee case passed muster in the D.C. Circuit Court, as opposed to eleven cases that were lost. Table 9.2 summarizes the results of the detainee *habeas* cases that went to the D.C. Circuit Court following the *Al-Adahi* case.[20]

Convincing Congress to defend the rights of detainees was equally frustrating for rights advocates. It is true, as two political scientists, Matthew Kroenig and Jay Stowsky (2006), find, that Congress modified the most extreme parts of the USA Patriot Act. And at the urging of Senator John McCain, Congress eventually reined in the more egregious abuses of detainees (Goldsmith 2012, 119–20, 185–88). But Congress has always modified administration proposals, and the worst Bush-Cheney policies—for example, the abuse and torture of

TABLE 9.2   Results of *habeas* cases coming before the Washington, D.C., Circuit Court of Appeals before and after the *Al-Adahi v. Obama* case in July 2010

	CASES DROPPED BY GOVERNMENT	CASES REVERSED BY D.C. CIRCUIT COURT OF APPEALS	CASES WON BY DETAINEES
Pre-*Al-Adahi* period	—	14 (41%)	20 (59%)
Post-*Al-Adahi* period	—	11 (92%)	1 (8%)
Uighur cases	17 (100%)	—	—

Source: Denbeaux et al. 2012.

prisoners—bypassed Congress. Nor was Congress adequately informed about what the CIA was doing in its black sites, a revelation that emerged only in 2014, long after the Obama administration announced that they had been suspended.[21]

Other practices were carried out through the administration's expanded interpretation of congressional mandates. When the Supreme Court, in *Hamdan v. Rumsfeld* (548 U.S. 557), held that the military commissions the government set up in Guantánamo had not been authorized by Congress, Congress promptly passed a law creating a new—and almost equally shoddy–system of commissions (Fisher 2008, 237–44). Moreover, the House and Senate Intelligence Committees that were set up in the Church Commission period never seriously tried to rein in the lawless actions of the executive. Using the law and the legislative process to protect rights is slow, frustrating, and reversible, and it provides the government with infinite opportunities for evasion, dissimulation, and stretching the use of permitted practices into shadowy areas of the law. More fundamentally, it can divert the energies of civil society groups and human rights lawyers from using more sustained and more public forms of contention. While dedicated lawyers spend years shepherding cases through reluctant and slow-moving courts, determined administrations can continue their practices—often under the shroud of secrecy—that these cases are intended to end. And even when the courts hold in favor of the legal advocates, Congress and the administration can find creative ways of side-stepping their decisions. To put this crudely: court cases lead to "retail" decisions that often do not extend to other, similar cases, but the government can make "wholesale" policies.

Dealing with legislators is even more frustrating for advocates attempting to use the legal process. Members of Congress, and those particularly in the House of Representatives who must face election campaigns every two years, are primarily interested in getting reelected. To do that, they focus much more on the demands of their constituents and on pleasing funders than on the public interest. It takes either an earth-shattering set of events—such as Watergate—or dissimulation so great that it outrages members' sense of their own and the institution's importance to induce members Congress to undertake serious reforms. This is what it took for Senator Dianne Feinstein, chair of the Senate Intelligence Committee, to publically castigate the CIA for evading the efforts of her Senate committee that was investigating the agency's dark sites in 2014. Not only had staff members found that the CIA lied about the abusive interrogation at its dark sites and about the lack of success of using torture to gain intelligence; the agency had also hacked into the computers that the staffers were using to investigate it.[22] The law on its own cannot constrain an administration that is willing to go outside the law to advance its purposes. Paradoxically, it is only by expanding into other forms of activism that the rule of law can be defended.

Activism in Civil Society

The first wave of civil society activism in the United States after 9/11 came from the nonprofit sector, when millions of Americans contributed to help support the victims of that tragedy and their families (Sidel 2004, 93–94). But activists soon had to contend with the government's efforts to surveil civil society. We saw in chapter 7 how deftly the administration manipulated the media to maintain the fear and uncertainty generated by the terrorist attacks. But this was not its only effort within civil society; there were also a number of understandable moves that took time to become public and for civil society activists to understand.

The first effort was limited to assisting Muslim-oriented groups that were suspected of helping terrorism soon after 9/11. Between 2001 and 2004, while denying any intention to target Muslims,[23] the administration began to close in on groups suspected of ties to the 9/11 terrorists. This was the first sign that the fight against terrorism was not going to be limited to the killers of 9/11 or to the organizations that had sent them. In December 2001, the FBI raided three Islamic charities—the Benevolence International Foundation, the Global Relief Foundation, and the Holy Land Foundation for Relief and Development—and froze their assets (Sidel 2004, 95–103). The attack on the third group signaled that the War on Terror was going to range well beyond the attackers of 9/11 because its funds went to support Hamas in Gaza—not the Al Qaeda organization (ibid, 102).

The effect of these actions was to chill Muslim-run civil society groups that were engaged in broader projects abroad. "In the wake of the government's actions, "writes Mark Sidel, "several charitable gift funds that funnel contributions from individual donors to charitable organizations declined to channel additional funds to over ten Muslim charities identified in government or press reports as possibly tied to terrorist activities" (ibid., 103, 107). This fear increased when the Treasury Department put forward a set of voluntary "best practices" to guide overseas giving. At this point, some groups became concerned that the "voluntary" guidelines "were in fact stealth laws, adopted without consideration by Congress or formal rulemaking by an agency" (ibid., 115).[24]

But, unexpectedly, the government's crackdown on Muslim transnational giving had the result of deflecting charity-giving to groups at home, increasing the vitality of Muslim community groups within the United States (Ewing 2008; Bakalian and Bozorgmehr 2009). Not only that—the highly integrated Muslim communities in places such as Dearborn, Michigan—facing discrimination, surveillance, and humiliating searches at airports—began to gain a greater sense of their religious identities. In an ironic twist, Muslim civil society was strengthened by the exercise of the state's hierarchical power.

As it became clear that the government was beginning to regard civil society as potentially "uncivil and a source of insecurity," the ripples of government pressure traveled well beyond the Muslim groups that were originally targeted (Sidel 2010, 5). Peace and humanitarian groups working in areas of conflict—such as the West Bank or Somalia—were, of course, carefully watched. As it became clear that the government was interested other groups, not only in those responsible for the 9/11 bombings, a variety of groups began to mobilize in defense of civil liberties. Many of them, such as Human Rights Watch, Human Rights First, Amnesty International, the Constitution Project, and even the American Bar Association, struggled energetically to rein in the emerging surveillance state. Here we can survey the efforts of only a few such groups.

Librarians against the Patriot Act

Among the most far-reaching provisions of the Patriot Act was Section 215, which permitted "law enforcement authorities to gain access to medical, financial, student, computer, and other personal records from third party holders of these records . . . without notice to the target of the investigation, without explicitly tying the search to terrorism or spying" (Sidel 2004, 12). Section 215 was conceived to include the records of public libraries, university libraries, bookstores, medical offices, doctors, Internet service providers, and other record holders. A gag order attached to the provision meant that those who were targeted by the FBI for investigation through a "third party," such as a library or an Internet service provider, could not be informed by that third party that they were subjects of an investigation.[25]

In 2003, a coalition of booksellers, libraries, gun owners, the American Conservative Union, and the ACLU formed to demand that Congress amend Section

215.[26] Among the first to become alarmed was the American Library Association (ALA), which had a history of defending freedom of speech that went back to World War Two.[27] In its 2002 Resolution on the USA Patriot Act, the ALA maintained that "privacy is essential to the exercise of free speech, free thought, and free association."[28] It followed this resolution with a broad-based lobbying campaign to get Congress to strike library surveillance from the Patriot Act when its "sunset provisions" came due in 2005.

Librarians' protests against Section 215 were not limited to national resolutions. In March 2003, in places as widely dispersed as Santa Cruz, California; Whatcom County, Washington; and Longmont, Colorado, librarians warned users that their library records might be subject to FBI searches and launched a series of "subversive book checkouts," including books by Molly Ivins, Michael Moore, and Howard Zinn, and offered readers a guidebook on the FBI's counterintelligence program (Blanc 2010, 194–95). Some librarians even shredded physical records of book take-outs or deleted electronic records to shield users from possible searches (ibid., 203). The ALA's protests, together with the legal efforts of the ACLU and the Electronic Frontier Foundation, led to modest revisions of section 215 when it was re-authorized in 2005.

Local Bill of Rights Campaigns

Civil liberties activists also became involved in opposing the Patriot Act through what came to be called Bill of Rights Resolutions. In early 2002, a group called the Bill of Rights Defense Committee launched a campaign asking municipalities and states to pass a resolution in defense of civil liberties.[29] Again, the ACLU was involved in the campaign, but this one spread much more rapidly than the librarians' protest. By the time the campaign had leveled off in 2005, almost four hundred municipalities had signed Bill of Rights Resolutions (see Vasi and Strang 2009).[30]

It soon emerged that opposition to executive overreach would not come from civil society in general. In fact, as we saw in the last chapter, the government was simultaneously penetrating vast reaches of American society through contracting, coopting, and recruiting from among private groups. Opposition soon settled down to groups that were formed to defend the rights of minorities and unpopular groups. Among these, from the beginning, two stood out: the Center for Constitutional Rights (CCR) and the American Civil Liberties Union (ACLU). But their protests were made around the law, using the law against a lawless administration. And although the two groups were allied in their general purpose, the small size and outsider standing of the first, and the age and institutional standing of the latter, produced important differences in how they contested hegemony. Let us see how effective this process was against an administration determined to govern through rule by law.

The Center for Constitutional Rights

CCR is not a mass membership organization, as is its larger partner, the ACLU, but the post-9/11 legal challenges had a dramatic impact on both its funding and its dimensions.[31] From a modest budget of $2.1 million in 2001 and about $2.2 million in 2002, its funding increased fourfold in the next decade to a budget of approximately $8 million in 2013. In 2001, not counting administration, the organization had fourteen employees—with four full-time lawyers, a legal director, one fellow, and a volunteer. By 2013, CCR had a staff of fifty-one, not counting administration, which included twelve full-time lawyers, three fellows, five paralegals, and a legal director. In addition, the organization has added an advocacy department of five new staff members, five communications specialists, and six development staffers.[32] The events of 9/11 were terrible for the country and its rule-of-law tradition, but it made CCR the center of a new social movement based on the defense of detainee rights.

On November 13, 2001, President Bush issued Military Order Number 1, creating military commissions without consulting Congress; asserting the power to detain any noncitizen defined as a terrorist, whether picked up on the battlefield or elsewhere; and denying detainees a remedy to challenge their detention in a court of the United States.[33] When he read the decision the next day, Michael Ratner, venerable president of the CCR, saw in it the threat of an American coup d'état. Ratner was not alone. That same morning, Joseph Margulies, death-penalty defender, and Sandra Babcock, human rights lawyer, organized a conference call with colleagues, including "experts in the laws of war, the death penalty, civil rights, and international human rights" (Margulies 2006, 9). Margulies called Ratner, who was already beginning to put together a group of lawyers to defend against what he saw as the wholesale abolition of *habeas corpus* rights (Goldsmith 2012, 162). These initial contacts led to the creation of a network of lawyers around the country that would be referred to—after the success of the *Rasul* case—tongue-in-cheek as the Guantánamo Bar.

The Guantánamo legal network was transnational from the beginning. When Stephen Kenny, an Australian lawyer who had been asked to defend David Hicks, an Australian detainee, contacted Ratner, the group met at CCR headquarters in New York City to decide on whether they wanted to take on Hicks's defense. The group was joined by Clive Stafford-Smith, another death penalty lawyer, and by Steven Watt, a Scottish legal intern who had just joined CCR from a stint as a legal defender for the British government in the Pacific. The Anglo-American connection was soldered more tightly when Ratner was contacted by Gareth Peirce, a British barrister. Peirce, who had been a defender of IRA prisoners, had been contacted by a young Birmingham man, Habib Rasul, who had seen on television "those first images of orange-suited detainees in Guantánamo just as a reporter . . . arrived at his door to inform him that his brother Shafiq was being held there" (Peirce 2012, 18). Two years later, the case of *Rasul v. Bush* reached the U.S. Supreme Court.[34]

Ratner was determined to take the case all the way to the Supreme Court, but there was concern in the CCR (whose offices are located only a few miles north of the World Trade Center) at the delicacy of representing clients who might turn out to have been conspirators in the 9/11 massacres. There was even difficulty finding an attorney in Washington who would help file the papers. Some law firms looked askance at attorneys who were willing to represent detainees, and as late as 2005, one Department of Defense official suggested that clients stop offering their business to firms that did so.[35] But winning cases had never been the CCR's strategy, like the lawyers who had founded the organization in the 1960s,[36] Ratner believed in placing controversial issues on the agenda to force the government to take a position. With his urging, the decision was made to go ahead: "The issue of denying habeas corpus was so fundamental," he told Goldsmith in an interview, "that no matter what, we had to do the case" (quoted in Goldsmith 2012, 162).

The core legal question at issue in the *Rasul* litigation was whether *habeas* applies to detainees held outside the United States and whether the president has the power to suspend those rights. It was a legal fiction that Guantánamo was outside the writ of the federal court system, but this did not deter the Bush administration from denying the detainees all rights, and less than a year after 9/11, in a conservative Court that had historically been deferential to the executive in times of war, the chances of winning the case seemed small. The administration and the lower courts reduced the chances still further, the former by limiting access to Rasul and his co-defendants and the latter when federal district and appeals courts dismissed the case.

But, given the administration's extreme position that Guantánamo was beyond the law, the Supreme Court ruled in favor of the plaintiffs. The administration tried to use as a precedent the *Eisentrager* holding, which had denied access to the civilian courts for citizens of a country at war with the United States.[37] But the Court denied the relevance of that ruling, delivering a stinging rebuke to the administration's claim that the president had unchecked authority to hold detainees outside any legal constraint.

Rasul's legal results appeared to be modest and largely procedural. On the one hand, it starkly revealed the administration's lawless behavior in Afghanistan and elsewhere; but on the other, the Court granted only modest procedural rights to the detainees and their lawyers. More substantial was the signal given by the decision to mainstream law firms that it was legitimate to participate in the campaign. From *Rasul* on, many lawyers joined the campaign to oppose the government's lawless actions, and CCR saw it as only a first step—one that would only lead to real change when the *Boumediene v. Bush* decision was handed down.

Even before *Rasul*, white-shoe law firms had begun to approach the CCR. The distinguished firm of Shearman and Sterling had filed a case on behalf of twelve Kuwaiti detainees in May 2002. Shearman's involvement was instrumental in convincing other large law firms to come on board. The *Rasul* decision made it legitimate for lawyers outside the usual ideological range of the CCR to stand up for the rights of the detainees. Using personal and law-office ties, professional associations, and the newly developed tools of the Internet, activist lawyers developed the Guantánamo Bar, made up of a rapidly growing number of lawyers who signed up and trained for the defense of detainees they had never met. Watt was sent to Yemen to meet families who had received postcards from detainees informing them that they were in detention. Different lawyers and different firms were assigned particular national groups of detainees—mainly Saudis, Yemenis, and Europeans.

Some law firms operated independently to defend Guantánamo detainees, but the CCR was the core of the movement—training, assigning, and recruiting legal defenders. Figure 9.3, which draws on the analysis of Chan S. Suh (2015), shows how central the CCR was in the network of firms and legal institutions contributing pro bono services to the defense of Guantánamo detainees between 2002 and 2008. Suh's data also show how the composition of the Guantánamo Bar changed as it expanded. Table 9.3 summarizes the backgrounds and professional roles of the initiators (pre-*Rasul* participants) and the late-comers (participants in 2004–2008) in the Guantánamo Bar.

The pre-*Rasul* legal pioneers mainly came from civil liberties and death penalty work, and were drawn disproportionately from lawyers with long professional careers who had been trained in elite law schools, had more autonomous positions, and could draw on their experience as lead litigators. The post-*Rasul* recruits were younger on average, were less likely to have come from elite law schools, held less autonomous positions, and were less likely to have served as lead litigators. The table "provides evidence of clear differences between the initiators and the late-comers" (ibid.) and of a fairly standard pattern of diffusion from higher- to lower-status individuals. The meaning of the table is that, after the success of *Rasul*, the movement "normalized." From a small organization with cases that focused predominantly on domestic issues such as civil rights,

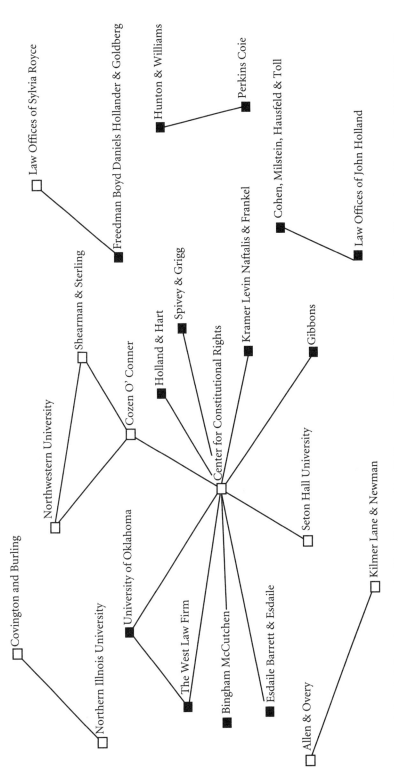

FIGURE 9.3 Collaborative network of law firms and institutions contributing to the Guantánamo Bar. Reproduced from Suh 2015, 300, with the kind permission of the author.

TABLE 9.3   Selected characteristics of Guantánamo lawyers: Initiators versus latecomers

	INITIATORS	LATECOMERS
Professional careers (years)	24.87	19.68
Elite law school training (%)	55.00	34.60
Professors (%)	22.00	5.30
Activists (%)	17.10	0.80
Lead litigators (%)	72.10	45.90
Total lawyers	26	55

Source: Suh 2015.

incarceration, and police abuse, the growing CCR's caseload shifted heavily to illegal detention and toward greater international involvements. At one point, there was a danger of the CCR becoming an organization that worked *only* on issues emerging from the War on Terror. This trend was reversed after 2008, when the CCR took on a number of challenging domestic issues, such as the NYPD's practice of "stopping and frisking" people—most commonly black or Hispanic people—on the street.

The Guantánamo years made CCR the center of the largest legal mobilization in U.S. history, apart from the civil rights movement, but its very success threatened to distract it from its historical commitment to civil rights. In 2008, it began expanding its cases under the rubric of Government Misconduct/Racial Justice, working on racial justice and prisoner's and immigrant rights, including cases against the NYPD's practice of "stop and frisk." At the same time, its international human rights work was shifting back from a near-exclusive focus on national security to its historical concerns with U.S. militarism in Central America; lesbian, gay, bisexual, and transgender (LGBT) rights; and even suing the pope for the Vatican's role in protecting priests guilty of sexual violence against children.[38]

The American Civil Liberties Union

What of the ACLU, which, as we saw in chapter 6, arose out of the antiwar movement during World War One?[39] It too has been a stalwart defender of civil rights and civil liberties, although with varying enthusiasm for unpopular causes, as when the organization was unwilling to take on the defense of communists in the Cold War (Keller 1989). But the ACLU regained its reputation for defending unpopular groups with a vengeance when it took on the defense of Frank Collin, American Nazi activist, in Skokie, Illinois, in 1977, to the outrage of much of its membership base (Strum 1999). Faced by the most aggressive domestic threat since Pearl Harbor, the organization had to decide whether to take on the defense of terrorist suspects being held in Guantánamo in the face of near-universal public opinion that favored locking them up and throwing away the key.

Compared to the small group of militant lawyers who were working around Michael Ratner in 2001, the ACLU is a vast organization with branches all over the country and major lobbying and communications wings alongside its extensive legal department. It was also engaged in trying to assist the hundreds of men who were swept off the streets in immigration raids or on other pretexts and was not as accustomed as CCR to doing international human rights cases.[40] Accordingly, it took longer to aggressively take up the defense of the detainees who might have had something to do with the massacres of September 11. But the organization filed amicus briefs in the big Guantánamo and Hamdi cases and, in 2008, established its John Adams Project to defend prisoners' rights.[41]

Whereas the CCR's post-9/11 work was based largely on legal defense, ACLU was also building coalitions, working with organizations that included Muslim organizations, the ALA, local Bill of Rights Defense committees, conservative privacy and libertarian groups, gun owners, antiabortion activists, and parts of the business community, to defend rights (Sidel 2004, 38). Coalition-building does not exclude legal defense, but it has a different political dynamic, requiring the organization to make compromises with partner groups and engaging it in public education and lobbying, as well as in legal action.

While CCR was forging ahead with the defense of detainees, the ACLU was developing a legal strategy more focused on the creative use of the FOIA (Freedom of Information Act) legislation. Starting in 2003, a group of ACLU lawyers began to file FOIA requests with the CIA and the Departments of Defense, Justice, and State for "records setting forth or discussing policies, procedures or guidelines relating to the torture or other cruel, inhuman or degrading treatment or punishment of Detainees."[42] The ACLU's campaign for FOIA releases forms the basis of much of what we now know about the administration's misdeeds, and the tactic of seeking freedom of information releases continues to produce revelations—for example, about the Obama administration's drone program and the NSA surveillance of U.S. citizens.

The ACLU was also concerned with the government's increasingly insistent surveillance and financial pressure on nonprofit groups and foundations. This extended to supporting groups that had been named as co-conspirators to the Holy Land Foundation, which was under indictment for financing terrorism. Filing a legal challenge in federal court in 2008, the national ACLU and its Texas affiliate alleged that the government was branding these groups as criminals without giving them the opportunity to clear their names (Sidel 2010, 29).[43] The

ACLU also filed suit against the Treasury Department's freezing of the funds of another organization, KindHearts, without providing it with an opportunity to challenge its designation as a "specially designated global terrorist" or the freezing of its funds (ibid., 30). While many other groups in the nonprofit sector rose to defend civil liberties only when their own interests were threatened, the ACLU became the default protector for groups of any kind that were caught up in the post-9/11 antiterrorist sweep.

As in the case of the CCR, opposing the government's post-9/11 policies produced internal changes in the ACLU. Whereas in 2000 the number of members/donors of the national ACLU was just over 285,000, by 2010 the number had grown to almost 522,000. And whereas in 2000 the total revenue declared to the IRS was $55.7 million, by 2010 it had nearly doubled, to $105.7 million. The staff of the national organization grew rapidly, too, from a total of 170 staff members in 2000 to 338 in 2013. Staffing grew more rapidly in the legal and communications divisions. In 2005, the national ACLU had a legal staff of 132 and a communications staff of 18 (the first year for which these breakdowns are available); the numbers had grown to 141 in the legal division and 29 in the communications division by 2013. At the same time, the size of its legislative division declined slightly, perhaps suggesting the hopelessness of lobbying Congress during a time of growing polarization.[44] The growth and diversification of the ACLU's activities following 9/11 can best be seen when we turn to the newest form of civil society activism—digital activism.

Contention on the Electronic Frontier

When Edward Snowden gave his first video interview to Glenn Greenwald for *The Guardian*, he was an unknown computer technologist working on contract for the government in Hawaii.[45] "But I didn't know Edward Snowden's name or his identity until you did, until *The Guardian* put on its website that first video interview . . .", said Ben Wizner, the ACLU's director of its Speech, Privacy, and Technology Project in 2014.[46] With a staff of seven lawyers and two technology experts, Wizner's group has taken up privacy cases relating to Facebook and other forms of social media and worked on intellectual property, patents, and cryptography law when Snowden's revelations were published in 2013.[47]

The ACLU was not alone. Since the early 1990s, when the government first became concerned about computer hacking, an archipelago of nonprofit groups—some of them supported by people who had pioneered in the electronic revolution of the late twentieth century—had been looking into issues such as intellectual property rights, hacktivism, the privacy of communications on the

Internet, and government electronic surveillance. These issues first came to public attention in a government operation against hacking in the early 1990s. On January 24, 1990, Secret Service agents entered an apartment in New York City where three young computer geeks calling themselves "Acid Phreak", "Phiber Optik", and "Scorpion" lived (Ludlow 1996, 468). The subjects of the investigation were members of a group called The Legion of Doom, which was thought to number fewer than twenty members, all of them in their teens or early twenties (ibid.). The government agents confiscated computers, software, floppy disks, and even, in one case, an answering machine, accusing the young men of hacking software from AT&T, BellSouth, MCI, U.S. Sprint, and other companies in the rapidly expanding world of electronic communications. These arrests were the beginning of a two-year investigation called Operation Sun Devil, involving 150 federal agents, a number of local and state law enforcement agencies, and the security resources of the affected companies.

Strange as it may seem, the dragnet eventually led to a visit to the office of a game publisher in Austin, Texas, named Steve Jackson Games (SJG). "They ransacked the premises, broke into several locked filing cabinets . . ., and eventually left carrying 3 computers, 2 laser printers, several hard disk, and many boxes of paper and floppy disks" (ibid., 472). The SJG investigation eventually led the FBI to John Perry Barlow, a rancher, computer activist, and one-time musician. An FBI agent, Barlow recalls, was sent to see if he was a member of a dread band of info-terrorists who had stolen and wantonly distributed source code normally used in the Macintosh ROMs. "As soon as I quit laughing," Barlow remembered, "I started to worry" (1990, 1).

Barlow had heard about the Secret Service raids on young hackers at a Harper's forum earlier in the year. As more information began to appear about the government's attempts to suppress a practice it did not yet understand, "It occurred to me that this might be the beginning of a great paroxysm of governmental confusion during which everyone's liberties would become at risk" (ibid.). He wrote up his experience for WELL, a computer board in Sausalito that was read by Mitch Kapor, the founder of Lotus 1–2–3, who had also had a visit from the FBI. Together, they involved John Gilmore, one of the founders of Sun Microsystems, and contacted a member of the same New York law firm that had defended Daniel Ellsberg against the government in the "Pentagon Papers" case two decades earlier.[48]

This was the origin of the Electronic Frontier Foundation (EFF), which became the leading nonprofit organization defending civil liberties in the electronic world. Over the next two decades, its activities ranged from the defense of hackers whose civil liberties were being threatened to the defense of electronic privacy, free expression on the Internet, technology development, and grassroots activism.[49] EFF began with a few activists working out of Kapor's office in Cambridge, Massachusetts, briefly moved to the nation's capital, before escaping from the beltway to offices in San Francisco, closer to its natural base in the tech industry and near the friendly precincts of Berkeley and Stanford. It began with the idea of serving as a source of funding for the legal costs of people whose rights it hoped to protect, but soon it began to take on cases of its own, hired staff, and began to engage in discussions about public policy and government invasions of privacy. The first important case it fielded involved a Berkeley student who wished to publish a paper on an encryption code system he had developed.[50] The EFF won that case, establishing the key principle that software source code is speech, protected by the First Amendment.

Encryption turned out to be a red thread in EFF's early history. As computer technology began to spread around the world, increasingly sophisticated encryption programs were being developed. In the United States, the National Bureau of Standards had adopted a Federal Information Processing Standard with the approval of the NSA, which was adopted around the world. By the 1990s, a more advanced Data Encryption Standard (DES) was developed, which raised concerns among technology experts about a backdoor that the government could use to get into encrypted messages. The EFF began to work on a project to crack the DES to demonstrate that it was unsafe. In 1999, it broke a DES key in just over twenty-two hours (Electronic Frontier Foundation 1998). As a result, a far more robust standard was developed for encryption.

The government had been using electronic surveillance for spying since the 1970s, but the 9/11 massacres and the attempt to locate the Islamist terrorists electronically led to a rapid expansion of its electronic surveillance efforts and to a willingness to go outside the law in doing so. Activists learned that something big was afoot only from contacts in the technology industry, but the information was vague and people were reluctant to discuss it. During the Clinton administration, several proposals for electronic surveillance had made their way through Congress, but the president had vetoed them; now the Bush administration's lawyers interpreted Section 215 of the USA Patriot Act to mean that the government could use its contacts with the industry to get the records of every single American phone call every day. Government stretching of the law went so far as to interpret the Fourth Amendment's strictures on searches and seizures to say that the amendment is silent "when it comes to intercepting and storing all our communications."[51]

But in a system that depended so intimately on cooperation among the government, private contractors, and industry, the details of what the government was doing could not remain secret forever. In 2005, the *New York Times*, based on anonymous tips, reported that the government was monitoring international financial transactions; picking up international communications that traveled through the United States; mining phone and e-mail data; analyzing automated teller machine (ATM) transactions, credit card purchases and wire transfers; and inducing private telecom companies to cooperate.[52] The government's response to the exposures was to introduce reforms in the secret FISA court that had been created in the 1970s to monitor government surveillance.

At the same time, more technically savvy actors were becoming concerned at what governmental secrecy was hiding. In 2006, a former hacker, Julian Assange, and his colleagues began a data-revealing enterprise called Wikileaks. No more than a pest to officials for its first few years of activities, Wikileaks struck pay dirt in 2010 when it published documents stolen by a U.S. army soldier, then called Bradley Manning. From a forward monitoring post in Iraq, Manning had downloaded diplomatic cables; secret government documents from Iraq and Afghanistan; and, most appalling, a video of a U.S. army airstrike in Iraq that savaged a group of civilians, including journalists and a child. When Assange played this video before the National Press Club in Washington, the story went viral, and the government realized its "secret files" were no longer secret.[53]

But neither Wikileaks nor the Manning files had anything like the effects on government secrecy that the Snowden files did. When Snowden looked into the NSA records, he discovered that the targets of NSA electronic spying were not only foreign suspects but U.S. citizens and that the agency was secretly going through the backdoor of Internet firms and phone companies—just as the EFF had supposed it would do in its cracking efforts in the 1990s.[54] The immediate effects were electric. Within days, much of the press and the blogosphere had fastened on the story; there was rising outrage in public opinion that the government was invading Americans' privacy; and Congress, so long indifferent to the abuses of rights the Bush administration had fostered, began to stir.[55] Indeed, Representative James Sensenbrenner (R-Wisconsin), who had written the Patriot Act, denied he had had any intention in 2001 of allowing it to be used as the legal authority to permit mass surveillance of Americans.[56] After the Snowden revelations, an outraged Sensenbrenner proposed revisions in the act that scaled back the government's ability to spy on Americans.

Obama's response, when he acted, was cautious. He appointed a blue-ribbon presidential committee that presented a report claiming the NSA had gone beyond its congressional mandate. In response, a watered-down version of Sensenbrenner's USA Freedom Act, intended to rein in the NSA programs, passed the House of Representatives.[57] As Ben Wizner, who has had more experience than most activists with the government's capacity to find new ways to invade citizens' privacy, said in an interview in March 2014, "And I think one of the most remarkable developments in the last eight or nine months has been how the surveillance state has lost control of the argument in the plot, that their efforts to say that they have stopped any number of terrorist attacks with these and we would all be in great danger if they lost these authorities just don't seem as credible anymore."[58]

Is Wizner's guarded optimism likely to prove justified? Past experience does not offer much hope. As Baher Azmy, legal director of CCR, writes, "Neither Congress, the courts, nor the mass public showed much interest in rolling back the expansion of the hierarchical state in the wake of 9/11" (2012, 23). As the narratives in this chapter indicate, a state rich in both hierarchical and infrastructural power has almost infinite resources to respond to civil society resistance with new or modified policies.

But, as Wizner also notes, the United States is far from the nation of September 12, 2001. There is a new generation of Americans who are more tech savvy, less traumatized from the massacres of 9/11 than their parents were, and more conscious of the potential for invading civil society. They are helping to transform the nature of contentious politics and perhaps making it more difficult for the state to restrict rights in wartime. And as the revelations of Manning, Wikileaks, and Snowden suggest, there is a "logic of connective action" that is opening up a new field of contentious politics (Bennett and Segerberg 2013).

Conclusions

The long cycle of contentious politics that began with the protests against the Iraq War and continued through legal efforts to defend the rights of detainees evolved into a broad coalition of contentious actors against a government that responded to the tragedy of 9/11 with the misuse of the law (as we saw in chapter 7) and the expansion of state power (as we examined in chapter 8). The Stop Watching Us rally following the Snowden revelations was not an antiwar protest or a legal mobilization, but it brought together veterans of the antiwar movement with people who had used the legal process to defend human rights, people dependent on the Internet for their business, and still others who were worried about government surveillance.

The activism of civil society groups such as the ACLU, the CCR, the EFF, and an archipelago of similar groups were the main source of resistance to the emergency state that expanded alarmingly after 9/11. They were responding in part to the expansion of hierarchical power, but also to the capacity of the state to penetrate society through its infrastructural power. Their partial success was due to their stubborn resistance to the former but also to the permeability of the archipelago of the state's reach into civil society.

Past episodes of war-making depended heavily on the use of hierarchical power. Recall what we have learned from previous episodes described in this book: how quickly the crafters of the French Declaration of the Rights of Man put opponents "outside the law"; how the Lincoln administration used military commissions to try civilians opposing the Civil War; how the Italian government installed military control over industrial relations during World War One; how the Wilson administration used the Sedition Act against foreigners during and after the same war; how the Roosevelt administration ignored constitutional guarantees and interned thousands of Japanese Americans during World War Two; and how the Truman and Eisenhower administrations forced government employees and teachers to sign loyalty oaths during the Cold War.

But infrastructural powers were increasingly used for social control and repression too. In Italy, patriotic groups served the state, reporting on "subversive" activities against intervention in World War One; in the same war, the American Committee on Public Information fostered a mood of fear, anger, and rabid patriotism against pacifists and foreigners; after Pearl Harbor, California's voluntary sector colluded in the internment of Japanese Americans; during the Cold War, civic groups opposed the First Amendment rights of communists and "fellow travelers"; and more recently, the government developed an enormous contracting sector and used its ties with tech companies to intrude on Americans' privacy rights.

But there are exceptions, and they are instructive. Think of the reversal of the *Dennis* precedent and other court decisions expanding free speech and association rights in the later years of the Cold War. Remember the antiwar mobilizations that led Congress to pass antiwar resolutions against the Vietnam War and convinced Nixon he could not continue the invasion into Cambodia. Think of the national shame at the Japanese internment tragedy under Presidents Ford and Reagan. Finally, reflect on the Church Commission reforms of the 1970s. In all these cases, when civil society groups built coalitions and took advantage of political opportunities, executive overreach in times of emergency was rolled back.

Such a combination was absent in the wars that were launched in the immediate wake of 9/11, as can be seen in the failure of the antiwar mobilization of February 15, 2003. It was only when the Iraq War began to go badly and the government's criminal behavior was exposed that the excesses of the Bush-Cheney emergency state began to be confronted. Even then, campaigners dropped away and the successes were partial, uneven, and often dependent on alliances with institutional actors that did not share all of the activists' goals (Cortright 2014). These coalitions took years of struggle, thousands of hours of dedicated work, and a willingness to believe, against the odds, that some of them might pay off.

Movements seldom seek only small changes, but their struggles sometimes have partial effects in the longer run. Remember the "Pentagon Papers" and the break-in at the FBI headquarters in Media, Pennsylvania? In the short-term, the former was diverted into a discussion of whether Daniel Ellsberg had broken the law, and the latter was kept off the front pages by an FBI that devoted thousands of agent-hours to trying to track down the burglars (Medsger 2013). But it is the indirect effects of these disclosures that we remember today. Our understanding of the Vietnam War was sharply redefined by what Ellsberg revealed when he published the "Pentagon Papers." The COINTELPRO exposure, along with persistent digging by Daniel Stern, investigative journalist, led to the temporary end of the FBI's infiltration of groups it had targeted for investigation. This was a "wholesale" outcome that came about through a set of "retail" actions on the part of civil society groups.

What of the future? Goldsmith believes that "when Presidents act aggressively to curtail civil liberties at the dawn of a war or an emergency in a way that is later regretted, those regrets are remembered in the next war or emergency and are not repeated" (2012, 240). But Goldsmith forgets that the government's capacity to invent new ways to evade civil society resistance does not stand still. New circumstances and new methods mean that the abuses of the past may no longer be a guide to the emergency practices of the next war. Whereas there was a libertarian ratchet in the reforms after Vietnam and Watergate (Posner and Vermeuele 2005), we have seen that a new statist ratchet followed, using new and more innovative forms of social control, media manipulation, and electronic surveillance.

There was something else that was new as well. In part because of the fabric of international ties and institutions created since World War Two and in part because of the dominant U.S. position within that matrix, the state of emergency after 9/11 was extended abroad. That led both to illegal actions, such as the kidnapping and rendition of suspects, and to the projection of the tools that the U.S. government had developed against terrorists at home to the international level. Those dual upward shifts in scale are the topic of chapter 10.

Part III

INTERNATIONALIZATION AND THE NEW WORLD OF CONTENTION

THE DARK SIDE OF
INTERNATIONALISM

Not long after the fall of Muammar Gaddafi, the Libyan dictator, a group of rebels, journalists, and Human Rights Watch activists stormed the offices of Gaddafi's former intelligence chief, Moussa Koussa. There they discovered a fax in which he was congratulated by Sir Mark Allen, then Britain's MI6 director, on the "safe arrival" of Libyan rebel Abel Hakin Belhadj in Libya in 2004. Belhadj's rendition, Allen glowed, "demonstrates the remarkable relationship we have built over recent years."[1] Belhadj, along with his pregnant wife, Fatima Bouchar, had been living in China when the couple became alarmed at what seemed to be surveillance of their home. They decided to seek asylum in Britain, but when they tried to fly there, with Belhadj traveling on a false passport, they were arrested, deported to Malaysia, and held there while the Malaysian authorities consulted other countries' authorities; Malaysian authorities then sent them to Bangkok.[2] But on arriving there, they were handed over to people they assumed to be U.S. agents and were detained in what they believed was a U.S. secret prison. The couple were separated, and Belhadj, in a later court filing, claimed that he suffered weeks of abuse from what he assumed to be U.S. agents. After several weeks, Belhadj and his wife were put on a plane in restraints by U.S. agents and transferred to Tripoli, where he was taken to the notorious Tajoura prison and tortured for about four years. During the initial part of his detention, according to his testimony, he was interrogated by a number of foreign agents, both British and American. When he agreed to participate in the "de-radicalization and reconciliation process" led by Gaddafi's son, Saif, his conditions were eased. He was eventually released from prison in March 2010 and reunited with his wife.

Based on the documents that came to light when Koussa's office was raided, Belhadj and Bouchar sued Jack Straw, then British foreign minister, Mark Allen, and other British officials, alleging false imprisonment and a host of other charges. On December 19, 2013, High Court Justice Sir Peregrine Simon ruled that Belhadj and his wife could not sue either MI6 or Straw "because to do so would damage Britain's relations with the US." Simon said he was ruling against Belhadj "because American, as well as British, officials were involved in the operation." The judge admitted that "the conduct of US officials acting outside the US was unlawful" and that there was "what appears to be a potentially well-founded claim that UK authorities were directly implicated in the extraordinary rendition."[3]

What was happening here, and what does it have to do with war, states, and contention? First, none of this was likely to have happened had it not been for the U.S. government's attempts after 9/11 to use its international contacts to defeat Islamist radicalism. There had been renditions during the Reagan and Clinton administrations, but only in extraordinary situations and never with the regularity and the degree of clandestine cooperation that followed the September 11 bombings. The new wars of the early twenty-first century produced a systematic willingness on the part of both Britain and the United States to ignore the rules of international behavior that the United States had helped to write in the decades after the passage of the Universal Declaration of Human Rights in 1947.

Second, although most cases of extraordinary rendition involved only two cooperating states—most often the United States and Egypt—the Belhadj-Bouchar rendition was multilateral; it involved China, where the couple were living; Malaysia and Thailand, which allowed Belhadj to be rendered to Libya; the United States, which took him to what was evidently a black-site prison in Thailand and then sent him to Libya; the United Kingdom, which connived in the rendition and interrogated him in Libyan prisons; and—only at the end of the story—Libya. Moreover, it involved a group of Libyan rebels, journalists, and the human rights activists who passed on the documents unearthed in Koussa's office to the British press and to nonprofit groups such as Human Rights Watch and the British group Reprieve. Unlike past periods of repression of terrorism, which were either unilateral or bilateral, the post-9/11 suppression of terrorism was built on a network of multilateral contacts.

Third, Judge Simon's decision not to allow the lawsuit to proceed was based on a threat from the United States. As in other cases we will examine, the judge virtually admitted that the state interest that concerned him was that Britain's U.S. partners would cut off intelligence cooperation between the two countries.

If this was internationalism, it was of a very different kind than what is taught in classes on international relations; it is part of "the dark side" of internationalism, which has grown both more multilateral and more clandestine in the twenty-first century in the name of fighting terrorism.

Students of American politics have long observed that liberalism has a dark side (Smith 2010; Katzenstein, Mohsen, and Rubin 2011). But liberal internationalists have ignored the possibility that the institutions and norms developed in a liberal internationalist spirit after World War Two could be employed for illiberal purposes. Stories such as this one—and there are many others—shift the focus of internationalism from the ministries traditionally dedicated to foreign relations to the executive and the clandestine world of national security (Scheppele 2006). And when the internationalization of security is pushed by a hegemonic power that feels itself to be threatened—as in the United States did after 9/11—even the internal politics of minor powers are affected.

In this chapter, I turn first to the doctrine of liberal internationalism and its practices in the post–World War Two period. I then turn to the progression from mainly national responses at the turn of the twentieth century, to the largely bilateral response to clandestine violence during the Cold War, and then to the uses that the Bush administration made of international norms and multinational cooperation in fighting terrorism after 9/11. I show how internationalist language and multilateral institutions became the platform on which far-reaching methods of surveillance and control were supported by the United States and its major ally, the United Kingdom, after 9/11. Finally, I turn to two examples of how dark-side internationalism manifested itself in two U.S. allies: the intrusion of extraordinary rendition into Italian domestic politics and the creation of a network of civil society groups in British civil society

Liberal Internationalism

The post–World War Two period saw the creation of a network of institutions, multinational agreements, and treaties in the fields of collective security, economic cooperation, and human rights, first in the North Atlantic area and then globally (Mazower 2012). Theorists were quick to identify the emerging structure of the postwar international system with liberal goals. In the 1950s, Karl W. Deutsch, Sidney A. Burrell, and Robert A. Kann (1957) already saw the North Atlantic area as a potential political community. In the 1970s, Robert Keohane and Joseph Nye (1971) identified a trend to greater transnational relations. Later in the same decade, they wrote of the "complex interdependence" they saw developing in world politics (Keohane and Nye 1977). These themes were taken up in the 1990s by a school of constructivists, whose instincts were essentially liberal (Risse-Kappen 1995; Keck and Sikkink, 1998; Risse, Ropp, and Sikkink 1999, 2013).

By the turn of the new century, the international institutions created after World War Two reflected both meanings of the term *liberal*: they were guided by economic neoliberalism, and they operated through weighted pluralistic decision making (O'Brien, Goetz, Scholte, and Williams 2000; Tarrow 2005). As G. John Ikenberry writes, "The United States shaped the governing arrangements of the Western system into an order tied together by partnerships, pacts, institutions, and grand bargains and built around multilayered agreements that served to open markets, bind democracies and anticommunist authoritarian regimes together, and create a far-flung security community" (2011, 159).[4]

The same period saw the parallel construction of a spectrum of transnational *non*state organizations that both mirrored and interacted with the official structures of international cooperation. These organizations were by no means all liberal, in the sense of seeking to liberalize the world. But their variety of form and function made them increasingly resemble the pluralistic template typical of liberal systems (Huntington 1973). As the Cold War ended, the human rights community began to mobilize on behalf of the rights of children, women, and prisoners and of human rights in general (Mazower 2012, chap. 13). The number of human rights treaties and conventions signed under the liberal internationalist umbrella grew gradually in the early Cold War but accelerated as tensions eased. Figure 10.1 lays out the cumulative number of major international and regional human rights treaties and conventions in the postwar period.

Notice how quickly this wave of liberal institution-building arose, producing the impression "that internationalization necessarily supported the constitutionalization of state power" (Scheppele 2006, 350–51). And because these instruments were associated with the efforts of liberal groups, they underscored the idea that internationalism was inherently liberal. But the same process of globalization that nurtured the diffusion of human rights and other liberal groups also provided the communication links for a new family of nonstate actors—transnational terrorist groups (Asal, Nusbaum, and Harrington 2007). As Harold Koh writes, "terrorists can exploit the same interconnectedness to turn airplanes into missiles, to use the global financial system to move money across borders, to turn ordinary mail into a delivery system for biological weapons, and to plant viruses into email as a tool for cyberterrorism" (2003, 1496). Terrorism was the spur to the use of multilateral institutions for purposes other than the founding ones of the international community. As figure 10.1 also shows, as the human rights curve leveled off after the 1980s, states began to sign an increasing number of treaties and conventions that required them to take measures against transnational terrorism.

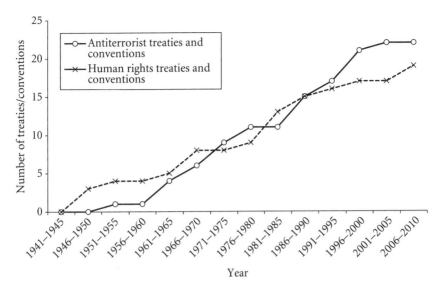

FIGURE 10.1 Human rights and antiterrorist conventions, 1945–2010. Bates et al. 2011, xxv–xxxi.

The United States had played the leading role in constructing the Bretton Woods Accords that governed the postwar international economic system (Mazower 2012, chap. 10). As the world's leading military power, it was also the lynchpin of NATO and of a series of NATO-like institutions around the world. As a pluralist state, it shaped the multilateral nature of the institutions that emerged in its image (Huntington 1973). And as a liberal state, it welcomed the addition of human rights treaties and conventions to the international framework—as long as these did not impose too much on its domestic behavior. This led to a peculiar combination of universalism and particularism. As Mark Mazower writes in *Governing the World*, "Washington's participation in the world body turned out to carry only minor risks of constraint since the United States was able to combine universalism and exceptionalism to an unprecedented degree, writing the rules in a way that mostly served its core interests and generally exempting itself from those rules its legislators disliked" (2012, xvi).

Trouble in Internationalism

From the start, there were ambiguities in the practice of liberal internationalism. With the exception of the European Court of Human Rights, international tribunals created to monitor human rights abuses lacked the legal authority to implement their judgments and were peppered with derogations. Opponents to these state interests could be framed as being outside the liberal consensus (Tsoulala 2008, 64–65). The same institutions that had been developed for mutual security, economic development, and human rights could be employed to freeze the assets of suspected groups and ignored the human rights treaties that had been created under the aegis of liberal internationalism (Gross and Ní Aoláin 2006, 400–401). This meant that even states with poor human rights records—such as Russia and China—could justify the suppression of internal insurgencies under the umbrella of United Nations antiterrorism resolutions. Before we turn to that inversion of liberal internationalism, however, it is important to understand how it developed out of purely national, and then bilateral, attempts to combat clandestine violence.

From Unilateralism to Bilateralism

The transnational features of terrorism are not new. "Many terrorist organizations . . . have operated and trained across jurisdictions for decades, and have been financed accordingly," (ibid., 380) but cooperation and mutual assistance in dealing with clandestine armed conflict took a long time to develop, first, because states were jealous of their sovereignty; second, because the Cold War impeded cooperation; and, finally, because of the absence of a consensual definition of terrorism. Early efforts to subdue terrorism were unilateral, as in the case of European anarchism at the turn of the twentieth century. By the Cold War, we can see largely bilateral arrangements, as in the efforts of the United Kingdom to involve, first, the Irish Republic and, then, the United States in peacemaking efforts in Northern Ireland.

The Anarchist Challenge

Although attempts to organize socialists internationally dated from the 1860s, it was only in the 1890s that something resembling a transnational network of anarchists was thought to exist. Italy was the first Western country to suffer the outrages of this "international." In 1898, a wave of violence led the government to attempt to organize its neighbors to fight what it saw as an international problem, convening the Rome Conference of 1898. As Giovanna Tosatti writes, "Italy, under accusation abroad as the source of anarchism, and deciding that surveillance of the anarchists was an international problem, proposed as an immediate remedy the convocation of a conference open to all the European states."(1997, 225–26).[5]

But the Italian initiative failed. Part of the reason was because countries such as Britain, Belgium, and Switzerland regarded the right of asylum as an essential component of sovereignty and would not agree to the automatic extradition of presumed anarchists (Aquarone 1981, 157). Another was a lack of trust of police agents, who, either through incompetence or provocation, sometimes facilitated terrorist acts (Jenson 2009, 97). But the major reason was the growing political and ideological divisions between rival governments in the years leading up to World War One.

After the Rome conference, European police officials met occasionally to discuss how to deal with transborder subversion (Bigo 1996, 61). The St. Petersburg protocol of 1904, which followed several spectacular assassinations, made progress in the coordination of antiterrorist policing, but it was never signed by the majority of European countries. Even the informal cooperation agreed on in Rome and St. Petersburg lapsed as Europe approached World War One (Jenson 2009, 98–99). But until the creation of Interpol in 1923, the only significant changes were normative; in both the 1892 resolution of the Institute of International Law and in the 1934 International Conference for the Unification of Penal Law, *anarchist violence* was defined as "criminal acts directed against the bases of the *entire social order*" and not against only a certain state or form of government (quoted in ibid., 103, emphasis added). But the first of these resolutions had no legal force and the second was never ratified. The important point is that transnational anarchism was dealt with largely by unilateral police efforts.

The Age of Bilateralism

The end of World War Two and the creation of the United Nations did not lead in short order to the creation of international policing agreements either, mainly because the world was quickly engulfed in the Cold War, which hamstrung international cooperation. The 1977 European Convention on the Suppression of Terrorism marked a first, but extremely modest, step toward collaboration (Guelke 2009, 166–67). But until the approach of the Single Market and the opening of EU borders, police cooperation was usually informal and bilateral rather than based on multilateral agreements (Jenson 2009, 92; Bigo 1996, 34).

Didier Bigo provides a sampling of these accords: an agreement of October 1986 between France and Italy for an exchange of experts in the domain of antiterrorism and drug control; an agreement of April 1987 between France and Germany to exchange antiterrorist intelligence; an agreement of May 1987 between France and Spain on terrorism, organized crime, and drug trafficking; an agreement of May 1989 between France and Britain on terrorism, organized crime, drug trafficking, and clandestine immigration; and an agreement between France and Belgium on organized terrorism (Bigo 1996, 32–33). Not even the longest episode of violence involving more than one EU member—the Northern

Irish conflict—produced significant multilateral intervention until late in the conflict, when the Cold War had ebbed and European institutions were beginning to take shape.

The Northern Irish Troubles

Soon after the signing of the United Nations' Universal Declaration of Human Rights in 1948, the newly formed Council of Europe moved quickly to create a binding multilateral treaty (Dickson 2010, 24). But, given the paramount issue of decolonization, the Irish conflict was scarcely mentioned, and the British government refused to ratify the 1977 Geneva Protocols as long as it persisted (Campbell and Connolly 2012, 18).[6]

The modern phase of the Northern Irish conflict, as we saw in chapter 5, erupted in the late 1960s with a civil rights movement modeled on the U.S. example. Bloody Sunday radicalized the Catholic population, and direct rule brought martial law, detention without trial, and the use of five "deep interrogation" techniques against IRA prisoners (Donahue 2008, 49–50). As in Abu Ghraib three decades later, these techniques were not the result of "a few rotten apples" but were mandated by the British Special Powers Act and by a 1972 Joint Directive on Military Interrogation in Internal Security Operations Overseas. A blue-ribbon committee headed by Hubert Lister Parker, Lord Parker, found that the Geneva Convention III, which governs the treatment of prisoners of war, did not apply to the conflict—because it was internal—nor did Britain's obligations under the European Convention on Human Rights or Article V of the Universal Declaration of Human Rights.[7]

But it was soon clear that, despite the British determination to regard the Troubles as internal to the United Kingdom, no solution could ignore the Republic of Ireland and its links to both Northern Ireland and to the United Kingdom. IRA combatants were known to cross the border almost at will, where they could lick their wounds, seek arms and financial support, and recruit new militants; until 1999, the Irish Constitution even maintained a territorial claim to the entire island. By the mid-1980s, it had become clear that the British would need the Republic of Ireland's cooperation to police the border, round up IRA suspects, and eventually resolve the conflict.

A first effort at British-Irish cooperation was the Sunningdale agreement of 1973, which fell apart when it was violently opposed by the Protestant majority in the North. After the British government backed off, there were no successful efforts at cooperation until the signature of the Anglo-Irish Agreement of 1985 (Neumann 2003, 142–47, 184–85). Among other things, the agreement was aimed at preventing IRA combatants from finding safe haven across the border and assuring that the republic would be on board for any future settlement. Many years of negotiations dragged on between the British government and all parties, including secret contacts with the IRA, before a new bilateral actor—the United States—entered the picture.

Despite the good offices of Irish-American politicians such as Senator Edward Kennedy (D-Massachusetts), the U.S. connection was not always helpful to its British allies. Irish American groups—some of them illegal—were known to support the cause of the Northern Irish militants.[8] The British government suspected—not without reason—that U.S. politicians were more influenced by local electoral considerations and by Irish American associations than by support for a settlement. Bill Clinton even broke briefly with his British allies by allowing Gerry Adams, Sinn Féin leader, to enter the United States (Cox 1997, 687–89). Yet it was the United States, through the peace negotiations led by Senator George Mitchell (D-Maine), that eventually produced the Good Friday Agreement of 1998.

What of international institutions? The European Union initially stayed out of the conflict but could not disguise its dark side from Europeans, who began to take more note of the conflict after the British began to use internment without trial and abusive interrogation techniques against IRA prisoners. European attention grew especially after the hunger strike and death of Bobby Sands, IRA leader, in May 1981 (Guelke 1988, 2). As the insurgency heated up, the Irish Republic brought a case in the European Court of Human Rights (*The Republic of Ireland v. United Kingdom*) against Britain's use of the five techniques against IRA detainees.[9] But both the European Commission and the Court decided that, although the British had engaged in inhuman and degrading treatment, they had not in fact used torture, presaging the use of Aesopian language for torture that was used in the U.S. War on Terror.

As the Cold War ebbed, multilateral institutions began to matter increasingly in states' responses to armed conflict. In the mid-1990s, the European Union agreed to pay a "peace dividend" to convince the Irish parties to come to the table (Meehan 2000; Neumann 2003, 174). In the same decade, the European Court of Human Rights began to take more seriously the accusations of abuse in Northern Irish prisons. But, as Brice Dickson writes of the European human rights treaty (European Convention on Human Rights, ECHR), "The Convention was very largely irrelevant both to the way the conflict was managed while it was raging and to the way it was largely resolved through the Belfast (Good Friday) Agreement of 1998. The Convention's political role, in other words, was minimal" (Dickson 2010, 362). Although international cooperation against armed conflict expanded during the wars in former Yugoslavia, it was only with the growing threat of Islamist terrorism that the United Nations and the European Union became centrally involved in the fight against clandestine violence.

Multilateral Counterterrorism

The advent of 9/11 brought the United States to the center of international efforts to track down and suppress terrorism. And when it did, a dark side began to emerge within the institutions that had grown up under the umbrella of liberal internationalism. Many observers, reflecting on the horrific events of September 11, 2001, have seen it in an "everything changed" framework. A great deal *did* change after 9/11, but the world never changes all at once. More often, institutions created for one purpose are adapted to another, and norms that emerge in earlier periods are adapted to confront later problems. Because the United States suffered the most horrific attack of all and remained the hegemonic center of the international system, there was a scale shift upward from its policies and its interests to the United Nations and other international institutions.

Bush Reframes Liberal Internationalism

In his first address to a joint session of Congress after 9/11, after thanking foreign friends for their sympathy, President Bush warned other nations, "Either you are with us, or you are with the terrorists. From this day forward, any nation that continues to harbor or support terrorism will be regarded by the United States as a hostile regime."[10] This threatening statement was certainly in line with the unipolar interpretation of the Bush Doctrine. But the president also struck an internationalist note. "This is not," he declared, "just America's fight, and what is at stake is not just America's freedom. This is the world's fight. This is civilization's fight. This is the fight of all who believe in progress and pluralism, tolerance and freedom." Evoking the spirit of multilateralism, Bush continued, "The United States is grateful that many nations and many international organizations have already responded with sympathy and with support, nations from Latin America to Asia, to Africa, to Europe, to the Islamic world. Perhaps the NATO Charter reflects best the attitude of the world: An attack on one is an attack on all."[11]

During his first State of the Union Speech following 9/11, even as he introduced his fateful "Axis of Evil" metaphor, Bush continued to link international cooperation against terrorism to liberal values. "America," he promised, "will lead by defending liberty and justice because they are right and true and unchanging for all people everywhere. No nation owns these aspirations, and no nation is exempt from them. We have no intention of imposing our culture. But America will always stand firm for the nonnegotiable demands of human dignity: the rule of law; limits on the power of the state; respect for women; private property; free speech; equal justice; and religious tolerance."[12] But from the beginning, these "productive international relationships" were to produce a dark side.

Putting People outside the Law

After September 11, instead of declaring a state of emergency or calling for a change in international human rights, the Bush administration tried to reshape existing international law, both by creating extralegal zones—most prominently at Guantánamo Bay, Cuba—and *extralegal persons*—"particularly those detainees labeled 'unlawful enemy combatants,'" who, "even if American citizens on American soil, are effectively accorded no recognized legal avenue to assert either substantive or procedural rights" (Koh 2003,1497–98). It is striking how often the administration used the language of internationalism to justify holding prisoners without due process. "Indeed," writes Frédéric Mégret, "the US authorities' case is often not a case to simply violate or do away with the law, as much as it is a characteristically strict, *almost legalistic* interpretation of the law" (2006: 27).

As we saw in chapter 7, the original "torture memo" written by Jay Bybee claimed that "to say that the President may suspend specific provisions of the Geneva Conventions *as a legal requirement* is by no means to say that the principles of the laws of armed conflict cannot be applied *as a matter of U.S. government policy*" (2005, 105, emphasis in original). The same was true of the opinion of Assistant Attorney General Jack Goldsmith, who tried to justify the extraordinary rendition of prisoners to countries where they were sure to be tortured without reference to international law. Article 49 of the Geneva Conventions, Goldsmith airily suggested, did not preclude "the temporary relocation of 'protected persons' . . . who have not been accused of an offense from occupied Iraq to another country for a brief but not indefinite period, to facilitate interrogation" (Goldsmith 2005, 367). As in Bush's State of the Union address, Goldsmith used universalist rhetoric to frame U.S. interests.

International Rule by Law

What would happen to the government's dedication to liberal internationalism when it came to justifying how it would treat its prisoners? Long ago, E. H. Carr, the British historian, described a fundamental divergence in the understanding of international law "between those who regard law primarily as a branch of ethics, and those who regard it primarily as a vehicle of power" (1939, 173). "More than six decades later," writes Matthew Evangelista, commenting on Carr's distinction, "the Global War on Terror exposed this divergence as still the fundamental source of disagreement on the purpose of the rules of war" (2008, 9). A whole range of definitional questions turned on this difference—beginning with the fundamental question of the definition of terrorism (ibid., chap. 2; Gross and Ní Aoláin 2006, 366–71). Rather than define the targets of the War on Terror as those who had committed the acts of September 11 and other related outrages, the Bush administration expanded the definition of terrorism to include all those who threaten human dignity, the rule of law, limits on the power of the state, respect for women, private property, free speech, equal justice, and religious tolerance. There was even a tendency to define states—or the armed forces of states—as terrorist. Thus, captured Taliban soldiers—who clearly represented a state—were treated with the same indifference to due process as Al Qaeda fighters, and in 2007, Iran's Revolutionary Guard Corps was labeled as "a foreign terrorist organization" (Evangelista 2008, 52–53). Law, in Carr's sharp distinction, was increasingly regarded as a vehicle of power.

From the beginning, Bush-era decision makers used rule-of-law arguments to respond to human rights organizations' efforts to bring the world's attention to the Guantánamo Bay prison camp. Consider what happened when the CCR, in early 2002, requested that the Inter-American Commission on Human Rights (IACHR) establish the legal status of the Guantánamo detainees. The CCR lawyers argued that the concept of "unlawful enemy combatants" had no status in international law, that the United States had ignored the Geneva Conventions by deciding on their status without reference to a competent tribunal, and that the detainees had been denied due process of law.[13] In a remarkably rapid response, the IACHR asked the U.S. government to take the urgent measures necessary to have the legal status of the detainees at Guantánamo Bay determined by a competent tribunal. The United States responded a month later by dismissing the commission's competence to apply the Geneva Convention to the detainees, arguing that, even if it did so, precautionary measures were neither necessary nor appropriate, and declaring the detainees to be unlawful combatants who were not entitled to POW status.[14]

The administration's response to the IACHR spoke the language of international law while ignoring its spirit. The government maintained that "the detainees are being treated humanely and consistent with the principles of the Geneva Convention";[15] it cited the Inter-American Declaration of the Rights and Duties of Man's admissibility requirements in claiming the groundless nature of the petition; it pointed to resolutions of the Organization of American States member states, the United Nations, and NATO in support of the U.S.-led war in Afghanistan; and it cited Article IV of the Geneva Conventions in maintaining that not even the Taliban detainees were entitled to POW status because "the Taliban have not effectively distinguished themselves from the civilian population of Afghanistan." International law and institutions had no effect on holding back the exercise of American power, but the U.S. government continued to justify its actions with the language of internationalism.

But what kind of internationalism? This was where the government's claim to be defending the values of freedom and internationalism broke down. From the beginning of the Bush presidency, international institutions and treaties were selectively employed. Richard Haass, the Department of State's director of policy planning, put this clearly when he called for "hard-headed multilateralism." "According to Haass, this hard-headed variety combines American leadership with a division of labour in dealing with foreign policy problems; it sometimes results in the creation of formal institutional structures, sometimes not" (Foot, MacFarlane, and Mastanduno 2003, 1). Like Bush's public declarations, this was a case of "international law à la carte."[16]

This was also a case—as Huntington (1973) saw long ago—of the projection of U.S. domestic practices onto the international scene. Scholars have noted the debt that post-9/11 counterterrorism policy owed much to the "punitive turn" in U.S. criminal law and to the wars on crime and drugs in particular (Margulies 2013). Even before 9/11, the U.S. administration had asked the United Nations to pass a series of resolutions supporting the national security policies it was pushing through Congress. For example, Security Council Resolution 1267 in September 1999 threatened sanctions on the Taliban government if it failed to expel the terrorist groups operating inside Afghanistan and created a Sanctions Committee that would be used to implement the various watchlists of suspected terrorists that the United States and its allies created. Council Resolution 1333, voted in the same month, prohibited states from selling arms or providing military assistance to the Taliban government.

The 9/11 crisis gave the U.S. government an opportunity to rework old approaches and to push a new wave of antiterrorist resolutions through the United Nations. The United States originated and drafted Resolution 1373, paving the way for its adoption by lobbying every member of the Security Council before introducing the text. For the first time, member states were required to change their domestic laws under Chapter VII of the UN Charter. The resolution directed states to criminalize the financing of terrorism;, freeze without delay any funds related to individuals involved in acts of terrorism; deny all forms of financial support for terrorist groups; suppress the provision of safe haven, sustenance, or support for terrorism; share information with other governments on any groups practicing or planning terrorist acts; cooperate with other governments in the investigation, detention, arrest, extradition, and prosecution of those involved in such acts; criminalize active and passive assistance for terrorism in domestic law; and bring violators to justice (Gross and Ní Aoláin 2006, 400–407).

Resolution 1373 had some remarkable features. First, as already mentioned, it required member states to change their domestic laws in specific ways. That meant that, for the first time, the Security Council was actually legislating (Scheppele 2006, 354; Szasz 2002; Rosand 2004), creating a new institutional structure—the Counter-Terrorism Committee—with actual enforcement teeth. Second, it moved beyond injunctions for state behavior "to a concern with a network of individuals that operated within states" (ibid., 356) and led to the freezing of the assets of a number of individuals and groups. Third, it failed to define terrorism, making it possible for states to apply the resolution to a wide range of states' opponents (ibid., 358). Finally, Resolution 1373 said nothing about the protection of human rights, either of citizens or of foreigners.[17] "In short," conclude Gross and Ní Aoláin, "there is a danger that the creation of a special hyper-regulatory category for some groups will inevitably involve slippage and the net will be cast more widely than is necessary to respond to the threat of those targeted" (2006, 401).

Unlike many Security Council resolutions, which were ignored, Resolution 1373 resulted in a flurry of national laws between autumn 2001 and spring 2002. In his exhaustive accounting of legislation pertaining to clandestine violence, Eran Shor has found that between 2001 and 2002 almost 150 laws and amendments to existing laws were passed around the world—largely in response to the UN Security Council's actions.[18] Figure 10.2, based on Shor's database, shows that more than twice as many laws and amendments to laws were passed in these two years than in the entire decade of the 1990s. The adoption of Resolution 1373 would have profound effects on other international institutions, such as the European Union.

The *Kadi* Cases

In late 2001, Resolution 1373 was adopted by the European Council of Ministers and thus became part of the European Union's regulations regarding the freezing of the assets of both its citizens and those who maintained bank accounts in Europe (Alter 2014; de Búrca, 2009; Fromuth 2009). This meant that decisions of the sanctions committee would effectively trump Europe's procedural rule of law traditions and would eventually come into conflict with the institution that had taken upon itself the protection of due process, the European Court of Human Rights.

Freezing the assets of individuals and institutions was a technique that the United States had used against organized crime and later in the War on Terror. Its terrorist watchlists became the main basis of the Security Council's sanctions committee, which had almost unlimited power to decide on the content of its

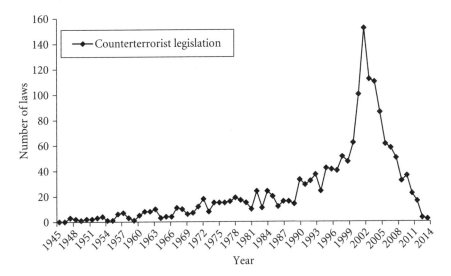

FIGURE 10.2 The Worldwide Passage of Counterterrorist Legislation, 1945–2014. The total number of counterterrorist laws is 1,687. From the Global Counterterrorist Legislation Database—2014 (GCLD), which Eran Shor has generously shared.

lists (Alter 2014, 299). As a result of this shift in scale, Yassin Abdullah Kadi, a Saudi national, and the Al Barakaad International Foundation ended up on the EU blacklist. He and the foundation, which was registered in Sweden, both challenged the designation.

The European Court of Justice (ECJ) held that the sanctions procedure afforded Kadi no opportunity to be heard, did not disclose the reasons for his listing, and used extra-judicial means for making listing decisions (Alter 2014, 299–92; Fromuth 2009, 3). The dispute went back and forth between Kadi, the European Commission, the first and second instances of the ECJ, and the United Nations. The case eventually led the Security Council to create an independent Office of the Ombudsperson to process the requests of individuals or entities to be deleted from the list (Alter 2014). But neither the decision nor the Office of the Ombudsperson persuaded the U.S. government or the Sanctions Committee to provide the evidence for why Kadi had been placed the blacklist in the first place.[19]

Internalizing the State of Emergency

The *Kadi* cases showed that the United States had a powerful influence over how international institutions responded to the terrorist threat, but it also showed that U.S. hegemony was not absolute—as liberal internationalism would predict. In addition, it demonstrated that the proliferation of international institutions could lead to conflict among these institutions, which could work to the advantage of private individuals and groups.[20] But for the most part, individuals and groups designated as supporters of terrorism by the United States and the UN Security Council lack the protections of due process that liberal ideology supposes. The creation of international institutions to "govern the world" opened channels for the powerful to externalize their internal legal innovations to the rest of the world. But it also created space for illegal and semi-legal intrusions on national autonomy and triggered domestic civil society groups to develop strategies to combat them. An Italian case illustrates how far the United States would go in illegal activities on an ally's soil, and a British case shows how civil society actors began to react to American pressures.

Stirring the Pot of Italian Politics

Many high-value detainees in the War on Terror were sent to black sites that were opened in U.S. allied states after 9/11. For example, Abu Zubayda and Abd Al Rahim Hussayn Muhammad Al Nashiri were both sent to a secret CIA-run facility in Poland in 2002 and held there until 2003, before ending up in Guantánamo.[21] Others—perhaps because they were "less valuable"—were rendered to authoritarian states, where they could be interrogated by local security forces. This was, of course, contrary to U.S. law because torture is a routine form of interrogation in many of those countries. Egypt, Syria, Jordan, and Morocco were the most frequent destinations for these detainees, some of whom turned out to have no connection to al Qaeda.

Each operation followed a pattern: local police or security agents would be asked to detain a suspect; he would be bundled onto a plane where he was stripped, fitted with a diaper, and spread-eagled on the floor of the plane, and flown to a black site in another country. He would then disappear into that country's dungeons, from where the results of his interrogation were shared with his abductors. As we have seen, Abel Hakin Belhadj was eventually released by his Libyan captors, but others languished for years in the prisons of Middle Eastern regimes. Most of these prisoners were kidnapped in countries with spotty human rights records—but not all of them were.

Abu Omar

In an extraordinary case of kidnapping and rendition, an Egyptian cleric was snatched by CIA officers from the streets of Milan. Italy—like Britain—had its

THE DARK SIDE OF INTERNATIONALISM

own experience with terrorism. Beginning in the early 1970s and continuing well into the 1980s, Italian police and magistrates had struggled to suppress groups of the extreme left and right (della Porta 1995, 2013). The secret services had played a shadowy role in abetting right-wing violence and in suppressing terrorism from the left. In fact, one secret service official, Vito Miceli, was arrested for conspiring with right-wing groups planning a coup against the government. This led to a restructuring of the intelligence services and to a division between the agency responsible for military and foreign intelligence (Servizio per le Informazioni e la Sicurezza Militare, SISMI) and the domestic intelligence agency (Servizio per le Informazioni e la Sicurezza Democratica, SISDE). The SISMI, as we will see, maintained a close relationship to the CIA.

During the Cold War, Italian foreign policy had been deeply influenced by the U.S. Department of State; indeed, some would say that it was *made* in Washington. The country's political shift to the left in the 1970s strained those ties, but under Prime Minister Silvio Berlusconi, the dominant political figure from the mid-1990s until 2013, ties with the United States were improved. This may have been why the CIA, with the collusion of officials of the SISMI, took the bold step of kidnapping a Muslim cleric from the streets of Milan.

"On February 17, 2003," writes John Foot, "a 39-year old Egyptian man was walking down a quiet street in suburban Milan on his way to daily prayers. . . . He was a cleric and political militant, an opponent of the Hosni Mubarak regime, and had refugee status in Italy. . . . A man in police uniform came up to him and asked in Italian to see his documents. As he reached for his passport, Omar was bundled into a white van by men who the police officer took to be Americans and driven away at high speed." He was transported to the U.S. airbase at Aviano and put on a plane to the U.S. air base in Ramstein, Germany, from where he was rendered to Cairo on a jet used for CIA operations (Foot 2007, 25). There he remained for over a year, before being temporarily released to his mother's home in Alexandria. When he phoned his wife to let her know he was still alive, he was re-arrested. Mubarak's police finally released him in February 2007 on the condition that he not return to Italy.[22]

Given the contentious nature of the Italian press, the story became public, but Prime Minister Berlusconi and his ministers denied any knowledge of the kidnapping. Over the next few years, both the Italian government and the U.S. and Italian secret services began laying down a tissue of false trails. First, it was claimed that Omar had traveled to another country on his own, then that he had been seen in Milan after the kidnapping—after he had already been transported to Aviano—and, finally, that he had staged his own kidnapping. Four prime ministers refused to cooperate in judicial investigations of the crime on the basis of state secrets, and five justice ministers declined to forward extradition requests to Washington for the suspected abductors. But Italy's investigative magistrates—in conflict with Berlusconi for years over his lapses of business and personal ethics—refused to back down. When Armando Spataro, a determined magistrate who had been investigating the cleric for terrorist ties,[23] began to look into the case, he discovered a trail of phone calls from near the site of the kidnapping and Aviano on cellphones that were discarded a few days later. The phone tree eventually led to Robert Lady, the CIA's man in Milan. When Lady's home near Turin was raided by the police in 2005, they found photos of Abu Omar taken on the street on which he had been seized, a map showing the route from Milan to Aviano, and an e-mail warning Lady to get out of Italy. The results of all this digging were indictments for twenty-six Americans and nine Italians, describing the rendition as "a serious crime against personal freedom and a breach of Italian state sovereignty" (ibid., 26).

The U.S. government was not happy with the magistrates' actions. When the CIA agents were put on trial in Milan in absentia, the U.S. ambassador, the Department of State, and even Secretary of Defense Robert Gates made strenuous efforts to prevent the case from going to court. Years later, the Wikileaks exposure of Department of State cables revealed "not-so-subtle threats" from Washington that "nothing would damage relations faster or more seriously than a decision by the GOI [government of Italy] to go forward with warrants for the arrest of the alleged CIA agents named in connection with the Abu Omar case." Berlusconi was reported in the same cables to have fulminated about the politicization of the Milan magistrates, who he complained were "dominated by leftists."[24]

The Dual Special Relationship

The indifference to human rights in the international repression of protest began to foster reactive webs of resistance soon after 9/11. In Germany, Spain, and the United Kingdom, human rights lawyers and civil society groups began to attempt to rein in U.S. excesses and their governments' concurrence in them. For example, in cooperation with the American Center for Constitutional Rights and other human rights groups, a group of German lawyers pursued a complaint in a German court against Defense Secretary Rumsfeld and other U.S. officials under the Code of Crimes against International Law (CCIL), which had been enacted in Germany to comply with the Rome statute creating the International Criminal Court. The case was thrown out by the German prosecutors, who deferred to the U.S. court system, but not before it raised the question of torture in the European justice system (Evangelista 2008, 88–89). The Abu Zubayda and Al Nashiri renditions to Poland, mentioned earlier, eventually reached the European Court of Human Rights, where Poland was judged to have "cooperated in the preparation and execution of the CIA rendition, secret detention and interrogation operations on its territory and it ought to have known that by enabling the CIA to detain the applicants on its territory, it was exposing them to a serious risk of treatment contrary to the Convention."[25]

Another case—this time in the United Kingdom—shows an even closer imbrication between allied states' responses to terrorism. But it also reveals how the extension of multilateral ties into dubious legal areas triggered the growth of cooperation among human rights groups and an expansion of a culture of civil liberties among some U.S. allies. As we have seen in the Belhadj case, U.S. and British intelligence agencies cooperated in the rendition of Muslim suspects to third countries. The case of Binyam Mohamed seriously embarrassed the British government because even the House of Lords and the British High Court were restless about the cooperation between the British secret services and their U.S. partners that it exposed. Unlike the case in Italy, the partnership between the British and U.S. intelligence wings spurred the creation of activism within British civil society to oppose Britain's role in the international rendition of suspects to countries where they would be tortured. Ties were formed between the U.S. lawyers who had formed the Guantánamo Bar and their British homologs, such as Gareth Peirce and Clive Stafford Smith, and between NGOs such as the ACLU and CCR and British charities such as Reprieve, which Stafford Smith founded on his return from the United States.

Binyam Mohamed

Binyam Mohamed was an Ethiopian who had sought asylum in the United Kingdom in 1995. Although that application was rejected, he was given leave to remain in the United Kingdom for seven years. In 2001, he went to Afghanistan, and from there he traveled to Pakistan, where in 2002 he was arrested by Pakistani authorities while trying to leave the country on a false passport. The arrest was reported to U.S. authorities. He was interviewed by the CIA, which informed the British security services that he was in custody. The UK officials asked to question him, and "with permission from U.S. authorities," a British security officer went to Pakistan and interviewed Mohamed "to obtain intelligence about possible security threats to the U.K." (Webber 2009, 4).

Mohamed was then rendered to Morocco on the theory that he had known many Moroccans in London and that the Moroccans "might be more likely to make Mohamed talk and he might know what Moroccans were up to in London." After being interrogated in "medieval" conditions, he was rerendered to U.S. custody—this time to Kabul—where he was again tortured before being transferred to Guantánamo, where he was charged under the Military Commissions

Act "as an alien unlawful enemy combatant," including the charge of participating in a "dirty bomb" plot. Uneasy about Mohamed's charges of mistreatment—or at least wanting him back in the United Kingdom for questioning—the British authorities wrote to their U.S. counterparts to ask for evidence of his claims of mistreatment but were unable to gain access to them. They were not alone; not even Mohamed's U.S. military attorney, Lt. Colonel Yvonne Bradley, was able to gain access to documents that his British attorneys claimed were exculpatory. When the initial request for the documents was refused, a civil law suit was filed in the UK High Court in 2008 seeking disclosure (ibid., 6).

Remarkably, the British court ordered that the documents be disclosed in a redacted form, prompting a US district court judge to order their disclosure to his U.S. attorney. Then, with no explanation, and without granting access to the documents, the Department of Justice dismissed the most serious charges against Mohamed—including the "dirty bomb" story—and the military authorities dismissed the rest. The heavily redacted documents were released to Mohamed's U.S. attorneys, and shortly afterward, the new U.S. administration agreed to release him to the United Kingdom (ibid., 8). This was a modest success—modest, in the light of the chain of injustices to which he had been subjected. But the redacted documents were still missing a crucial seven paragraphs in which, Mohamed's attorneys alleged, the evidence of his torture was contained. Two years into the litigation, Foreign Secretary David Miliband was still arguing that a court would be "irresponsible" to reveal the material for reasons of "national security."[26] In the same year, the U.S. Court of Appeals for the Ninth Circuit turned down an ACLU lawsuit on behalf of Mohamed and four other former prisoners against Jeppesen Dataplan, a Boeing subsidiary accused of arranging for extraordinary rendition flights for the CIA. The court ruled that "former prisoners of the C.I.A. could not sue over their alleged torture in overseas prisons because such a lawsuit might expose secret government information."[27]

Like the Abu Omar case, the Binyam Mohamed story reveals a tangled web of official and secret relations, and legal and illegal ties, between the United States and its allies in the fight against terrorism. It also shows how openly the U.S. government was willing to threaten to cut an ally off from security cooperation if it revealed evidence of U.S. misdeeds. As in the case of the Bush administration's warnings to the Italians, the Obama Department of Justice threatened the British, saying that, if the evidence of torture was revealed, "we will necessarily have to review with the greatest care the sensitivity of the information we can provide you in the future."[28]

The global War on Terror, mounted against transnational clandestine violence, has not created an international superstate. But it has transposed both the formal use of multilateral institutions and informal, and sometimes illegal, cooperation between the United States and its allies into an international state of emergency. This has begun to foster a countermovement against those ties in the form of a growing network for the defense of human rights. In terms of the legal cases it has won, this network is weak and tiny; but with the occasional support of the courts, by combining the tools of legal defense, investigative reporting, and public exposure, it has begun to establish a small beachhead for the defense of personal rights against the dark side of internationalism.

Conclusions

The world has changed a lot since the Rome Conference of 1898, when the Italian government tried unsuccessfully to coordinate international efforts to defeat European anarchism. It has also moved beyond bilateral approaches to end conflicts such as the Northern Irish Troubles during the Cold War. The creation of international institutions to "govern the world" has made possible successful campaigns against dread diseases and international criminal conspiracies, and has increased the visibility of states' abuses of human rights and perhaps even increased their willingness to punish human rights abusers. But it has also created channels for powerful states to export their domestic concerns to the rest of the world under the umbrella of universalism (Mazower 2012, 391–94).

True, the Bush administration sought UN agreement for the war it launched on Iraq. But when the United Nations withheld its support, the administration went ahead anyway, leaving the credibility of Secretary of State Colin Powell in the dirt and many U.S. allies appalled. And when the Security Council passed Resolution 1373 without reference to human rights, the UN Human Rights Commission proved to be helpless to stop the move (Gross and Ní Aoláin 2006, 406–7). Not even the European Union questioned the normative shift in international institutions from the protection of human rights to the repression of terrorism.

Internationalization is a complex and contradictory phenomenon, as we have seen in this chapter. The same UN Security Council that adopted the U.S. watchlists without vetting the criteria on which they were developed also created an Ombudsperson to monitor complaints by people who claimed they had been wrongly blacklisted. Whereas the European Council extended the watchlist to the European Union, the ECJ has emerged as a defender of due process and the European Court of Human Rights has taken on the cause of individual rights against member states. Seven decades after the creation of the UN system, a kind of institutional pluralism has emerged, willy-nilly, that may eventually develop into something resembling an international balance of powers that could result in the defense of individual rights against aggressive state interests (Morse and Keohane 2014).

The real danger is hidden from view. International moves against terrorism, such as those that followed 9/11, hold the danger of allowing a vertical scale shift from the national to the international level (Tarrow 2005, chap. 7). We saw this in the United States projecting its terrorist watchlists upward to the United Nations Security Council in Resolution 1373. But there has also been evidence of a horizontal shift from one area of policy to adjoining ones that have no relation to clandestine violence. For example, there is evidence of the extension of measures against terrorism to the control of immigrants and the surveillance of peace protesters. Already cross-border police cooperation, created to repress terrorism, has threatened to become a transnational police "guild," one that escapes democratic control (Bigo 2013).[29]

In some ways, an international scale shift in repression is more invidious than its domestic counterpart. In domestic politics—at least in the United States—the executive's responsibility for abusing civil liberties was eventually publicized by the press and contested in the courts and in grassroots mobilizations. Groups such as the ACLU, the CCR, the Electronic Frontier Foundation, and even mainstream groups such as the American Bar Association fought the state's expanding power with the traditional tools of lobbying, exposure, and contentious politics. They often failed, but when they formed broad civil liberties coalitions and gained access to the courts, to Congress, or to public opinion, they could hold an aggressive administration's feet to the fire.

But it was very different in the case of United Nations resolutions. When, under U.S. pressure, the USA Patriot Act was transposed into international resolutions, the source of the policy was unreachable by ordinary citizens, who were told by their leaders that they had no choice but to adopt sanctions imposed from abroad. When British and U.S. intelligence operatives colluded with the Pakistanis, the Moroccans, and the Libyans to render suspects to CIA dark sites, there were no nonprofits, courts, or legislators available to protest their actions. When the web of international institutions began to grow after World War Two, they had been infused with the language and the logic of human rights. That language and that logic remain, but their glow obscures the nooks and crannies in which illiberal policies can fester—the dark side of internationalization.

CONCLUSIONS

This book began with the events that exploded in Ukraine in late 2013. A revolution had dislodged a Russian ally, Victor Yanukovych, installing a weak pro-Western provisional government in March 2014. Enraged by what he saw as a Western-engineered coup on his border, President Vladimir Putin of Russia sent special forces to the Crimea to join pro-Russian militants in a separatist movement of surprising rapidity and effectiveness. The Crimea, the Russians maintained, was really part of Russia; it had been handed to the Ukrainian Republic by Nikita Khrushchev under the old Soviet Union. By the next month, following a hastily organized referendum, the Crimea was entrenched in the Russian sphere.

The conflict that began in Kiev and the Crimea did not end there. For no sooner was the peninsula detached from Ukraine than Russian-speaking militants, backed by their Russian allies, took over government buildings in twelve southeastern cities of Ukraine and declared "People's Republics" in Donetsk and Luhansk. They were helped by the inability of the new Ukrainian government to mount an effective response and by a propaganda campaign and "volunteers" sent in from Moscow.

But this time, the Russians and their separatist allies were confronted—although ineptly—by the Western powers, who backed the Ukrainian government and imposed sanctions on Putin's closest cronies in Russia. In May, the conflict began to escalate toward civil war.[1] "What began three months ago as a protest against the Ukrainian government," wrote the *New York Times* with foreboding, "has now turned into a big-power confrontation reminiscent of the Cold War and a significant challenge to international agreements on the sanctity of the borders of the post-Soviet nations."[2]

As spring turned to summer, the Ukrainian army, backed by nationalist militias that grew out of the Kiev uprising, began to gain ground against the rebels, pushing them back toward the Russian border. But not for long. In late August, President Putin of Russia sent tanks, supplies, and regular Russian troops to the aid of the militants, beating back the Ukrainian army; threatening Mariapul, a strategic port city; and forcing the new Ukrainian president, Petro Poroshenko, to negotiate a truce with the separatists. As this book goes to press, we do not yet know the ultimate shape of the Ukrainian state and what its relations will be with its aggressive neighbor and with the West.[3]

I return to the Ukrainian conflict here because it embodies the three main elements on whose interactions this book is based—contention, war, and states. The collapse of the Ukrainian government was triggered by a mass movement of pro-Western activists; the military conflicts in the Crimea and eastern Ukraine were mobilized by pro-Russian militants empowered by Russian agents; and whatever geopolitical state structure emerges from this conflict will be heavily marked by the interaction of war and contention.

The Ukrainian episode also embodies three factors from the new shape of transnational politics we sketched in chapter 5. First, there was a direct influence from external actors. The revolution in Kiev was encouraged by the European Union; the takeover of the Crimea was the result of the Russians' desire to return Ukraine to its sphere of influence; and while the West exerted pressure through the European Union, NATO, and the international financial system, the Russians used their oil and gas exports as leverage for their claims. Globalization and internationalization shaped the story from beginning to end.

Second, the conflict resembled those described in chapter 5 in its combination of conventional war-making and social movements. The Kiev government was taken over by a combination of pro-Western militants and political opponents of the Yanukovych regime; the peaceful occupation of the central square of Kiev rapidly gave way to armed confrontations with security forces; the mobilization of Russian-inspired militants in the Crimea and in the east demonstrated the porosity of the Ukrainian state; and the separatist movement was combined with ill-disguised special forces from across the border. The Ukrainian conflict was a composite conflict with intermingled internal and external, movement and state interactions.

Third, there was a rapid diffusion of protest performances—the occupation of public squares, the organization of social movements and their militarization, the use of the Internet and social media—that were also present in the Arab Spring and other contemporary conflicts. Like these other conflicts, this led to the creation of countermovements and to repressive state responses. The

Ukrainian episode had some unusual twists and turns, but it was representative of the composite contention we find in many episodes of modern contentious politics.

In chapter 1, I raised five big questions about the processes that relate war to states and contention: Does war-making produce state-building, and what are their joint effects on citizenship? How do states control contention in times of war? How do states interact with civil society in wartime? How does war affect contention in the wake of war? And, finally, how does war affect the relationships between states and contention in the future? In this concluding chapter, drawing on the episodes in this book, I propose answers to these questions before asking how the book's findings might be applied to a very different set of wars, states, and contention—the nationalist movements in the global South after World War Two.[4] Of these, I briefly examine four : the liberation of Burma and Indonesia from Japanese rule at the end of World War Two, the Arab-Jewish war in Mandate Palestine in 1947–1948; and the Algerian war, both there and what it led to in France. The object of these examples is to examine how far the findings of the book can be extended to different kinds of wars in different parts of the world.

Does War Makes States, and Do States Create Citizens?

Let us begin where this book began, with Charles Tilly's argument that war and preparations for war were at the origin of the modern state. "States," he famously wrote, "make war, but war makes states" (Tilly 1975, 42). But another part of his thesis is less familiar; in a little-remembered 1992 paper, Tilly wrote, "I think that citizenship rights came into being because relatively organized members of the general population bargained with state authorities for several centuries" (1992c, 10). Citizens and states, he reasons, first bargained over the means of war and then bargained over enforceable claims that would serve their interests outside of the area of war; that, in turn, helped to enlarge states' obligations to their citizens. The leverage that citizens gained from war broadened the range of their enforceable claims and expanded the population groups who could claim them (ibid., 10).

One way in which citizenship is linked to war is in the creation of the citizen army. In France and the United States, revolutionary armies were foundations of the modern concept of the citizen. Soldiers coming from villages and small towns met others like themselves and gained a sense of national unity. This socialization pattern, evident as long ago as the French *levée en masse*, has been most developed in the recruitment of immigrants into the Israeli army; for many new immigrants, this was their first encounter with the new state and, for some, even with the Hebrew language (Shapira 2005).

But three things are incomplete in this hypothesized connection between war and citizenship. First, citizen armies were, until quite recently, entirely *male*, and this may explain why women's suffrage was so long in coming. Second, the citizen armies of the nineteenth and early twentieth centuries became the professional armies of the late twentieth and early twenty-first centuries. Not only that—when Britain and France sent soldiers abroad, they were not fighting for democracy but on behalf of their empires. Finally, we have seen in the recent wars in Afghanistan and Iraq the expanded use of military contractors, whose motivations for fighting are largely for profit and not the defense of the homeland. If there was a link between citizenship and the military, it has become so thin as to be practically nonexistent.

Nevertheless, we have found other links between war and citizenship. Through the post–Civil War Reconstruction amendments to the U.S. Constitution, the war created citizens out of slaves; World War One gave voting rights to millions of working men and to women; in World War Two, mass migration and war work gave black Americans a sense of their own worth; and, finally, contention over the Vietnam War was responsible for expanding the vote to eighteen-year-olds and for providing greater protections of civil liberties. Even in the wake of 9/11, Paul Starr, a sociologist, writes, "Liberalism isn't just a set of fine aspirations. Historically, it has emerged from the pressures of political conflict, domestic and international, *not least of all from the pressures of war* (2007, x, emphasis added).

But where does contentious politics fit in? Wars need financing, and extracting taxes often leads to resistance. Wars also need soldiers, and that too can lead to contention. Making war weakens states internally, which produces opportunities for war's opponents and others to forward their claims. Intervening between war-making and the extension of citizenship is contention. The question is: Does the contention triggered by war enhance or reduce citizenship?

In the episodes analyzed in this book, we have seen much evidence of how war triggers contention. Draft resistance led to the Vendée rebellion in the wars of the French Revolution, to draft riots in the U.S. Civil War, and to the burning of draft cards during the Vietnam War. Military experience and the weakening of the Italian state in World War One created opportunities for Mussolini's fascists to attack their political enemies and topple the regime. In the United States, the passage of the Espionage and Sedition acts during World War One led to the repression of antiwar activism but the war opened the gates to women's suffrage. The pressure of that war on civil liberties was also the origin of the ACLU.

These examples could be endlessly replicated. But does the link between war and contention invariably expand citizenship? Remember that the French revolutionary wars led to the reversal of the Declaration of the Rights of Man; that Italy's intervention in World War One produced a postwar cycle that reversed the country's march toward democracy; that the Cold War produced a powerful anticommunist movement in the United States that curtailed free speech and association; and that the Vietnam war heightened government surveillance and threatened the Constitution. Once we insert contention into Tilly's causal chain from war-making to state-building to rights, the relationship between war-making and citizenship becomes indeterminate.

In summary, war can expand citizenship through contention on behalf of rights, but modern armies have become increasingly professionalized, and movements emerging from war can as easily take states in illiberal directions as in liberal ones, as we saw in Napoleonic France and fascist Italy. Where there is a rollback of wartime restrictions on rights, it depends not on war itself but on the mobilization of opinion in civil society.

How Do States Contain Contention during Wartime?

Modern states possess powerful instruments of hierarchical power. As early as the late 1930s, as he observed the Japanese bombing of Chinese cities, Harold Lasswell feared the coming of a garrison state, "a world in which the specialists on violence are the most powerful group in society" (1998, 56). Lasswell worried that, as state power expanded to fight wars, technology tied to militarism would pose a threat to democracy (ibid., 64). Fascism's defeat reduced his fears, but with the advent of the Cold war, he foresaw a militarization of American society that would lead to the self-perpetuation of elites "specialized to the planning and implementation of coercive strategies of power" (ibid., 95). Although Lasswell could not have imagined the ability of the state today to surveil its citizens, he already saw that the control of technology would give governments the tools and incentives with which to control public opinion.

Clandestine armed conflict is not as lethal a threat as nuclear war. But after 9/11, the fear of further attacks and the government's response to that threat lent credence to Lasswell's concerns. As fear of terrorism grew, the military-industrial complex expanded into a military-intelligence inkblot. The state gained greater control over information, secrecy was justified by fear of attack, and public officials behaved as if the country was threatened (Huddy, Feldman, Lahav, and Taber 2003; Sunstein 2003). This led the government to extend its reach, expand its intelligence apparatus, and curtail rights that had been considered central to the American creed (Margulies 2013). As Ronald Krebs writes, "Events of and since 11 September

2001 have renewed interest in age-old questions about liberal-democratic governance in the shadow of insecurity, crisis, and war" (2009, 177).

In some ways, post-9/11 security practices resembled aspects of the emergency script we have seen in earlier episodes. Like the citizens who were declared "outside the law" in revolutionary France, the Italian pacifists who were sent into internal exile during World War One, and Japanese Americans in World War Two, detainees suspected of complicity with al Qaeda were essentially declared nonpersons. Despite the Supreme Court's rejection of the military commissions unilaterally created by the Bush administration, they were re-instated by Congress in 2006. Immigrants were increasingly regarded with suspicion, leading to practices that recall the excesses of the Wilson administration. Muslim charities had their funds placed under special controls and sometimes frozen. To some, the United States after 9/11 seemed to be sinking into a Schmittian state.

On the other hand, despite the claims of prophets such as Giorgio Agamben (2005), no state of siege was declared, no mass arrests of antiwar protesters were made, no mass expulsions or interning of population groups were declared, and no censorship of the press or other media was imposed; and on at least four occasions, the Supreme Court defended minimal rights of detainees. In fact, as we have seen in chapter 9, in a classic reflex against government overreach, civil society groups such as the ACLU and the CCR were strengthened as alarmed citizens lent their support to rolling back the government's excesses.

The real danger to rights lay not in the trend toward a Schmittian state but that, under cover of the rule of law, the government would expand its ability to rule *by* law. For example:

- The Supreme Court's defense of detainee rights was largely emasculated by the D.C. Circuit Court of Appeals, which gave the government's allegations against detainees a presumption of accuracy.
- Restrictions on rights were aimed mainly at "alien enemies" and not at citizens, but once applied, these restrictions sometimes spread beyond their original targets (Cole 2003).
- Section 215 of the USA Patriot Act was written to contain foreign threats, but secret presidential orders permitted the warrantless wiretapping of U.S. citizens' communications.
- Based on the opinions of the Bush administration's Office of Legal Counsel (OLC), torture was sanitized into "enhanced interrogation" and used to squeeze information from prisoners in open defiance of U.S. law and UN treaties.
- Based on opinions of the Obama administration's OLC, the president was assured that the killing of U.S. citizens through targeted drones was legal.[5]

In summary, states at war enact some version of emergency rule, which limits rights and constrains contention. But the real danger for liberal states is not a Schmittian inversion but legal manipulation under the umbrella of rule of law.

How Do States and Civil Societies Interact during Wartime?

The United States after 9/11 retreated from the advances in the civil liberties that marked the post-Vietnam years. From survey evidence, we know that, after an initial rejection of torture against detainees, Americans increasingly came to see torture as legitimate, despite growing evidence of its ineffectiveness and its disavowal of solemn U.S. signature on international treaties (Margulies 2013, chap. 9). We also know that despite, President Bush's initial warning that most Muslims are not terrorists, millions of Americans became increasingly intolerant of Islam (ibid., chap. 6). Events such as the attempt of Muslim groups to open a religious center in New York City and the opening of the 9/11 museum near Ground Zero kept the image of the tragedy alive in the public mind. If nothing else, something as prosaic as being made to remove their shoes in airports reminded Americans of the danger of clandestine violent groups transgressing their borders.

In the 1990s, scholars saw the diffusion of human-rights norms across the globe as a linear trend (Meyer, Boli, Thomas, and Ramirez 1998 ; Risse, Ropp, and Sikkink 1999). It was assumed by many that these trends were universal, but to observers in the global South they looked remarkably Western. The history of human rights after 9/11 suggests not only that such norms are not universal but that what seemed like inexorable progress in human rights can be reversible (Evangelista 2013). Unless there is a determined effort within civil society to defend such norms, in the name of defending the citizenry, citizens' rights are put at risk.

In chapter 9, I argued that civil society activism is the only sure way to restrain the tendency of modern governments to sacrifice civil liberties in wartime. Antiwar movements are almost never successful in braking war's initiation. We saw this in the preparations for the U.S. Civil War, in the failure of antiwar groups to stop Italian and U.S. entry into World War One, in the capacity of the Bush administration to invent false threats from Iraq, and especially in the failure of the February 15, 2003, protests against the Iraq War. Legal mobilization in times of war is almost as unsuccessful as antiwar protests, as we saw in the evisceration of the Supreme Court's decisions in *Boumediene* by the D.C. Circuit Court of Appeals.

Critics of the Bush administration pointed to the ability of the "Vulcans" (the powerful neoconservative group within the Bush administration) to use the 9/11 tragedy to advance their project of going to war against Iraq.[6] Others pointed to the anger of President George W. Bush that Sadaam Hussein had attempted to assassinate his father. Still others pointed to the national security state, which could use its hierarchical power to begin the inexorable move to war based on groupthink and the inertia of motion. These critics were not wrong, but they generally underestimated the fact that liberal states—and the United States more than most—depend on their infrastructural power within civil society to promote and maintain war-making.

Throughout this book, the distinction between hierarchical and infrastructural power has served us well. We have seen how, after the fall of the Old French Regime, the vacuum in both kinds of power led the besieged republicans to invent the emergency script in wartime. Then we saw how the Lincoln administration, despite the weakness of its hierarchical power, drew on civil society to batter the Confederacy with a combination of popular mobilization and capitalist financing. The Italian state entered World War One with a weak civil society and attempted to control workers and peasants through coercion; in contrast, as Elizabeth Kier (2010) shows in a revealing comparison, during the same war, the British state combined the instruments of hierarchical and infrastructural power to mobilize the British population to fight a devastating war.

Mobilizing citizens for war is, of course, nothing new. We saw it in the *levée en masse* in the French Revolution, in the creation of the Committee on Public Information to support the U.S. entry into World War One, and in the Freedom Train and other patriotic initiatives during the Cold War. But the capacity of the American state to mobilize actors in civil society has been increased by what Linda Weiss (2014) calls governed interdependence. This is a trend that has been growing since President Eisenhower warned of the power of the military-industrial complex. After 9/11, as we have seen, literally hundreds of government-funded firms grew up around Washington, D.C., and across the country, not to mention the thousands of military contractors who were sent to Iraq, Afghanistan, and elsewhere. The military-industrial complex has become a military-intelligence complex, one that is reinforced by the War on Terror and the wars in Iraq and Afghanistan.

The advent of these wars also demonstrated the modern state's powerful influence on the media. This is not the result of hierarchical control, as in Russia or China, but of the state's infrastructural power. For example, during Operation Desert Storm, journalists were "embedded" in military units, insuring that they would report the war from the viewpoint of the troops. In the run-up to that war, the media depended on the state for information, much of which turned out to be inaccurate. When reports of the NSA's massive surveillance program began to leak out, the president was able to convince the *New York Times*, in 2005, to hold off on printing the story for over a year. It took the avalanche of documents stolen by Edward Snowden eight years later to make the public aware that the government had been reading its e-mail and tapping its telephones for the past decade. It was not the state's hierarchical power but its infrastructural links to civil society that allowed the American state to mount and sustain three wars and to infiltrate Americans' private lives.

In summary, citizens sometimes oppose but more commonly support states when they go to war, and liberal states use their infrastructural power to mobilize and maintain consent in wartime.

How Does War Affect Contention in War's Wake?

Aaron Friedberg (2000) has argued that, guided by their antistate political culture, Americans retreat rapidly from wartime state expansion. True, after almost every war, the costs of maintaining an army and the public's weariness with wartime measures lead to a rollback in the armed forces and in the parts of the civilian state that expand in wartime. This was certainly the case after World War Two, the case that Friedberg examines. But the postwar rollback of the American state was brief; the Cold War and the Korean War expanded the military again (see figure 6.2). Of our four cases, in only one—the postbellum U.S. North—was there a permanent rollback of the size of the army, and that was largely the result of the deadlocked 1876 election, which forced the eventual winner, Rutherford B. Hayes, to end military reconstruction. The evidence for Friedberg's rollback thesis is decidedly mixed.

The War on Terror and the wars in Iraq and Afghanistan have had both rollback and ratchet effects on the American state. Although both the military effort and the civilian efforts expanded after 2001, the military did not substantially increase in size, both because of the modern army with which Secretary Rumsfelt invaded Iraq and because of the government's massive employment of contractors. As for the civilian state, it did not grow in numbers but expanded through the practices of governed interdependence, we discussed in chapter 8.

More important than the size of the state in war's wake has been the ratchet effect of emergency powers after the emergency passes. We saw this in the extension of the state of siege after the French Revolution. We saw it again in the U.S. Civil War, as Lincoln's suspension of *habeas corpus* was expanded through an act of Congress.[7] Similarly, the British government extended its emergency measures from Northern Ireland in the 1970s to the whole country in the War against Terror. As for twentieth-century America, the Espionage Act, passed to prevent interference with military operations during World War One, has been amended many times and been used for purposes that went well beyond its drafters' original intentions, both in times of war and in peacetime.[8]

What of the administration that followed? Barack Obama campaigned for the presidency on a platform of ending human rights abuses and increasing transparency in government. His first acts after his inauguration were consistent with these pledges: he announced his desire to close the facility in Guantánamo Bay and to abandon enhanced interrogation and extraordinary rendition. There was also a sharp difference in the tone of the new administration. Obama and his deputies quickly discarded the trope of the War on Terror, reaffirmed liberal internationalism, and, in a much-publicized speech in Cairo, signified a desire to work with Muslim countries. These were important differences from the practices and the tone of the Bush administration, but, as Matthew Evangelista writes, "The practices of the Obama administration do not differ a great deal from those of its predecessors in key respects—particularly regarding indefinite detention and targeted killing of suspected terrorists" (2013, 25–26).

When we compare the early Bush administration security measures to those of Barack Obama's after 2008, a mixture of change and continuity is evident in the use of military commissions, the diffusion of surveillance, the migration of assets freezing to the international level, and the militarization of the police.

As we have seen, military commissions have been used intermittently in the United States since the 1840s. Employed during the Civil War, and then against insurgents opposing U.S. domination of the Philippines, they were not used again until World War Two, when they were used to try German saboteurs, whose conviction was approved by the Supreme Court in the landmark case of *Ex Parte Quirin* (317 U.S. 1). This was the precedent cited by the Bush administration to defend the original version of the military commissions created after 9/11. The Supreme Court invalidated these early commissions, but they were re-instituted by Congress in 2006 and, again, under Obama in 2009 when he was unable to convince Congress to close Guantánamo.[9]

The mass surveillance measures announced in Section 215 of the USA Patriot Act charged the FBI with responsibility for surveillance.[10] But the practice had already been secretly initiated by the NSA as the result of a presidential order drafted by the Office of the Vice President. We now know that during the Vietnam War, the NSA was spying on prominent American war critics.[11] After the Watergate era, the agency held to a strict respect for Americans' privacy, but it had a greater technological capacity than the FBI, and after 9/11, it had the willingness to use it aggressively. No one in Congress complained about this sliding expansion of the act until it was demonstrated by the Snowden exposures that the agency was tapping the phone calls of millions of Americans.

There has also been an international ratchet effect. As we have seen, cooperation against terrorism began to gain institutionalized form in the 1990s, but it took the shock of 9/11 for the UN Security Council to set up an effective UN institution, the Counter-Terrorism Committee, to process claims against individuals and groups thought to be providing support for terrorism. The measures had migrated upward from the USA Patriot Act to the United Nations, where they could be used by illiberal states as justification for measures they were already taking against their domestic insurgents.

There has also been a downward ratchet effect: local police departments show a growth of militarization. Until the Cold War, with the exception of the FBI, U.S. police powers were almost entirely restricted to state and local governments. The increase in protest movements and urban crime in the 1960s led the Nixon administration to begin a policy of financial and technical support for state and local police forces (Button 1978), one that has grown through subsequent administrations, especially as a result of the start of the War on Drugs. But the aftermath of 9/11 and the wars in Iraq and Afghanistan produced a massive transfer of military equipment to local police forces, as was vividly demonstrated in the police response to the Ferguson riots in August 2014.[12]

But it was the post-9/11 creation of the DHS and the construction of "fusion centers" around the country that increased federal cooperation with state and local police forces, as we have seen in chapter 8. This can be seen in the shift from a practice of peaceful management of protest from the 1970s through the 1990s (McPhail, Schweingruber, and McCarthy 1999) to the practice of "protester incapacitation" that began soon after 9/11 (Wood 2014).

These continuities in the American state's emergency powers in war's wake by no means exhaust the many ways in which bureaucratic inertia, intentional diffusion, and public indifference lead to a carryover of wartime emergency measures. The irony is that this expansion in hierarchical power depends at least in part on the type of powers that have grown up in liberal states—their infrastructural power within civil society. Against the power of the state to make its war-created innovations permanent, enormous labor, activism, and commitment are needed to hold this power in check. This takes us to the most important issue in this book: how war and infrastructural power affect contentious politics.

War, Infrastructural Power, and Future Contention

A state's capacity to control contention differs, depending on its relative dependence on hierarchical or infrastructural power. Autocratic states such as tsarist

Russia employed constraint to force young men to serve under arms and to extract a surplus from the population. Conversely, infrastructural power rests on a reciprocal relationship between the state and civil society. This provides leverage, not only to powerful industrial groups that produce war materiel and private contractors who perform services for the state; it also provides openings for peace movements, human rights lawyers, and civil society advocates who can use these ties to oppose going to war and its attendant human rights abuses and encroachments on civil liberties.

In the course of this book, we saw many examples of civil society groups that mobilized against war, during wartime, and in war's wake. Six main examples demonstrate such resistance: the Vendée counterrevolution in France; resistance to the draft in the North during the U.S. Civil War; the working-class insurrection in Turin in World War One; left-wing activists' opposition to U.S. intervention in World War One; the mass movement against the Vietnam War; and the varied forms of mobilization against the Bush-Cheney administration's global War on Terror and the wars in Iraq and Afghanistan.

All these movements struggled against the emergency powers their states adopted and from the hostility or indifference of the general public. All were met with rejection and, in the first four cases, with repression. Like invasion, regime change, or economic or governmental collapse, war has "profound effects on the structuring of strategic action fields across society. This is because such crises undermine all kinds of linkages in society and make it difficult for groups to reproduce their power" (Fligstein and McAdam 2012, 101). But war also allows for the "attribution of new opportunities and threats leading to the appropriation or creation of new organizational vehicles for the purpose of engaging in innovative, contentious interaction with other field actors" (ibid.).

Cycles of antiwar protest are crucibles in which new forms of collective action are cast. The burning of draft cards, religious vigils for peace, mass mobilizations around the country, and symbolic and then digital attacks on the Pentagon—these are all modes of protest that arose during recent wars. Some of them tended to disappear in war's wake; others were adopted by other groups; and still others were institutionalized as part of the recognized repertoire of contention (Tarrow 1995). The burning of draft cards to protest the Vietnam War stopped when the draft was ended. The vigils organized by Catholic peace organizations against the same war became part of the ordinary repertoire of contention (Tilly and Tarrow 2007). Mass mobilizations against the war went into abeyance during the relatively peaceful 1980s and 1990s, but re-appeared in the protests against the invasion of Iraq. Demonstrations outside the Pentagon ended after the Vietnam War, but digital hacking took its place, without the attendant physical contact. The repertoire of contention and the state's strategies of social control evolve in an unending reciprocal spiral of move and countermove (McAdam 1983) in which war is a major incentive and structuring element.

After Vietnam, mass demonstrations and legal mobilization became a fixture of antiwar movements, both in the United States and around the world. We have seen how the largest mass demonstration in history failed to stop the rush to war in Iraq. We also saw that, although legal mobilization on the part of groups such as the CCR and the ACLU had some success, the government's ability to reshape the law stymied these tactics. But the wars of the post-9/11 era and the abuses they justified led to a new opportunity, a new organizational format, and a new form of innovative collective action—the use of digital communication to reveal government misconduct. First in the Wikileaks files leaked by army Private First Class Chelsea (Bradley) Manning, and then in the downloading of what the government claimed were "millions" of documents by Edward Snowden, many of the illegal practices of the Bush and Obama administrations were exposed.

At this writing, the Snowden story is still unfolding. But it reveals what could turn out to be a major shift in the logic of collective action. Snowden had stumbled on a classified 2009 report by the NSA's inspector general while spring-cleaning the system. The report was an account of how the Bush administration had carried out an illegal wiretapping program following 9/11. It demonstrated from inside the government "that senior U.S. officials were breaking the law" (Harding 2014, 53–54). When James Clapper, director of national intelligence, lied to Congress about what his agency was doing, it pushed Snowden over the edge and led him to contact a small group of journalists and a documentary filmmaker, who helped him to publicize his findings. This turned him into a fugitive from U.S. justice but made him a hero to civil libertarians. In the wake of the Snowden revelations, even advocates from the libertarian right began to mobilize against government overreach. A lone individual embedded in the networks of the government's infrastructural power penetrated its hierarchical power and showed how "the logic of connective power" may be changing the nature of contentious politics (Bennett and Segerberg 2013).

Nevertheless, the state's ability to mold the law to its political purposes leads most efforts to rein in emergency powers to fail—at least in the short run. But the link among war, contention, and efforts to control the state is both contingent and long term. It is contingent because it depends on the balance of social and political forces at any given time. For example, Congress, which had caved in when the Nixon administration infiltrated the Black Panthers and antiwar groups in the 1960s, went on in the next decade to pass reforms reining in the state and protecting civil liberties. Similarly, the post-9/11 Congress gave President Bush almost unlimited power to employ force. Yet another Congress, however, worked to restrain the NSA, whose electronic spying had gone beyond the powers it had been granted a decade earlier.

The struggle to rein in government is–a slow process because states have an almost infinite capacity to rework and reconfigure parts of the emergency script into new forms under different conditions. Another way of putting the equation is to say that, states have the flexibility, the resources, and the durability to find new ways to exercise their emergency powers in war's wake, whereas movements are, by their nature, evanescent and lack durable permanent organizations. Some social movements have a natural base and go into abeyance during slack times (Taylor 1989); but peace movements have little reason to survive in times of peace and need to re-create themselves each time a new emergency arises.

In summary, infrastructural power offers protesters resources with which to frame and mobilize their claims. The same links that enable states to operate within civil society afford civil society groups opportunities and resources to oppose war-making and its domestic effects. We have seen how war and contention structured the shape of the state in the episodes in this book. Together they centralized the Jacobin state in France, strengthened the power of the federal state and its links to business in post–Civil War United States, created the fascist movement that destroyed the Liberal Italian state, and expanded both the hierarchical and infrastructural power of the contemporary state in the United States.

How far can these generalizations, drawn from only four Western liberal states, be extended in time and space? Other scholars with greater expertise will have to examine this question, but one kind of wartime experience—the national liberation movements following World War Two—shows that war and contention combined to produce fundamental changes in state structures in very different settings than those examined in this book. Space constraints and lack of expertise limit the number of these experiences we can examine, but four of them demonstrate how war and contention shaped states that emerged from World War Two and nationalist movements.

War, Nationalist Movements, and Militarization

As World War Two came to an end, some former imperial powers—such as the British in India or the Americans in the Philippines—realized that the Age of Empire was over and organized transfers of power to postcolonial elites. But where large European populations were settled or the control of resources was too valuable to give up without a fight, long and ruthless wars ensued. In Kenya, the British prosecuted a vicious war against the Mau Mau; in Rhodesia (today's Zimbabwe) a white-led regime resisted decolonization long after the British had given up the ghost. In Indochina and Algeria, postwar French governments tried to hold onto power against well-organized nationalist movements. The case of the territories west of the Jordan River that were mandated to Britain after World War One is unusual in that the British were opposed by two rival nationalist movements, but it too illustrates the interaction of social movements and war for future state-building.

From Mandate Palestine to the Israeli Movement-State

Even before World War Two, the British were faced with rival movements in the territories west of the Jordan River: nationalists drawn from the indigenous Palestinian population and the Zionist movement that had been organizing the immigrant Jewish population since early in the twentieth century (Avineri 1971). Both groups included veterans of previous conflicts, and each had powerful external allies: the Palestinians in the form of the armies of the nearby Arab countries and the Jews in the form of the diaspora Zionist movement. The former had the strategic advantage of Palestine's common borders with its Arab neighbors; the latter had greater financial resources and lobbying links to the great powers and had enjoyed the patronage of the Mandate authorities which had seen the Jews as allies for their ambitions in the Middle East (Segev 2000). The Holocaust provided the lesson that a people without a state was subject to genocide, but it also provided the Zionist movement with thousands of refugees, most of whom had lost their homes and their families. They created a movement-state, formed a citizen army, and were guided by a militant nationalism that eventually hardened the country into a garrison state with an extensive security network to sustain it in civil society (Sheffer and Barak 2013).

In 1947, as the British were preparing to withdraw under pressure from both sides, the United Nations offered a plan for the partition of the area. The plan would have reserved half of the country to the Palestinians, including all the highlands and a third of the coastline, and the rest to the Jews, including a densely populated strip along the coast around Tel Aviv, the Negev desert, and an interior area around the sea of Galilee. Jerusalem and its hinterland was to be governed by a UN mandate. Realizing that the possession of their own state was far more important than how much territory they were allotted, the Zionist leaders were quick to accept the plan, but the Palestinians, who would have been forced to accept the legitimacy of a Jewish state, refused it.

The war that followed matched well-trained Jewish Haganah forces, drawn both from Kibbutz defenses and from service with the British army in Europe, against the outmatched Palestinians, who were soon reinforced by an army and by volunteers sent to defend them by the Arab League. David Ben-Gurion declared the State of Israel a few hours before the midnight termination of the British mandate and a significant portion of the Arab population was either forced to leave their homes or chose refugee status over staying in the areas of the country under Jewish control.

The history that followed is too complicated to survey here, but three issues stand out that are important for what it tells us about the relationship among war, movements and state. formation. First, the Israeli state was created by a social movement, one that modeled itself on other European nationalisms. But unlike most of those movements, the Zionists did not seek to take control of an existing state; they had to establish a new one on territory that had been governed by others for two millennia. Their capacity to establish a postcolonial state, when so many other new states failed, was due to their involvement in the Mandate state, their long and careful preparation, an ideology reinforced by the Holocaust, and an organizational format that owed much to the experience of the European social democracy.

Second, surrounded by hostile Arab states and by a restive internal Arab population and periodic Palestinian uprisings, the Israeli military gained a central role in both state- and society-building. The army was not only an instrument needed to defend the tiny new Israeli state; as thousands of refugees from Europe and the Middle East began to flock to the Jewish state, it served as an institution for the socialization of new immigrants (Ben-Eliezer 1998, 201). Conscription was universal and compulsory—even for women—and service in the army became a rite of passage for Israeli young people. Especially in the years after the creation of the state, the army also served as a recruiting source for the country's political elite and the glue that held a contentious society together (Barak and Sheffer, 2010).

Third, especially after the 1967 war, which added significant new territories to the area conquered in the 1947–1948 war, Israeli governments governed significant Arab populations in areas where they operated under a permanent state of emergency. The security dilemma was exacerbated when a Jewish movement called the Bloc of the Faithful created settlements in the newly occupied Palestinian territories. The result was to rely increasingly on methods of managing suspect populations and defining citizenship using emergency models inherited from the British mandate (Berda 2013, 2014; Hofnung 1996). Israel-Palestine became a composite state made up of a "normal" parliamentary system for Jews and a military-run colonial state for Palestinians, in which the Palestinians living in Israel proper occupied an increasingly tenuous position (Alimi and Hirsch-Hoefler 2012; Tilly and Tarrow 2007, chap. 6). In terms that have been used repeatedly in this book, they governed through infrastructural power in Israel proper and through hierarchical power over the Palestinians.

Burma and Indonesia

A second region—Southeast Asia—also demonstrates the intimate relations among war, contention, and state-building after World War Two.[13] It was in Indochina that the most protracted war was fought in this region—first against the French and then against their U.S. successors. But the Indochinese nationalists were also communists, and their history of state-building was rapidly engulfed by the logic of the Cold War (Kahin 1986; Logevall 2012). In two other countries emerging from Japanese occupation, Burma and Indonesia, British and Dutch forces attempted to make retake control but were quickly discouraged, both by the strength of the movements they faced and by the lack of support they received from their U.S. allies. In both countries, the post-colonial states were heavily influenced by the movements that had emerged from war, Japanese occupation, and the militarization of postwar politics.

The Dutch had been in the Indonesian archipelago for four centuries, and the British had been in Burma since the nineteenth century. How did such long-established imperial domination dissolve in a period of a few years? Three structural factors had much to do with the rapid success of indigenous nationalist movements. World War Two weakened both empires, leaving them with shattered economies, empty coffers, and little inclination to spill the blood of their youth. In addition, both the Japanese occupation policies and Western gestures toward independence created at least the illusion that the war would bring independence. Finally, the emerging global hegemon, the United States, was unwilling to finance its allies' occupation of their colonial empires, if only because such efforts would deflect resources from the center of its attention in Europe.

But the close of the imperial era was not only the result of these structural factors. Between them and the collapse of the Dutch and British empires were nationalist movements that were empowered by the war, by the policies of both the Japanese and the Allies, and by internal conflicts that emerged in the transition to peacetime politics. In both countries, thousands of young people gained experience in military organization and a bitterness against the former colonial powers. Wherever the Japanese army went, it established organizational networks and a military ethos (Anderson 1972). These not only provided the germ for the movements that would oppose the occupation as the war drew to its close; it provided solidarity and military organizational forms that could be transformed into anti-Dutch and anti-British militancy after the Japanese surrendered (Callahan 2003; Anderson 1972).

For most of its history under the British, Burma was run, not as a directly administered colony but as a buffer to protect the eastern borders of India, the "jewel in the crown" of Britain's empire. The northern part of the country remained outside the range of British administration and "colonial administration sailed over from the other three provinces of India, complete with English-speaking, mostly civilian Indian personnel to operate it" (Callahan 2003, 23, 27). Like the British before them, the Japanese had little interest in establishing control over the Burmese periphery or in creating a strong central administration in Rangoon. The result, according to Mary Callahan, was that after 1941 "the country disintegrated into an array of autonomous local enclaves" in which indigenous Burmans "emerged as local state builders," establishing "an enduring pattern of political strength—often backed by force of arms—in the countryside accompanied by paralysis in Rangoon" (ibid., 45–46).

At war's end, tribal and territorial identities reemerged, strengthened by the guerilla insurgencies they had fought against the Japanese. Once armed, writes Callahan, "most of these guerilla groups stayed armed" and became the basis of the postwar anticolonial movement against the British and the postcolonial insurgency that followed (ibid., 66–67). "One limp structure lay in the civilian realm," writes Mary Callahan, "the other, more robust structure in the military bureaucracy" (ibid., 205). The result was a militarized state that descended into a dictatorship that endured until the new century.

In Indonesia too, the new nationalist elite chose a military route. Here, too, there were separate insurgencies across the archipelago, but even on Java, the core of the country, different coalitions and different conflicts developed across this extended island (Anderson 1972). The result was to shift the balance of power toward the military. But in Indonesia the transfer of power to the military came later and was more abrupt than in Burma. In 1965, an attempted *coup d'état* led the military to remove President Sukarno from power and destroyed the grassroots structure of the Indonesian Communist Party (PKI), the only major party that had emerged from the independence movement. Both countries were ruled by their militaries for most of their postwar histories.

The French in Algeria; Algeria in France

While the Japanese occupation was responsible for politicizing young people in Indonesia and the highland tribes in Burma, in North Africa it was the Free French forces that recruited young men from the slums of Algiers and Oran to fight against the Axis Powers. Seeming to ignore the fact that Algeria held a significant European population, General Charles de Gaulle had declared that France was under an obligation to *indigène* soldiers for the sacrifices they made for *la patrie*. Nevertheless, their treatment in the French army was atrocious, and at war's end, the *indigène* soldiers' military pensions were frozen; moreover, faced by the political power of almost a million European settlers, French promises of Algerian independence came to nothing.

The Algerian nationalist movement began when a display of nationalist flags in Sétif in May 1945 led French soldiers to fire on a group of demonstrators. This produced a postwar uprising in which European settlers were killed. The movement did not take its ultimate military shape, however, until 1954, when a number of postwar currents came together to form the FLN (Front de Libération Nationale). The FLN never completely controlled the resistance, and until the end, there were Arabs and Europeans who sought a compromise solution within the French sphere.[14] But once begun, the spiral of mutual violence in Algeria was polarizing, and the moderate positions on both sides collapsed.

This was a composite conflict. The FLN had both political and military wings; it fought both guerilla actions and conventional warfare—the latter from camps across the border in Morocco and Tunisia; and its militants viciously attacked the settlers, especially those on isolated farms in the countryside. Against this unconventional enemy, the French adopted the counterinsurgency strategy they had learned in Indochina, dislocated parts of the Arab population, and used torture against detainees. What was more unusual was that—and unlike the British and Dutch in their distant territories—the conflict produced a near civil war in France.

Unlike many French colonial possessions, Algeria contained a large, prosperous, and heterodox European minority, mainly living in the cities on the coast. More unusual, it was juridically and politically part of France (Delarue and Rudelle 1990, 52). Algerian independence was therefore opposed not only by important sectors of the French army—still smarting from its 1955 defeat in Indochina—but by over a million European residents, all of whom held French citizenship, and by a sector of the political elite in France.

By the late 1950s, it was clear that the French army was failing and that the Fourth Republic was failing with it. But what could replace it? In May 1958, a group of generals, frustrated with the inability of the civilian leaders to give them the tools they needed to win, took over Algiers in the name of *Algèrie fran-çaise* and moved on to Corsica in preparation for an operation to take Paris as well (Operation Resurrection). A Committee of Public Safety pressed General Charles de Gaulle—the charismatic leader of the wartime Resistance—to return to power, confident that he would both hold onto Algeria and eject the detested parties of the Fourth Republic from power. So, the Fourth Republic ended like the first one—with a "man on horseback" who was brought into power to create a new and more authoritative system. De Gaulle was no Napoleon, but he was ready with a plan for a strong presidential regime in which the powers of the

Fourth Republic parties would be reduced. Supported by most of the political class, by the press, and by public opinion, the referendum that he proposed for a Fifth Republic passed with a majority of 80 percent.

But the conflict soon shifted from Algeria to France proper. When it began to appear that de Gaulle was going back on his commitment to keep Algeria French, a group of civilians and military officers formed a clandestine movement, the OAS (Organisation de l'armée secrète), and attempted to take power in Algiers and assassinate the president in August 1962 (Delarue and Rudelle 1990, chap. 1). The assassination attempt failed, and the politically astute de Gaulle used it to call another referendum, creating the first directly elected presidency since 1848. World War Two had weakened the French Republic and provided the opportunity for the nationalist movement in Algeria, which started another war that led to a countermovement that created a fundamentally new French state.

The post-colonial states that evolved in Israel, Burma, Indonesia, and Algeria looked nothing like the Jacobin state in France, the fascist state in Italy, or either the post-Reconstruction or post-Vietnam states in the United States. But in all four cases, nationalist movements used their military experience to organize against colonial states and—in the case of the Jews in Palestine—against a rival nationalist movement. All four created states with enduring militaristic characteristics. War, and movements generated during warfare, profoundly shaped the future state. As for France, both the Indochinese and the Algerian wars left profound fissures in the Fourth Republic, brought a victorious general to the presidency, and led to an attempted *coup d'état* by embittered military officers.

Back to America

It seems fitting that a book that began with a chapter on the wars of the first movement-state—the French First Republic—should end with those of the Fifth Republic, in which a general-turned-politician closed the long imperial parenthesis that was begun by an earlier general and was fought by the first citizen army. The story also shows what had happened to the citizen army in the interim—it had become both professionalized and authoritarian—and how war had changed from conventional interstate conflicts to composite, transnational conflict that involved both civilians and armed forces. For not only did the Algerian FLN combine conventional warfare with guerilla war and attacks on civilians but the French fought a conventional war in the countryside even as they abused and attacked civilians in the cities. Not only that—in response to the emergency, the French, who had invented the emergency script in wartime, created a state of siege on both sides of the Mediterranean. The press was censored, civil liberties were compromised, Algerians in Paris were killed and thrown into the Seine, and prisoners were tortured—all in the name of protecting freedom.

In these respects, the French-Algerian War was a predecessor of the wars of the United States after 9/11. Those who fought to keep Algeria French used methods with which Vice President Dick Cheney would have been comfortable: the displacement of population groups, attacks on civilians, and the torture of detainees. All of these recall the dark side of the War on Terror. Cheney would probably also have sympathized with the conviction of the French that they were fighting on behalf of freedom and civilization. As a French officer who had fought in both Indochina and Algeria said, "We are not making war for ourselves, not making a colonialist war. . . . We are fighting right here right now for them, for the evolution, to see the evolution of these people and this war is for them. We are defending their freedom as we are, in my opinion, defending the West's freedom. We are here ambassadors, Crusaders. . . ."[15]

But there is a final, and more positive resemblance between the French war in Algeria and the U.S. wars of the twenty-first century. The abuses of the Algerian war and the exposure of the army's systematic use of torture helped to create an antiwar movement among French intellectuals, civil society groups, and organized Catholics, much like the antiwar, antitorture, and antisurveillance movements we have seen in the United States in the wake of 9/11. Both movements protested their countries' wars, emergency rule, and especially the use of torture.[16] Like their U.S. homologs, these French groups sought to rebuild a state that would be worthy of their respective democratic traditions (Andrieu 2002).

In the short run, these activists were unsuccessful in opposing hegemonic power in both countries. But by organizing within vibrant and creative civil societies, they helped to alert the public of the crimes that were being committed in their names and pushed reluctant officials to end the worst of their abuses. Civil society activism often fails. At best, it is hard, slogging, and frustrating work. But it is the only recourse for those who believe in the defense of rights against expanding state powers. Like Sisyphus rolling a stone up the hill only to find that it rolls down again when he reaches the summit, activists continue to seek new and innovative forms for their struggles. As Albert Camus—himself a native of Algeria—wrote under the occupation in 1942, "Struggling to the summit is enough to fill the human heart. We have to imagine that Sisyphus was happy."[17]

Notes

INTRODUCTION

1. Alison Smale and Steven Erlanger, "Ukraine Mobilizes Reserve Troops, Threatening War," *New York Times*, March 1, 2014, http://www.nytimes.com/2014/03/02/world/europe/ukraine.html?_r=0.

2. For the chronology and geography of the crisis through the end of August, 2014, when this book went to press, go to http://www.bbc.com/news/world-europe-27308526.

CHAPTER 1

1. From Howarth 1932, quoted in Tomalin, 2002, 75, from which I have accepted the modern spellings.

2. There are, of course, many definitions of social movements, some of which emphasize disorderly, noninstitutional politics and even sort-term riots. My capacious definition recognizes that movements engage in both institutional and extra-institutional actions in durable interaction with opponents. For a more thorough examination, see Tilly and Wood 2009; della Porta and Diani 2006.

3. But see Anderson 1977 and Callahan 2003 for historical analyses of the colonial state, World War Two, and the nationalist movements that overthrew them, in Java and Burma.

4. The definition is extended for modern states by Poggi (1990, chap. 2) but not essentially changed. The new sociological reflections on the state culminated in Evans, Rueschemeyer, and Skocpol, *Bringing the State Back In* (1985), particularly in the introductory and concluding sections and in Tilly's contribution to that collection.

5. The major works of Schmitt that have resurfaced in the debate over the expansion of executive power are his *Political Theology* (1985), *The Concept of the Political* (1995), *The Theory of the Partisan* (2007), and *Dictatorship* (2013). I argue in chapter 7 that Schmitt is the wrong target for critics of U.S. executive expansion.

6. As Milton Esman summarizes Lasswell's argument, "military priorities preempt a larger share of the nation's resources and military values are accorded higher and higher levels of social prestige. Military officers as a ruling elite achieve expertise in the management of civilian affairs. Civil liberties are subordinated to the requirements of national security" (2013, 5).

7. Rossiter wrote during the early days of the Cold War, "In terms of power, crisis government in a constitutional democracy—whatever the character of the emergency and whatever the dictatorial institutions temporarily adopted—entails one or two, or more probably all, of three things: *concentration, expansion,* and *liberation*. Generally these three features are fused together and evidence themselves as an increase in the authority and prestige of the state and a decrease in the liberty and importance of the individual" (1963, 288).

8. It is not clear why Mann reduces his important distinction between despotic and infrastructural power, which framed his key 1987 article, into a side issue in *The Sources of Social Power* (1993). For a creative application of his concepts to the political economy of East Asia, see Linda Weiss's article "Governed Interdependence" (1995). For

an appreciation and critique of Mann's work, see her "Infrastructural Power, Economic Transformation, and Globalization" (2006).

9. Weiss argues that the power of modern industrial states is infrastructural—not despotic: "They possess the capacity to reach into society to extract and redistribute resources on the basis of consent and negotiation" (2014, 17). King and Lieberman argue that the state's capacity and strength are increasingly based on the links formed with social networks "rather than as necessarily independent or autonomous from society" (2008, 18). Daniel Slater uses the term "infrastructural power" in a narrower sense to mean the power to implement policies (2010, 3).

10. The diversionary theory of war holds that, at times, leaders go to war to divert attention from domestic issues, as in for example the French revolutionary war of 1792. For a summary of the research on this strategy, go to en.wikipedia.org/wiki/Diversionary-_foreign_policy.

11. Neorealists, in particular, have tended to downplay the impact of domestic politics on international warfare in favor of systemic factors (Walt 1996, 3; cf. Waltz 1979). But constructivists also seldom focus on war-making, reacting against neorealism by turning their attention to the role of nonstate actors in transnational relations (Keck and Sikkink 1998). To find concerted attention paid to domestic politics in war-making, we must turn to statists, such as Stephen Krasner (1999), or to historians who study how leaders go to war as a function of domestic incentives, such as Frederik Logevall (1999, 2001).

12. Also see Moaz 1989 and Adelman 1985, for the empirical sources for Walt's striking generalization. Note that Walt is writing only of revolutionary *states*—that is, of successful revolutions. I am unaware of a data set that measures the proportion of all revolutions that go to war. Even more lacking are quantitative data on the correlation between social movements and war-making.

13. The term *protection*, in Tilly's lexicon had a double meaning: first, the obligation to protect citizens and, second, government as a "protection racket." See Tilly 1985 for the starkest statement of this thesis.

14. In both the 1980s and after the turn of the twenty-first century, scholars working in the social movement tradition carried out excellent research on the antiwar movement in the United States. Representative research can be found for the earlier period in Klandermans 1991; Meyer 1990, 1990–91; Rochon 1988; and for the later period in Walgrave and Rucht 2012; Heaney and Rojas 2015; Woehrle, Coy, and Maney 2008.

CHAPTER 2

1. I am grateful to Sébastien Le Gal for suggesting this concise definition.

CHAPTER 3

1. Aside from the immense historiographic work on individual civil wars, modern comparative work began with a series of quantitative analyses of contemporary civil wars, starting with the pathbreaking work by Ted Robert Gurr (1968, 1970). Important markers in this development are the econometric models of Collier and Hoeffler (1998) and the more politically attuned work of James Fearon and David Laitin (2003) and Lars-Erik Cederman, Kristian Skrede Gleditsch, and Halyard Buhaug (2013). For important case studies, see Collier and Sambanis 2005; Trejo 2012; Weinstein 2006; Wood 2000, 2003. For a critical analysis of this literature, see Tarrow 2007.

2. For this section and the next one, I am in debt\to Barry Weingast's (1998, 2002) important analyses. Weingast 2002 is an unpublished manuscript, graciously provided to the author.

3. Weingast 2002 (table 4.1) provides a useful summary, showing how, until the admission of California, the number of slave and free states as represented in the Senate remained largely in balance. Weingast 2002 (table 6.2) shows how consistently antislavery measures in the House failed to win passage until 1858, when Northerners in the House defeated the Democrats' attempt to admit Kansas as a slave state (ibid., 98).

4. *Dred Scott v. Sandford* 60 US (19 How.) 393 (1857). The analysis that follows draws on the accounts of Christopher Eisgruber (2009), Aziz Rana (2010), and Don E. Fehrenbacher (1978).

5. This is interesting because Taylor Blow later took up Scott's cause and supported his long fight for freedom. For this part of the story, see Fehrenbacher (1978, 240–41).

6. Buchanan was widely believed to have been in cahoots with Taney, based on a whispered conversation between the two at Buchanan's inauguration immediately before the Court announced its decision.

7. After analyzing data on capital markets to grasp the economic effect of the decision, two economists found that the decision had a substantial and negative impact on the expected profits in those industries and firms with a stake in the expansion of the free northern economy (Calomiris and Schweikart 1991).

8. An NGram Viewer analysis shows that the term *slave power* first gained currency in the 1830s but that its use surged after 1845, and especially in the 1850s. I am grateful to Richard Valelly for pointing this out.

9. The data are from Silbey 1977 (tables 1.2, 6.1). Four additional states did not hold congressional elections in 1862.

10. See the thoughtful critique by Ira Katznelson (2002).

11. This absence of the national state from local affairs was in line with what Aziz Rana calls "a faith in mass rationality and commitment to expanding popular knowledge ... far beyond rhetoric. In fact, it shaped much of the legal approach to matters of emergency and security during the mid-nineteenth century. Such an approach emphasized the capacity of deliberative bodies and ordinary citizens to sit in judgment of the emergency practices of military officers and pointedly rejected the notion of judicial deference to claims of military necessity" (2012,1445).

12. 67 U.S. 635 (1862). "[T]he Court boldly declared that the president had authority *juri belli* (by right of war) to order a blockade of ports of seceding states" (Brandon 2005, 24).

13. In the 1850s, the writ was widely used by abolitionist lawyers, such as Salmon P. Chase, as a device to free fugitive slaves; but it never became a widespread tool in the antislavery controversy, and it was happily used by southern courts to deny freedom to African Americans. "Antislavery forces employed writs to free black people claimed by Southerners in free states, but a New York law of 1828, for example, also allowed claimants to request the issuance of writs that would cause the sheriff to bring in an alleged runaway" (Neely 1991, xiv–xv).

14. 17 Fed. Cas. No. 9,487 (1861).

15. Stone (2004, 98–120) devotes most of his chapter on the Civil War to the Vallandigham case, which indeed was notorious at the time, but this leaves the reader with the impression that partisan arrests of civilians were more important than they in fact were. The analysis here rests more on the accounts of Hyman (1975) and Neely (1991), who both see the partisan motives for repression of civil liberties as far less important.

16. Although the *Milligan* decision was hailed by civil libertarians, during World War One it was disregarded; President Wilson got Congress to pass the Espionage Act of 1917, which threatened civil liberties far more generally than military commissions could have done (Neely 1991, 181; Stone 2004, chap. 3). In World War Two, and again during the War

on Terror, military commissions were also employed against saboteurs and suspected terrorists (see chapter 5).

17. Du Bois's essay "Of the Dawn of Freedom" (2005, 29–58) remains one of the most balanced analyses of the promise and the pitfalls of Reconstruction. It was first published in the *Atlantic Monthly* in March 1901.

CHAPTER 4

1. For these expansions, and for comparisons with other European countries during the same period, see Rokkan 1970, 84–85

2. Sonnino wrote, "Beyond the concessions [which we are demanding] that are intended to satisfy national sentiments . . . the only two alternatives are war or revolution" (quoted in Rusconi 2014, 210).

3. Too much has been written about Italy's North-South division to require elaboration here. The classical source in English is Putnam 1993; see also Tarrow 1967. For the origins of the North-South cleavage in the unified Italian state, see Macry 2012.

4. The exceptions were the *tavogliere* of Puglia and the fertile enclaves around Naples and Palermo. The best analysis of the geographical structure of southern agriculture is still Rossi-Doria 1982; a summary in English is found in Tarrow 1967, 48–54.

5. This period is perhaps the best studied of any period of modern Italian history. For the success—but also the contradictions—of Garibaldi's invasion of Sicily, see Mack Smith 1954; for the subsequent period of royal conquest of the South, see Macry 2012.

6. Farini was sent to Naples to prevent Giuseppe Garibaldi—whose guerilla army defeated the Bourbon army of King Ferdinand in Sicily—from moving on Rome and the Vatican. It was at this point that the Piedmontese faced the daunting problem of transferring power to a new state against the hostility of the pope, the suspicions of the French, and a rising tide of civil unrest throughout the South.

7. The term is that of Antonio Gramsci, who famously compared the Italian passive revolution to the French bourgeois revolution. See Gramsci 1949; it is translated in Forgacs 1988. See also Davis 1975.

8. The necessarily brief summary in this section is based on the work of John Davis (1988), Carlo Guarnieri (1995), Antonella Meniconi (2013), Stefano Rodotà (1995), Giovanna Tosatti (1997), and Luciano Violante (1976).

9. Bordogna's and Provasi's analysis appears in their essay "Il movimento degli scioperi in Italia (1881–1973)" (1979). The time series data in figure 4.1 begins in 1901 because data on the percentage of strikers in agriculture do not appear in the official statistics until that year. I am grateful to Lorenzo Bordogna for providing me with the statistical data in this chapter.

10. Even the most vulnerable soldiers—those who had surrendered—were left to starve in Austrian prison camps because the General Staff refused to send them shipments of food (Procacci 1993).

11. For a detailed analysis of the IM, see Luigi Tomassini 1992. Tomassini's analysis, like this one, is much in debt to the report of Luigi Einaudi, economist and future Italian president, to the Rockefeller Foundation, *La condotta economica e gli effetti sociali della guerra italiana* (1933).

12. The concept of cycles of contention owes much to the contributions of Alessandro Pizzorno (1978). It was further developed in Tarrow 1989 and 2011b, and in Koopmans 1993.

CHAPTER 5

1. A related strand of research uses the concept of *hybrid warfare*, which is defined as "conflict involving a combination of conventional military forces and irregulars (guerillas,

insurgents, and terrorists), which could include both state and nonstate actors, aimed at achieving a common political purpose" (Murray and Mansoor 2012, 2). The hybrid warfare literature is much more oriented toward strategies to defeat hybrid warriors than to understanding the nature of this enemy.

2. As warrants such an original and skillful analysis, Kaldor's book stimulated a lively debate among specialists. For a useful synthesis of the debate and proposals for resolving some of the issues raised by *New Wars*, see Masullo Jiménez and Bajo 2014.

3. *Globalization* I define as the increasing volume and speed of flows of capital and goods, information and ideas, people, and forces that connect actors between countries (Keohane 2002, 194); *internationalization* is the increasing network of links among state actors and between states and international institutions (Tarrow 2005).

4. This literature is too vast to effectively summarize here. Three studies that mark its progression are Keck and Sikkink 1998, della Porta 2007, and Smith 2008. For evidence that the spectrum of transnational NGOs is not all liberal, see Bob 2012 and Miodownik and Barak 2013.

5. A sprawling literature has grown out of the growing number of civil wars in the global South of the end of the twentieth century, much of it using tools of cross-national statistical analysis but much of it engaged with insurgencies in single countries. Among the former, see Cederman, Gleditsch, and Buhaug 2013; Collier and Hoeffler 1998; and Fearon and Laitin 2003. Among the latter, see Collier and Sambanis 2005; Kalyvas 2003, 2006; Weinstein 2006; and Wood 2000 and 2003.

6. I exclude the ongoing conflict between Israel and the Palestinians because Engene's data set does not go beyond Western Europe. For the best analysis of the conflict, see Alimi 2007. For the most thorough analysis of the Israeli state's national security policies in response to it, see Hofnung 1996. For a more up-to-date analysis, see Levy 2012.

7. The TWEED data set and codebook are available at the project's website, http://folk.uib.no/sspje/tweed.htm. In what follows, for clarity, I adopt Engene's use of the terms *terrorism* and *terrorist*, despite my preference for the more precise term used by della Porta 2013, *clandestine political violence*.

8. Indeed, the army officer who was sent to Belfast to plan a campaign of resistance had earned his spurs in the repression of independence movements in Southeast Asia and Kenya. The same was true in the French war against the Front de Libération Nationale (FLN) in Algeria. The official sent to organize the suppression of the underground wing of the FLN, General Marcel Bigeard, had earned his spurs in Indochina. I return to the Algerian war in the conclusion.

9. The journalistic and scientific literature on the Northern Irish Troubles is too vast to even attempt to summarize. A convenient, if now dated, starting point is Whyte 1990. A sociological analysis can be found in McGarry and O'Leary 1995. Contentious politics accounts can be found in Maney 2006; Gupta 2007; and Ruane and Todd 1996 . On the role of the British state in the conflict, see Smith 2011. On the state of emergency and the abuse of prisoners, see Donahue 2008, and Gross and Ní Aoláin 2006.

10. Kitson put his strategy into theory in a manual called *Low-Intensity Operations: Subversions, Insurgency, Peace-Keeping* (1971), which drew on his colonial experiences and was the guide for security operations in Northern Ireland.

11. Two recent studies that deliberately compare al Qaeda with Western clandestine movements are della Porta 2013 and Alimi, Demetriou, and Bosi, forthcoming. The first studies of Islamic radicalism to use a social movement approach were Wiktorowicz 2004 (based on field research in Britain) and 2005. Also important is the empirical research of Wickham (2002). More recent work by social movement scholars has drawn effectively on this research tradition. See Wickham 2013, Goodwin 2006 and 2012, and especially della Porta 2013.

CHAPTER 6

Gracious comments were offered on a draft of this chapter by my colleagues Josh Chafetz, Mike Dorf, Matt Evangelista, Fred Logevall, and Joe Margulies.

1. For the Media break-in story, see Mark Mazzetti, "Burglars Who Took on FBI Abandon Shadows," *New York Times* January 7, 2014, http://www.nytimes.com/2014/01/07/us/burglars-who-took-on-fbi-abandon-shadows.html?_r=0.

2. I use the term *suppression* as Jules Boykoff does, to include both overtly repressive state actions and those that depend on indirect means, such as making it harder and more expensive to organize and creating a hostile climate of opinion. For this distinction, see Boykoff 2007.

3. U.S. Bureau of the Census 1965, 736–37.

4. Wilson's speech asking Congress to declare war can be found at http://historymatters.gmu.edu/d/4943/, accessed December 4, 2013.

5. This section is inspired by my colleague Aziz Rana's paper, "Constitutionalism and the Foundations of the Security State" (forthcoming), http://papers.ssrn.com/sol3/papers.cfm?abstract_id=2392666. See also Rana 2010 and 2012.

6. For the concept of social movement spillover, see Meyer and Whittier 1994.

7. Interestingly enough, although the same war produced a radical escalation of emergency powers, we have a much thinner record of that term in American history, as figure 6.1 also shows. This may have been because of the belated presence of the federal state in American life; because the legal concepts we currently include under emergency powers are referred to in more specific terms, such as *habeas corpus*; or because Americans do not like to think of themselves acting outside the rule of law.

8. In a third case, *Ex Parte Endo* 323 US 283 (1944), the Court actually invalidated detention for a citizen of undoubted loyalty but did so one day after the administration announced an end to internment.

9. As Biddle—who was forced to go along with the move—later speculated about Roosevelt's decision, "Nor do I think that the constitutional difficulty plagued him—the Constitution has never greatly bothered any wartime President. That was a question of law, which ultimately the Supreme Court must decide. And meanwhile—probably a long meanwhile—we must get on with the war" (quoted in Stone 2004, 296).

10. In my emphasis on these early documents, I follow closely the analysis of Michael Hogan (1998, 10–12).

11. Jackson argued that there are three tiers of presidential authority. When a president acts in conjunction with Congress, executive power is at its zenith because the president may rely on his own authority plus that of the legislative branch. When a president acts contrary to congressional will, executive power is at its nadir because the president must rely solely on his expressly delegated authority minus that of the legislative branch. And when a president acts in an area where Congress has been silent, executive power is uncertain and may fluctuate depending on the circumstances. For a summary of the various opinions of the Court, go to http://legal-dictionary.thefreedictionary.com/Steel+Seizure+Case.

12. Eisenhower's 1960 "Military-Industrial Complex" speech originally included Congress, but he seems to have removed this third pole of the triangle from his speech at the suggestion of his aides.

13. http://coursesa.matrix.msu.edu/~hst306/documents/indust.html.

14. Some of the films the FBI targeted would surprise many moviegoers. For example, Lou Budin's 1951 filming of *Alice in Wonderland* was criticized because "its puppet characters were identified to a certain extent with supposedly real personages"; *The Best Years of Our Lives* was criticized because it "portrayed the 'upper class' in a bad light"; and the antiracist *Gentlemen's Agreement* was criticized as "a deliberate effort to discredit law enforcement" (Sbardellati 2012, app., 197, 198, 200).

15. This moveable ritual has not been given sufficient attention by students of post-war political culture. For example, it is not even mentioned in Friedberg's (2000) *In the Shadow of the Garrison State*. In addition to Hogan's lively account, see Bodnar 1992 and Little 1989.

16. For example, most were unwilling to allow an atheist to speak in public or to allow a socialist to teach in a college or university (Stouffer 1955, 34, 30, 51). The special fear of communism could be measured indirectly during the Korean War when Americans were asked two different versions of a question about support for the war by the National Opinion Research Center. In the first version, respondents were asked, "As things stand now, do you feel that the war in Korea has been [was] worth fighting, or not?" In the second, the members of the public were asked, "Do you think the United States was right or wrong in sending American troops to stop the Communist invasion of South Korea?" Although both versions of the question tracked opinion similarly between the start of the war in June 1950 and April 1953, the level of support for the second, "anticommunist" version ranged between 10 and 20 percent higher than the "worth fighting for" version of the question (Berinsky 2009,15–16).

17. On the "lavender scare" and its origins in the early Cold War, see Valelly 2014. I am grateful to Professor Valelly for sharing with me an early draft of part of his unpublished manuscript.

18. An NGram analysis of Google Books shows that the expression *constitutional loyalty* peaked in 1966 and began to decline as the unpopularity of the Vietnam War increased, well before the Watergate scandal. http://books.google.com/ngrams/graph?content=constitutional+loyalty&year_start=1945&year_end=2000&corpus=17&smoothing=3&share=/.

19. Next to the Civil War, the Vietnam War is probably the most studied episode of armed conflict in U.S. history. General histories that I consulted for this section are Campbell and Logevall 2009; Ely 1993; Fisher, 2004, chap. 6; Griffin 2013, chap. 4; Herring 1979; Logevall 1999 and 2012; and Kahin 1986.

20. Gitlin (1980, 27–28) lists some of the framing devices he found in the media's coverage of the movement—particularly of the movement he identified with, the SDS: trivialization, polarization, emphasis on internal dissension, marginalization, undercounting, disparagement of its effectiveness, reliance on statements by government authorities, emphasis on the presence of communists and the carrying of Viet Cong flags, and, increasingly, emphasis on violence in demonstrations.

21. The literature on the FBI's assault on the New Left is too broad to be effectively summarized here. For basic accounts sympathetic to the movement, see DeBenedetti 1990, Davis 1997, Keller 1989, Medsger 2013, and Small 2002. A skeptical view of the effectiveness of the movement in changing public policy is Garfinkle 1997. The programs of the Departments of Justice and Defense have received less attention, but see the study by Scott (2009), a Senate historian.

22. A list of disruptive FBI activities against New Left groups was compiled by James Kirkpatrick Davis (1997, 58–59) from FBI internal memoranda. All of chapter 3 of his book bears careful reading to determine how far the FBI, in its New Left COINTELPRO, had moved from its early Cold War programs.

23. The full text of the "Pentagon Papers" can be found at www.archives/gov/research/pentagon-papers/.

CHAPTER 7

1. The problem of determining whether and how the laws of war apply to conflict between a state and a nonstate actor such as al Qaeda has divided international lawyers and political theorists since the beginning. For a thoughtful summary and analysis, see Ohlin, 2015, chap. 5.

2. Article 5 of the Third Geneva Convention offers only limited protection for the rights of belligerents who do not wear uniforms. The full text is available at www.icrc.org/Web/Eng/siteeng0.nsf/html/genevaconventions. For a summary and analysis, see Evangelista 2008, chap. 3. See also Newton 2005 and Goldman and Tittemore 2002.

3. The team came from Harvard, MIT, Stanford, and the University of Virginia and involved experts on national security, terrorism, intelligence, law enforcement, constitutional law, technologies of catastrophic terrorism and defenses against them, and government organization and management. Organized by the Stanford-Harvard Preventive Defense Project, it was part of the Kennedy School of Government's Visions of Governance for the Twenty-First Century project. For the group's report, go to http://belfer center.hks.harvard.edu/publication/652/catastrophic_terrorism.html.

4. The term *homeland security*, which had been uncommon in public discourse until the mid-1990s, shot up in frequency after 2001, as can be found in an NGram search of Google Books from 1990 to 2008, https://books.google.com/ngrams/graph?content=ho meland+security&year_start=1945&year_end=2008&corpus=17&smoothing=3&share =&direct_url=t1%3B%2Chomeland%20security%3B%2Cc0.

5. Reported in the *Washington Post*, November 1, 2007.

6. When Homeland Security Secretary Tom Ridge hesitated to announce a red alert against the advice of hard-liners in the Cabinet, he reports that he was called on the carpet by the president and told "bluntly that counterterrorism is one of the administration's highest priorities, and that a united front had to be presented" (2009, 228).

7. In the wake of the 2004 campaign, the term *swiftboating* became part of the American political lexicon, meaning "undercutting a candidate's legitimacy with rumors of his or her past life." For the flavor of the swiftboat campaign, go to http://urbanlegends.about.com/library/bl_swift_boat_veterans.htm.

8. "After that episode," Ridge concludes, "I knew I had to follow through on my plans to leave the federal government". Quoted in "Ridge Cites Pressure before 2004 Election," *Washington Post*, August 21, 2009, p. 1, available at http://www.washingtonpost.com/wp-dyn/content/article/2009/08/20/AR2009082003993.html.

9. See, in particular, Brooks and Manza 2013, chaps. 1, 4, 5; Margulies 2013, chaps. 7–10; and Nacos, Bloch-Elkon, and Shapiro 2011, chap. 3.

10. In *Turkmen v. Ashcroft*, a class action civil rights lawsuit was filed by the Center for Constitutional Rights on behalf of a class of Muslim, South Asian, and Arab noncitizens who had been swept up by the Immigration and Naturalization Service (INS) and FBI following 9/11. http://ccrjustice.org/ourcases/current-cases/turkmen-v.-ashcroft. The case was still tied up in the courts in 2013 after a federal judge dismissed the charges against Attorney General Ashcroft and other federal officials.

11. This admission was made on the *Times*'s editorial page in the form of an apology a few days later, http://www.nytimes.com/2004/05/26/international/middle east/26FTE_NOTE.html?ex=1400990400&en=94c17fcffad92ca9&ei=5007&partner=USERLAND, accessed December 6, 2013. To my knowledge, only the *Times* admitted that it had been taken in by the administration's unsubstantiated claims.

12. The original act, Public Law 107–56, can be found at http://www.gpo.gov/fdsys/pkg/PLAW-107pub156/pdf/PLAW-107publ.56. With minor revisions, it was reauthorized in 2005 and signed by President Bush in March 2006.

13. A convenient summary and a review of the controversy over Section 215 can be found at http://www.slate.com/blogs/weigel/2013/06/07/nsa_prism_scandal_what_patriot_act_section_215_does.html. The Sensenbrenner protest can be found in his letter to Attorney General Holder at http://sensenbrenner.house.gov/uploadedfiles/sensen brenner_letter_to_attorney_general_eric_holder.pdf. The political impact of the Snowden affair will be examined in chapter 9.

14. Authorization for the Use of Military Force (AUMF), Pub. L. No. 107–40, 115 Stat. 224 (2001).

15. Joseph Margulies, who was one of the first lawyers to gain access to his client at the facility, has written up his experiences in *Guantánamo and the Abuse of Presidential Power* (2006, chap. 1).

16. Military Commissions Act of 2009, # 848a. This expansion of the targets legitimated by the AUMF to include "associated forces" was continued under the Obama administration. *In Re Guantánamo Bay Detention Litigation* (District Court of the District of Columbia, March 13, 2009), 2. I am grateful to Jens Ohlin for calling this continuity in language to my attention.

17. In its *al-Bihani* decision (590 F.3d 866, 872 [D.C. Cir. 2010]) the D.C. Circuit Court of Appeals adopted the "associated forces" standard proposed by the government for legitimate detention and did not seem bothered by the fact that the term did not appear in the AUMF passed by Congress.

18. For an overview of the new act and how it related to the federal court systems, see Segal and Kimura 2011, chaps. 1 and 2. See also Ni Aolain and Gross 2013.

19. Memorandum for William J. Haynes II, General Counsel, Department of Defense, "Possible *Habeas* Jurisdiction of Aliens Held in Guantanamo Bay, Cuba, December 28, 2001," reprinted in Greenberg and Dratel 2005, 29–37.

20. *Rasul* is discussed in detail by Margulies (2006), who was attorney of record for the case. Although it was made irrelevant by Congress, responding to administration pressure, the case was an important benchmark for U.S. lawyers, many of whom responded by joining what came to be called the "Guantánamo Bar." See chapter 9 for this remarkable example of legal mobilization.

21. Memo to William J. Haynes, General Counsel, Department of Defense, "Application of Treaties and Laws to al Qaeda and Taliban Detainees," reprinted in Greenberg and Dratel 2005, 38–79.

22. Article 5 of the Third Geneva Convention holds that unauthorized combatants will enjoy the protection of the Convention until their status can be determined by a competent tribunal. http://avalon.law.yale.edu/20th_century/geneva03.asp#art5.

23. The original quotation is from the report of General George Fay, "Investigation of the Abu Ghraib Detention Facility and the 205th Military Intelligence Brigade," http://www.thetorturedatabase.org/document/fay-report-investigation-205th-military-intelligence-brigades-activites-abu-ghraib.

24. There were actually two memos on that day: (1) Jay S. Bybee, Memorandum to Alberto R. Gonzales Counsel to the President, "Standards of Conduct for Interrogation under 18 U.S.C." (reprinted in Greenberg and Dratel 2005, 172–217), and (2) a letter to Gonzales from Yoo regarding "the views of our Office concerning the legality under international law, of interrogation methods to be used on captured al Qaeda operatives" (reprinted in ibid., 218–22).

25. It emerged only in 2014 in a report to the Senate Intelligence Committee that the CIA had misled the government and the public about aspects of its brutal interrogation program, concealing details about the severity of its methods, overstating the significance of plots and prisoners, and taking credit for critical pieces of intelligence that detainees had in fact surrendered before they were subjected to harsh techniques (*Washington Post*, April 1, 2014). At the time of this writing, the report is still awaiting vetting by the White House and the CIA before being released.

26. Memorandum for William J. Haynes, General Counsel of the Department of Defense, "Military Interrogation of Alien Unlawful Combatants Held Outside the United States, March 14, 2003," http:///fas.org/irp/agency/doj/olc-interrogation.pdf.

27. Memo to Timothy Flanigan, Deputy Counsel to the President, "The President's Constitutional Authority to Conduct Military Operations against Terrorists and

Nations Supporting Them, September 25, 2001," reprinted in Greenberg and Dratel, 2005, 3–24.

28. "When the President takes measures incompatible with the expressed or implied will of Congress," wrote Justice Jackson in an important concurrence in the Steel Seizure case, "his power is at its lowest ebb, for then he can rely only upon his own constitutional powers minus any constitutional powers of Congress over the matter" (*Youngstown Sheet and Tube v. Sawyer* 343 U.S. 637 [1952]).

29. For Mora's memorandum, go to http://www.newyorker.com/images/pdfs/mo ramemo.pdf. The Mora affair was revealed in a *New Yorker* article, Mayer 2006.

30. Goldsmith's opinions were greeted with consternation in the White House and with rage by David Addington, Vice President Cheney's chief-of-staff. "Why are you trying to give away the President's power," Addington expostulated when Goldsmith urged the administration to gain congressional approval for its detention policies (quoted in Goldsmith 2012, 124).

31. Memorandum for John A. Rizzo, "Re: Application of 18 U.S. C. 2340–2340A to the Combined Use of Certain Techniques in the Interrogation of High Value al Qaeda Detainees," reprinted in Cole and Sands 2009, 158–59, 171.

32. Pub. Law No 109–148, 1003, U.S. Statute 2739.

33. http://www.whitehouse.gov/the-press-office/2013/05/23/remarks-president-national-defense-university.

CHAPTER 8

1. The suit was filed under the False Claims Act 31 USC sections 3729–33. The government's complaint can be found at http://apps.washingtonpost.com/g/documents/world/justice-department-joins-suit-against-usis/757/.

2. In the wake of the scandal, the Office of Personnel Management decided to scale back the amount of business it would give USIS in the future. Dion Nussenbaum, "US Scales Back USIS's Role in Security Clearances," *Wall Street Journal*, February 16, 2014, p. 1, http://online.wsj.com/news/articles/SB10001424052702304680904579367351 9252.

3. Reagan's speech and its interpretation as a neoliberal manifesto can be found on the website of the Heritage Foundation, one of the avant-garde organizations in the neoliberal movement, http://www.heritage.org/initiatives/first-principles/primary-sources/reagans-first-inaugural-government-is-not-the-solution-to-our-problem-government-is-the-problem.

4. These figures are from the U.S. Office of Personnel Management, http://www.opm.gov/feddata/ (accessed October 25, 2012).

5. The data are from the *Global Security Mailing List*, www.globalsecurity.org/intell/library/budget/index.html (accessed October 21, 2013). Obviously, these figures do not include secret appropriations. the *Washington Post* report was published on September 17, 2009.

6. Former Pennsylvania Governor Tom Ridge's (2009) recounting of his experiences as the first Secretary of DHS describes both the immense tasks assigned to the new hybrid agency and the difficulties he had in establishing its authority amid competing preexisting agencies.

7. The case of Rahinah Ibrahim, a PhD student at Stanford, is archetypical. Ibrahim was stopped at an airport by the FBI after an FBI agent had mistakenly placed her on the government's vastly overbroad no-fly list. In 2005, the mistake was rectified, but when she tried to return from her native Malaysia, she found that her student visa had been revoked. Ibrahim sued the government and found that the word *terrorist* had been written on her visa application to attend her trial. For the best examination of the watchlist issue, see the ACLU report, "U.S. Government Watchlisting: Unfair Process and Devastating Consequences," March 2014, https://www.aclu.org/sites/default/files/

assets/watchlist_briefing_paper_v3.pdf. For the Ibrahim story, go to http://www.nytimes. com/2014/04/19/opinion/terror-watch-lists-run-amok.html.

8. For reports on the activities of the fusion centers in relation to the Occupy movement, see Colin Moynihan, "Officials Cast Wide Net in Monitoring Occupy Protests," *New York Times*, May 23, 2014, www.nytimes.com/2014/05/23/us/officials-cast-wide-net-in-monitoring-occupy-protests.html?_r=0.

9. Research and development spending from the intelligence agencies is not included in the data set because their budgets are classified.

10. Among the most useful academic studies on military contracting are those by Deborah Avant (2005, 2010, 2013), Peter Singer (2003), and Allison Stanger (2009). The best-documented journalistic studies of intelligence outsourcing are by Arkin (2013) and Priest and Arkin (2011). The most damning journalistic account of a military contractor is of the Blackwater—now Academi—company by Jeremy Scahill (2007).

11. For this report, go to http://www.businessinsider.com/108000-contractors-are-in-afghanistan-2013-6 (accessed October 25, 2013). A more detailed analysis can be found at http://www.thefiscaltimes.com/Articles/2013/06/03/Pentagon-Has-No-Idea-What-108K-Contractors-Are-Doing.aspx#page1#ixzz2ilPdkD4x.

12. Governmental intrusion on private-sector communications also dates to the Cold War. "From the late 1940s to the mid-1970s," writes Tim Shorrock, "Western Union, AT&T, and several other communication companies allowed the NSA to read and listen in on every international telegram and phone call placed to the United States" (2008, 74–76).

13. Shorrock's source for these data was an unclassified PowerPoint presentation that was prepared for a Defense Intelligence Agency conference and unwittingly released by the Office of the Director of National Intelligence. See the description of how he derived his estimates in his informative book, *Spies for Hire* (2008, 392n. 18).

14. The ACLU has tracked these programs and filed lawsuits against them, https://www.aclu.org/blog/national-security-religion-belief/nypd-shutters-muslim-spying-unit-what-about-its-tactics.

15. http://www.huffingtonpost.com/2014/04/15/nypd-muslims-_n_5155467.html.

16. For information on the ACLU campaign against MATRIX, go to https://www.aclu.org/technology-and-liberty/feature-matrix.

17. An archetypical case is that of Cofer Black, a former high CIA official who joined Blackwater and lent legitimacy to the firm in Washington (Scahill 2007, 278–79).

18. For an accurate account, see Jon Swaine and Amanda Holpuch, "Ferguson Police: A Stark Illustration of Newly Militarised Law Enforcement," *The Guardian*, August 14, 2014, p. 1, http://www.theguardian.com/world/2014/aug/14/ferguson-police-military-restraints-violence-weaponry-missouri.

19. The coalition included Google, Apple, Facebook. Twitter, AOL, Microsoft, LinkedIn, and Yahoo (http://www.bbc.co.uk/news/tehcnology-25297044).

CHAPTER 9

1. The government at one point accused Snowden of stealing "millions of pages of documents," a number that has no known source in reality but that the press picked up on as if it was a fact.

2. At this writing, it is too soon for scholarly assessments of the Snowden affair to have appeared, but two insider accounts are more or less reliable: Luke Harding's *The Snowden Files* (2014), and Glenn Greenwald's *No Place to Hide* (2014), which is a more serious account than its thrilling title suggests.

3. Jason Leopold, "Revealed: NSA Pushed 9/11 as Key 'Sound Bite' to Justify Surveillance," 2013, http://america.aljazeera.com/articles/2013/10/30/revealed-nsa-pushed-911askeysoundbitetojustifysurveillance.html.

4. "That assignment," according to the *New York Times*, "helps explain how Mr. Snowden got hold of documents laying bare the top-secret capabilities of the nation's largest intelligence agency." July 1, 2013, www.nytimes.com/2013/07/01/us.job-title-key-to-inner-access-held-by-snowden.html?pagewanted=all&_r=0.

5. Andrew Ross Sorkin, "Tech Companies Tread Lightly in Statements on U.S. Spying," *New York Times*, June 10, 2013, http://dealbook.nytimes.com/2013/06/10/tech-companies-tread-lightly-in-statements-on-u-s-spying/?_php=true&_type=blogs&_r=0.

6. When James Clapper, director of National Intelligence, was asked by Senator Ron Wyden (D-Oregon) of the Senate Intelligence Committee whether Americans' private communications were being surveilled, Clapper lied to the American people; Clapper testimony to the Senate Intelligence Committee, March 2013, http://www.youtube.com/watch?v=T9ss2_0emOY. In June 2013, Clapper apologized to Dianne Feinstein (D-California), Intelligence Committee chair, for "erroneous testimony," http://www.forbes.com/sites/andygreenberg/2013/07/02/national-intelligence-director-clapper-apologizes-for-clearly-erroneous-congressional-testimony-on-nsa-surveillance/. Six months later, Clapper issued a directive barring officials at the seventeen intelligence agencies he controls from speaking to journalists without permission, www.dne.gov/files/documents/ICD/ICD%20119.pdf.

7. The first question that Snowden asked the ACLU attorney in charge of Speech, Privacy, and Technology, Ben Wizner, was "Do you have standing now?" See Wizner's interview with *Forbes Magazine*, March 2014, http://www.forbes.com/sites/kashmirhill/2014/03/10/how-aclu-attorney-ben-wizner-became-snowdens-lawyer/.

8. As late as April 2014, there were still 131 million hits for the search *Snowden + NSA* on Google.

9. The rally is described at https://rally.stopwatching.us/, accessed October 28, 2013.

10. For Obama's reaction to the NSA revelations, see his January 2014 speech, http://www.washingtonpost.com/politics/full-text-of-president-obamas-jan-17-speech-on-nsa-reforms/2014/01/17/fa33590a-7f8c-11e3-9. For the report of the committee he appointed to advise him on reforming the agency, see "Presidential Advisory Committee's Recommendations for NSA," http://www.nytimes.com/interactive/2013/12/19/us/politics/19nsa-review.html?_r=0. For Obama's response to the committee report, see Peter Baker and Charlie Savage, "Obama to Place Some Restraints on Surveillance," *New York Times*, January 15, 2014, http://www.nytimes.com/2014/01/15/us/politics/judge-warns-proposed-safeguards-could-hamper-surveillance-court.html?_r=0&gwh=FDC7D881C524E85A09C29D424671DB13&gwt=pay.

11. See also Edwards and Marullo 1995. On the nuclear freeze movement of the 1980s, see Meyer 1990.

12. The Battle of Seattle and its diffusion to other sites inspired much excitement among scholars and activists. For the history of the Seattle movement, see "The WTO History Project," edited by Lance Bennett and Margaret Levi, depts.washington.edu/wto hist/. For the broader Seattle campaign, see Lichbach and DeVries 2007. For its diffusion, see Lesley Wood's (2012) study of New York and Toronto.

13. For profiles of the fifteen groups in the sample, see Woehrle, Coy, and Maney 2008, app. 1.

14. A Pew survey a few weeks after 9/11 found that "The public has little discomfort with the widespread expressions of patriotism and religious expression—just 8% say there has been too much showing of the flag, 10% believe there has been too much playing of patriotic songs, and 12% say the expressions of religious faith and prayer by politicians have been excessive." On the other hand, about 70 percent were open to allowing peaceful protests of military action. "Americans Open to Dissenting Views on the War on Terrorism," Pew Research Center for the People and the Press, October 4, 2001, http://www.people-press.org/2001/10/04/americans-open-to-dissenting-views-on-the-war-on-terrorism/.

15. I am grateful to Michael Heaney and Fabio Rojas for allowing me to consult and quote from their forthcoming book.

16. Obama's 2002 speech can be found at http://www.politisite.com/2013/09/05/the-44th-presidents-2002-speech-on-waging-war-with-syria-update/.

17. For a telescopic survey of the literature on law, movements, and organizations, see Edelman, Leachman, and McAdam 2010. The new field owed much to Stuart Scheingold's *The Politics of Rights* (1974), which was followed by a number of collective volumes edited by Austin Sarat and Scheingold (1997, 2001, 2006). Michael McCann's reader, *Law and Social Movements* (2006), provides a solid introduction to this growing field. For the growing interest in law and movements among social scientists, see Boutcher and Stobaugh 2013 and Sarat 2011. For a cautionary approach, see Rosenberg 2008.

18. The major cases are *Rasul v. Bush* 542 U.S. 542, *Hamdi v. Bush* 542 U.S. 507, *Hamdan v. Rumsfeld* 548 U.S. 557, and *Boumediene v. Bush* 553 U.S. 723. All four cases are discussed dispassionately by Goldsmith (2012), with more engagement Louis Fisher (2008), and with real passion by Jess Bravin (2013).

19. Center for Constitutional Rights, "Legal Analysis: Boumediene v. Bush/Al Odah v. United States," 2008, http://ccrjustice.org/learn-more/faqs/legal-analysis%3A-boumediene-v.-bush/al-odah-v.-united-states.

20. http://www.lawfareblog.com/wiki/the-lawfare-wiki-document-library/post-911-era-materials/post-911-era-materials-court-cases/al-adahi-v-obama-613-f-3d-1102-d-c-cir-2010/#.UsbivbThM1E.

21. http://www.mcclatchydc.com/2014/04/11/224085/cias-use-of-harsh-interrogation.html.

22. http://www.washingtonpost.com/world/national-security/feinstein-cia-searched-intelligence-committee-computers/2014/03/11/982cbc2c-a923–11e3–8599-ce7295b6851c_story.html.

23. The government's claim was not quite accurate. In the case of *Turkmen v. Aschcroft*, the Center for Constitutional Rights took up the claim of a group of Muslim men from a number of countries that they had been held illegally in the Metropolitan Detention Center in Brooklyn after 9/11. Although five of the original claimants received a settlement from the government for $1.26 million, as of May 2014 the case was still in the federal court system. http://ccrjustice.org/Turkmen-v-Ashcroft.

24. The federal government's Combined Federal Campaign, which integrates charitable giving for thousands of government workers, issued a memorandum requiring nonprofits receiving funds to certify that they do not knowingly employ representatives of or distribute funds to groups found on one of the government's many watchlists. At this point, many nonprofit groups became truly alarmed, particularly given the chaotic and expansive nature of these lists (Sidel 2004, 125). A number of groups refused to sign the certification, and others protested openly against it. The ACLU Board even turned down money from the federal campaign in protest and ended its long cooperation with the Ford and Rockefeller foundations when these two signed on to the government's restrictive funding requirements.

25. Section 215 of the USA Patriot Act (P.L.107–56, passed on October 26, 2001, http://www.ala.org/advocacy/advleg/federallegislation/theusapatriotact.

26. For the ACLU's campaign, go to https://www.aclu.org/free-speech-national-security-technology-and-liberty/reform-patriot-act-section-215.

27. For the role of the ALA and local public libraries in opposing Section 215, see Blanc 2010, chap. 3. For the ALA's position against section 215, go to http://www.ala.org/advocacy/advleg/federallegislation/theusapatriotact. Its 2002 Resolution can be found at http://www.ala.org/ala/washoff/woissues/civillberties/theusapatriotact/alaresolution/cfm.

28. The ALA's statement can be found at http://www.ala.org/advocacy/intfreedom/librarybill/interpretations/privacy.

29. For the details of the campaign and a list of the cities and states that had passed Bill of Rights resolutions as of the end of 2013, go to http://www.constitutioncampaign.org/map/resos.php.

30. For evidence on statewide Bill of Rights resolutions, see Riverstone-Newell 2012.

31. This section draws on interviews with Baher Azmy, Gitajali Gutierrez, Joseph Margulies, Gareth Peirce, Michael Ratner, Steven Watt, and Vince Warren and on the original research of Chan S. Suh (forthcoming), Florent Blanc (2010), and Devyani Prabat (2011).

32. I am grateful to Baher Azmy, legal director of CCR, for providing these data.

33. "Detention, Treatment, and Trial of Certain Non-Citizens in the War Against Terrorism," http://www.fas.org/irp/offdocs/eo/mo-111301.htm.

34. Shafiq, it seemed to Peirce, could serve as a "named litigant" to challenge the administration's assertion that the Geneva Conventions did not apply to the detainees. She gathered the background information on Rasul in Britain as the legal team in New York was preparing its legal case. Interview with Gareth Peirce, London, September 21, 2013.

35. Charles "Cully" Stimson, assistant secretary of defense for detainee affairs, was forced to resign from the Department of Defense after the controversy that followed his remark that "corporate CEOs seeing this [the representation of detainees] should ask firms to choose between lucrative retainers and representing terrorists." *New York Times*, January 13, 2007, http://www.nytimes.com/2007/01/13/washington/13gitmo.html?_r=0.

36. The CCR was founded in the 1960s by a group of radical lawyers—Morton Stavis, Arthur Kinoy, Ben Smith, and William Kunstler—to defend civil rights activists in the South. Although its motto is "success without victory," in practice, the group won a number of victories, both before and after *Rasul*, in the fields of civil rights, immigrant rights, surveillance, police abuse, and detainee rights.

37. *Johnson v. Eisentrager*, 339 U.S. 763 (1950) held that military tribunals were an appropriate venue in which to try German spies who were arrested in China during World War Two.

38. In August 2013 in a historic ruling, a federal district court found the NYPD liable for a pattern and practice of racial profiling and unconstitutional "stop and frisks." For the CCR's stop-and-frisk case, go to http://ccrjustice.org/newsroom/press-releases/judge-rules-floyd-case. On Central American intervention, go to http://ccrjustice.org/honduras-foia. On the defense of LGBT rights in Africa, go to http://ccrjustice.org/our-cases/current-cases/sexual-minorities-uganda-v.-lively. On the Catholic church's sexual violence, http://ccrjustice.org/icc-vatican-prosecution-0.

39. In preparing this section, I was lucky to have the cooperation of Susan Herman, Jameel Jaffer, Zachary Katznelson, Steven Shapiro, Steven Watt, and Ben Wizner.

40. Susan Herman, national president of the ACLU, points out (personal communication to the author) that "(the) very fact that CCR was taking the lead on Guantánamo made it less necessary that we figure out how to shift the nature of our work, so that we could devote our attention to the tremendous amount of work we were doing domestically on behalf of detainees and others."

41. https://www.aclu.org/national-security/john-adams-project-american-values. The name was chosen because Adams had famously defended a British soldier's rights during the height of revolutionary ferment in Boston.

42. "Letter from the ACLU to the Freedom of Information Officer," October 7, 2003, http://aclu.o0rg/torturefoia/legaldocuments/nnACLUFOIA request.pdf. This campaign looms large in Goldsmith 2012, 112–21.

43. The ACLU claimed that "By publicly branding these groups as criminals without providing a forum for them to defend themselves or clear their names, the government has acted with blatant disregard for their constitutional rights." https://www.aclu.org/national-security/aclu-challenges-governments-stigmatizing-mainstream-muslim-groups-holy-land-case.

44. I am grateful to Terence Dougherty, chief operating officer and general counsel of the ACLU for providing these figures.

45. I am grateful to Ben Wizner of ACLA and to Cindy Cohn of the EFF for helping me to understand some of the complexities of digital contention.

46. Ben Wizner's interview on *Moyers and Company* on March 11, 2014, http://bill moyers.com/2014/03/11/our-chat-with-edward-snowdens-legal-counsel/.

47. https://www.aclu.org/free-speech-technology-and-liberty/about-aclus-project-speech-privacy-and-technology.

48. For basic information about the law firm, which specializes in constitutional law, go to http://rbskl.com/about-the-firm/.

49. For basic information on EFF, go to https://www.eff.org/.

50. http://epic.org/crypto/export_controls/bernstein_decision_9_cir.html.

51. Wizner interview, *Moyers and Company*, 6.

52. See David Sanger and John O'Neil, "White House Begins New Effort to Defend Surveillance Program," http://www.nytimes.com/2006/01/23/politics/23cnd-wiretap.html?_r=0.

53. For the "collateral murder" tape that Assange presented to the National Press Club, go to http://www.collateralmurder.com/.

54. Scott Shane, "No Morsel Too Minuscule for All-Consuming NSA," *New York Times*, November 3, 2013, http://www.nytimes.com/2013/11/03/world/no-morsel-too-minuscule-for-all-consuming-nsa.html.

55. A Marist Poll taken shortly after the Snowden revelations showed that majorities of Democrats, Independents, and Republicans thought the NSA had gone too far. http://www.mcclatchydc.com/2013/07/24/197519/marist-poll-for-mcclatchy-on-edward.html.

56. http://sensenbrenner.house.gov/news/documentsingle.aspx?DocumentID=360167.

57. See Jonathan Weisman and Charlie Savage, "House Passes Restraints on Bulk Data Collection," *New York Times*, May 22, 2014, http://www.nytimes.com/2014/05/23/us/poli tics/house-votes-to-limit-nsas-collection-of-phone-data.html. As of this writing, in September 2014, the Senate had not yet taken action on the Sensenbrenner proposal.

58. Quoted in ibid., 8.

CHAPTER 10

1. See Reprieve, "Gaddafi Opponents Sue Ex-MI6 Counter-Terror Chief Sir Mark Allen over Libya Torture Complicity," press release, www.reprieve.org.uk/press/2011_01_31_allen_lawsuit.

2. These facts, and the remainder of this narrative, come from Belhadj and his wife's Letter of Claim for Damages, dated November 9, 2011, to the British High Court of Justice of October 8, 2012, kindly provided by Reprieve, the British nonprofit group that supported their claims. I am grateful to Cori Chider, Katherine Craig, and Clive Stafford-Smith for their help in investigating this case.

3. Richard Norton Taylor, "Libyan Told He Cannot Pursue Rendition Claim in Case It Harms UK Interests," *The Guardian*, December 20, 2013, www.theguardian.com/world/2013/dec/20/libyan-rendition-claim-uk-interests.

4. I cite Ikenberry's theory of liberal internationalism because it is theoretically uncomplicated and closely reveals the link between liberal values and the U.S. foreign policy preference for working through institutions. For a theory that is more self-conscious about the tension between liberal values and structures of power and interest, see Robert Keohane 1984 and 2012.

5. The proceedings of the conference can be found at Ministero degli Affari Esteri 1898.

6. As Prime Minister Margaret Thatcher once put it, Northern Ireland is "part of the United Kingdom as much as my constituency is" (quoted in Neumann 2003, 20).

7. The Parker Committee Report, http://cain.ulst.ac.uk/hmso/parker.htm.

8. The most ruthless of these American friends was Whitey Bulger, a Boston gangster who attempted to ship them arms, possibly with the collusion of an FBI handler. On Bulger's involvement, see Cullen and Murphy 2013.

9. http://hudoc.echr.coe.int/sites/eng/pages/search.aspx?i=001–57506#{%22ite mid%22:[%22001–57506%22]}.

10. This and the following quotations and citations are from the American Presidency Project, www.Presidency.ucsb.edu/ws/index.php?pid=64731&st=&st1=.

11. The full text of Bush's address can be found at http://www.washingtonpost.com/ wp-srv/nation/specials/attacked/transcripts/bushaddress_092001.html.

12. American Presidency Project, www.Presidency.ucsb.edu/ws/index.php?pid=2964 4&st=&st1=.

13. See "Request by the Center for Constitutional Rights, et al. to the Inter-American Commission on Human Rights, Organization of American States," February 25, 2002, www.photius.com/roghe_nations/guantanamo.html. The commission's response can be found at www1.umn./edu/humanrits/cases/Guantanamo-2003.html. The government's denial of the commission's competence can be found at www.derechos.org/nizkor/excep/ usresp1.html. I am grateful to Steven Watt of the American Civil Liberties Union for putting these documents and his memory of the case at my disposal for this chapter.

14. For legal precedents, the United States was forced back on a Supreme Court case (*Ex Parte Quirin* 317 U.S. 1, 31 [1942]) from World War Two and for its authority in denying the detainees a legal status on a grab-bag of foreign military manuals and law textbooks. See "Response of the U.S. to the Request for Precautionary Measures on behalf of the detainees in Guantanamo Bay, Cuba," http://www.derechos.org/nizkor/excep/usresp1. html, n. 4.

15. "Request by the Center for Constitutional Rights, et al. to the Inter-American Commission on Human Rights, Organization of American States," February 25, 2002, 4.

16. I am grateful to Steven Watt for this felicitous phrase.

17. In fact, the first chair of the Counter-Terrorism Committee, Sir Jeremy Greenstock, "rejected the idea that the Security Council had any responsibility for ensuring human rights compliance while it pushed states to combat terrorism" (quoted in Scheppele 2006, 357).

18. I am grateful to Professor Shor for allowing me to access his database for the time line of antiterrorist legislation. For a report on his methodology and a preliminary accounting of his findings, see Shor 2011. Updated data appear in figure 10.2.

19. In 2012, Mr. Kadi was taken off the UN Security Council blacklist, followed a week later by removal from the EU blacklist. See "Kadi De-Listed: A Cause for Celebration?" *European Law Blog*, October 30, 2012, http://europeanlawblog.eu/?p=1192.

20. On the dynamics of interinstitutional conflicts, using the *Kadi* case an example, see Morse and Keohane 2014.

21. Both detainees took an accusation against Poland to the European Court of Human Rights. For their case, go to http://hudoc.echr.coe.int/webservices/content/pdf/003-483 2205-5894802.

22. The Rendition Project provided this succinct account of the story, http://www. therenditionproject.org.uk/global-rendition/the-detainees/hassan-mustafa-osama-nasr-%28abu-omar%29.html. For a more detailed analyses, see Foot 2007 and Messineo 2009.

23. In December 2013, Abu Omar was condemned in absentia by a Milanese magistrate to six years in prison for conspiracy (*associazione per delinquere*) with the goal of international terrorism (*La Repubblica*, December 14, 2013, 6).

24. We have this and other information about the efforts to throttle the case against the CIA thanks to the cables released by Wikileaks and reported by Glenn Greenwald,

the *Guardian* journalist who exposed the Snowden NSA revelations, in 2013; see "Italy's Ex-Intelligence Chief Given 10-Year Sentence for Role in CIA Kidnapping," http://www. theguardian.com/commentisfree/2013/feb/13/italy-cia-rendition-abu-omar.

25. http://hudoc.echr.coe.int/webservices/content/pdf/003-4832205-5894802, p. 1. For a report of the Court's judgment, A brief description of the plaintiffs' claims and the disposition of the case will be found in http://www.washingtonpost.com/ world/national-security/european-court-finds-poland-complicit-in-cia-torture-orders-detainee-compensation/2014/07/24/7ce81f02-133a-11e4-98ee-daea85133bc9_story.html.

26. Clive Stafford Smith, "Binyam Mohamed: A Shameful Cover-Up," *The Guardian*, February 10, 2010, www.guardian.co/uk/commentsfree/libertycentral /2010/feb/10/ torture-guantanamo-bay.

27. Charlie Savage, "Court Dismisses a Case Asserting Torture by CIA," *New York Times*, September 9, 2010, http://www.nytimes.com/2010/09/09/us/09secrets.html?page wanted=all&_r=.

28. Glenn Greenwald, "Obama Administration Threatens Britain to Keep Torture Evidence Concealed," *Salon*, May 12, 2009, http://www.salon.com/2009/05/12/obama_101/.

29. For example, the European Police College (CEPOL), created in 2000, responded to the transnational protests at the Gothenburg and Genoa international conferences in 2001 as if it was dealing with terrorism. Many of these protesters were students attempting to cross borders to participate in rallies at summit meetings of the G-8, the International Monetary Fund, or the European Union (Reiter and Fillieule 2006; della Porta, Andretta, Mosca, and Reiter 2006).

CONCLUSIONS

1. David M. Herszenhorn, "As Ukrainian Election Looms, Western Powers and Russia Compete for Influence," *New York Times*, May 7, 2014, http://www.nytimes. com/2014/05/07/world/europe/ukraine.html.

2. Alison Smale and Steven Erlanger, "Ukraine Mobilizes Reserve Troops. Threatening War," *New York Times*. March 1, 2014, http://www.nytimes.com/2014/03/02/world/ europe/ukraine.html?_r=0/.

3. *Al Jazeera* offers a reasonably complete time line of the Ukrainian conflict from November 21, 2013, when President Yanukovich announced the abandonment of a trade agreement with the European Union, to late August 2014, when Russian troops began to enter Ukraine, http://www.aljazeera.com/news/europe/2014/03/timeline-ukraine-political-crisis-201431143722854652.html.

4. I am grateful to my colleague Tom Pepinsky for suggesting I attempt the sketches that appear later in this chapter and to Benedict Anderson and Barak Oren for looking them over.

5. The head of the OLC, David Barron, was nominated by the Obama administration to the Court of Appeals for the First Circuit, ACLU, "Urgent: Barron Nomination Could Be on the Senate Floor as Early as This Week," https://www.aclu.org/sites/default/files/ assets/letter_re_barron_nomination.pdf, accessed May 5, 2014.

6. Especially important was the role of Paul Wolfowitz, Donald Rumsfeld's deputy in the Department of Defense. On Wolfowitz's role, see Bill Keller, "The Sunshine Warrior," *New York Times*, September 22, 2002, http://www.nytimes.com/2002/09/22/magazine/ the-sunshine-warrior.html.

7. 12 State 755.

8. 18 USC, chap. 37.

9. The Military Commissions Act of 2006, http://www.gpo.gov/fdsys/pkg/BILLS-109s3930enr/pdf/BILLS-109s3930enr.pdf. The 2009 act can be found at https://www.fas. org/sgp/crs/natsec/R41163.pdf.

10. Section 215 reads, "the Director of the Federal Bureau of Investigation or a designee of the Director (whose rank shall be no lower than Assistant Special Agent in Charge) may make an application for an order requiring the production of any tangible things (including books, records, papers, documents, and other items) for an investigation to obtain foreign intelligence information not concerning a United States person or to protect against international terrorism or clandestine intelligence activities, provided that such investigation of a United States person is not conducted solely upon the basis of activities protected by the first amendment to the Constitution." http://www.law.cornell.edu/uscode/text/50/1861.

11. Matthew M. Aid and William Burr, eds., "'Disreputable If Not Outright Illegal': The National Security Agency versus Martin Luther King, Muhammad Ali, Art Buchwald, Frank Church, *et al.*," National Security Archive Electronic Briefing Book No. 441, posted September 25, 2013 (originally posted November 14, 2008), http://www2.gwu.edu/~nsarchiv/NSAEBB/NSAEBB441/.

12. Niraj Chokshi, "Militarized Police in Ferguson Unsettles Some; Pentagon Gives Cities Equipment," *Washington Post*, August 14, 2014, http://www.washingtonpost.com/politics/militarized-police-in-ferguson-unsettles-some-pentagon-gives-cities-equipment/2014/08/14/4651f670-2401-11e4-86ca-6f03cbd15c1a_story.html.

13. Too late to enrich the brief discussions of Burma and Indonesia here, I discovered Dan Slater's *Ordering Power: Contentious Politics and Authoritarian Leviathans in Southeast Asia* (2010). As I do in these narratives, Slater traces the rise of military dictatorships to contentious politics, but he gives less specific emphasis to the importance of war in influencing the type of contentious politics that developed in these states.

14. Among them was Albert Camus, who was Algerian-born and caught between his loyalty to his Mediterranean roots and his desire to keep Algeria in some kind of association with France. For his tormented history see Susan Tarrow 1985.

15. General Marcel Bigeard, speaking to journalist Jean Lartéguy in 1959, http://alolu.com/algerian_war71157.htm.

16. On the displacement of the Arab population, see, for example, Michel Rocard and Vincent Dudert 2003. On the role of the intellectuals in opposing torture and the war, see, for example, Vidal-Naquet 1972, and Rioux and Sirinelli 1991. The most active Catholic group agitating against the war was Témoignage chrétien.

17. "La lutte elle-même vers les sommets suffit à remplir un coeur d'homme. Il faut imaginer Sisyphe heureux" (Camus 1965, 198, author's translation).

References

Ackerman, Bruce. 1998. *We the People: Transformations.* Cambridge, MA: Harvard University Press.

———. 2006. *Before the Next Attack: Preserving Civil Liberties in an Age of Terrorism.* New Haven: Yale University Press.

Adelman, Jonathan R. 1985. *Revolution, Armies, and War: A Political History.* Boulder: Luynne Reinner.

Agamben, Giorgio. 2005. *State of Exception.* Chicago: University of Chicago Press.

Alimi, Eitan. 2007. *Israeli Politics and the First Palestinian Intifada: Political Opportunities, Framing Processes and Contentious Politics.* London: Routledge.

Alimi, Eitan, Lorenzo Bosi, and Chares Demetriou. 2012. "Relational Dynamics and Processes of Radicalization: A Comparative Framework." *Mobilization* 17:7–26.

Alimi, Eitan, Chares Demetriou, and Lorenzo Bosi, eds. Forthcoming. *The Dynamics of Radicalization: A Comparative Perspective.* New York: Oxford University Press.

Alimi, Eitan, and Sivan Hirsch-Hoefler. 2012. "Structure of Political Opportunities and Threats and Movement-Countermovement Interaction in Segmented Composite Regimes." *Comparative Politics* 4:331–49.

Alter, Karen J. 2014. *The New Terrain of International Law: Courts, Politics, Rights.* Princeton: Princeton University Press.

Amato, Giuliano. 1967a. *Individuo e autorità nella disciplina della libertà personale.* Milan: Giuffrè.

———. 1967b. "La libertà personale." In *La tutela del cittadino*, vol. 2. *La pubblica sicurezza.* Edited by Paolo Barile, 51–180. Milan: Neri Pozza.

Anderson, Bendict. 1972. *Java in a Time of Revolution.* Ithaca: Cornell University Press.

Andreas, Peter. 2003. "Redrawing the Line: Borders and Security in the Twenty-First Century." *International Security* 28:78–111.

Andreski, Stanislav. 1954. *Military Organization and Society.* Berkeley: University of California Press.

Andrieu, Claire. 2002. *Pour l'amour de la République: Le Club Jean Moulin, 1958–1970.* Paris: Fayard.

Aquarone, Alberto. 1965. *L'organizzazione dello Stato totalitario.* Turin: Einaudi.

———. 1981. *L'Italia giolittiana I. Le Premesse politiche ed economiche.* Bologna: Il Mulino.

———. 2003. *Alla ricerca dell'Italia liberale.* Firenze: Le Monnier.

Arkin, William M. 2013. *American Coup: How a Terrified Government Is Destroying the Constitution.* New York: Little, Brown and Company.

Asal, Victor, Brian Nusbaum, and D. William Harrington. 2007. "Terrorism as Transnational Advocacy: An Organizational and Tactical Examination." *Studies in Conflict and Terrorism* 30:15–39.

Associazione per lo sviluppo dell'industria nel Mezzogiorno (Svimez). 1961. *Un secolo di statistiche italiane: Nord e Sud 1861–1961.* Roma.

Avant, Deborah. 2005. *The Market for Force: The Consequences of Privatizing Security.* New York: Cambridge University Press.

———. 2010. "War, Recruitment Systems, and Democracy." in *In War's Wake: International Conflict and the Fate of Liberal Democracy*, edited by Elizabeth Kier and Ronald R. Krebs. New York: Cambridge University Press.

———. 2013. "The Mobilization of Private Forces after 9/11: Ad Hoc Response to Inadequate Planning." In *How 9/11 Changed Our Ways of War*, edited by James Burk, 209–32. Stanford: Stanford University Press.

Avant, Deborah, and Renee De Nevers. 2013. "Military Contractors and the American Way of War." In *The Modern American Military*, edited by David M. Kennedy, 135–52. Oxford: Oxford University Press.

Avineri, Shlomo, ed. 1971. *Israel and the Palestinians: Reflections on the Clash of Two National Movements*. New York: St. Martin's.

Azmy, Baher. 2012. "An Insufficiently Accountable Presidency: Some Reflections on Jack Goldsmith's *Power and Constraint*." *Case Western Reserve Journal of International Law* 45:23–63.

Badinter, Robert. 1989. *Une autre justice 1789–1799*. Paris: Fayard.

Bakalian, Anny P., and Mehdi Bozorgmehr. 2009. *Backlash 9/11*. Berkeley: University of California Press.

Barak, Oren, and Gabriel Sheffer, eds. 2010. *Militarism and Israeli Society*. Bloomington: Indiana University Press.

Barkan, Steven E. 1984. "Legal Control of the Southern Civil Rights Movement." *American Sociological Review* 49:552–65.

Barlow, John Perry. 1990. "A Not Terribly Brief History of the Electronic Frontier Foundation." https://w2.eff.org/Misc/Publications/John_Perry_Barlow/not_too_brief_history.eff.txt.

Barnes, Gilbert Hobbs. 1957. *The Antislavery Impulse, 1830–1844*. Gloucester, MA: Peter Smith.

Bates, Elizabeth Stubbins, IBA Task Force on Terrorism, Richard Goldstone, Eugene Cotran, Gijs de Vries, Julia A. Hall, Juan E. Méndez, and Javaid Rehman. 2011. *Terrorism and International Law: Accountability, Remedies, and Reform*. Oxford: Oxford University Press.

Beissinger, Mark R. 2011. "Mechanisms of Maidan: The Structure of Contingency in the Making of Colored Revolution." *Mobilization* 16:25–43.

Bell, David A. 2007. *The First Total War: Napoleon's Europe and the Birth of Warfare As We Know It*. Baltimore: Johns Hopkins University Press.

Ben-Eliezer, Uri. 1998. *The Making of Israeli Militarism*. Bloomington: University of Indiana Press.

Bennett, W. Lance, Regina Lawrence, and Steven Livingston. 2007. *When the Press Fails: Political Power and the News Media from Iraq to Katrina*. Chicago: University of Chicago Press.

Bennett, W. Lance, and Alexandra Segerberg. 2013. *The Logic of Connective Action*. New York: Cambridge University Press.

Bensel, Richard F. 1991. *Yankee Leviathan: The Origins of Central Authority in America, 1859–1877*. New York: Cambridge University Press.

Berda, Yael. 2013. "Managing Dangerous Populations: Colonial Legacies of Security and Surveillance." *Sociological Forum* 28:627–30.

———. 2014. "Colonial Legacy and Administrative Memory: The Legal Construction of Citizenship in India, Israel, and Cyprus." PhD diss., Princeton University.

Berinsky, Adam J. 2009. *In Time of War: Understanding American Public Opinion from World War II to Iraq*. Chicago: University of Chicago Press.

Bermeo, Nancy. 2003. *Ordinary People in Extraordinary Times: The Citizenry and the Breakdown of Democracy*. Princeton: Princeton University Press.

Bertaud, Jean-Paul. 1988. *The Army of the French Revolution: From Citizen-Soldiers to Instrument of Power*. Princeton: Princeton University Press.

Bigo, Didier. 1992. "L'Europe de la sécurité intérieure." In *L'Europe des polices et de la sécurité intérieure*, edited by Didier Bigo, 13–94. Brussels : Editions Complexe.

———. 1996. *Polices en reseaux: L'expérience européenne*. Paris: Presses de Sciences Po.

———. 2013. "The Transnational Field of Computerized Exchange of Information in Police Matters and Its European Guilds." In *Transnational Power Elites: The New Professionals of Governance, Law, and Security*, edited by Niilo Kauppi and Mikael R. Madsen, 155–66. New York: Routledge.

Blanc, Florent. 2010. "Dissent after September 11: Mobilization of Librarians, ACLU, Cities and Lawyers." PhD diss., Northwestern University.

Blanning, Timothy C. W. 1986. *The Origins of the French Revolutionary Wars*. London: Longman.

Bob, Clifford. 2012. *The Global Right Wing and the Clash of World Politics*. Cambridge, UK: Cambridge University Press.

Bodnar, John. 1992. *Remaking America: Public Memory, Commemoration, and Patriotism in the Twentieth Century*. Princeton: Princeton University Press.

Bordogna, Lorenzo, and Giancarlo Provasi. 1979. "Il movimento degli scioperi in Italia, 1881–1973." In *Il Movimento degli scioperi nel XX secolo*, edited by Gian P. Cella, 169–304. Bologna: Il Mulino.

Boutcher, Steven A., and James E. Stobaugh. 2013. "Law and Social Movements." In *Wiley-Blackwell Encyclopedia of Social and Political Movements*, edited by David Snow, Donatella della Porta, Bert Klandermans, and Doug McAdam, 683–87. New York: Blackwell.

Boykoff, Jules. 2007. *Beyond Bullets: The Suppression of Dissent in the United States*. Oakland, CA: AK Press.

Braman, Sandra. 2006. *Change of State: Information, Policy, and Power*. Cambridge, MA: MIT Press.

Brandon, Mark E. 2005. "War and the American Constitutional Order." In *The Constitution in Wartime: Beyond Alarmism and Complacency*, edited by M. Tushnet, 11–38. Durham: Duke University Press.

Bravin, Jess. 2013. *The Terror Courts: Rough Justice at Guantanamo Bay*. New Haven: Yale University Press.

Brewer, John. 1990. *Sinews of Power: War, Money and the English State, 1688–1783*. Cambridge, MA: Harvard University Press.

Brewer, Susan A. 2009. *Why America Fights: Patriotism and War Propaganda from the Philippines to Iraq*. New York: Oxford University Press.

Brinton, Crane. 1965. *The Anatomy of Revolution*. Rev. ed. New York: Vintage Books.

Brooks, Clem, and Jeff Manza. 2013. *Whose Rights? Counterterrorism and the Dark Side of American Public Opinion*. New York: Russell Sage Foundation.

Brown, Howard G. 2006. *Ending the French Revolution: Violence, Justice, and Repression from the Terror to Napoleon*. Chartlottesville: University of Virginia Press

Burstein, Paul, and William Freudenberg. 1978. "Changing Public Policy: The Impact of Public Opinion, Anti-War Demonstrations, and War Costs on Senate Voting on Vietnam War Motions." *American Journal of Sociology* 84:99–122.

Button, James W. 1978. *Black Violence: The Political Impact of the 1960s Riots*. Princeton: Princeton University Press.

Bybee, Jay S. 2005. "Memorandum for Albert R. Gonzales, Counsel to the President and William J. Haynes II, General Counsel of the Department of Defense "In *The Torture Papers: The Road to Abu Ghraib*, edited by Karen J. Greenberg and Joshua L. Dratel, 81–117. New York: Cambridge University Press.

Callahan, Mary P. 2003. *Making Enemies: War and State Building in Burma.* Ithaca: Cornell University Press.

Calomiris, Charles W., and Larry Schweikart. 1991. "The Panic of 1857: Origins, Transmission, and Containment." *Journal of Economic History* 51:807–34.

Campbell, Colm, and Ita Connolly. 2012. "The Sharp End: Armed Opposition Movements, Transitional Truth Processes and the *Rechtsstaat.*" *International Journal of Transitional Justice* 10:1–29.

Camus, Albert. 1965. *Essais.* Paris: Gallimard.

Cardoza, Anthony L. 1979. "Agrarians and Industrialists: The Evolution of an Alliance in the Po Delta, 1896–1914." In *Gramsci and Italy's Passive Revolution*, edited by John A. Davis, 172–212. London: Croon Helm.

——. 1982. *Agrarian Elites and Italian Fascism: The Province of Bologna, 1901–1926.* Princeton: Princeton University Press.

Carr, Edward H. 1939. *The Twenty Years' Crisis: 1919–1939.* London: Macmillan.

Carter, Ashton B., John M. Deutsch, and Philip D. Zelikow. 1998. "Catastrophic Terrorism: Tackling the New Danger." *Foreign Affairs* 77:80–94.

Cassese, Sabino. 1974. *La formazione dello Stato amministrativo.* Milan: Giuffrè.

——. 2010. *Lo stato fascista.* Bologna: Il Mulino.

Cederman, Lars-Erik, Kristian Skrede Gleditsch, and Halyard Buhaug. 2013. *Inequality, Grievances, and Civil War.* New York: Cambridge University Press.

Centeno, Miguel. 2002. *Blood and Debt: War and the Nation-State in Latin America.* University Park: Penn State University Press.

Chadwick, Andrew, and Simon Collister. 2014. "Boundary-Drawing Power and the Renewal of Professional News Organizations: The Case of the *Guardian* and the Edward Snowden NSA Leak." *International Journal of Communication* 8. http://ijoc.org/index.php/ijoc/article/view/2883.

Chafetz, Joshua. 2010. "Impeachment and Assassination." *Minnesota Law Review* 95:347–423.

Checkel, Jeffrey T., ed. 2013. *Transnational Dynamics of Civil War.* Cambridge: Cambridge University Press.

Chomsky, Noam. 1993. "The Pentagon System." *Z Magazine (Reason).* http://www.thirdworldtraveler.com/Chomsky/PentagonSystem_Chom.html.

Cobb, Richard. 1987. *The People's Armies: Instrument of the Terror in the Departments: April 1793 to Floréal Year II.* New Haven: Yale University Press.

Cole, David. 2003. *Enemy Aliens: Double Standards and Constitutional Freedoms in the War on Terrorism.* New York: The New Press.

——. 2012. "Where Liberty Lies: Civil Society and Individual Rights after 9/11." *Wayne State Law Review* 57:1203–67.

Cole, David, and Philippe Sands. 2009. *The Torture Memos: Rationalizing the Unthinkable.* New York: The New Press.

Collier, Paul, and Anke Hoeffler. 1998. "On the Economic Causes of Civil War." *Oxford Economic Papers* 50:563–73.

Collier, Paul, and Nicholas Sambanis, eds. 2005. *Understanding Civil War: Evidence and Analysis.* Washington, DC: World Bank.

Commission on Wartime Contracting in Iraq and Afghanistan. 2011. "At What Risk? Correcting Over-Reliance on Contactors in Contingency Operations." Commission on Wartime Contracting in Iraq and Afghanistan, Washington, DC. http://cybercemetery.unt.edu/archive/cwc/20110929221313/http:/www.wartimecontracting.gov/docs/CWC_InterimReport2-lowres.pdf.

Condorcet, Jean-Antoine-Nicolas de. 1847–1849 [1968]. *Oeuvres de Condorcet.* Vol. 9. Paris: Firmin Didot Frères.

Corner, Paul 1975. *Fascism in Ferrara, 1915–1925*. Oxford: Oxford University Press.

——. 2002. "The Road to Fascism: An Italian Sonderweg?" *Contemporary European History* 11:273–95.

Corner, Paul, and Giovanna Procacci. 1997. "The Italian Experience of 'Total' Mobilization, 1915–1920." In *State. Society and Mobilization in Europe during the First World War*, edited by John Horne, 223–40. Cambridge, UK: Cambridge University Press.

Cortright, David. 2014. "Protest and Politics: How Peace Movements Shape History." In *The Handbook of Global Security Policy*, edited by Mary Kaldor and Iavor Rangelov, 482–504. Hoboken: Wiley-Blackwell.

Cox, Michael. 1997. "Bringing in the International: The IRA Ceasefire and the End of the Cold War." *International Affairs* 73:671–93.

Craig, Campbell, and Frederik Logevall. 2009. *America's Cold War: The Politics of Insecurity*. Cambridge, MA: Harvard University Press.

Crane, David M., and Daniel Reisner. 2011. "'Jousting at Windmills': The Laws of Armed Conflict in an Age of Terror-state Actors and Nonstate Elements." In *New Battlefields, Old Laws: Critical Debates on Asymmetric Warfare*, edited by William C. Banks, 67–84. New York: Columbia University Press.

Cullen, Kevin, and Shelley Murphy. 2013. *Whitey Bulger: America's Most Wanted Gangster and the Manhunt That Brought Him to Justice*. New York: W. W. Norton.

Cumings, Bruce E. 1981. *Origins of the Korean War*. Princeton: Princeton University Press.

Danner, Mark. 2004. *Torture and Truth: America, Abu Ghraib, and the War on Terror*. New York: New York Review Books.

Davis, David Brion. 1969. *The Slave Power Conspiracy and the Paranoid Style in American Politics*. Baton Rouge: Louisiana State University Press.

Davis, James Kirkpatrick. 1997. *Assault on the Left: The FBI and the Sixties Antiwar Movement*. Westport, CT: Praeger.

Davis, John A. 1979. "Introduction: Antonio Gramsci and Italy's Passive Revolution." In *Gramsci and Italy's Passive Revolution*, edited by John A. Davis, 11–30. London: Croon Helm.

——. 1988. *Conflict and Control: Law and Order in Nineteenth-Century Italy*. London: Macmillan.

DeBenedetti, Charles. 1990. *An American Ordeal: The Antiwar Movement of the Vietnam Era*. Syracuse: Syracuse University Press.

de Búrca, Grainne. 2009. "The European Court of Justice and the International Legal Order after Kadi." Jean Monnet Working Paper no. 01/09. New York University Law, New York.

Delarue, Jacques, and Odile Rudelle. 1990. *L'attentat du Petit-Clamart*. Paris: La Documentation Française.

della Porta, Donatella. 1995. *Social Movements, Political Violence and the State: A Comparative Analysis of Italy and Germany*. New York: Cambridge University Press.

——, ed. 2007. *The Global Justice Movement: Cross-National and Transnational Perspectives*. Boulder: Paradigm Publishers

——. 2010. "Paths to the February 15 Protest: Social or Political Determinants?" In *The World Says No to War: Demonstrations against the War in Iraq*, edited by Stefaan Walgrave and Dieter Rucht, 119–40. Minneapolis: University of Minnesota Press.

——. 2013. *Clandestine Political Violence*. New York: Cambridge University Press.

della Porta, Donatella, Massimo Andretta, Lorenzo Mosca, and Herbert Reiter. 2006. *Globalization from Below: Transnational Activists and Protest Networks*. Minneapolis: University of Minnesota Press.

della Porta, Donatella, and Mario Diani. 2006. *Social Movements: An Introduction*. 2nd ed. Oxford: Blackwell.

della Porta, Donatella, and Herbert Reiter, eds. 1998. *Policing Protest: The Control of Mass Demonstration in Western Democracies*. Minneapolis: University of Minnesota Press.

della Porta, Donatella, and Sidney Tarrow. 1986. "Unwanted Children: Political Violence and the Cycle of Protest in Italy." *European Journal of Political Research* 14:607–32.

———, eds. 2005. *Transnational Protest and Global Activism*. Lanham, MD: Rowman and Littlefield.

de Mari, Eric. 1991. "La Mise Hors de la Loi Sous la Révolution française: 19 mars 1793–9 Thermidor Ann II." PhD diss., University of Montpellier I.

Denbeaux, Mark P., Jonathan Hafetz, Sara Ben David, Nicolas Stratton, and Lauren Winchester. 2012. "No Hearing Habeas: DC Circuit Restricts Meaningful Review." Seton Hall Public Law Research Paper No. 2145554. Center for Policy and Research, Seton Hall School of Law, Newark, NJ.

Deutsch, Karl W., Sidney A. Burrell, and Robert A. Kann. 1957. *Political Community and the North Atlantic Area: International Organization in the Light of Historical Experience*. Princeton: Princeton University Press.

Dickson, Bryce. 2010. *The European Convention on Human Rights and the Conflict in Northern Ireland*. Oxford: Oxford University Press.

Donahue, Laura K. 2008. *The Cost of Counterterrorism: Power, Politics and Liberty*. Cambridge, UK: Cambridge University Press.

Du Bois, William E. B. 2005. *The Illustrated Souls of Black Folk*. Boulder: Paradigm Publishers.

Dudziak, Mary L. 2000. *Cold War Civil Rights*. Princeton: Princeton University Press.

———. 2010. *War-Time: An Idea, Its History, Its Consequences*. New York: Oxford University Press.

Edelman, Lauren B., Gwendolyn Leachman, and Doug McAdam. 2010. "On Law, Organizations, and Social Movements." *Annual Review of Law and Society* 6:653–85.

Edwards, Bob, and Sam Marullo. 1995. "Organizational Mortality in a Declining Social Movement: The Demise of Peace Movement Organizations in the End of the Cold War Era." *American Sociological Review* 60:908–27.

Einaudi, Luigi. 1933. *La condotta economica e gli effetti sociali della guerra italiana*. Bari and New Haven: Laterza and Yale University Press.

Eisenhower, Dwight D. 1960 [1999]. "Military-Industrial Complex Speech." In *Public Papers of the Presidents, Dwight D Eishehower, 1960–61*, 1035–40. Washington DC: Government Printing Office.

Eisgruber, Christopher L. 2009. "The Story of Dred Scott: Originalism's Forgotten Past." In *Constitutional Law Stories*, 2nd. ed., edited by Michael C. Drof, 155–86. New York: Foundation Press.

Electronic Frontier Foundation. 1998. *Cracking DES—Secrets of Encryption Research, Wiretap Politics & Chip Design*. Sebastapol, CA: Oreilly and Associates.

Ely, John Hart. 1993. *War and Responsibility: Constitutional Lessons of Vietnam and Its Aftermath*. Princeton: Princeton University Press.

Engene, Jan Oskar. 2004. *Terrorism in Western Europe: Explaining the Trends since 1950*. Northhampton, MA: Edward Elgar.

Ertman, Thomas. 1997. *Birth of the Leviathan: Building States and Regimes in Medieval and Early Modern Europe*. New York: Cambridge University Press.

Esman, Milton J. 2013. *The Emerging American Garrison State.* New York: Palgrave Macmillan.

Evangelista, Matthew. 2008. *Law, Ethics, and the War on Terror.* Cambridge, UK: Polity.

———. 2013. "A 'War on Terror' by Any Other Name . . . What Did Obama Change?" Publication 2012-02, Mario Einaudi Center, Cornell University, Ithaca, NY.

Evangelista, Matthew, and Nina Tannenbaum. Forthcoming. "How the Geneva Conventions Matter?" Cornell University and Brown University.

Evans, Peter, Dietrich Rueschemeyer, and Theda Skocpol. 1985. *Bringing the State Back In.* New York: Cambridge University Press.

Ewing, Katherine Pratt, ed. 2008. *Being and Belonging: Muslims in the United States since 9/11.* New York: Russell Sage.

Farneti, Paolo. 1978. "Social Conflict, Parliamentary Fragmentation, Institutional Shift, and the Rise of Fascist Italy." In *The Breakdown of Democratic Regimes,* vol. 2: *The Breakdown of Democratic Regimes: Europe,* edited by Juan J. Linz and Alfred Stepan, 3–33. Baltimore: Johns Hopkins University Press.

Favre, Pierre. 1990. *La Manifestation.* Paris: Presses de la Fondation Nationale des Sciences Politiques.

Fearon, James D., and David Laitin. 2003. "Ethnicity, Insurgency, and Civil War." *American Political Science Review* 97:75–90.

Fehrenbacher, Don E. 1978. *The Dred Scott Case: Its Significance in American Law and Politics.* New York: Oxford University Press.

Fellman, Michael 1979. "Rehearsal for Civil War: Antislavery and Proslavery at the Fighting Point in Kansas, 1854–1856." In *Antislavery Reconsidered: New Perspectives on the Abolitionists,* edited by Lewis Perry and Michael Fellman, 287–307. Baton Rouge: Louisiana State University Press.

Ferrand, Jerôme. 2010. "Aux confins du politique et du juridique . . . ou du bon usage des declarations de droits par les corps administratifs et judiciaires de la Révolution." *Clio@Themis* 3:1–62.

Finer, Samuel E. 1975. "State and Nation Building in Europe: The Role of the Military." In *The Formation of National States in Western Europe,* edited by Charles Tilly, 84–163. Princeton: Princeton University Press.

Fisher, Louis. 2004. *Presidential War Power.* 2nd, ed. Lawrence: University Press of Kansas.

———. 2008. *The Constitution and 9/11: Recurring Threats to America's Freedoms.* Lawrence: University Press of Kansas.

Fligstein, Neil, and Doug McAdam. 2012. *A Theory of Fields.* New York: Oxford University Press.

Flores-Macías, Gustavo and Sarah Kreps. 2013. "Political Parties at War: A Study of American War Finance, 1789–2010." *American Political Science Review* 107:833–48.

Foner, Eric. 1995. *Free Soil, Free Labor, Free Men: The Ideology of the Republican Party before the Civil War.* Oxford: Oxford University Press.

Foot, John. 2007. "The Rendition of Abu Omar." *London Review of Books* 29:24–25. lrb.co.uk/v29/n15/john-foot/the-rendition-of-abu-omar.

Foot, Rosemary, S. Neal MacFarlane, and Michael Mastanduno. 2003. *U.S. Hegemony and International Organizations.* Oxford: Oxford University Press.

Forgacs, David, ed. 1988. *An Antonio Gramsci Reader: Selected Writings, 1916–1935.* New York: Schocken Books.

Frank, Jason. 2010. *Constituent Moments: Enacting the People in Postrevolutionary America.* Durham: Duke University Press.

Franzosi, Roberto. 1997. "Mobilization and Counter-Mobilization Processes: From the 'Red Years' (1919–20) to the 'Black Years' (1921–22) in Italy." *Theory and Society* 26:275–304.

Fredrickson, George M. 1971. *The Black Image in the White Mind*. Middletown, CT: Wesleyan University Press.

Friedberg, Aaron L. 2000. *In the Shadow of the Garrison State: America's Anti-Statism and Its Cold War Grand Strategy*. Princeton: Princeton University Press.

Fromuth, Peter. 2009. "The European Court of Justice Kadi Decision and the Future of UN Counterterrorism Sanctions." *American Society of International Law Insight* 13:1–9.

Furet, François. 1981. *Interpreting the French Revolution*. London: Cambridge University Press.

——. 1989. "The Terror." In *A Critical Dictionary of the French Revolution*, edited by François Furet and Mona Ozouf, translated by Arthur Goldhammer, 137–50. Cambridge MA: Harvard University Press.

Gallman, J. Matthew. 1994. *The North Fights the Civil War: The Home Front*. Chicago: Ivan R. Dee.

Gamson, William A. 1990. *The Strategy of Social Protest*. Belmont, CA: Wadsworth.

Garfinkle, Adam. 1997. *Telltale Hearts: The Origins and Impact of the Vietnam Antiwar Movement*. New York: St. Martin's.

Gauchet, Marcel. 1989. "Rights of Man." In *A Critical Dictionary of the French Revolution*, edited by François Furet and Mona Ozouf, translated by Arthor Goldhammer, 818–28. Cambridge MA: Harvard University Press.

——. 1995. *la Révolution des pouvoirs: La souveraineté, le peuple et la représentation, 1788–1799*. Paris: Gallimard.

Genovese, Eugene. 1992. *The Slaveholders' Dilemma: Freedom and Progress in Southern Conservative Thought, 1820–1860*. Columbia: University of South Carolina Press.

Gentile, Emilio. 1989. *Storia del Partito fascista, 1919–1922: Movimento e milizia*. Bari: Laterza.

Giddens, Anthony. 1985. *A Contemporary Critique of Historical Materialism*, vol. 2: *The Nation-State and Violence*. Berkeley: University of California Press.

Gillham, Patrick, and Bob Edwards. 2003. "Global Justice Protesters Respond to the September 11 Terrorist Attacks: The Impact of an Intentional Disaster on Demonstrations in Washington, D.C." In *Beyond September 11: An Account of Post-Disaster Research*, edited by Jacquelyn L. Monday, 483–520. Boulder: Natural Hazards Research and Information Center, University of Colorado.

Gitlin, Todd. 1980. *The Whole World Is Watching : Mass Media in the Making & Unmaking of the New Left*. Berkeley: University of California Press.

Glénard, Guillaume. 2010. *L'executif et la Constitution de 1791*. Paris: PUF.

Godechot, Jacques. 1968. *Les Institutions de la France sous La Révolution et l'Empire*. Paris: Presses Universitaires de France.

Godfrey, James Logan. 1951. *Revolutionary Justice: A Study of the Organization, Personnel, and Procedure of the Paris Tribunal, 1793–1795*. Chapel Hill: University of North Carolina Press.

Goldman, Robert, and Brian Tittemore. 2002. "Unprivileged Combatants and the Hostilities in Afghanistan." American Society of International Law Task Force on Terrorism. http://www.asil.org/taskforce/goldman.pdf.

Goldsmith, Jack. 2005. "Memorandum for Alberto Gonzales on 'Permissibility of Relocating Certain "Protected Persons" from Occupied Iraq,' March 19, 2004." In *The Torture Papers: The Road to Abu Ghraib*, edited by Karen J. Greenberg and Joshua L. Dratel, 367–80. Cambridge, UK: Cambridge University Press.

———. 2007. *The Terror Presidency: Law and Judgment Inside the Bush Administration.* New York: W. W. Norton.

———. 2012. *Power and Constraint: The Accountable Presidency after 9/11.* New York: W. W. Norton.

Goodheart, Adam. 2011. *1861: The Civil War Awakening.* New York: Knopf.

Goodwin, Jeff. 2006. "A Theory of Categorical Terrorism." *Social Forces* 84:2027–46.

———, ed. 2012. *Political Violence as Contentious Politics.* Special issue of *Mobilization* 17(1).

Gramsci, Antonio. 1949. *Il Risorgimento.* Turin: Giulio Einaudi.

Greenberg, Karen J., and Joshua L. Dratel, eds. 2005. *The Torture Papers: The Road to Abu Ghraib.* Cambridge, UK: Cambridge University Press.

Greenwald, Glenn. 2014. *No Place to Hide: Edward Snowden, the NSA, and the US Surveillance State.* London: Metropolitan Books.

Greer, Donald. 1935. *The Incidence of the Terror during the French Revolution: A Statistical Interpretation.* Cambridge, MA: Harvard University Press.

Griffin, Stephen M. 2013. *Long Wars and the Constitution.* Cambridge, MA: Harvard University Press.

Gross, Oren, and Fionnuala Ní Aoláin. 2006. *Law in Times of Crisis: Emergency Powers in Theory and Practice.* Cambridge, UK: Cambridge University Press.

Guarnieri, Carlo. 1995. "L'ordine pubblico e la giustizia penale." In *Storia dello stato italiano dall'Unità a oggi*, edited by Raffaele Romanelli, 365–407. Rome: Donzelli.

Guelke, Adrian. 1988. *Northern Ireland: The International Perspective.* New York: St. Martin's.

———. 2009. *The New Age of Terrorism and the International Political System.* London: I. B. Tauris.

Gueniffey, Patrice. 2000. *la politique de la terreur: Essai sur la violence révolutionnaire, 1789–794.* Paris: Fayard.

Gupta, Devashree. 2007. "Militant Flanks and Moderate Centers." PhD diss., Cornell University.

———. 2013. "The Strategic Logic of the Radical Flank Effect: Theorizing Power in Divided Social Movements." Paper presented at the 71st conference of the Midwest Political Science Association, Chicago, April 11–14.

Gurr, Ted Robert. 1968. "A Causal Model of Civil Strife: A Comparative Analysis Using New Indices." *American Political Science Review* 62:1104–24.

———. 1970. *Why Men Rebel.* Princeton: Center for International Studies, Princeton University.

Hadden, Jennifer, and Sidney Tarrow. 2007. "Spillover or Spillout: The Global Justice Movement in the United States after 9/11." *Mobilization* 12:359–76.

Hafez, Mohammed M. 2007. *Suicide Bombers in Iraq.* Washington, DC: United States Institute of Peace.

Hafez, Mohammed M., and Quentin Wiktorowicz. 2004. "Violence as Contention in the Egyptian Islamic Movement." In *Islamic Activism: A Social Movement Theory Approach*, edited by Quentin Wiktorowicz, 61–88. Bloomington: Indiana University Press.

Haines, Herbert H. 1984. "Black Radicalization and the Study of Civil Rights: 1957–1970." *Social Problems* 32:21–43.

Halpérin, Jean-Louis. 1987. *Le Tribunal de Cassation et les pouvoirs sous la Révolution (1790–1799).* Paris: Librairie Générale de Droit et de Jurisprudence.

Hanagan, Michael. 1998. "Transnational Social Movements, Deterritorialized Migrants, and the State System: A Nineteenth Century Case Study." *Mobilization* 3:107–24.

Hans, Valerie, and Claire Germain. 2011. "The French Jury at a Crossroads." *Chicago-Kent Law Review* 86:737–68.

Harding, Luke. 2014. *The Snowden Files: The Inside Story of the World's Most Wanted Man*. New York: Vintage Books.

Heaney, Michael T., and Fabio Rojas. 2015. *The Party in the Street: The Antiwar Movement and the Democratic Party after 9/11*. New York: Cambridge University Press.

Herbst, Jeffrey. 2000. *State and Power in Africa*. Princeton: Princeton University Press.

Herring, George C. 1979. *America's Longest War: The United States and Vietnam, 1950–1975*. New York: Wiley.

Higonnet, Patrice. 1998. *Goodness beyond Virtue: Jacobins during the French Revolution*. Cambridge, MA: Harvard University Press.

Hintze, Otto. 1975. "Military Organization and the Organization of the State." in *The Historical Essays of Otto Hintze*, edited by Felix Gilbert, 178–215. Oxford: Oxford University Press.

Hironaka, Ann. 2005. *Neverending Wars: The International Community, Weak States, and the Perpetuation of Civil War*. Cambridge, MA: Harvard University Press.

Hirsch-Hoefler, Sivan. 2008. "Mobilizing Politics: The Mobilization Strategies of the Israeli Settlement Movement." PhD diss., University of Antwerp.

Hofnung, Menachem. 1996. *Democracy, Law and National Security in Israel*. Aldershot, UK: Dartmouth.

Hogan, Michael J. 1998. *A Cross of Iron: Harry S. Truman and the Origins of the National Security State, 1945–1954*. New York: Cambridge University Press.

Huddy, Leonie, Stanley Feldman, Gallya Lahav, and Charles Taber. 2003. "Fear and Terrorism: Psychological Reactions to 9/11." In *Framing Terrorism: The News Media, the Government, and the Public*, edited by Pippa Norris, Montague Kern, and Marion Just, 255–78. New York: Routledge.

Hughes-Hallett, Lucy. 2013. *Gabriele d'Annunzio: Poet, Seducer, and Preacher of War*. New York: Alfred A. Knopf.

Hunt, Lynn. 1984. *Politics, Culture and Class in the French Revolution*. Berkeley: University of California Press.

———. 2007. *Inventing Human Rights: A History*. New York: W. W. Norton.

Huntington, Samuel P. 1973. "Transnational Organizations in World Politics." *World Politics* 25:333–68.

Hyman, Harold M. 1975. *A More Perfect Union: The Impact of the Civil War and Reconstruction on the Constitution*. Boston: Houghton Mifflin.

Ikenberry, G. John. 2011. *Liberal Leviathan: The Origins, Crisis. and Transformation of the American World Order*. Princeton: Princeton University Press.

Jenne, Erin. 2006. *Ethnic Bargaining: The Paradox of Minority Rights*. Ithaca: Cornell University Press.

Jenson, Richard Bach. 2009. "The International Campaign against Anarchist Terrorism, 1880–1930s." *Terrorism and Political Violence* 21:89–109.

Istituto Centrale di Statistica (ISTAT). 1966. *X Censimento generale della popolazione*, Vol. 3. Roma.

Kahin, George M. 1986. *Intervention: How America Became Involved in Vietnam*. New York: Knopf.

Kaldor, Mary. 2006. *New and Old Wars: Organized Violence in a Global Era*. 2nd rev. ed. Cambridge, UK: Polity Press.

Kalyvas, Stathis N. 1996. *The Rise of Christian Democracy in Europe*. Ithaca: Cornell University Press.

———. 2003. "The Ontology of 'Political Violence': Action and Identity in Civil Wars." *Perspectives on Politics* 1:275–94.

———. 2006. *The Logic of Violence in Civil War*. New York: Cambridge University Press.

Kant, Immanuel. 1991. *Kant: Political Writings*. Edited by Hans S. Reis. Translated by H. B. Nisbet. Cambridge, UK: Cambridge University Press.

Kaplan, Steven L. 1982. *The Famine Plot: Persuasion in Eighteenth-Century France*. Philadelphia: American Philosophical Society.

———. 1984. *Provisioning Paris: Merchants and Millers in the Grain and Flour Trade during the Eighteenth Century*. Ithaca: Cornell University Press.

Katz, Milton S. 1974. *Ban the Bomb: A History of SANE, the Committee for a Sane Nuclear Policy, 1957–1985*. New York: Greenwood Press.

Katzenstein, Mary F., Leila Mohsen, and Katherine D. Rubin. 2011. "The Dark Side of American Liberalism and Felony Disenfranchisement." *Perspectives on Politics* 8:1035–54.

Katzenstein, Peter J. 2005. *A World of Regions*. Ithaca: Cornell University Press.

Katznelson, Ira. 2002. "Flexible Capacity: The Military and Early American Statebuilding." In *Shaped by War and Trade: International Influences on American Political Development*, edited by Ira Katznelson and Martin Shefter, 82–110. Princeton: Princeton University Press.

———. 2013. *Fear Itself: The New Deal and the Origins of Our Time*. New York: Liveright.

Keck, Margaret, and Kathryn Sikkink. 1998. *Activists beyond Borders: Transnational Activist Networks in International Politics*. Ithaca: Cornell University Press.

Keller, William. 1989. *The Liberals and J. Edgar Hoover: The Rise and Fall of a Domestic Intelligence State*. Princeton: Princeton University Press.

Kennedy, Michael K. 1982. *The Jacobin Clubs in the French Revolution: The First Years*. Princeton: Princeton University Press.

Keohane, Robert O. 1984. *After Hegemony: Cooperation and Discord in the World Political Economy*. Princeton: Princeton University Press.

———. 2002. *Power and Governance in a Partially Globalized World*. New York: Routledge.

———. 2012. "Twenty Years of Institutional Liberalism." *International Relations* 26:125–38.

Keohane, Robert O., and Joseph S. Nye, eds. 1971. *Transnational Relations and World Politics*. Cambridge, MA: Harvard University Press.

———.1977. *Power and Interdependence: World Politics in Transition*. Boston: Little, Brown.

Kestnbaum, Meyer. 2002. "Citizen-Soldiers, National Service and the Mass Army: The Birth of Conscription in Revolutionary Europe and North America." In *The Comparative Study of Conscription in the Armed Forces*, edited by Lars Mjøset and Stephen van Holde, 117–44. Oxford: Elsevier Science.

Kier, Elizabeth. 2010. "War and Reform: Gaining Labor's Compliance on the Homefront." In *In War's Wake: International Conflict and the Fate of Liberal Democracy*, edited by Elizabeth Kier and Ronald R. Krebs, 139–61. New York: Cambridge University Press.

Kier, Elizabeth, and Ronald R Krebs. 2010a. "Introduction: War and Democracy in Comparative Perspective." In *In War's Wake: International Conflict and the Fate of Liberal Democracy*, edited by Elizabeth Kier and Ronald R. Krebs, 1–20. New York: Cambridge University Press.

———, eds. 2010b. *In War's Wake: International Conflict and the Fate of Liberal Democracy*. New York: Cambridge University Press.

King, Desmond S., and Robert C. Lieberman. 2008. "Finding the American State: Transcending the 'Statelessness' Account." *Polity* 40:368–78.

Kitson, Frank. 1971. *Low-Intensity Operations: Subversion, Insurgency, Peace-Keeping*. London: Faber and Faber.

Klandermans, Bert, ed. 1991. *Peace Movements in Western Europe and the United States.* Greenwich, CT: JAI Press.

Koh, Harold Hongju. 2003. "On American Exceptionalism." *Stanford Law Review* 55:1479–525.

Koopmans, Ruud. 1993. "The Dynamics of Protest Waves: West Germany, 1965 to 1989." *American Sociological Review* 58:637–58.

Krasner, Stephen D. 1999. *Sovereignty; Organized Hypocrisy.* Princeton: Princeton University Press.

Krebs, Ronald R. 2009. "In the Shadow of War: The Effects of Conflict on Liberal Democracy." *International Organization* 63:177–210.

Kroenig, Mathew, and Jay Stowsky. 2006. "War Makes the State but Not as It Pleases." *Security Studies* 15:225–70.

Krueger, Alan, and David Laitin. 2004. "Faulty Terror Report Card." *Washington Post*, May 17, 1.

Kryder, Daniel. 2000. *Divided Arsenal: Race and the American State during World War Two.* New York: Cambridge University Press.

Kurzman, Charles. 2011. *The Missing Martyrs: Why There Are So Few Muslim Terrorists.* New York: Oxford University Press.

Laffan, Brigid. 2002. "Ireland and the European Union." In *Ireland on the World Stage*, edited by William Crotty and David E. Schmitt, 83–94. Harlow: Pearson Education Limited.

Lascoumes, Pierre, and Pierrette Poncela. 1989. "Classer et punir autrement: Les incriminations sous l'Ancien Régime et sous la Constituante." In *Une autre justice, 1789–1799*, edited by Robert Badinter, 73–104. Paris: Fayard.

Lascoumes, Pierre, Pierrette Poncela, and Pierre Lenoël. 1989. *Au nom de l'ordre : Une Histoire poliique du code penal.* Paris: Hachette.

Lasswell, Harold. 1941. "The Garrison State." *American Journal of Sociology* 46:455–68.

———. 1998. *Essays on the Garrison State.* New Brunswick, NJ: Transaction Press.

Le Gal, Sebastien. 2005. "La suspension du Droit en Révolution: Entre volonté de rupture et permanence d'une tentation : l'article 92 de la Constitution de l'an VIII " In *Le Droit en Révolution*, edited by AFHIP, 59–73. Aix-en-Provence: PUAM.

———. 2011. "Les Origines de l'État de siège en France (Ancien Régime—Révolution)." PhD diss., University of Lyons.

———. 2012. "Aux origines du droit à la sureté." In *Le Droit à la sureté: Etat des lieux, état du droit*, edited by Ludovic Garrido, 19–42. Paris: Editions Cujas.

Lepetit, Bernard. 1988. *Les villes dans la France moderne, 1740–1840.* Paris: Albin Michel.

Levi, Margaret. 1988. *Of Rule and Revenue.* Berkeley: University of California Press.

———. 1997. *Consent, Dissent, and Patriotism.* New York: Cambridge University Press.

Levi, Margaret, and Laura Stoker. 2000. "Political Trust and Trustworthiness." *Annual Review of Political Science* 3:475–507.

Levy, Jack S. 1983. *War in the Modern Great Power System, 1495–1975.* Lexington: University Press of Kentucky.

Levy, Jack S., and William R. Thompson. 2011. *The Arc of War: Origins, Escalation, and Transformation.* Chicago: University of Chicago Press.

Levy, Yagil. 2012. *Israel's Death Hierarchy.* New York: New York University Press.

Lichbach, Mark, and Helma DeVries. 2007. "Mechanisms of Globalized Protest Movements." In *The Oxford Handbook of Comparative Politics*, edited by Carles Boix and Susan C. Stokes, 461–96. New York: Oxford University Press.

Lipset, Seymour Martin. 1960. *Political Man: The Social Bases of Politics.* Garden City, NY: Doubleday.

Little, Stuart Jon. 1989. "The Freedom Train and the Formation of National Political Culture, 1946–1949." PhD diss., University of Kansas.

Logevall, Frederik. 1999. *Choosing War: The Lost Chance for Peace and the Escalation of the War in Vietnam.* Berkeley: University of California Press.

———. 2001. *The Origins of the Vietnam War.* Harlow, UK: Longman.

———. 2012. *Embers of War: The Fall of an Empire and the Making of America's Vietnam.* New York: Random House.

Ludlow, Peter. 1996. *High Noon on the Electronic Frontier.* Cambridge, MA: MIT Press.

Luebbert, Gregory M. 1991. *Liberalism, Fascism, or Social Democracy: Social Classes and the Political Origins of Regimes in Interwar Europe.* New York: Oxford University Press.

Lussu, Emilio. 2000. *Un anno sull'Altopiano.* Bologna: Il Mulino.

Lynn, John A. 1983. *The Bayonets of the Republic: Motivation and Tactics in the Army of Revolutionary France, 1791–94.* Urbana: University of Illinois Press.

Mack, Andrew J. R. 1975. "Why Big Nations Lose Small Wars: The Politics of Asymmetric Conflict." *World Politics* 27:175–200.

Mack Smith, Dennis. 1954. *Cavour and Garibaldi, 1860: A Study in Political Conflict.* Cambridge, UK: Cambridge University Press.

———. 1959. *Italy; A Modern History.* Ann Arbor: University of Michigan Press.

Macry, Paolo. 2012. *Unità a Mezzogiorno: Come l'"Italia ha messo assieme i pezzi.* Bologna: Il Mulino.

Madison, James. 1795 [1865]. "Political Observations (April 20, 1795)." In *Letters and Other Writings of James Madison,* Vol. 4, 485–505. Philadelphia: Lippincott.

Mahnken, Thomas G. 2013. "The Growth and Spread of the Precision-Strike Regime." In *The Modern American Military,* edited by David M. Kennedy, 59–78. New York: Oxford University Press.

Maier, Charles. 1975. *Recasting Bourgeois Europe: Stabilization in France, Germany, and Italy in the Decade after World War I.* Princeton: Princeton University Press.

Maney, Gregory M. 2000. "Transnational Mobilization and Civil Rights in Northern Ireland." *Social Problems* 47:153–79.

———. 2006. "From Civil War to Civil Rights and Back Again: The Interrelation of Rebellion and Protest in Northern Ireland, 1955–1972." *Research in Social Movements, Conflicts, and Change* 27:3–35.

Mann, Michael. 1986. *The Sources of Social Power,* vol. 1: *The Rise of Classes and Nation-States, 1760–1914.* Cambridge, UK: Cambridge University Press.

———. 1987. "The Autonomous Power of the State: Its Origins, Mechanisms and Results." In *States in History,* edited by John H. Hall, 109–36. Oxford: Basil Blackwell.

———. 1988. *States, War and Capitalism: Studies in Political Sociology.* Oxford: Blackwell's.

———. 1993. *The Sources of Social Power,* vol. 2: *The Rise of Classes and Nation-States, 1760–1914.* New York: Cambridge University Press.

———. 2012. *The Sources of Social Power,* vol. 3: *Global Empires and Revolution, 1890–1945.* Cambridge, UK: Cambridge University Press.

———. 2013. *The Sources of Social Power,* vol. 4: *Globalizations, 1945–2011.* Cambridge, UK: Cambridge University Press.

Maranini, Giuseppe. 1967. *Storia del potere in Italia, 1848–1967.* Florence: Vallecchi.

Margulies, Joseph. 2006. *Guantanamo and the Abuse of Presidential Power.* New York: Simon and Schuster.

———. 2013. *What Changed When Everything Changed: 9/11 and the Making of National Identity.* New Haven: Yale University Press.

Martin, Jean-Clément. 1998. *Contre-révolution, révolution et nation en France, 1789–1799*. Paris: Seuil.

———. 2006. *Violence et révolution*. Paris: Editions du Seuil.

Martinage, René. 1989. "Les innovations des constituants en matière de répression." In *Une autre justice*, edited by Robert Badinter, 103–26. Paris: Fayard.

Martineau, François. 1989. "Accaparement et maximum: La Répression de la cupidité mercantile sous la Terreur." In *Une autre justice*, edited by Robert Badinter, 127–47. Paris Fayard.

Masullo Jiménez, Juan, and Jone Lauzurika Bajo. 2014. "Bringing the 'New Wars' Debate Back on Track: Building on Critiques, Identifying Opportunities, and Moving Forward." *Global Policy* 5:1–10.

Mayer, Jane. 2006. "How an Internal Effort to Ban the Abuse and Torture of Detainees Was Thwarted." *New Yorker*, February 27, 112–21. http://www.newyorker.com/fact/content/articles/0602227fa_fact.

Mazower, Mark. 2012. *Governing the World: The History of an Idea*. New York: Penguin.

McAdam, Doug. 1983. "Tactical Innovation and the Pace of Insurgency." *American Sociological Review* 48:735–54.

———. 1988. *Freedom Summer*. New York: Oxford University Press.

———. 1998. "On the International Origins of Domestic Political Opportunities." In *Social Movements and American Political Institutions*, edited by Ann Costain and Andrew McFarland, 251–267. Lanham, MD: Rowman and Littlefield.

McAdam, Doug, and Yang Su. 2002. "The War at Home. Antiwar Protests and Congressional Voting, 1965 to 1973." *American Sociological Review* 67:696–721.

McAdam, Doug, and Sidney Tarrow. 2010. "On the Reciprocal Relationship between Elections and Social Movements." *Perspectives on Politics* 8:529–42.

———. 2013. "Social Movements and Elections: Towards a Better Understanding of the Political Context of Contention." In *The Changing Dynamics of Contention*, edited by Conny Roggeband, Bert Klandermans, and Jacquelien Van Stekelenburg, 325–46. Minneapolis: University of Minnesota Press.

McAdam, Doug, Sidney Tarrow, and Charles Tilly. 2001. *Dynamics of Contention*. New York: Cambridge University Press.

McCann, Michael W., ed. 2006. *Law and Social Movements*. Burlington, VT: Ashgate.

McConnell, Grant. 1966. *Private Power and American Democracy*. New York: Alfred Knopf.

McGarry, John, and Brendan O'Leary. 1995. *Explaining Northern Ireland: Broken Images*. Oxford: Blackwell.

McPhail, Clark, David Schweingruber, and John McCarthy. 1999. "Policing Protest in the United States, 1960–1995." In *Policing Protest: The Control of Mass Demonstrations in Western Democracies*, edited by Donatella della Porta and Herbert Reiter, 49–69. Minneapolis: University of Minnesota Press.

McPherson, James M. 1988. *Battle Cry of Freedom: The Civil War Era*. New York: Ballantine Books.

Medsger, Betty. 2013. *The Burglary: The Discovery of J. Edgar Hoover's Secret FBI*. New York: Random House.

Meehan, Elizabeth. 2000. "Bringing in Europe: The Peace Process and the Europeanization of the Irish Question." *Irish Studies in International Affairs* 11:179–91.

Mégret, Frédéric. 2006. "From 'Savages' to 'Unlawful Combatants': A Postcolonial Look at International Law's 'Other.'" In *International Law and Its Others*, edited by Anne Orford, 265–318. Cambridge, UK: Cambridge University Press.

Melis, Guido. 1988. *Due modelli di amministrazione fra liberalismo e fascismo*. Rome: Ministero per i beni culturali e ambientali.

———. 1995. "L'amministrazione." In *Storia dello stato italiano dall'Unità a oggi*, edited by Raffaele. Romanelli, 187–252. Rome: Donzelli.

Meniconi, Antonella. 2013. *Storia della magistratura italiana*. Bologna: Il Mulino.

Merlini, Stefano. 1995. "Il governo costituzionale." In *Storia dello stato italano dall'Unità a oggi*, edited by Raffaele Romanelli. Rome: Donzelli.

Merolla, Jennifer L., and Elizabeth J. Zechmeister. 2009. *Democracy at Risk: How Terrorist Threats Affect the Public*. Chicago: University of Chicago Press.

Messineo, Francesco. 2009. "The Abu Omar Case in Italy: Extraordinary Renditions and State Obligations to Criminalize and Prosecute Torture under the UN Torture Convention." *Journal of International Criminal Justice* 7:1023–44.

Meyer, David S. 1990. *A Winter of Discontent: The Nuclear Freeze and American Politics*. New York: Praeger.

———. 1990–91. "How We Helped End the Cold War (and Let Someone Else Take All the Credit)." *Nuclear Times* 8(4): 9–14.

———. 1993. "Institutionalizing Dissent: The United States Political Opportunity Structure and the End of the Nuclear Freeze Movement." *Sociological Forum* 8:157–79.

Meyer, David S., and Sidney Tarrow, eds. 1998. *The Social Movement Society: Contentious Politics for a New Century*. Lanham, MD: Rowman and Littlefield.

Meyer, David S., and Nancy Whittier. 1994. "Social Movement Spillover." *Social Problems* 41:277–98.

Meyer, John, John Boli, George Thomas, and Francisco O. Ramirez. 1998. "World Society and the Nation-State." *American Journal of Sociology* 103:144–81.

Ministero degli Affari Esteri. 1898. *Conférence Internationale de Rome pour la Défense Sociale contre les Anarchistes*. Rome: Ministero Affari Esteri.

Miodownik, Dan, and Oren Barak. 2013. *Nonstate Actors in Intrastate Conflicts*. Philadelphia: University of Pennsylvania Press.

Moaz, Zeev. 1989. "Joining the Club of Nations: Political Development and International Conflict, 1816–1876." *International Studies Quarterly* 33:199–231.

Molfese, Franco. 1964. *Storia del brigantaggio dopo l'Unità*. Milan: Feltrinelli.

Mondini, Marco. 2006. *La politica delle armi: Il ruolo dell'esercito nell'avvento del fascismo*. Bari: Laterza.

Moore, Barrington Jr. 1966. *The Social Origins of Dictatorship and Democracy: Lord and Peasant in the Modern World*. Boston: Beacon Press.

Morse, Julia, and Robert O. Keohane. 2014. "Contested Multilateralism." *Review of International Organizations* 9. http://link.springer.com/article/10.100 7%2Fs11558-014-9188-2.

Murray, Williamson, and Peter R. Mansoor. 2012. *Hybrid Warfare: Fighting Complex Opponents from the Ancient World to the Present*. New York: Cambridge University Press.

Nacos, Brigitte L., Yaeli Bloch-Elkon, and Robert Y. Shapiro. 2011. *Selling Fear: Counterterrorism, the Media, and Public Opinon*. Chicago: University of Chicago Press.

Neely, Mark E. Jr. 1991. *The Fate of Liberty: Abraham Lincoln and Civil Liberties*. New York: Oxford University Press.

Neppi Modona, Guido. 1969. *Sciopero, potere politico e magistratura*. Bari: Laterza.

———. 1973. "La magistratura e il fascismo." In *Fascismo e società italiana*, edited by Guido Quazza, 125–82. Turin: Einaudi.

Neumann, Peter R. 2003. *Britain's Long War: British Strategy in the Northern Ireland Conflict, 1969–98*. Houndmills, UK: Palgrave Macmillan.

Newton, Michael. 2005. "Unlawful Belligerency after September 11." In *New Wars, New Laws?: Applying the Laws of War in 21st Century Conflicts*, edited by David Wippman and Matthew Evangelista, 75–110. Leiden: Martinus Nijhoff.

Ní Aoláin, Fionnuala, and Oren Gross. 2013. *Guantanamo and Beyond: Exceptional Courts and Military Commissions in Comparative Perspective*. New York: Cambridge University Press.

Noftsinger, John B. Jr., Kennet F. Newbold Jr., and Jack K. Wheeler. 2007. *Understanding Homeland Security: Policy, Perspectives, and Paradoxes*. New York: Palgrave Macmillan.

Oakes, James. 2012. *Freedom National: The Destruction of Slavery in the United States, 1861–1985*. New York: W. W. Norton.

O'Brien, Robert, Anne Marie Goetz, Jan Aart Scholte, and Marc Williams. 2000. *Contesting Global Governance: Multilateral Economic Institutions and Global Social Movements*. Cambridge, UK: Cambridge University Press.

Ohlin, Jens David. 2015. *The Assault on International Law*. Oxford: Oxford University Press.

Oshinsky, David. M. 1996. *Worse Than Slavery: Parchman Farm and the Ordeal of Jim Crow Justice*. New York: Free Press.

Palmer, Beverly Wilson, and Holly Byers Ochoa. 1998. *The Selected Papers of Thaddeus Stevens*. Vol. 2. Pittsburgh: University of Pittsburgh Press.

Palmer, Robert R. 1964. *The Age of the Democratic Revolution: A Political History of Europe and America, 1760–1800*. Vol. 2. Princeton: Princeton University Press.

Pedahzur, Ari, and Amie Perlinger. 2006. "The Changing Nature of Suicide Attacks: A Social Network Perspective." *Social Forces* 84:1933–2004.

Peirce, Gareth. 2012. *Dispatches from the Dark Side: On Torture and the Death of Justice*. London: Verso.

Piretti, Maria Serena. 1996. *Le elezioni politiche in Italia dal 1848 a oggi*. Rome-Bari: Laterza.

Pizzorno, Alessandro. 1978. "Political Exchange and Collective Identity in Industrial Conflict." In *The Resurgence of Class Conflict in Western Europe*, edited by Colin Crouch and Alessandro Pizzorno, vol. 2, 277–95. London: Macmillan.

Poggi, Gianfranco. 1990. *The State: Its Nature, Development, and Prospects*. Cambridge, UK: Polity.

Poole, Keith T., and Howard Rosenthal. 1997. *Congress: A Political-Economic History of Roll Call Voting*. New York: Oxford University Press.

Porter, Bruce D. 1994. *War and the Rise of the State: The Military Foundations of Modern Politics*. New York: Free Press.

Posner, Eric A., and Adrian Vermeule. 2005. "Accommodating Emergencies." In *The Constitution in Wartime: Beyond Alarmism and Complacency*, edited by Mark Tushnet, 55–93. Durham: Duke University Press.

Poulantzas, Nicos. 1975. *Political Power and Social Classes*. London: New Left Books.

Prabhat, Devyani. 2011. "Terrorism, State Action, and Rights Lawyering in the U.K. and the U.S.A.: Illegal Violence, Legal Force, and Legal Response?" PhD diss., New York University.

Priest, Dana, and William M. Arkin. 2011. *Top Secret America: The Rise of the New American Security State*. New York: Little, Brown.

Procacci, Giovanna. 1992. "State Coercion and Worker Solidarity in Italy (1915–1918); The Moral and Political Content of Social Unrest." In *Strikes, Social Conflict and the First World War: An International Perspective*, edited by Leopold Haimson and Guilio Sapelli. 145–78. Milano: Fondazione Giangiacomo Feltrinelli.

——. 1993. *Soldati e prigionieri italiani nella Grande guerra. Con una raccolta di lettere inedite*. Rome: Editori Riunite.

——. 2006. "Osservazioni sulla continuità della legislazione sull'ordine pubblico tra fine Ottocento, prima guerra mondiale e fascismo." In *Militarizzazione e nazionalizzazione nella storia d'Italia*, edited by Pierre Del Negro, Nicola Labianca, and Alessandra Staderini, 83–96. Milano: Unicopli.

———. 2009. "Stato di guerra, regime di eccezione e violazione delle libertà: Francia, Inghilterra, Germania, Austria, Italia dal 1914 al 1918." In *Le guerre mondiali in Asia orientale e in Europa: Violenza, collaborazionismi, propaganda*, edited by Bruno Bianchi, Laura De Giorgi, and Guido Samarini, 33–52. Milano: Unicpoli.

———. 2011. "Alcune note sulle eredità della prima guerra mondiale." In *Pensare la contemporaneità: Studi di storia per Mariuccia Salvati*, edited by Paolo Capuzzo, Chiara Giorgi, Manuela Martini, and Carlotta Sorba, 49–66. Roma: Viella.

———. 2013. *Warfare-Welfare: Intervento dello Stato e diritti dei cittadini (1914–1918)*. Roma: Carocci.

Putnam, Robert D. 1993. *Making Democracy Work: Civic Traditions in Modern Italy*. Princeton: Princeton University Press.

Rana, Aziz. 2010. *The Two Faces of American Freedom*. Cambridge, MA: Harvard University Press.

———. 2012. "Who Decides on Security." *Connecticut Law Review* 44:1–75.

———. 2015. "Constitutionalism and the Foundations of the Security State." California Law Review 103.

Ransom, Roger L. 1989. *Conflict and Compromise: The Political Economy of Slavery, Emancipation and the Civil War*. New York: Cambridge University Press.

Rasler, Karen A., and William R. Thompson. 1989. *War and State Making: The Shaping of the Global Powers*. Boston: Unwin Hyman.

Rials, Stephane, ed. 1982. *Textes constitutionnels français*. Paris: PUF.

———. 1988. *La déclaration des droits de l'homme et du citoyen*. Paris: Hachette.

Ridge, Tom. 2009. *The Test of Our Times: America under Siege . . . and How We Can Be Safe Again*. New York: Thomas Dunne Books.

Reiter, Dan, and Allan C. Stam. 2002. *Democracies at War*. Princeton: Princeton University Press.

Reiter, Herbert, and Olivier Fillieule. 2006. "Formalizing the Informal: The EU Approach to Transnational Protest Policing." In *The Policing of Transnational Protest*, edited by Donatella Della Porta, Abby Peterson, and Herbert Reiter, 145–73. London: Ashgate.

Riley, Dylan. 2010. *The Civic Foundations of Fascism in Europe: Italy, Spain, Romania*. Baltimore: Johns Hopkins University Press.

Rioux, Jean-Pierre, and Jean-François Sirinelli. 1991. *La guerre d'Algèrie et les intellectuels*. Brussels: Editions Complexe.

Risse, Thomas, Stephen Ropp, and Katherine Sikkink, eds. 1999. *The Power of Human Rights: International Norms and Domestic Change*. Cambridge, UK: Cambridge University Press.

———. 2013. *The Persistent Power of Human Rights: From Commitment to Compliance*. New York: Cambridge University Press.

Risse-Kappen, Thomas, ed. 1995. *Bringing Transnational Relations Back In: Non-State Actors, Domestic Structure and International Institutions*. New York: Cambridge University Press.

Riverstone-Newell, Lori. 2012. "The Diffusion of Local Bill of Rights Resolutions to the States." *State and Local Government Review* 45:14–24.

Rocard, Michel, and Vincent Dudert. 2003. *Rapport sur les camps de regroupement et autres textes sur la guerre d'Algerie*. Paris: Mille et une nuits.

Rochat, Giorgio. 1967. *L'esercito italiano da Vittorio Veneto a Mussolini (1919–1925*. Bari: Laterza.

——. 1973. "L'esercito e il fascismo." In *Fascismo e società italiana*, edited by Guido Quazza, 90–124. Turin: Einaudi.

——. 1976. "L'Italia nella prima guerra mondiale. Problemi di interpretazione e ipotesi di ricerca oggi." *Rivista di storia contemporanea* 5:161–207.

Rochon, Thomas R. 1988. *Mobilizing for Peace: The Antinuclear Movements in Western Europe*. Princeton: Princeton University Press.

Rodotà, Stefano. 1995. "Le libertà e i diritti." In *Storia dello stato italiano dall'Unità a oggi*, edited by Raffaele Romanelli, 301–64. Rome: Donzelli.

Rokkan, Stein. 1970. *Citizens, Elections, Parties*. New York: McKay.

Romanelli, Raffaele, ed. 1995. *Storia dello Stato italiano dall'Unità a oggi*. Rome: Donzelli.

Rosand, Eric. 2004. "The Security Council as 'Global Legislator': Ultra Vires or Ultra Innovative?" *Fordham International Law Journal* 28:542–90.

Rosenberg, Gerald. 2008. *The Hollow Hope: Can Courts Bring About Social Change?* Chicago: University of Chicago Press.

Rossi-Doria, Manlio. 1982. *Scritti sul Mezzogiorno*. Turin: Einaudi.

Rossiter, Clinton. 1963. *Constitutional Dictatorship: Crisis Government in the Modern Democracies*. 2nd. ed. Princeton: Princeton University Press.

Ruane, Joseph, and Jennifer Todd, eds. 1996. *The Dynamics of Conflict in Northern Ireland: Power, Conflict, and Emancipation*. Cambridge, UK: Cambridge University Press.

Rudelle, Odile. 1993. "Le legicentrisme republicain." In *Le siècle de l'avenement républicain*, edited by François Furet and Mona Ozouf, 441–72. Paris: Gallimard.

Rumsfeld, Donald H. 2002. "Transforming the Military." *Foreign Affairs* 81:20–32.

Rusconi, Gian Enrico. 2014. *Attacco a Occidente*. Bologna: Il Mulino.

Sabbatucci, Giovanni. 1974. *I combattenti nel primo dopoguerra*. Bari: Laterza.

Sageman, Mark. 2004. *Understanding Terror Networks*. Philadelphia: University of Pennsylvania Press.

Saint-Bonnet, François. 2001. *L'Etat d'exception*. Paris: PUF.

Salamone, A. William. 1960. *Italy in the Giolittian Era: Italian Democracy in the Making, 1900–1914*. Philadelphia: University of Pennsylvania Press.

Salvemini, Gaetano. 1955. *Scritti sulla questione meridionale*. Turin: Einaudi.

Salvemini, Gaetano, Sergio Bucchi, and Gaetano Arfé. 2000. *Il ministro della malavita*. Turin: Bollati Boringhieri.

Sarat, Austin, ed. 2011. Special issue of *Studies in Law, Politics, and Society* 54.

Sarat, Austin, and Stuart Scheingold, eds. 1997. *Cause Lawyering : Political Commitments and Professional Responsibilities*. Oxford: Oxford University Press.

——, eds. 2001. *Cause Lawyering and the State in the Global Era*. Oxford: Oxford University Press.

——, eds. 2006. *Cause Lawyering and Social Movements*. Stanford: Stanford University Press.

Sarkees, Meredith R., and Frank W. Wayman. 2010. *Resort to War, 1816–2007*. Washington, DC: Congressional Quarterly Press.

Sbardellati, John. 2012. *J. Edgar Hoover Goes to the Movies: The FBI and the Origins of the Cold War*. Ithaca: Cornell University Press.

Scahill, Tim. 2007. *Blackwater: The Rise of the World's Most Powerful Mercenary Army*. New York: Nation Books.

Scheingold, Stuart. 1974. *Politics of Rights: Lawyers, Public Policy. and Political Change*. New Haven: Yale University Press.

Scheppele, Kim Lane. 2005–2006. "Small Emergencies." *Georgia Law Review* 40:835–62.

——. 2006. "The Migration of Anti-Constitutional Ideas: The Post-9/11 Globalization of Public Law and the International State of Emergency." In *The Migration of Constitutional Ideas*, edited by Sujit Choudhry, 347–73. Cambridge, UK: Cambridge University Press.

——. 2010. "Exceptions That Prove the Rule: Embedding Emergency Government in Everyday Constitutional Life." In *The Limits of Constitutional Democracy*, edited by Jeffrey K. Tulis and Stephen Macedo, 124–54. Princeton: Princeton University Press.

Schmitt, Carl. 1985. *Political Theology: Four Chapters on the Concept of Sovereignty.* Chicago: University of Chicago Press.

——. 1995. *The Concept of the Political.* Chicago: University of Chicago Press.

——. 2007. *Theory of the Partisan: Intermediate Commentary on the Concept of the Political.* New York: Telos Press.

——. 2013. *Dictatorship.* Cambridge, UK: Polity

Schnapper, Bernard. 1989. "Le jury criminel." In *Une autre justice*, edited by Robert Badinter, 149–72. Paris: Fayard.

Scott, Katherine A. 2009. *Reining in the State: Civil Society and Congress in the Vietnam and Watergate Eras.* Lawrence: University Press of Kansas.

Segal, David R., and Lawrence J. Korb. 2013. "Manning and Financing the Twenty-First Century All-Volunteer Force." In *The Modern American Military*, edited by David M. Kennedy, 111–34. Oxford: Oxford University Press.

Segal, Joshua, and Soto Kimura, eds. 2011. *The Military Commissions Act and Detainee Trials.* New York: Nova Science Publishers.

Segev, Tom. 2000. *One Palestine, Complete: Jews and Arabs under the British Mandate.* New York: Henry Holt.

Seidman, Gay. 2001. "Guerillas in Their Midst: Armed Struggle in the South African Anti-Apartheid Movement." *Mobilization* 6:111–27.

Sereni, Emilio. 1956. *Vecchio e nuovo nelle campagne italiane.* Roma: Editori Riuniti.

Sergio, Marialuisa-Lucia. 2002. *Dall'antipartito al partito unico: La crisi della politica in Italia agli inizi del '900.* Roma: Edizioni Studium.

Sewell, Richard H. 1976. *Ballots for Freedom: Antislavery Politics in the United States, 1837–1860.* New York: W. W. Norton.

Shapira, Anita. 2005. *L'Imaginaire d'Israël: Histoire d'une culture politique.* Paris: Calmann-Lévy.

Sheffer, Gabriel, and Oren Barak. 2013. *Israel's Security Networks: A Theoretical and Comparative Perspective.* New York: Cambridge University Press.

Shor, Eran. 2011. "Constructing a Terrorism Database." *Journal of Terrorism Research* 2:49–77.

Shorrock, Tim. 2008. *Spies for Hire.* New York: Simon and Schuster.

Sidel, Mark. 2004. *More Secure, Less Free?: Antiterrorism Policy and Civil Liberties after September 11.* Ann Arbor: University of Michigan Press.

——. 2010. *Regulation of the Voluntary Sector: Freedom and Security in an Era of Uncertainty.* New York: Routledge.

Silbey, Joel H. 1967. *The Transformation of American Politics, 1840–1860.* Englewood Cliffs: Prentice-Hall.

——. 1977. *A Respectable Minority: The Democratic Party in the Civil War Era, 1860–1868.* New York: W. W. Norton.

Simonin, Anne. 2007. *Deshonneur dans la Révolution.* Paris: Grasset.

Singer, Peter W. 2003. *Corporate Warriors: The Rise of the Private Military Industry.* Ithaca: Cornell University Press.

Skocpol, Theda. 1979. *States and Social Revolutions: A Comparative Analysis of France, Russia and China*. New York: Cambridge University Press.

Skowronek, Stephen. 1982. *Building a New American State: The Expansion of National Administrative Capacities, 1877–1920*. New York: Cambridge University Press.

Slater, Dan. 2010. *Ordering Power: Contentious Politics and Authoritarian Leviathans in Southeast Asia*. New York: Cambridge University Press.

Small, Melvin. 2002. *Antiwarriors: The Vietnam War and the Battle for America's Hearts and Minds*. Lanham, MD: Rowman and Littlefield.

Smith, Jackie. 2008. *Social Movements for Global Democracy*. Baltimore: Johns Hopkins University Press.

Smith, Jackie, and Hank Johnston, eds. 2002. *Globalization and Resistance: Transnational Dimensions of Social Movements*. Lanham, MD: Rowman and Littlefield.

Smith, Rogers. 2010. "The Strangers in Ourselves: The Rights of Suspect Citizens in the Age of Terrorism." In *Law and the Stranger*, edited by Austin Sarat, Lawrence Douglas, and Martha M. Umphrey, 65–96. Stanford: Stanford University Press.

Smith, William Beattie. 2011. *The British State and the Northern Irish Crisis, 1969–73*. Washington, DC: United States Institute of Peace.

Spriano, Paolo. 1975. *The Occupation of the Factories: Italy, 1920*. London: Pluto.

Spruyt, Hendrik. 1994. *The Sovereign State and Its Competitors: An Analysis of System Change*. Princeton: Princeton University Press.

Stanger, Allison. 2009. *One Nation under Contract: The Outsourcing of American Foreign Policy*. New Haven: Yale University Press.

Starr, Paul. 2007. *Freedom's Power: The True Force of Liberalism*. New York: Basic Books.

——. 2010. "Dodging a Bullet: Democracy's Gains in Modern War." In *In War's Wake: International Conflict and the Fate of Liberal Democracy*, edited by Elizabeth Kier and Ronald R. Krebs, 50–66. New York: Cambridge University Press.

Stein, Arthur A., and Bruce Russett. 1980. "Evaluating War: Outcomes and Consequences." In *Handbook of Political Conflict: Theory and Research*, edited by Ted R. Gurr, 399–422. New York: The Free Press.

Steinberg, Ronen. 2010. "The Afterlives of the Terror: Dealing with the Legacies of Violence in Post-Revolutionary France, 1794–1830s." PhD diss., University of Chicago.

——. 2013. "Transitional Justice in the Age of the French Revolution." *International Journal of Transitional Justice* 7:267–85.

Stone, Geoffrey R. 2004. *Perilous Times: Free Speech in Wartime*. New York: W. W. Norton.

Stouffer, Samuel A. 1955. *Communism, Conformity and Civil Rights: A Cross-Section of the Nation Speaks Its Mind*. Garden City, NY: Doubleday.

Strum, Philippa. 1999. *When the Nazis Came to Skokie: Freedom for Speech We Hate*. Lawrence: University of Kansas Press.

Suh, Chan S. 2015. "Differential Participation in Professional Activism: The Case of the Guantánamo Habeas Lawyers." *Mobilization* 19:287–307.

Sunstein, Cass R. 2003. "Terrorism and Probability Neglect." *Journal of Risk and Uncertainty* 26:121–36.

Szasz, Paul. 2002. "The Security Council Starts Legislating." *American Journal of International Law* 96:901–5.

Tarrow, Sidney. 1967. *Peasant Communism in Southern Italy*. New Haven: Yale University Press.

——. 1977. *Between Center and Periphery: Grassroots Politicians in Italy and France*. New Haven: Yale University Press.

———. 1989. *Democracy and Disorder: Protest and Politics in Italy, 1965–1974*. Oxford: Oxford University Press.

———. 1995. "Cycles of Collective Action: Between Moments of Madness and the Repertoire of Contention." In *Repertoires and Cycles of Collective Action*, edited by Mark Traugott, 89–116. Durham: Duke University Press.

———. 2005. *The New Transnational Activism*. Cambridge, UK: Cambridge University Press.

———. 2007. "Inside Insurgencies: Politics and Violence in an Age of Civil War." *Perspectives on Politics* 5:587–600.

———. 2011a. "The French Revolution, War and State-Building: Making One Tilly Out of Three." In *Contention and Trust in Cities and States*, edited by Michael Hanagan and Chris Tilly, 79–94. New York: Springer.

———. 2011b. *Power in Movement*. 3rd rev. ed. New York: Cambridge University Press.

———. 2013a. *The Language of Contention: Revolutions in Words, 1789–2012*. New York: Cambridge University Press.

———. 2013b. "War, Rights, and Contention: Lasswell v. Tilly." In *Sovereignty, Citizenship, and Cosmopolitan Alternatives*, edited by Sigal Ben-Porath and Rogers M. Smith, 35–67. Philadelphia: University of Pennsylvania Press.

Tarrow, Susan. 1985. *Exile from the Kingdom: A Political Rereading of Albert Camus*. Tuscaloosa: University of Alabama Press.

Taylor, Brian D., and Roxana Botea. 2008. "Tilly Tally: War-Making and State-Making in the Contemporary Third World." *International Studies Review* 10:27–56.

Taylor, Verta. 1989. "Social Movement Continuity: The Women's Movement in Abeyance." *American Sociological Review* 54:761–75.

te Brake, Wayne. 1998. *Shaping History: Ordinary People in European Politics, 1500–1700*. Brekeley: University of California Press.

Tilly, Charles. 1964. *The Vendée*. Cambridge, MA: Harvard University Press.

———, ed. 1975. *The Formation of National States in Western Europe*. Princeton: Princeton University Press.

———. 1984. *Big Structures, Large Processes, Huge Comparisons*. New York: Russell Sage Foundation.

———. 1985. "War Making and State Making as Organized Crime." In *Bringing the State Back In*, edited by Peter Evans, Dietrich Rueschemeyer, and Theda. Skocpol, 169–87. New York: Cambridge University Press.

———. 1986. *The Contentious French*. Cambridge, MA: Harvard University Press.

———. 1992a. *Coercion, Capital, and European States, AD 990–1992*. Cambridge, MA: Blackwell.

———. 1992b. "Conclusions." In *Strikes, Social Conflict and the First World War*, edited by Leopold Haimson and Giulio Sapelli, 587–98. Milano: Fondazione Giangiacomo Feltrinelli.

———. 1992c. "Where Do Rights Come From?" In *Contributions to the Comparative Study of Development*, edited by Lars Mjoset, 9–37. Oslo: Institute for Social Research.

———. 1993. *European Revolutions, 1492–1992*. Oxford: Blackwell.

———. 2003. *The Politics of Collective Violence*. New York: Cambridge University Press.

———. 2004. *Contention and Democracy in Europe, 1650–2000*. New York: Cambridge University Press.

———. 2008. *Contentious Performances*. New York: Cambridge University Press.

Tilly, Charles, and Sidney Tarrow. 2007. *Contentious Politics*. Boulder: Paradigm.

Tilly, Charles, and Lesley Wood. 2009. *Social Movements, 1768–2008*. Boulder: Paradigm.

Tocqueville, Alexis de. 1955. *The Old Regime and the French Revolution*. Garden City, NY: Doubleday.

Tomalin, Claire. 2002. *Samuel Pepys: The Unequalled Self*. New York: Vintage.

Tomassini, Luigi. 1992. "Industrial Mobilization and State Intervention in Italy in the First World War: Effects on Labor Unrest." In *Strikes, Social Conflict and the First World War: An International Perspective*, edited by Leopold Haimson and. Guilio Sapelli, 179–212. Milano: Fondazione Giangiacomo Feltrinelli.

Tosatti, Giovanna. 1997. "La repressione del dissenso politico tra l'etá liberale e il fascismo. L'organizazzione della polizia." *Studi Storici* 38:217–55.

Traugott, Mark. 2010. *The Insurgent Barricade*. Berkeley: University of California Press.

Trejo, Guillermo. 2012. *Popular Movements in Autocracies: Religion, Repression, and Indigenous Collective Action in Mexico*. New York: Cambridge University Press.

Tsoukala, Anastassia. 2008. "Defining the Terrorist Threat in the Post-Sepember 11 Era." In *Terror, Insecurity and Liberty: Illiberal Practices of Liberal Regimes*, edited by Didier Bigo and Anastassia Tsoukala, 49–99. New York: Routledge.

Tushnet, Mark. 2005. "Defending Koramatsu: Reflections on Civil Liberties in Wartime." In *The Constitution in Wartime: Beyond Alarmism and Complacency*, edited by Mark Tushnet, 124–42. Durham: Duke University Press.

U.S. Bureau of the Census, Social Science Research Council. 1965. *The Statistical History of the United States from Colonial Times to the Present*. Stamford, CT: Fairfield Publishers.

Valelly, Richard M. 2004. *The Two Reconstructions: The Struggle for Black Enfranchisement*. Chicago: University of Chicago Press.

———. 2014. Exile and Return: Gays, Lesbians, and the American State. Unpublished manuscript, Swarthmore College.

Vasi, Ion Bogdan. 2006. "The New Anti-War Protests and Miscible Mobilizations." *Social Movement Studies* 5:137–53.

Vasi, Ion Bogdan, and David Strang. 2009. "Civil liberty in America: The Diffusion of Municipal Bill of Rights Resolutions after the Passage of the USA PATRIOT Act." *American Journal of Sociology* 114:1716–64.

Vaughn, Stephen. 1980. *Holding Fast the Inner Lines: Democracy, Nationalism, and the Committee on Public Information*. Chapel Hill: University of North Carolina Press.

Verhulst, Joris. 2010. "February 15, 2003: The World Says No to War." In *The World Says No to War: Demonstrations against the War on Iraq*, edited by Stefaan Walgrave and Dieter Rucht, 1–19. Minneapolis: University of Minnesota Press.

Vidal-Naquet, Pierre. 1972. *La Torture dans la République*. Paris: Editions du Minuit.

Violante, Luciano. 1976. "La repressione del dissenso politico nell'Italia liberale: Stato d'assedio e giustizia militare." *Rivista di storia contemporanea* 5:481–524.

Vladeck, Stephen I. 2004. "Emergency Power and the Militia Acts." *Yale Law Journal* 114:114–49.

Walgrave, Stefaan, and Dieter Rucht, eds. 2010. *The World Says No to War: Demonstrations against the War on Iraq*. Minneapolis: University of Minnesota Press.

Walgrave, Stefaan, Dieter Rucht, and Peter Van Aelst. 2010. "New Activists or Old Leftists? The Demographics of Protesters." In *The World Says No to War: Demonstrations against the War in Iraq*, edited by Stefaan Walgrave and Dieter Rucht, 78–97. Minneapolis: University of Minnesota Press.

Walt, Stephen M. 1996. *Revolution and War*. Ithaca: Cornell University Press.

Waltz, Kenneth N. 1979. *Theory of International Politics*. Reading, MA: Addison-Wesley.

Webber, Diane. 2009. "The Case of Binyam Mohamed: National Security or National Embarrassment?" *ExpressO*. http://works.bepress.com/diane_webber.

Weingast, Barry R. 1998. "Political Stability and Civil War: Institutions, Commitment, and American Democracy." In *Analytic Narratives*, Robert Bates et al., 148–93. Princeton: Princeton University Press.

———. 2002. Institutions and Political Commitment: A New Political Economy of the American Civil War Era. Unpublished manuscript, Stanford, CA.

Weinstein, Jeremy. 2006. *Inside Rebellion. The Politics of Insurgent Violence.* New York: Cambridge University Press.

Weiss, Linda. 1995. "Governed Interdependence: Rethinking the Government-Business Relationship in East Asia." *Pacific Review* 8:589–616.

———. 2006. "Infrastructural Power, Economic Transformation, and Globalization." In *An Anatomy of Power: The Social Theory of Michael Mann*, edited by John A. Hall and Ralph Schoeder, 167–86. Cambridge: Cambridge University Press.

———. 2014. *America, Inc.?: Innovation and Enterprise in the National Security State.* Ithaca: Cornell University Press.

Westad, Odd Arne. 2005. *The Global Cold War: Third World Interventions and the Making of Our Times.* Cambridge, UK: Cambridge University Press.

Whyte, John. 1990. *Interpreting Northern Ireland.* Oxford: Oxford University Press.

Wickham, Carrie Rosofsky. 2002. *Mobilizing Islam: Religion, Activism and Political Change in Egypt.* New York: Columbia University Press.

———. 2013. *The Muslim Brotherhood: Evolution of an Islamist Movement.* Princeton: Princeton University Press.

Wiktorowicz, Quentin. 2005. *Radical Islam Rising: Muslim Extremism in the West.* Lanham, MD: Rowman and Littlefield.

Wilson, Valerie Plame. 2007. *Fair Game: My Life as a Spy, My Betrayal by the White House.* New York: Simon and Shuster.

Witt, John Fabian. 2007. *Patriots and Cosmopolitans: Hidden Histories of American Law.* Cambridge, MA: Harvard University Press.

———. 2012. *Lincoln's Code: The Laws of War in American History.* New York: The Free Press.

Wittes, Benjamin, and Hannah Neprash. 2009. "The Story of the Guantánamo Cases: Habeas Corpus, the Reach of the Court, and the War on Terror." In *Constitutional Stories*, edited by Michael C. Dorf, 513–53. New York: Foundation Press.

Woehrle, Lynne, Patrick G. Coy, and Gregory M. Maney. 2008. *Contesting Patriotism: Culture, Power, and Strategy in the Peace Movement.* Lanham, MD: Rowman and Littlefield.

Woloch, Isser. 1994. *The New Regime: Transformations of the French Civic Order, 1789–1820s.* New York: W. W. Norton.

Wood, Elisabeth Jean. 2000. *Forging Democracy from Below: Insurgent Transitions in South Africa and El Salvador.* New York: Cambridge University Press.

———. 2003. *Insurgent Collective Action and Civil War in El Salvador.* New York: Cambridge University Press.

Wood, Lesley J. 2012. *Direct Action, Deliberation, and Diffusion. Collective Action after the WTO Protests in Seattle.* New York: Cambridge University Press.

———. 2014. *Crisis and Control: The Militarization of Protest Policing.* London: Pluto Press.

Wright, J. Kent. 1993. "Les sources républicaines de la Déclaration des droits de l'homme et du citoyen." In *Le Siècle de l'avènement républicain*, edited by François Furet and Mona Ozouf, 127–64. Paris: PUF.

Zangheri, Renato, ed. 1960. *Le lotte agrarie in Italia. La Fedeazione nazionale dei lavoratori della terra, 1901–1926.* Milan: Feltrinelli.

Zelizer, Julian E. 2010. *Arsenal of Democracy: The Politics of National Security—from World War II to the War on Terrorism.* New York: Basic Books.

Acknowledgments

I am grateful to a number of colleagues and institutions for help in developing the arguments that guided this book over more years than they would probably care to remember. Eitan Alimi, Mike Dorf, Donatella della Porta, Matt Evangelista, Roger Haydon, Peter Katzenstein, Joe Margulies, Aziz Rana, and Susan Tarrow read The Whole Thing and thankfully never worried about hurting my feelings when I had travelled too far off base. For that, I thank them warmly.

An early version of the argument was presented at a seminar at the City University of New York (CUNY) Graduate Center colloquium on politics and protest in 2008. My colleagues at that seminar—especially John Krinsky and Wayne te Brake—bear some responsibility for encouraging me to turn it into this book. Chapter 1 grew out of a lecture presented at the University of Pennsylvania, which appears in modified form as a chapter in *Sovereignty, Citizenship, and Cosmopolitan Alternatives*, edited by Sigal Ben-Porath and Rogers Smith (Tarrow 2013b). Parts of chapter 2 were presented at the University of California at Irvine, the University of Colorado, the Hebrew University, and Haifa University and were published as "The French Revolution, War and State-Building," in *Contention and Trust in Cities and States*, edited by Michael Hanagan and Chris Tilly (Tarrow 2011a). The origin of chapter 3 was my contribution to a conference on authoritarian inversions organized by Valerie Bunce at Cornell University in 2011. The arguments in part II were developed while I was a visiting professor at the Cornell Law School. Parts of chapter 10 grew out of my Gorecki Lecture at the University of Illinois.

I wish to thank the Andrew Mellon Foundation and the Cornell Association of Professors Emeritus, each of which contributed financially to the research reported in the book. Laurie Coon, Stacy Kesselring, and Judy Virgilio patiently administered these grants well past the time when I could expect the kindness with which they always greeted my requests. The staff of the Bibliothèque Historique de la Révolution Française at the Sorbonne and of the Fondazione Lelio and Lisli Basso in Rome deserve warm thanks for meeting my requests with courtesy and efficiency. Chan S. Suh loyally and creatively prepared the figures, tables, and maps, and shared his original work on the Guantánamo lawyers that is cited in chapter 9.

Because my previous work was far removed from the study of either war or state-building, in preparing this book I leaned heavily on the advice and criticism of many friends and colleagues. In international relations, I am grateful to Matthew Evangelista, Peter Katzenstein, Bob Keohane, Beth Kier, Ron Krebs, Frederik Logevall, Sarah Kreps, Karen Rasler, and Kathryn Sikkink. For help in understanding American politics and history, I thank Glenn Altschuler, Richard Bensel, Ira Katznelson, Doug McAdam, Steven Skowronek, Rogers Smith, Linda Weiss, and Richard Valelly. Most of what I know about the French Revolution I learned from Jérome Ferrand, Jean-Clément Martin, Steven Laurence Kaplan, Sébastien le Gal, and Ronen Steinberg. Sabino Cassese, Paul Corner, Donatella della Porta, Guido Melis, Antonella Meniconi, Marco Mondini, and, especially, Giovanna Procacci were sources of expertise as I plunged back into Italian history after a long absence. Cornell colleagues Jason Frank and Isaac Kramnick were always ready with incisive responses to impossible questions about their area of expertise. Eitan Alimi, Benedict Anderson, Juan Masullo, and Tom Pepinsky taught me that the scope conditions of the study could be extended beyond my home turf to theirs.

Much of the book engages the legal literature on war, rights, and national security. I thank Baher Azmy, Josh Chafetz, David Cole, Michael Dorf, Jens Ohlin, Aziz Rana, and Steve Shiffrin for guiding me through this literature during a stimulating visiting professorship at the Cornell Law School. As for the movement against the abuse of rights in the War on Terror, I am grateful for help from the American Civil Liberties Union, the Center for Constitutional Rights in the United States, Reprieve in the United Kingdom, and lawyers in the United Kingdom and the United States who were willing to share their experiences defending the rights of detainees with me. I also thank Roger Haydon of the Cornell University Press, who continues to believe—against the odds—that the job of an editor is to help authors produce the best work of which they are capable.

My deepest intellectual and personal debt is to Charles Tilly. His *Coercion, Capital and European States* was the inspiration for the book. In the preface to his last book, *Contentious Performances*, Chuck joked that he hoped some day to write a book of which I would approve (2008, xvi). Reverse the subject and the object in this sentence, and you will know why I have undertaken this one. I offer it in homage to Chuck in the spirit he would have most appreciated: never take on anything less than big structures, large processes, and huge comparisons (1984)—even if it causes enormous headaches!

Not a single excessive citation or infelicitous Americanism escaped the eagle eye of Susan Tarrow. For that, and for everything else, I am eternally grateful.

Index